MW00343051

Adult Learning

Theories, Principles and Applications

SHARAN B. MERRIAM
ROSEMARY S. CAFFARELLA
RAYMOND J. WLODKOWSKI
P. CRANTON

UNIVERSITY OF PHOENIX

JOHN WILEY & SONS, INC.

Copyright © 2001 by Jossey-Bass Inc.
            Jossey-Bass is a registered trademark of Jossey-Bass Inc., A Wiley Company.

All rights reserved.

Reproduction or translation of any part of this work beyond that permitted by Sections 107 and 108 of the 1976 United States Copyright Act without the permission of the copyright owner is unlawful. Requests for permission or further information should be addressed to the Permission Department, John Wiley & Sons.

Printed in the United States of America.

EISBN 0-471-22775-7

ISBN 0-471-43298-9

BRIEF CONTENTS

SECTION ONE

SECTION TWO

SECTION THREE

SECTION FOUR

SECTION FIVE

SECTION SIX

TABLE OF CONTENTS

SECTION ONE

SECTION TWO

SECTION THREE

SECTION FOUR

SECTION FIVE

SECTION SIX

SECTION ONE

BIOLOGICAL AND PSYCHOLOGICAL DEVELOPMENT

Sʜᴀʀᴀɴ B. Mᴇʀʀɪᴀᴍ
Rᴏsᴇᴍᴀʀʏ S. Cᴀғғᴀʀᴇʟʟᴀ

That children change as they age is well understood and anticipated; but it is only within the last few decades that it became equally clear that adults also change as they age. It is not unusual to hear someone talk about her "age-thirty transition," "midlife crisis," or "biological clock" running out. Indeed, separating facts, ideas, and theories about adult development from the popularized and fictionalized versions of research findings and then linking those findings to learning in adulthood is the challenge. Efforts to integrate development and learning have focused on why and how we physically age, our psychological makeup, and more recently on how social and cultural forces shape our development (Tennant and Pogson, 1995). In addition, there have been major discussions about how our thinking processes themselves change in adulthood.

The concept of development, as with learning, is most often equated with change. Some view change resulting from development as an orderly progression, while others find little that is preprogrammed. The goal of development is similarly controversial. Some think that adults move toward closely specified goals such as self-actualization (Maslow, 1970) or a fully integrated sense of ego (Loevinger, 1976). Others, like Riegel (1973) and Tennant and Pogson (1995), view development as more dialectical in nature, with development a function of the "constant interaction of the person and the environment" (Tennant and Pogson, 1995, p. 199). Still others view development as a political construct "because different versions of development serve the interests of different groups" (Tennant and Pogson, 1995, p. 199).

Most of the work in adult development has been driven by the psychological tradition and focuses on the individual's internal process of development. Out of this tradition have grown the most prevalent theories of development, which often have been conceptualized as a patterned or ordered progression tied to chronological time. Some theorists, such as Havighurst (1972) and Levinson and Levinson (1996), have been highly specific, tying each developmental period to a particular age, while others (Erikson, 1963, 1982; Vaillant, 1977) have left the age frame open-ended and speak rather of life periods such as young adulthood and middle age. Still others within the psychological paradigm have concentrated on life's transitions, such as marriage, birth of a child, or death. Although the psychological framework for development is most often cited, other perspectives on adulthood, such as biological aging, are equally important, especially when thinking about learning. Moreover, there has been a growing awareness (though some might term it a resurfacing of interest) of how social and cultural forces such as gender, race, and social class affect adult development (Dannefer, 1984; Elder, 1995; Tennant and Pogson, 1995). A number of authors have even called for the creation of "a new perspective that ... draws equally on biology, psychology, and social science, as well as on the humanities" (Levinson, 1986, p. 13), to understand fully the complex and intricate patterns of development in adulthood.

In this section we discuss the developmental characteristics of adults from two major orientations, biological aging and psychological changes, each explained through illustrative theories and ideas. We interweave in the discussion of these theories and ideas how educators and others have linked these perspectives to learning in adulthood.

BIOLOGICAL AGING

Biological aging is a fact of life, although rarely a welcome one. When we ask groups of adults to describe physical changes that have happened to them over the previous five to ten years, there are usually a collective sigh and mumblings about weight gain, graying hair, and the like. It is not a subject most people care to discuss. Yet with advances in nutrition and health care, our overall outlook for continued health and well-being has never been better. As Erikson (1982) so keenly observed, we have moved from an elite of elderlies to a mass of elderlies.

Although life expectancy has almost doubled since the beginning of this century, from approximately forty to seventy-six years, our capacity to live longer does not mean we have been able to halt the primary process of aging—those time-related physical changes governed by some kind of maturational process, as in vision and hearing, for example, that happen to all of us (Bee, 1996; Lefrancois, 1996). Although life expectancy has increased, the human life span, usually given as 110 to 120 years, has not changed. Rather, our increased longevity stems from overcoming some of the problems related to secondary aging—aging that is "the product of environmental influences, health habits, or disease and is . . . not shared by all people" (Bee, 1996, p. 83). Improved nutrition, hygiene, medical discoveries, and lifestyle changes have accounted for most of this increased longevity.

Since most bodily functions reach their maximum capacity and efficiency in young adulthood, this period is a time of optimal health, physical strength, and endurance for many adults (Berger, 1998). Decline in the actual functioning of the major biological systems is slow. The fourth and fifth decades tend to be the physiological turning point for most adults, although the effects of these changes may not be felt until the sixth or seventh decade of life (Bee, 1996; Berger, 1998). The most obvious changes are the ones we see when we return to our twenty-fifth college reunion. Suddenly our classmates look middle-aged. We see gray and thinning hair, more wrinkles, and different contours of the body. Yet these changes, although noticeable, really have little effect on our physical functioning, unless we take to heart the negative stereotypes society has placed on "looking old." Less obvious to the eye are the more pervasive internal changes. For example, most adults begin to experience changes in their vision, their cardiovascular systems, their bones and connective material, and their reproductive function (for women) sometime in their forties and early fifties.

Yet it is not until the sixties and the seventies, when the degenerative biological process overtakes the regenerative process for most adults, that major effects on all structures and functions of the body are seen. Even these major changes are being questioned in the popular and scientific literature alike, implying "that virtually all previously presumed changes with age are either illusory or insignificant" (Bee, 1996, p. 84). Still, for most adults "there are real changes occurring with age. It is important not to exaggerate those changes, but neither should we gloss over or ignore them" (Bee, 1996, p. 84). Although it appears that we will all experience many major changes in our physical beings at some point in our lives, the effect of these changes on our capacity to learn is largely unknown. In fact, many of these changes may prove to be very minor, except in cases of underlying disease processes. Three specific physical changes have been shown to affect learning in adulthood: changes in two of the senses, changes in the central nervous system, and changes as a result of major disease processes.

Senses

Deterioration in the ability to see and to hear can create problems with the learning process. Specific changes in vision are well documented (Kline and Scialfa, 1996; Marsh, 1996). One of the most notable changes is in the ability to perceive small detail on the printed page and computer screen. A loss of close vision starts to decline for most people between the ages of forty and fifty and results primarily from the lens's becoming larger and denser and losing elasticity. By the age of seventy-five, poor visual acuity is common, although many problems can be corrected with eyeglasses or surgery.

A second major sight-related change concerns light. As people age, they need more illumination to see both near and far (Bee, 1996; Marsh, 1996). This results from a combination of lens and iris changes that allow less light and a different quality of light to reach the retina. These latter changes make those especially past the age of seventy less responsive to sudden changes in illumination, such as oncoming headlights. In addition, "peripheral vision, depth perception, color vision, and adaption to the dark also become poorer and sensitivity to glare increases" with age (Lefrancois, 1996, p. 505).

While changes in vision happen primarily at set periods in life, hearing loss is a progressive but gradual process throughout adulthood. Most adults do not notice any discernible change until their fifties and sixties, when sounds, especially in the high-frequency range, become more difficult to hear (Kline and Scialfa, 1996; Marsh, 1996). This loss is most often noted by males, who are more affected than females by hearing loss. Even greater hearing losses are noticed in the seventh and eighth decades. An estimated 35 percent of the population has some detectable amount of hearing difficulty between the ages of seventy-five and eighty-five, and 51 percent of the population over age eighty-five experiences hearing impairment (Bee, 1996). According to Bee (1996, p. 92), the basic cause of this loss appears to be "from wear and tear on the auditory nerves and structures of the inner ear." One of the obvious results of this loss of hearing is the difficulty of older adults to understand the spoken word. Some people become completely deaf, but most often people who are hard of hearing miss pieces of words and phrases, so they may not understand what was said. As some grandchildren have observed, asking their grandparents one question often elicits an answer to a totally different question. Some hearing losses can be compensated for with the use of hearing aids or by adding such devices as amplifiers in large meeting rooms, but such adjustments do not often help those with major hearing losses. Those with acute hearing loss and the people who interact with them often become frustrated with the whole communication process, and adults with serious hearing losses may become increasingly isolated.

The aging of the eyes and ears "serves as a good example of how the effects of aging need not interfere with the capacity for learning" (Cross, 1981, p. 156). Except for major degenerative and other disease processes, corrective measures, such as the wearing of eyeglasses and teaching people to find alternative ways of communicating, can help ensure the best use of the vision and hearing that remain. Adults learning on their own have fewer problems than those who choose to learn in formal settings. For the most part, our institutions do not take into consideration the physical differences of adult learners. Both teachers and learners must see to it that the educational environment is conducive to all adult learners, ensuring, for example, that rooms are adequately illuminated and acoustics are good.

The Nervous System

Consisting of the brain and the spinal cord, the central nervous system forms the primary biological basis for learning. We have only limited knowledge about how changes in this system affect learning in healthy adults as they age (Bruer, 1997; Scheibel, 1996). For example, although we know that both the weight and the number of cells in the brain decline and the connections between these cells become less numerous with age, we do not know what impact, if any, these changes have on the learning process. During the perinatal period, for example, unborn babies lose many more cells as a consequence of normal brain maturation than the cell loss adults experience later in life (Scheibel, 1996).

The most consistent finding related to changes in the central nervous system has to do with declining reaction time as people age (Bee, 1996; Lefrancois, 1996; Schaie and Willis, 1986). Reaction time is usually measured as the time it takes a person to complete a psychomotor task, such as putting together a puzzle or responding to a specific stimulus by hitting a lighted button. Although "it is not true that all elderly people are markedly slower than young people … , on the average people over the age of 65" react less rapidly (Lefrancois, 1996, p. 506). Numerous explanations have been posited for this change, such as possible sensory deprivation or changes in actual brain activity (Baltes and Lindenberger, 1997). Not only are the physiological causes unclear, but it has also been found that such factors as the nature of the task and a person's familiarity with the task also affect reaction time. (Additional implications of the slowing of reaction time with regard to memory and other intellectual processes are discussed in Intelligence and Aging and Memory, Cognition, and the Brain later.)

Disease Processes

As one grows older, it becomes difficult to distinguish between the normal or primary aging processes and those physical changes that are disease related. Although changes in health can affect the ability to learn at any age, the greatest effect is felt in older adulthood, when "the concept of disease as distinguishable from normal aging (i.e., physical changes unrelated to disease) has many implications for studying cognitive processes" (Elias, Elias, and Elias, 1991, p. 27).

Although a number of health impairments may affect the learning process, two specific disease processes affect learning profoundly, depending on the severity and stage of the disease (Bee, 1996; Lefrancois, 1996). The first is cardiovascular disease, especially when it results in a stroke or cerebrovascular incident in which the blood supply is cut off to a part of the brain. This can lead to a loss of memory and aphasia, restricting the ability to reproduce verbal speech. Moreover, other physical changes, such as loss of mobility, can occur, depending on which part of the brain is affected. If the stroke is mild or intervention comes quickly, full or at least partial functioning may be restored so that people can once again communicate normally and be cognizant of the world around them. In the case of massive brain damage, chronic organic brain disorder might result—the second class of health problems that, even in their milder forms, affect learning. One of the major causes of chronic brain dysfunction is Alzheimer's disease. Alzheimer's disease often develops so slowly that it may take years to recognize, although certain forms of the disease appear to develop more rapidly. The cause of this disease process is not known, but its effects become very apparent over time. Symptoms range from impaired memory and disorganization of thought, to changes in judgment and emotion, and finally to the inability to care for oneself.

In addition to these direct effects, disease processes indirectly influence adults' ability to learn. Pain and fatigue often accompany both acute and chronic illnesses, leaving one with little energy or motivation to engage in learning activities. Different medications and treatments may affect the way one thinks and behaves, side effects that may go unrecognized. Moreover, the financial drain on resources may be enormous, particularly in coping with chronic illness, leaving little support for learning activities of any kind.

PSYCHOLOGICAL CHANGES

The psychological perspective encompasses a broad array of ideas on how adults develop over the life span. The focus of this framework is how development occurs within the individual, whether development is primarily an internal process or results from interactions with the environment. The material can be divided into three major categories: cognitive development, intelligence and aging, and psychological development. Here we focus on the third category: psychological development.

A number of diverse concepts have been placed in the category of psychological development, including the theories of ego development (Erikson, 1963; Loevinger, 1976), self development (Gould, 1978; Jordan, 1997c; Josselson, 1996; Kegan, 1982, 1994; Levinson and others, 1978; Levinson and Levinson, 1996; Vaillant, 1977), moral development (Gilligan, 1982; Kohlberg, 1973; Kohlberg and Ryncarz, 1990), and faith and spiritual development (Fowler, 1981; Jones, 1995). The common theme in this vast array of work is the changing nature of the internal self as we develop.

The literature on psychological development is grounded primarily in clinical studies and qualitative biographies obtained through in-depth interviews. In addition to the limited nature of the research designs, the samples, except in a few notable studies (Clausen, 1993; Costa and McCrae, 1980, 1994; Eichorn and others, 1981; Neugarten and others, 1964), have been relatively small and highly selective. Subjects of the most often quoted studies have been primarily white and middle class. There also was a male bias in many of the earlier studies (for example, Kohlberg, 1973; Levinson and others, 1978). More recently there has been a substantial increase in the study of women's development (see, for example, Caffarella and Olson, 1993; Estes, 1992; Gilligan, 1982; Jordan, 1997c; Jordan and others, 1991; Josselson, 1996; Levinson and Levinson, 1996). Although the majority of subjects of many of these studies have also been white and middle class, there is a growing trend to acknowledge class, race, ethnicity, and sexual orientation as critical factors in affecting development (D'Augelli and Patterson, 1995; Etter-Lewis and Foster, 1996; Jordan, 1997c; Ponterotto, Casas, Suzuki, and Alexander, 1995). Still the theory building in psychological development is at best tentative in terms of people of color, gay men and women, and people from different social backgrounds and cultures.

Although this material on psychological development is somewhat tenuous and at times unclear, adult educators over the years, such as Knox (1977), Cross (1981), Merriam (1984), Daloz (1986), and Tennant and Pogson (1995), have proposed a number of useful ideas on how this material can help us understand learning in adulthood. We especially like Daloz's notion of using these developmental theories as alternative maps of how adults can develop—without saying which specific roads should be taken or whether in some cases this developmental journey should be taken at all (Daloz, 1986, 1988b). This best fits our stance: that there is no right or best way of developing as we age. With this caveat in mind, we have organized the literature into three categories: sequential models of development, life events and transitions, and relational models. Interwoven within each major theme are implications for learning in adulthood.

Sequential Models

Although all of the sequential models provide for an unfolding of adult life in a series of phases or stages, they have different end points, from becoming autonomous and independent to finding wisdom and a universal sense of faith and moral behavior. Levinson and his colleagues (Levinson, 1986; Levinson and Levinson, 1996; Levinson and others, 1978), Gould (1978), and Sheehy (1976, 1995) assert that development is bound to very specific ages. Levinson and Levinson (1996), for example, from their studies of both men and women, suggest that people evolve through an orderly sequence of stable and transitional periods that correlate with chronological age. One's life structure, that is, "the underlying pattern or design of a person's life at any given time" (Levinson and Levinson, 1996, p. 22), tends to be established and maintained during stable periods and then questioned and changed during transitional periods. The specific time periods they outline for both men and women are as follows (p. 18):

Early Adult Transition	*Ages 17–22*
Entry Life Structure for Early Adulthood	Ages 22–28
Age 30 Transition	Ages 28–33
Culminating Life Structure for Early Adulthood	Ages 33–40
Mid-Life Transition	*Ages 40–45*
Early Life Structure for Middle Adulthood	Ages 45–50
Age 50 Transition	Ages 50–55
Culminating Life Structure for Middle Adulthood	Ages 55–60
Late Adult Transition	*Ages 60–65*
Era of Late Adulthood	Ages 60–?

Components of this changing life structure include marriage and family, occupation, friendships, relationships to politics, religion, ethnicity, and community, and leisure, recreation, and memberships and roles in many social settings. The *central components* are those that have the greatest significance for the self and the life. They receive the greatest share of one's time and energy, and they strongly influence the character of the other components (Levinson and Levinson, 1996, p. 23).

Although Levinson and his colleagues hold that both men and women follow these alternating sequences of structure building and transitional periods, these periods "operate somewhat differently in females and males.... Women ... work on the developmental tasks of every period with different resources and constraints, external as well as internal" (pp. 36–37). Levinson and Levinson's central concept for these differences in gender is gender splitting, which "refers not simply to gender differences but of a splitting asunder—the creation of a rigid division between male and female, masculine and feminine, in human life" (p. 38). More specifically they describe four forms of gender splitting that have an impact on how the life structure evolves in men and women (pp. 38–39):

1.   The splitting of the domestic sphere and the public sphere as social domains for women and for men;
2.   The Traditional Marriage Enterprise and the split it creates between the female homemaker and the male provisioner;
3.   The splitting of "women's work" and "men's work";
4.   The splitting of feminine and masculine in the individual psyche.

This framework of relating development to specific age periods has led a number of educators to propose a link between age-appropriate tasks and behavior and the fostering of learning activities for adults. Havighurst (1972) was one of the earliest writers to link these ideas into what he termed the *teachable moment*. The idea of the teachable moment is grounded in the concept of developmental tasks tasks that arise at a certain period in a person's life, such as selecting a mate, starting a family, and getting started in an occupation. Although the time frame and some of the tasks Havighurst suggested are somewhat dated, the idea of specific life tasks' giving rise to a teachable moment is not. Knowles (1980, p. 51) has also viewed developmental tasks as producing "a 'readiness to learn' which at its peak presents a 'teachable moment' " and outlines his own list of "life tasks" for young, old, and middle-aged adults.

For other theorists writing from a sequential perspective, there is a step-wise upward movement, but it is not necessarily tied to chronological age (Erikson, 1963, 1982; Erikson, Erikson, and Kivnick, 1986; Fowler, 1981; Kegan, 1982; Kohlberg, 1973; Loevinger, 1976; Vaillant, 1977). These scholars assert that whether the stages or steps they describe are related to age or not, they are hierarchical in nature and therefore build on one another. There is disagreement among these writers about what causes the movement between stages and whether this movement is upward only to higher stages or whether it is back and forth across stages. Kohlberg (1973) and Loevinger (1976), for example, view the movement as primarily upward only and internally driven, while Erikson (1982) perceives it to be a function of internal and environmental forces and allows for movement back and forth between the stages throughout the life cycle.

Erikson is by far the most often quoted theorist representing sequential development from this perspective. Erikson has posited eight stages of development, each representing a series of crises or issues to be dealt with over the life span. For each stage there is a choice between opposites—one negative and the other positive—and it is imperative that persons achieve a favorable ratio of positive over negative prior to moving to the next stage. In young adulthood, the successful resolution between intimacy versus isolation results in love. In middle adulthood, resolving the tensions between generativity and self-absorption allows people to care for others; in older adulthood, resolutions between integrity versus despair provide the capacity for wisdom. Although Erikson characterized his fourth stage, that of identity versus identity confusion, as being tied primarily to the period of adolescence, researchers in adult development have also included the examination of this stage as part of their research on adults (for example, Josselson, 1987). Erikson maintains that as adults we may revisit earlier stages to resolve or re-resolve conflicts from earlier periods in different ways. For example, because of a loss of a spouse, we may need to work again through issues of both intimacy and identity. In addition, Erikson, Erikson, and Kivnick (1986) go on to suggest that it is vital involvement in old age and the interdependence among people that allow adults to complete the life cycle successfully and leave a positive legacy for the next generation.

Cross (1981, p. 240) proposes that "if one accepts a hierarchy of developmental stages, and if one believes that the role of educators is to help each individual develop to the highest possible level, then the role of educators is to challenge the learner to move to increasingly advanced stages of personal development." One way of accomplishing this is to assist adult learners in examining the basic assumptions on which they operate in order to help them move to these higher levels of development and thinking. The process of facilitating adult learning in this manner has been best described by Daloz (1986, 1988b), Krupp (1987, 1992), Levine (1989), Mezirow and Associates (1990), and Kegan (1994). For example, Daloz, who has directly linked his work with developmental theory, clearly uses the work of Kegan (1982) and others as the foundation for his notions of helping learners through their "transformational journeys" through formal mentoring and teaching activities.

Life Events and Transitions

One of the alternatives to the paradigm of development as a set of sequential stages is the concept of life events and transitions (Brim and Ryff, 1980; Creel, 1996; Evans, Forney, and Guido-DiBrito, 1998; Hultsch and Plemons, 1979; Schlossberg, Waters, and Goodman, 1995). In this framework, "life events are benchmarks in the human life cycle," markers that give "shape and direction to the various aspects of a person's life" (Danish and others, 1980, as quoted in Sugarman, 1986, p. 131). Unlike the stage and phase theorists, those who describe life events as providing key growth periods do not usually connect these life events to specific age periods, although some events seem to be more tied to age than others (Hughes, Blazer, and George, 1988).

There are two basic types of life events: individual and cultural (Hultsch and Plemons, 1979). Individual life events, such as birth, death, marriage, and divorce, define one person's specific life. Schlossberg (1989) has categorized individual life events into those that are anticipated or unanticipated, nonevents or sleeper events. Nonevents are events that were expected but do not occur, like infertility and the child who never leaves home; sleeper events are ones that you are not sure when they started, such as becoming bored with work or falling in love (Schlossberg, 1989; Schlossberg, Waters, and Goodman, 1995). Societal and historical happenings that shape the context in which a person develops, such as wars, the women's movement, and natural catastrophes, make up cultural life events. A number of factors affect how a person might experience any particular event (Brim and Ryff, 1980; Reese and Smyer, 1983; Schlossberg, Waters, and Goodman, 1995; Sugarman, 1986). Among the most salient are *timing* (the event is congruent with either personal or societal expectations of when it should happen), *cohort specificity* (the event may affect only certain generations, or it may affect different cohorts of people in different ways), and *probability* (normative being high, nonnormative being low) (Brim and Ryff, 1980; Neugarten, 1976; Peterson, 1996; Tennant and Pogson, 1995).

In addition to being viewed as milestones, life events are also seen as a process that may begin well before the event itself happens and continue well beyond it (Reese and Smyer, 1983; Schlossberg, Waters, and Goodman, 1995; Sugarman, 1986). The sequence of this process is not necessarily smooth or continuous. In the case of certain disease processes such as cancer, for example, the prognosis may be terminal, with the resulting event being death. But the process of dying is much more than just the day of death and often takes unplanned twists and turns prior to death itself. There is also a time needed after the event of death for survivors to assimilate the loss and make sense out of a seemingly different world. The notion of life events as a process is often equated with the idea of transitions (Schlossberg, Waters, and Goodman, 1995).

Transitions are viewed as "the natural process of disorientation and reorientation that marks the turning points of the path of growth ... involving periodic accelerations and transformations" (Bridges, 1980, p. 5). Adults continually experience transitions, whether anticipated or unanticipated, and react to them depending on the type of transition, the context in which it occurs, and its impact on their lives. "Transitions may lead to growth, but decline is also a possible outcome, and many transitions may be viewed with ambivalence by the individuals experiencing them" (Evans, Forney, and Guido-DiBrito, 1998, p. 112).

"Whereas a transition may be precipitated by a single event or non-event, dealing with a transition is a process that extends over time" (Evans, Forney, and Guido-DiBrito, 1998, p. 112). Three authors have provided transition models that are especially helpful in understanding the notion of transition as a process (Bridges, 1980, 1991; Schlossberg, 1989; Schlossberg, Waters, and Goodman, 1995; Sugarman, 1986). Bridges's (1980, 1991) model begins with endings, that is, "letting go of something" (Bridges, 1991, p. 5). People then move into what he calls the neutral zone, "the no-man's land between the old reality and the new.... It is a time when the old way is gone and the new doesn't feel comfortable yet" (p. 5). His final phase is that of new beginnings, whereby people consciously choose to launch into their new ways of being and doing. Bridges emphasizes that these phases are not necessarily separate; people often find themselves in more than one phase at a time.

Sugarman (1986), who agrees with Bridges that transition cycles are not an orderly or sequential process, has identified seven stages that accompany a wide range of transitions: (1) immobilization—a sense of being overwhelmed or frozen; (2) reaction—a sharp swing of mood from elation to despair depending on the nature of the transition; (3) minimization—minimizing one's feelings and the anticipated impact of the event; (4) letting—go breaking with the past; (5) testing—exploration of the new terrain; (6) searching for meaning—conscious striving to learn from the experience; and (7) integration—feeling at home with the change. And Schlossberg, Waters, and Goodman (1995) endorse a three-phase model: "moving in," "moving through," and "moving out." Bridges (1980, 1991) stresses that letting go of the past, which is included in all three models, is often overlooked. We want to get on with the change rather than deal with the loss of the way we were before. When first having a child, for example, we must let go of what being childless was all about.

Schlossberg and her colleagues (Schlossberg, 1987, 1989; Schlossberg, Lynch, and Chickering, 1989; Schlossberg, Waters, and Goodman, 1995) specifically describe how people in transition have both strengths and weaknesses—resources and deficits—to cope with the transition. She divides them into "four major categories, the four S's: situation, self, supports, and strategies" (1987, p. 75). How does a person assess the transition—as positive, negative, or indifferent—and what is her sense of control as she encounters and acts on the transition? What are the person's inner strengths for dealing with the transition? What kinds of social supports does the person have? And, finally, does the person have a wide repertoire of strategies for coping with the transition? The ratio of strengths to weaknesses helps to explain "why different individuals react differently to the same type of transition and why the same person reacts differently at different times" (Schlossberg, Waters, and Goodman, 1995, p. 49).

A number of educators have proposed that engaging in learning activities is one way in which adults cope with life events and transitions (Aslanian and Brickell, 1980; Knox, 1977; Merriam and Clark, 1991; Merriam and Yang, 1996; Schlossberg, Waters, and Goodman, 1995; Tennant and Pogson, 1995; Wolf and Leahy, 1998). Indeed, Aslanian and Brickell (1980) found that most adults "learn in order to cope with some change in their lives" (p. 111) and concluded that this learning is tied to a triggering event. The learning resulting from these triggering events is not always related to the event itself. For example, a divorce (the triggering event) may motivate a woman to return to school (the learning activity) so she may become more employable and therefore self-sufficient. These triggering events were most often related to career and family changes, such as moving to a new job or becoming pregnant. Blaxter and Tight (1995) have challenged Aslanian and Brickell's findings that most adults learn as a result of life events. Their study of adult students revealed that their respondents "split into two, almost equal groups: those for whom a clear linkage between their current educational participation and one or more transitional events can be identified, and those for whom no such linkage is readily apparent. Indeed, the latter may be continuously resisting such linkages" (p. 231).

Merriam and Clark (1991, 1992), based on a qualitative study of work, love, and learning in adult life, also found that issues related to one's work life and personal life, including family changes, are sources of learning. Furthermore, respondents identified the learning related to these events as highly significant, to the point, in some cases, of bringing about a change in their worldviews. Merriam and Yang (1996), using a totally different methodology, confirmed these findings, with "work-related variables ... being particularly powerful in predicting" developmental changes.

Merriam and Clark (1991, 1992) also found links between the transition times created by these life events and learning. They observed that more learning happens in periods that people perceive as good versus bad times. Yet although nearly ten times more significant learning occurred in the good times than in the bad, learning that is more likely to be transformative occurred in the bad times. In other words, the more difficult the transition is perceived to be by learners, the more potential this transition may have for learning, and especially for changing how learners see themselves and their worlds.

Merriam, Mott, and Lee (1996) also explored transition times that resulted in what they termed negative learning versus growth and development. They speculated that learning from life experience can also result "in debilitating, growth-inhibiting outcomes" (p. 1). Intensive interviews were held with eighteen adults who self-identified a negative outcome from a life experience. The researchers found that these respondents interpreted their experiences negatively if some defining aspect of themselves had been challenged. For example, becoming divorced challenged one man's definition of self as a caretaker; being attached challenged another women's sense of self as in control. When this challenge was too daunting or made them feel too vulnerable, these respondents made sense of the experience by adopting self-protective behaviors or attitudes, "including blaming others, becoming angry, withdrawing or becoming distrustful" (p. 18). Therefore, rather than opening themselves up to what we might term positive learning or growth, they closed themselves off. Another major finding from the study was that "when and if the threat to the self was reduced by time, having support, and gaining a larger perspective and personal agency, the process began to reverse itself toward more growth-oriented outcomes" (p. 21). Thus, to extract deeper and more expanded leaning from some of our most difficult times, adults often need an extended period of time and the active support and caring from others.

Building on this work, as well as the work of others, such as Mezirow (1981) and Daloz (1986), Merriam and Heuer (1996) have proposed a useful model for extracting meaning from our more complex life-altering transitions (see Figure 1-1). More specifically, this model addresses life experiences that are difficult to accommodate or explain. For example, there is a poor fit between the event and the person's current meaning system. Or there is a challenge to the fundamental assumptions, beliefs, or values a person holds about life. In taking on this challenge, adults must be willing to engage themselves cognitively, affectively, and even physically with the experience and be given the time and support to do so. For example, many parents have their fundamental belief systems about sexuality and the meaning of family heavily challenged when they learn their son or daughter is gay. They may refuse to think about it, react in anger, or become highly stressed. As these parents continue to work through this challenge to their way of thinking and being, Merriam and Heuer posit that they need to move in their thinking beyond just their personal experience of learning their child is gay to "the larger context, both personal and sociocultural, in which [they] live. In doing so, space is created whereby the self can be defined or restructured" (p. 251). One way they might do this is to go into counseling or join a parent support group, where they can share stories and ways of coping with this new reality in their lives. Another strategy might be to support a local group of community activists for gay rights, whereby they could see the broader

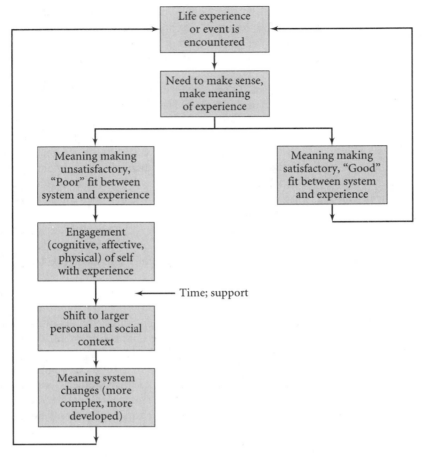

Figure 1-1.   Meaning Making, Learning, and Development.
Source: Merriam and Heuer, 1996, p. 252.

lives of people who are gay. Hopefully through all of these learning activities, they might become more accepting both of their child and of the gay lifestyle as a way of life for many people.

Schlossberg and her colleagues (Schlossberg, Lynch, and Chickering, 1989; Schlossberg, Waters and, Goodman, 1995) have suggested areas of knowledge and skill that would be helpful to people in transition, including exploration of the transition event and process, problem-solving techniques, and skills for coping with the transition. Moreover, they believe that personal support in the form of family, friends, self-help groups, or professionals is needed to help adults in transition examine their current situation and future scenarios. They and others, like Daloz (1986) and Bloom (1995), have provided more specific guidance for how this could be done in a learning environment. Daloz and Bloom believe that a mentoring relationship is especially powerful when adult learners are in periods of transition in their lives.

And finally, Wolf and Leahy (1998, p. 4) have edited a useful book that gives educators of adults "guidance and support for creating learning environments to meet the needs of learners undergoing life transitions." These authors explore five specific transitional areas (such as career changes, homelessness, and caring for and loss of an aging parent) and examples of specific ways educators have assisted learners in responding to these transitions. Although many learners do not necessarily "speak of their own [transitional] circumstances, the educational community would do well to prepare for and honor such growth" (p. 7).

Relational Models of Development

Yet another model of development has come from scholars who view the centrality of relationships as key to development. The majority of studies from this framework are grounded in research on women's development, including studies of women's moral development, identity development, and sources of well-being (Baruch, Barnett, and Rivers, 1983; Bateson, 1989, 1994; Brown and Gilligan, 1992; Caffarella and Olson, 1993; Crose, 1997; Estes, 1992; Gilligan, 1979, 1982; Hancock, 1985; Jordan, 1997c; Jordan and others, 1991; Josselson, 1996; Miller, 1986; Peck, 1986). The metaphor of an ever-changing web of interconnectedness is often used to describe how women grow and develop throughout their lives. These webs often have very different patterns, sometimes intricate and other times simple, and yet always changing.

The Stone Center relational model provides an excellent example of a model of development that views relationships as central to development (Jordan, 1991a, 1991b, 1997a, 1997b; Surrey, 1991). This model "goes beyond saying that women value relationships; we are suggesting that the deepest sense of one's being is continuously formed in connection to others and is inextricably tied to relational formation. The primary feature, rather than structure marked by separateness and autonomy, is increasing empathic responsiveness in the context of interpersonal mutuality" (Jordan, 1997a, p. 15). Empathy—being able to understand authentically and be a part of the experiences of others—is central to the relational model. Mutual empathy, "characterized by the flow of empathic attunement between people" (Jordan, 1997a, p. 15), then becomes the key to development. Jordan observes that in Western cultures, "there has been a split along gender lines between the ideal of a separate, autonomous, objective male self and a relational, connected, and empathic female self" (Jordan, 1997a, p. 21). Although most authors agree with Jordan's beliefs that the relational model best fits with women, at least white women within Western cultures, there are others who would argue that the importance of connectedness to development also applies to women of color and perhaps even to men in general (Erikson, Erikson, and Kivnick, 1986; Jones, 1995; Levinson and Levinson, 1996; Tatum, 1997; Turner, 1997).

Numerous scholars, writing primarily from their knowledge of women's development and feminist pedagogy, have spoken to the importance of relationships and connectedness to the learning process in adulthood (Belenky, Clinchy, Goldberger, and Tarule, 1986; Caffarella, 1992, 1996; Fiddler and Marienau, 1995; Goldberger, Tarule, Clinchy, and Belenky, 1996; Hayes, 1989; Maher and Tetreault, 1994; Taylor and Marienau, 1995). For example, Belenky, Clinchy, Goldberger, and Tarule (1986) coined the term *connected teaching,* which describes a process of collaborative knowing among learners and instructors, and Fiddler and Marienau (1995, p. 76) offer a model of learner-centered teaching that includes the notion that learning is "promoted by interactions among one's experiences and ideas, and those of others." More specifically, Caffarella (1996, pp. 40–42) advocates that adult educators incorporate four key ideas into their practice relating to the theme of centrality of relationships: "(1) use collaborative interaction as one of the fundamental ways to plan and organize learning experiences; (2) foster a climate for learning where learners and instructors support each other in the learning process, both in and out of formal learning situations; (3) use a cooperative communication style; and (4) recognize that feelings are a critical part of fostering relationships in learning experiences." Although Caffarella speaks to the role of educators in primarily formal settings, these same ideas are also relevant for both nonformal and informal learning activities. This can be seen, for example, in studies of learning through social action programs and through informal or self-directed methods.

Recurring Developmental Issues

Recurring developmental issues is yet another way of organizing the literature on psychological development. We have chosen the issues of identity and intimacy as two examples, although other themes could be explored. These themes of identity and intimacy, which some authors equate with the time-honored notions of work and love (for example, Freud, as cited in Rohrlich, 1980; Baruch, Barnett, and Rivers, 1983; Vaillant, 1977), are fundamental to the lives of adults. The theme of intimacy centers on building meaningful relationships, while identity issues focus on questions of who we are and what we believe in. Some developmental theorists, like Erikson (1982) and Levinson (Levinson, 1986; Levinson and Levinson, 1996), place these developmental markers on a time continuum, most often during the adolescent and young adulthood phases. In Erikson's theory, for example, "adolescents face *identity* versus *identity diffusion* and learn the virtue of fidelity. Young adults face *intimacy* versus *isolation* and learn the virtue of love" (Chickering and Reisser, 1993, p. 22). Other scholars, including many who study women's development, argue that these themes are salient throughout adult lives (Apter, 1995; Caffarella and Olson, 1993; Chickering and Reisser, 1993; Josselson, 1996; Merriam and Clark, 1991, 1992).

Josselson (1987, 1996), through her longitudinal study of women, found four pathways to identity formation: guardians, pathmakers, searchers, and drifters. Guardians seem to have always known who they were and where they were going without considering alternative paths. The pathmakers, in contrast, consider and try out alternative ways of being and believing before making any commitments to who they are and what they want to be. Searchers continually struggle with making choices about their identities. They are uncertain about who they are or want to be, but they are trying to figure it out. And drifters "are without commitments and not struggling to make them, either feeling lost or following the impulse of the moment" (Josselson, 1996, p. 36). Josselson (1996, p. 40) stresses that adults can move in and out of these different pathways and that one's "identity continues to be modified through adult life.... Identity is always both product and process; it embodies continuity and change."

Our stance is in agreement with Josselson and others: these two major themes of identity and intimacy are salient throughout adult lives, and therefore educators of adults need to be aware of these continuing developmental issues in working with adult learners. Issues of who we are and how we fit in the world are never totally resolved. Rather, finding our identity is "an evolving narrative quest.... The story is created and revised across the adult years as the changing person and the person's changing world negotiate niches, places, opportunities, and positions within which the person can live, and live meaningfully" (McAdams, 1994, pp. 306–307). Men and women also revisit issues of intimacy over and over again in their lives through multiple contexts: in families with the birth and growth of children; in the loss of a spouse or partner through divorce or death; and in wider social networks of building friendships, as well as structuring relationships with colleagues at work.

Merriam and Clark's study (1991, 1992) gives a clear picture of the patterns of the intersection of work and love and how these patterns relate to learning. More specifically, these authors discovered three broad patterns: the parallel pattern, the steady/fluctuating pattern, and the divergent pattern. In the *parallel pattern,* work and love are intertwined; "change in one area is reflected by change in the other. The *steady/fluctuating pattern* ... shows one area remaining steady ... , while the other fluctuates. In this pattern the steady domain whether it be work or love—appears to function as a stabilizer or source of security, and people tend to locate their identity in this area" (Merriam and Clark, 1991, p. xv). In the *divergent pattern,* work and love exist independently and often in opposition to one another. Although Merriam and Clark caution against generalizability of these patterns because their sample was limited (well educated, white, and heavily female), they assume these patterns might also be present in more diverse populations. In summary, they view work and love events of people's lives as functioning in two ways: "as a stimulus for other learning, and as a source of learning in and of themselves" (Merriam and Clark, 1991, p. 213). Learning, as noted earlier, was often a result of coping with a specific life event and the transition period triggered by that life event. And finally, learning was most likely to occur when "things were going well in both the work and love arenas. Apparently people need the energy and resources available in good times to engage in significant learning" (p. 213).

A number of authors have suggested specific ways that educators of adults can relate one or both of these two fundamental themes of development to their practice (Beatty and Wolf, 1996; Caffarella, 1992, 1996; Chickering and Reisser, 1993; Maher and Tetreault, 1994; Pratt and others,

1998; Wolf and Leahy, 1998). Pratt and others (1998), for example, in offering five perspectives on teaching, speak to the importance of the nurturing perspective. In this perspective, an instructor is "fundamentally concerned with the development of each learner's concept of self as learner per se" (Pratt and others, 1998, p. 49). "Learners' efficacy and self-esteem issues become the ultimate criteria against which learning success is measured" (p. 164). Pratt stresses that nurturing educators are caring and sincerely interested in their learners and can enter their learners' worlds in an empathic manner. And Caffarella (1996, p. 44) has offered three specific suggestions for responding to these developmental themes of identity and intimacy:

1. Recognize that some [learners] may be wrestling with the issues of who they are and what they want to be as educators, especially in times of major changes in their work situations or [personal lives].
2. Encourage [learners] to find, fashion, and use what has been termed the "authentic self" or one's voice in the instructional process. The heart of sharing one's authentic self is the use of "I" and "we" versus "her" or "them."
3. Have instructors serve as role models in helping [learners] share their changing sense of selves.

Beatty and Wolf (1996) have added to these suggestions by outlining an assistance pattern for older adult learners that includes activities such as establishing relationships of trust and credibility with learners and guiding learners in the pursuit of alternative avenues of change.

SUMMARY

Adult developmental theory and research offer a rich array of material from which numerous implications can be drawn about learning in adulthood. This section has reviewed the developmental characteristics of adults from two perspectives: biological aging and psychological change. With regard to biological aging, all adults experience some changes as they age. Many of these changes, such as weight gain, graying hair, and wrinkles, while unwelcome and unsettling perhaps, have no effect on learning. The changes that can affect learning, such as deterioration of sight and hearing, changes in reaction time, and disease, vary widely from person to person. Not all adults will lose their hearing, be unable to complete a task in a specified time, or be impaired by acute or chronic illness. Furthermore, we know that adults compensate for physical changes such that learning may not seem affected at all.

Psychological changes in adulthood have been charted by a number of researchers. This work can be loosely grouped into three categories: sequential, life events and transitions, and relational models of development. The sequential models of development of Levinson, Gould, Erikson, Kohlberg, and others attempt to delineate the common themes of adult life according to what phase or stage of life one is in. The characteristics and concerns of a particular time of life have been linked to learning through what Havighurst (1972) called the "teachable moment." Educators who frame programs according to these models believe their role is to help each individual move vertically to the highest possible stage of development or horizontally through the various life phases.

One alternative to the sequential models of development is the life events and transitions framework. Life events are happenings that shape people's lives. Although life events are usually not thought of as connecting to specific age periods, some seem to be tied more to age than others. Transitions, which are precipitated by life events or even nonevents, are processes that over time can, but not necessarily do, lead to learning and change. Adults often engage in learning as one way to cope with the life events they encounter, whether that learning is related to or just precipitated by a life event. Learning within these times of transition is most often linked to work and family, with the most significant amounts of learning happening during what we would term the good times of our lives. Yet although a great deal more learning happens during the good times than the bad, extracting deeper meanings from these events more often occurs during what we perceive as the difficult times, such as a death in the family, divorce, or serious illness.

A third approach to development, based primarily in studies of women, is grounded in the notion that relationships are central to development. The relational model emphasizes that our sense of self is continuously formed in connection to others, with empathic attunement to others as central. From this model and other writings on women's development and feminist pedagogy has come the emphasis on the importance of relationships and collaboration in learning, including the significance of recognizing feelings as a critical part of fostering relational learning.

The section concluded with a discussion of recurring developmental themes. The two themes of identity and intimacy, often equated as the time-honored notions of work and love, are seen as fundamental to the lives of adults. Although some theorists place these themes on a time continuum, others view them as the ones that most adults revisit throughout their lives as relationships and roles in life change. Educators in formal and nonformal settings will likely have at least a few learners in their activities who are wrestling with issues of who they are and what they want to be, especially in times of major changes in their work situations or personal lives. In addition, identity and intimacy issues may lead to seeking out adult learning activities.

SOCIOCULTURAL AND INTEGRATIVE PERSPECTIVES ON DEVELOPMENT

Sharan B. Merriam
Rosemary S. Caffarella

Scholars have taken many different perspectives about what development in adulthood is all about. For years, the major assumption was that the nexus of development lay with the individual person, whether those forces were genetically preprogrammed or chosen by that person. This belief led to a plethora of books and manuals on how to get adulthood "right," from the many books on the power of loving ourselves to those that advocate ways to use and enhance own our inborn personalities. More recently, there has been an increasing recognition that explaining development in adulthood is more than just focusing on the individualized self. Rather, emphasis has been placed on our collective selves as defined by society. Equally important to development is how society characterizes defining aspects of adulthood, such as age, race, gender, class, ethnicity, and sexual orientation. For example, older people in many Westernized countries are accorded lesser status than young and middle-aged adults. People of color are shunned by many whites, either openly or through less overt ways, like where they choose to live and whom they associate with. Poor people become invisible in the social structure, other than being told regularly to pull themselves up by their bootstraps and get their lives in order. And gays and lesbians fear losing their jobs or being ridiculed for their lifestyle. In addition, there is an increasing interest in viewing adult development from many perspectives. Although this kind of theorizing is difficult to operationalize, it holds much promise; many adults are aware of the complex and interrelated nature of their biological, psychological, and sociocultural selves.

Highlighted in this section are two additional perspectives of adult development: sociocultural factors that influence development and what we are calling the integrative paradigm of development. Addressed first are three strands of work from the sociocultural perspective that have figured prominently in our discussion of the connections of adult development and learning: work on social roles and timing of life events; on the socially constructed notions of race, gender, ethnicity, and sexual orientation; and on cross-cultural studies of adulthood. Interwoven within the discussion of each of these ideas is their connection to adult learning. In the second portion of this section we discuss theories exemplifying an integrative perspective of development. The section concludes with a short overview of why educators of adults need to consider multiple perspectives of adulthood in their research and practice.

SOCIOCULTURAL FACTORS

The sociocultural perspective of adult development moves us from focusing on how development is primarily an internal process to one which acknowledges the importance of the social world in which we live (Dannefer, 1984, 1989, 1996; Levenson and Crumpler, 1996). With in this perspective the emphasis is placed on how the world about us defines who and what we ought to be as adults based on our age, the color of our skin, whether we are male or female, how rich or poor we are, what our ethnic backgrounds are, and our sexual orientation. Scholars writing from this perspective view "the sociocultural environment as a point of departure" for studying the life course of adults (Elder, 1995, p. 103) and stress the socially constructed nature of how adulthood is defined. Bee (1996, p. 41), for example, has listed how adult lives differ in our society based on social status or social class, which "are typically defined or measured in terms of three dimensions: education, income, and occupation." She goes on to observe that "distinctions between 'blue collar' and 'white collar', or 'middle class' and 'working class', are fundamental status distinctions" (p. 41), at least in North American culture. More specifically

Bee asserts that people with higher status, compared to those of lower status, have the following characteristics (pp. 41–42):

- In the United States, over the past several generations at least, the majority of both men and women end up in occupations at the same broad level of social status as their parents.
- Middle class adults, as a group, marry later and have fewer children than do working-class adults. Both of these differences affect the timing of various subsequent adult life experiences, such as the departure of the last child.
- The life course of middle-class adults is more likely to be advantaged in a variety of ways: They are less likely to experience periods of unemployment; they are healthier and live longer; … retain a higher level of intellectual functioning longer into old age … ; and are, in general, more satisfied with their lives.

Bee has developed similar lists for people of different racial and ethnic, and gender groups.

We offer three salient strands of work from the literature on the sociocultural perspective of adulthood that provide us with different ways of looking at adult development: adult social roles and the timing of life events; the socially constructed notions of race, ethnicity, gender, and sexual orientation and how these affect development; and cross-cultural studies of adulthood. Interwoven within the discussion of each of these strands of work are implications for learning in adulthood.

Social Roles and the Timing of Life Events

The earlier work on the sociocultural dimensions of adulthood focused on social role taking and the notion of the timing of life events. Social roles are defined as both positions and associated expectations determined primarily by normative beliefs held by society (Hughes and Graham, 1990). Examples of these various roles include parent, spouse, worker, child, and friend. Changes in one's social position result from modifications of these roles (such as redefining the role of parent when both parents assume employment) and the taking on of new roles (such as wife to widow or paid worker to retired person). These changes may be initiated by the individual or by others; a parent might ask an older child to take on the role of worker to help pay for her college expenses, for example, or changes in legislative policy might give a specific group in society, such as minorities or women, more or perhaps less control over their own lives. This focus on social roles has fostered a number of research traditions in such areas as career development and marriage and family roles (see Bee, 1996; Berger, 1998; Lefrancois, 1996).

The research on the timing of life events, which is exemplified by the work of Neugarten and others (Neugarten, 1976, 1979; Neugarten and others, 1964; Neugarten and Danton, 1973), suggests that "every society is age-graded, and every society has a system of social expectations regarding age-appropriate behavior. The individual passes through a socially regulated cycle from birth to death as inexorably as he [sic] passes through the biological cycle: a succession of socially delineated age-statuses, each with its recognized rights, duties and obligations" (Neugarten, 1976, p. 16). Although the timing of events has changed somewhat and the deadlines for completing such events have become more variable since Neugarten completed her original work, adults are still very much aware of when they should be doing what (Settersten and Hägestad, 1996). Neugarten goes on to point out that it is not the events themselves that necessarily precipitate crisis or change. "What is more important is the timing of those events. If they occur off-time, that is, outside the 'normal, expectable life cycle' (being widowed in young adulthood or fired close to retirement, for example), they are much more likely to cause trauma or conflict" (Merriam, 1984, p. 22). From this vantage point, the study of adult development then becomes a study of life events construed from socially constructed beliefs, whereas in the psychological tradition, the focus is on the life events themselves as markers and processes. More recent work on this concept of the timing of life events has been completed by such scholars as Clausen (1995), Bengtson (1996), and Settersten and Hägestad (1996).

The idea that learning in adulthood is related to appropriate role taking, as defined by society's expectations, has a long history in adult education, from the early citizenship education program for immigrants to today's workplace learning programs. Several writers have suggested that programs be developed related to the social roles of adults. Kidd (1973) and Knox (1977), for example, explored how changes in social roles can be related to learning activities. Specially, Kidd (1973) outlined a taxonomy suggested by Malcolm Knowles at a UNESCO seminar in Hamburg in 1972 that takes into account not only roles but also the competencies related to those roles. The implied assumption underlying this taxonomy is that learning programs could be built to address these competencies for adults going through role changes or wishing to become more competent in their current roles (for example, family member, worker, and citizen). Even learning on our own may be driven by what society expects of us, such as learning parenting skills or taking care of aging parents. For the most part, adult educators have developed programs around role taking to the age-normative times of life events and have not taken into account those people who are "off-time." More recently there has been some change in this thinking. For example, hospice programs, which both offer support and teach caretakers how to care for dying people, do not discriminate whom they will serve based either on the age of the patient or the caretaker.

Socially Constructed Notions of Race, Ethnicity, Gender, and Sexual Orientation

Researchers have been especially interested over the past decade in the socially constructed notions of race, ethnicity, gender, and sexual orientation as they relate to adult development (Bakari, 1997; Bem, 1993; Cross, 1991; D'Augelli and Patterson, 1995; Etter-Lewis and Foster, 1996; Evans, Forney, and Guido-DiBrito, 1998; Helms, 1993; Mashengele, 1997; Ponterotto, Casas, Suzuki, and Alexander, 1995; Tennant and Pogson, 1995; Wilson, 1996). Discussing these different constructs in relationship to development is difficult because they often overlap and have been given different meanings by researchers. For example, some use the terms *race* and *ethnicity* interchangeably, while others clearly distinguish between these two concepts. What makes it even more difficult to establish the connection between these ideas and development is that adults are rarely just black or white, male or female, homosexual or heterosexual, or of one cultural origin. Rather most adults come in many shades and variations. For example, they may be female, but also white, of Hispanic origin, and a lesbian; or they may be male, but also black of African origin and heterosexual. Although this complexity makes it difficult to form any generalizations, researchers nevertheless are working to untangle the intersections of race, class, gender, sexual orientation, and ethnicity.

Prominent theories of racial and ethnic identity development grounded at least in part on the assumption that views of adulthood are socially constructed include those of Cross (1991, 1995), Helms (1993, 1995), Phinney (1990), and Sodowsky, Kwan, and Pannu (1995). Cross (1995, p. 98), for example, defines his model of Nigrescence as one "that explains how assimilated as well as deracinated, deculturalized, or miseducated adolescents or Black adults are transformed, by a series of circumstances and events, into persons who are more Black or Afrocentrically aligned." Moving through the five stages of pre-encounter, encounter, immersion-emersion, internalization, and internalization-commitment, though not necessarily in a linear journey, blacks are able to change "the salience of race and culture in [their lives] ..., define what is important [to them] in adult life, and ... feel totally new" (pp. 114–115). One of the consequences of this movement is that "a person's conception of Blackness tends to become more open, expansive, and sophisticated" (p. 114). They become more at peace and comfortable with themselves as black and replace "an 'I' or egocentric perspective with a 'we' or 'group' perspective" (Evans, Forney, and Guido-DiBrito, 1998, p. 76). Helms (1993, 1995), on the other hand, proposes a process model of white racial identity that consists of two phases: abandonment of racism and defining a nonracist white identity. In this process individuals give up their white privilege and "abandon cultural and institutional racism as well as personal racism. [Rather, they] actively seek opportunities to learn from other cultural groups.... It is a process wherein [persons are] continually open to new information and new ways of thinking about racial and cultural variables" (Helms, 1993, p. 66).

Defining gender influences on development from the sociocultural perspective is somewhat different from the psychological tradition. Although scholars writing from a psychological perspective on women and development also often acknowledge the importance of context and environment in development, they do not necessarily see this as the major determinant in women's development. Rather, they more often speak to the lack of women's voices in developmental theory and how that theory might differ if those voices were included. Researchers drawing primarily on the sociocultural perspective view gender as embedded in our cultural discourses and systems of social organization. The perceived differences between males and females become a way to organize our lives. "It is thus not simply that women and men are seen to be different but that this male-female difference is super-imposed on so many aspects of the social world that a cultural connection is thereby forged between sex and virtually every other aspect of human experience, including modes of dress and social roles and even ways of expressing emotion and experiencing sexual desire" (Bem, 1993, p. 2). Thus, a change in perspective about how women and men grow and develop can happen only if we assist adults in examining what they believe about how men and women "act and be" in terms of the dominant culture in which they live. Bem (1993, p. 2) observes, for example, that at least in the United States, males and male experiences are viewed as "a neutral standard or norm, and females' experience as a sex-specific deviation from that norm."

Theories of sexual identity formation of heterosexuals are discussed quite often in the literature. In fact, most developmental theories, whether psychologically or socioculturally based, are primarily drawn from samples of heterosexual individuals or sexual orientation is either not known or not even considered. What is less common are theories that conceptualize gay, lesbian, and bisexual development and especially those that view development as a social construction. D'Augelli's (1994, p. 317) work represents one such model in that he takes into account "the complex factors that influence the development of people in context over historical time." More specifically he identifies six interactive processes that involve individuals' choosing to give up their prescribed heterosexual identity and the privileges associated with that identity to take on one that is still not well accepted by mainstream society. D'Augelli views this as a relatively slow process due to the prevalent social and cultural norms against homosexual or bisexual orientations. Brooks and Edwards (1997) believe that the sharing of narrative stories of people of different sexual orientations is one way to understand better sexual identity development as well as other developmental issues where culture is acknowledged as a key component of the developmental process. Brooks and Edwards go on to observe that "to experience our lives as different from the dominant narrative is frightening. If this experience is supported by a strong counter narrative such as that of lesbians or certain minority and racial and ethnic groups, we can find a space to live out our knowledge knowing there are others like ourselves. However, when our experience remains unarticulated and inchoate, we come to know ourselves as misfits" (p. 69).

This sentiment to share the narratives of one another's lives has been the impetus for many of the studies that address a mixture of two or more of these categories of race, ethnicity, gender, and sexual orientation (Neuman and Peterson, 1997). One such seminal work are the vivid descriptive studies of Coles and Coles (1978, 1980) of women from all walks of life. Through a biographical approach, the story is told of "the daily battles, the losses, the small victories, the long, burdened marches across time and space" (1978, p. 273) of black, Chicano, Eskimo, and Pueblo American Indian women, among others. Coles and Coles conclude that the interwoven factors of gender, race, and social class have had a major impact on these women's lives: "The enemy is a given social order, yes; an economic system, yes; but also and quite distinctly—or as George Eliot might want to say quite definitely—a certain number of men" (p. 232).

More current examples of the use of narratives to tell the stories of development across categories include the work of Etter-Lewis and Foster (1996) and A. Wilson (1996). *Unrelated Kin*

(Etter-Lewis and Foster, 1996) tells the stories of women of color: African American, Native American, Asian American, Latina, and non-Western women. Etter-Lewis and Foster observe that "documentation of women's lives has tended to be difficult due to a variety of factors, including women's relatively low social status and marginalization within society" (p. 8). In their work, these authors "place women of color at the center of their communities rather than at the periphery. They are the authorities and standard-bearers of their own lives" (p. 10). Patricia Bell-Scott and Juanita Johnson-Bailey also tell the stories, or what they term the "flat-footed truths," of women of African American origin. "To tell the flat-footed truth means to offer a story or statement that is straightforward, unshakable, and unembellished" (Bell-Scott, 1998, p. xix). Bell-Scott, like Etter-Lewis and Foster (1996), views this as risky business for the twenty-seven creative spirits who tell of their lives as women artists: "This kind of truth telling, especially by and about Black women, can be risky business because our lives are often devalued and our voices periodically silenced" (p. xix). Yet Bell-Scott also observes that there have always been women, both within and outside the African American communities, like Audre Lorde and Anita Hill, "who insist on speaking truths in the face of disbelief and public criticism" (p. xix). Through essays, interviews, poetry, and photographic images, the contributors to *Flat-Footed Truths* (Bell-Scott with Johnson-Bailey, 1998) have created extended conversations about "the challenge of telling one's own life ..., the adventure of claiming lives neglected or lost, ... the affirmation of lives of resistance, and the optimism and healing of lives transformed" (p. xix).

Wilson (1996, p. 303) speaks directly to the problems of trying to treat "sexual and racial identity as independent developmental pathways. While this simplifying division may make it easier to generate theory, it may also make it less likely that the resulting theory will describe people's real-life developmental experiences." Wilson describes her experiences of trying to find herself as a lesbian indigenous American—"a two-spirited person." She notes that it was "in the context of Native spirituality [that] I learned about the traditions of two-spirit people. I acquired strength from elders and leaders who were able to explain that as an indigenous woman who is also a lesbian, I needed to use the gifts of difference wisely" (p. 313). Wilson's strength and identity are, in her words, "inseparable from [my] culture" (p. 315). She also makes the point that the mainstream lesbian and gay communities rarely recognize the two-spirit identity and often discriminate against gay and lesbian indigenous Americans.

Chávez, Guido-DiBrito, and Mallory (1996) have presented an intriguing and complex model of how we learn to value what they have termed "the other": anyone who is different from ourselves in race, ethnicity, social class, gender, or sexual orientation. This diversity development model, built on the work of Kegan (1994), Cass (1979), Devine (1989), and others, provides "a framework in which individuals develop in a non-linear way toward valuing and possibly choosing to validate those who are 'other'" (p. 8). As shown in Figure 1-2, the framework consists of five periods: unawareness, awareness, questioning/self-exploration, risk-taking/other exploration, and integration. This process "can be experienced at various ages, simultaneously [if dealing with more than one form of "the other"], repeatedly, or not at all" (p. 9). The outcome for individuals who go through this process is that they are "able to interact confidently in and out of their own 'culture' and have the ability to affirm choices different than their own" (p. 14). Although this model has not been tested empirically, it holds much promise for understanding how to embrace diversity within our lives.

Numerous scholars, primarily within the past decade, have acknowledged the importance of the socially constructed notions of race, ethnicity, gender, and sexual orientation to understanding learning in adulthood (Hawkesworth, 1997; Hayes and Colin, 1994a; Maher and Tetreault, 1994; Resides, 1996; Ross-Gordon, Martin, and Briscoe, 1990a, 1990b; Tennant and Pogson, 1995; Tisdell, 1995). Not everyone wants to admit that the issues of race, ethnicity, gender, and sexual orientation have or should have any educational relevance, either in relationship to the content being taught or the instructional techniques being used. Some learners become uncomfortable, angry, or just plain turned off when these issues are brought forward.

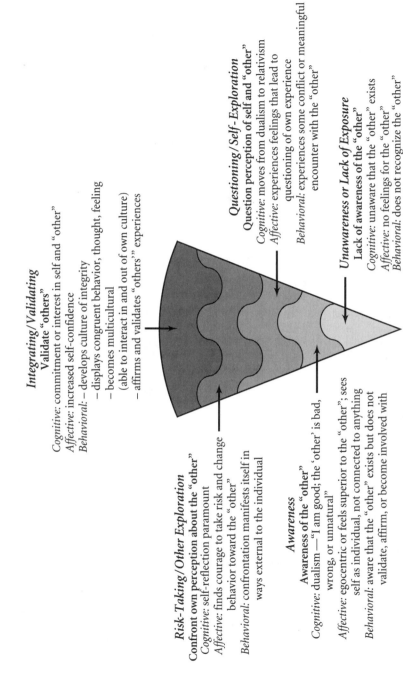

Integrating/Validating
Validate "others"
Cognitive: commitment or interest in self and "other"
Affective: increased self-confidence
Behavioral: – develops culture of integrity
– displays congruent behavior, thought, feeling
– becomes multicultural
(able to interact in and out of own culture)
– affirms and validates "others" experiences

Questioning/Self - Exploration
Question perception of self and "other"
Cognitive: moves from dualism to relativism
Affective: experiences feelings that lead to questioning of own experience
Behavioral: experiences some conflict or meaningful encounter with the "other"

Unawareness or Lack of Exposure
Lack of awareness of the "other"
Cognitive: unaware that the "other" exists
Affective: no feelings for the "other"
Behavioral: does not recognize the "other"

Risk-Taking/Other Exploration
Confront own perception about the "other"
Cognitive: self-reflection paramount
Affective: finds courage to take risk and change behavior toward the "other"
Behavioral: confrontation manifests itself in ways external to the individual

Awareness
Awareness of the "other"
Cognitive: dualism —"I am good; the 'other' is bad, wrong, or unnatural"
Affective: egocentric or feels superior to the "other"; sees self as individual, not connected to anything
Behavioral: aware that the "other" exists but does not validate, affirm, or become involved with

Figure 1-2. Frameworks in Learning to Value the "Other."

Source: Chávez, Guido-DiBrito, and Mallory, 1996.

Some have never considered the idea that some of these groups (for example, women and Native Americans) may have different views on how adults learn or how organizations should be managed and led. They instead want context-free ideas of adult learning and leadership, free from social or political orientations, including the socially constructed notions of race, ethnicity, gender, or sexual orientation.

Tisdell (1995), among others (Ellsworth, 1989; Hayes and Colin, 1994a; Maher and Tetreault, 1994), has pointed out the important role that power plays when introducing socially constructed notions of race, ethnicity, gender, and sexual orientation into formal and even non formal programs of adult learning. Tisdell observes that "what counts as knowledge in a particular learning context—and decisions about what gets included in the curriculum for a given learning activity—are decisions made with attention to the politics of this particular educational context and to what is seen as 'real' knowledge relevant to this educational context" (p. 11). Teaching strategies that allow participants to connect the material to their own life experiences, allow for reflective time, confront differences, and bring together theory and practice seem to provide useful starting points for doing this (Caffarella, 1992; Mezirow and Associates, 1990; Wlodkowski and Ginsberg, 1995). Storytelling, critical incident techniques, role plays, small group work, case studies, and problem-posing strategies seem especially appropriate for promoting different voices, self-disclosure, and alternative ways of looking at these issues.

Other authors have depicted what effective adult education programs might look like that serve people from diverse backgrounds. Ross-Gordon, Martin, and Briscoe (1990a), for example, outline nine characteristics that they found were associated with effective programs that serve minority populations. Among these nine are preserving the cultural distinctness of groups, accommodating preferred learning strategies or learning environments, reaching out to the most disenfranchised, and sponsoring activities that increase the level of intercultural sensitivity of staff (pp. 103–104). These authors also suggest that we "improve our own knowledge and understanding of other cultural groups, particularly those within our respective service areas" (p. 106), and ensure that they have access to all programs of adult education, even if this means changing the way we practice. Tisdell (1995) also speaks eloquently to this issue in her description of what she terms "inclusive learning environments for all adults": environments that take into account the atmosphere of both "the specific learning context of the classroom or learning activity and the organizational context in which one is working" (p. 83).

Cross-Cultural Studies of Development

Although a vast number of cross-cultural studies have been completed in the anthropological tradition, this material has rarely been incorporated into the adult development literature. The lack of cross-cultural material is especially evident when development is viewed from the sociocultural versus psychological paradigm. There are, however, some notable exceptions. Erikson (1978), for example, has provided an excellent sampling of adulthood in other cultures. His essays, primarily linked to the religious orientation of each cultural grouping, give a diverse picture of how the life cycle is depicted according to religious traditions. More recent examples include an edited book by Valsiner (1995), which contains two essays about adult life in India, and the work of Pratt (1991), which focuses on the different conceptions of self within China and the United States. These three studies provide helpful illustrations of how culture is often one of the defining factors in the way that adults develop and change.

In the Valsiner volume, Ullrich (1995) describes a co-constructivist perspective of life course changes among Havik Brahmins in a South India village. She vividly portrays how men and women of this culture, over a sixteen-year period, negotiated and accommodated to new situations, which resulted in changes in many of the ways they carried out their roles in life. She describes J.A., for example, who opened the way for women in her village to pursue careers by being the first woman to take a salaried teaching position at a nursery school prior to her marriage: "At that time a salary provided a person with economic resources to spend as desired. Women had traditionally been dependent on men for every cent, just as sons and younger brothers were dependent on fathers and older brothers.... After J.A.'s marriage, nursery school teaching became an option for women awaiting marriage [and] was reserved for unmarried women.... Now there are [even] Havik Brahmin women employed elsewhere as nursery school teachers who have decided against marriage" (pp. 183–184). J.A.'s story was an exemplar for unmarried women to have more choices in their developmental journeys.

Verma (1995) also analyzed the changes that have taken place in the social roles of women over the past three generations in India. Using a cultural-historic paradigm, she describes how the roles of rural, middle-class, and higher-upper-class affluent women have been altered over time. More specifically Verma depicts changes in the relationship between the mother-in-law and the daughter-in-law, the *purdah* (or veiling), and women as home managers. For example, the

> change in the *purdah* system across generations in India has been quite notable.... *Purdah* did not mean just veiling, but some strict rules that forbade women to go outside their homes for visiting relatives and friends, for shopping or entertainment, or even for getting an education.... *Purdah* meant almost total seclusion of women from the outside world, and it was a manmade rule for safeguarding women's chastity and modesty from outsiders and the "evil eyes." [p. 148]

The changes in the *purdah* system have allowed women to obtain a higher educational level and employment outside the home, which have expanded their developmental potential and options. Verma concludes "that the transformation in women's social role in India has been gradual but surely taking place at a number of manifest levels. However, the pace of the transformation has been relatively 'fast' or 'slow' for different categories of women, depending on their socioeconomic status, education, and place of habitation" (p. 161).

And finally, Pratt (1991) and Pratt, Kelly, and Wong (1998) have challenged us to look at the conceptions of self from two different cultural perspectives, that of China and the United States. He stresses that definitions of the self in China are tied to family continuity, socially prescribed roles, the acceptance of hierarchical relationships as supreme, compliance with authority, a value on stability versus change, and the current political ideology. "The resulting self," he writes, "finds an identity that is externally ascribed, subordinated to the collective, seeks fulfillment through the performance of duty, and would have little meaningful existence apart from ordained roles and patterns of affiliations. If this is true, the Chinese self is, largely, an externally ascribed, highly malleable, and socially constructed entity" (Pratt, 1991, p. 302). In contrast, Pratt views the self as defined by cultural tradition in the United States as driven "primarily by individual autonomy and the right to choose as central values to be protected and promoted" (Pratt, 1991, p. 303). Although this way of viewing the self is often equated with the masculine view of self versus the more feminine connected self, these different ways of conceptualizing the self lead to important implications for the practice of adult education.

Pratt (1991) and Pratt, Kelly, and Wong (1998) go on to provide a link between how these different views of the idealized self, and thus the end point of development, need to be considered when designing learning situations for adults. More specifically, Pratt questions whether we can impose as part of our practice of adult education our Westernized assumptions about adult development on people who have a very different sense of what characterizes how mature adults should function. "For example [in China], attempting to get adult students to express their opinions and feelings, choose among learning assignments, participate in self-evaluation, or challenge the stated positions of those in authority, for example, the instructor's opinions, usually meets with some resistance.... What lies beneath these patterns is far more than simple reticence or courtesy. These behaviors are deeply rooted in a culture and society that is profoundly different than those that expect students to be outspoken and autonomous" (Pratt, 1991, p. 305). We have made similar observations in working with adult learners from other parts of Asia, such as Taiwan and Indonesia.

Pratt concludes that "adult education within any country is not simply a neutral body of knowledge and procedures.... There are significant cultural and ideological differences [in how adulthood is defined] ... which must be considered when exporting (or importing) educational practices and procedures" (Pratt, 1991, p. 307).

One other example of the importance of cross-cultural studies of adult development and learning is the recognition of the value and worth of indigenous ways of learning. In a provocative book, Cajete (1994) advocates that American Indian educators develop "a contemporary, culturally based, educational process founded upon traditional Tribal values, orientations and principles, while *simultaneously* using the most appropriate concepts, technologies, and content of modern education" (p. 17). In making this statement he assumes that "American Indians view life through a different cultural metaphor than mainstream America" and therefore have been "forced to adapt to an educational process not of their making" (p. 19). Greater opportunities for learning could be developed for American Indians if the foundations of education are "indigenously inspired and ecologically based" (p. 21). Cajete outlines a number of elements that characterize indigenous educational processes. These elements are grounded in the beliefs that "environmental relationships, myths, visionary tradition, traditional arts, Tribal community, and Nature centered spirituality have traditionally formed the foundations in American Indian life for discovering one's true face (character, potential, identity), one's heart (soul, creative self, true passion), and one's foundation (true work, vocation), all of which lead to the expression of a complete life" (p. 23).

Other scholars who have spoken to the importance of acknowledging indigenous culture in adult learning include Brennan (1997) and Kidd and Coletta (1980).

INTEGRATIVE PERSPECTIVES ON DEVELOPMENT

The challenge to create integrative perspectives of adult development that reflect a more holistic picture of adult life has received attention in the literature over the past two decades. Observations by long-term scholars of development (Levinson, 1986, Levinson and Levinson, 1996; Moen, Elder, and Luscher, 1995; Rodin, Schooler, and Schaie, 1990; Tennant and Pogson, 1995) and those who have studied adulthood for the first time (Bryant, 1989) make us cognizant of the incompleteness of our narrow definitions of adulthood, whether from the psychological, the biological, or the sociocultural perspective. As Bryant (1989, pp. 3–4) put it so eloquently, "One need only look at the plights of those in even very recent history who were out of sync with their time, the forerunners of new criteria for normal adult development—the women who could not be patently subservient to men, the men who could not be independent of emotions, the oldsters who persist in physical and sexual vigor.... It seems virtually impossible that psychologists and sociologists could concurrently accommodate the change that these individuals represent. What they can do is only observe, compute and rhapsodize over statistics, and inject some of their own thought and personal dispositions." There have been attempts to respond to the call for a more integrated theory of adult development, through combining two or more of the perspectives reviewed in this section (Baltes, 1982; Bronfenbrenner, 1995; Kahana and Kahana, 1996; Levenson and Crumpler, 1996; Magnusson, 1995; Peck, 1986; Perun and Bielby, 1980; Peters, 1989). Four models of adult development—those proposed by Baltes (1982), Magnusson (1995), Perun and Bielby (1980), and Peters (1989)—are illustrative of this new wave of theory building.

Baltes (1982, p. 18) introduced one of the earlier comprehensive models that emphasized a "multicausal and interactive view" of adult development. Drawing on the work of Havighurst, Neugarten, and others, he hypothesized that biological and environmental forces constitute the basic determinants of development. These are then influenced by three major sets of factors: normative age-graded influences (forces normally correlated with age), normative history-graded influences (events that are widely experienced by one age group of people), and nonnormative influences (factors significant to one particular person). The interaction of these influences results in developmental changes over the life span. Baltes hypothesizes that the relative significance of the three developmental influences may vary at different points in the life span—"for example, age-graded influences may be especially important … in old age, whereas history-graded nonnormative influences may predominate in early and middle adulthood" (Schaie and Willis, 1986, p. 22).

These three developmental influences (age graded, history graded, and nonnormative) have been subsumed in a later work by Baltes (1987) under the concept of contextualism as one of six theoretical propositions he proposed to guide the thinking and research in the life span perspective of development. In addition to the concept of contextualism, his other propositions are that there is no single direction for change in adulthood (multidirectionality), development consists of the joint occurrences of both growth and decline (development as gain or loss), development can take many forms (plasticity), development varies substantially in accordance with historical and cultural conditions (historical embeddedness), and further understanding of development will come from collaborative work among several disciplines, including psychology, anthropology, biology, and sociology (multidisciplinary approach). Within this life span perspective, Baltes and others (Baltes, 1982, 1987; Baltes and Reese, 1984) assume "there is *lawfulness* to the changes we see in adult life.… Our task … is to uncover and understand the nature of that lawfulness. They do *not* assume that the specific pathways followed by adults will necessarily all be the same; they do not assume that all pathways lead toward either decline or toward higher efficacy. They do assume that the underlying lawfulness will create many surface patterns" (Bee, 1996, p. 74). Baltes has also stressed the need for new "development-specific" research methodologies to address the more interactive and complex models of adult development.

One response to Baltes's concern related to methodology is a recent integrative model proposed by Magnusson (1995). Grounded in four basic assumptions, Magnusson argues that his model "can serve as a general theoretical framework for planning, implementation, and interpretation of empirical research on specific aspects of individual development" (p. 19). His four assumptions are as follows (pp. 25–29):

1. The individual functions and develops as a total integrated organism. Development does not take place in single aspects, taken out of context.
2. The individual functions and develops in a continuously ongoing, reciprocal process of interaction with his or her environment.
3. At each specific moment, individual functioning is determined in a process of continuous, reciprocal interaction between mental factors, biological factors, and behavior—on the individual side—and situational factors.
4. The individual develops in a process of continuous reciprocal interaction among psychological, biological, and environmental factors.

What is key to this model is that "individuals do not develop in terms of single variables but as total integrated systems. In this perspective, all changes during the life span of a person are characterized by lawful continuity" (p. 39). Magnusson emphasizes that his model "does not imply that the whole system of an individual must be studied at the same time. The essential function of the model is that it enables us to formulate problems at different levels of the functioning of the total organism, to implement empirical studies, and to interpret the results in a common, theoretical framework" (p. 50).

The third model we discuss is not widely known, but we have found it useful in framing development from the integrative perspective. Perun and Bielby (1980) view adulthood as "consisting of a large number of *temporal progressions*—sequences of experiences or internal changes each of which follow some timetable" (Bee, 1996, p. 75). Pictured as a set of disks, similar to machine gears rotating on a central rod, each disk represents a part of the developmental picture: physical changes, changes in nuclear family roles (like marrying and having children), changes in other family roles (such as death of a parent), changes in work roles, and changes in emotional and personal tasks of adulthood (Perun and Bielby, 1980). Each of these gears or disks moves at different rates for different people, "thus creating a unique pattern for each adult" (Bee, 1996, p. 76). For example, one person may delay having children until her early forties so she can establish herself in a career, while another may start a family in her teens and then start a career once her children are grown. The first person would have speeded up her career or work progression, while slowing down her family life cycle, while the second person would be doing just the opposite. In addition, the entire developmental process is embedded in historical time, which also affects the developmental progression in each of the major areas.

Developmental changes come from two sources within this model. The first is the basic changes that happen within each of the temporal progressions, some of them inevitable and others chosen. Second, asynchrony, which "occurs when one or more dimensions is off-time in relation to others" (Perun and Bielby, 1980, p. 105), triggers other changes. For example, when a person's spouse or partner dies in early adulthood, the nuclear family roles and possibly the work roles often change dramatically, especially if there are minor children involved. Bee (1996, p. 77) has outlined a number of "intriguing and potentially useful implications or expansions of this model." Among these are that the rate of movement along any of the temporal dimensions may be influenced by gender, race, class, ethnicity, and sexual orientation.

The final illustrative model, that of Peters (1989), is more practical in nature. Peters, as part of a framework for extension education programming through the adult life span and similar to the other models discussed, brings together the biological, psychological, and sociological aspects of adult development. The model's first key element is the changing nature of the life structure, consisting of three task-related subsystems—work, other, and self. Work consists of the job-related activities in which the person engages; other consists of the many relationships adults have, such as family, friends, and social acquaintances; and self is the individualized nature of each person. It is the interrelationship of these subsystems that depicts "who the person is" at a particular time in his or her life (p. 86). Internal forces (psychological, biological) and external forces (social expectations, economic conditions) make up the second major element in the model. These forces influence the choices people make about their work, their relationships with others, and how they see themselves as individuals. Young adults, for example, often concern themselves with building and maintaining a job or career; therefore, the work subsystem predominates, with lesser attention paid to the other aspects of life. A person's life structure does not remain stable but changes as a result of both the internal and external forces and the individual's choices. It is the reconfiguration of this life structure that is assumed to be the "essence of development" (p. 86). In addition to mapping out the model itself, Peters has outlined specific implications for educational programming in terms of both the needs assessment process and the educational strategies for learning.

Although application of these integrated models to learning in adulthood has been limited, the message conveyed by the theorists is clear: to understand development in adulthood fully, one must move beyond explanations fostered only by one or two perspectives. Educators of adults must be mindful of the impact of single-perspective theories "on shaping and maintaining conventionally held views about what it means to be a mature and healthy adult" (Tennant, 1988, p. 65). The psychological perspective, which has been used as the major lens through which educators of adults have viewed development, can be widened to include the other lens of biological, sociocultural, and integrated perspectives. Tennant and Pogson (1995) observe that "the raw material in the process of development are the organism, with its constitutionally endowed equipment; and the social environment, with its historical and cultural formations. Development thus proceeds through a constant interaction between the person and the environment. [Further], because development is contested, and because different versions of development serve the interests of different groups, it is as much a political as it is a psychological construct" (p. 199). Therefore, it is important to foster a multiperspective focus in our study and practice of how adult development theory is linked to learning in adulthood.

SUMMARY

We have reviewed in this section adult development from two perspectives: the influence of sociocultural factors on development and the integrative paradigm of development. From the sociocultural perspective, change in adulthood is determined more by sociocultural factors, such as social roles, race, and gender, than by individual maturation. Three strands of work from the sociocultural perspective were described, and implications for this work for adult learning were addressed. Discussed first was the importance of social roles, such as parent, worker, or friend. Social roles are determined primarily by societal expectations and change over time. Adult educators have often designed programs tied to social roles, such as parenting classes or workshops on retirement. Society still determines at what age we ought to be engaged in which life events.

Addressed next was the socially constructed nature of the concepts of race, gender, ethnicity, and sexual orientation and how defining these concepts as social constructions versus individual traits has affected the way we think about adult development. Representative developmental theories of Cross, Helms, Bem, and D'Augelli were reviewed, with the caveat that understanding development through their lens is difficult because scholars have given different meanings to each of these concepts. In addition, most adults rarely represent just one of these categories. For this reason, other scholars, like Wilson and Chávez, Guido-DiBrito, and Mallory, have posited developmental ideas and models that address multiple social categories. Educators of adults have more recently been interested in how race, gender, ethnicity, and sexual orientation might be linked to learning. Mention was also made of cross-cultural studies of adult development, although these types of studies are scarce. Pratt, through his work in China, and Cajete, who studied indigenous American Indian education, have contributed a great deal to our understanding of how cross-cultural studies can add to our knowledge of learning in adulthood.

The section concluded with a description of integrated perspectives on development with salient examples of theorists who have included the biological, psychological, and sociological perspectives in their models of adult development (for example, Baltes and Magnusson). To understand fully how adult development is linked to adult learning, we suggested that educators of adults move to multiple explanations of what adulthood is all about, rather than rely on just one or two paradigms. We especially need to acknowledge perspectives beyond the psychological lens that has driven our research and practice on learning in adulthood for the past three decades. The more we know about adult learners, the changes they go through, and how these changes motivate and interact with learning, the better we can structure learning experiences that both respond to and stimulate development.

COGNITIVE DEVELOPMENT IN ADULTHOOD

Sharan B. Merriam
Rosemary S. Caffarella

That other people can think so differently from us about the same things comes as no surprise. We all know people who think in absolutes; it is either right or it is wrong, good or bad. Witness some of the talk show hosts who make it clear to their listeners that their opinions are the only way to think. They voice their sentiments in many arenas, from how to bring up the kids to who not to vote for in the upcoming elections. For others, everything is relative to everything else. It seems as if these people not only change their minds a lot, but it takes them forever to get closure. And then we have all found ourselves in situations where we really do not know what to think; there is no one right answer, however long we puzzle over the question or problem. Should we quit a job because those in power act in ways we find offensive when our family depends on our salary to survive? Should we speak up in public forums about issues of race, gender, and class, if in speaking we cause enormous pain to ourselves and those closest to us? Should we be allowed to help someone we love die more peacefully, even if it means using illegal methods? Examining the myriad ways that adults think has intrigued scholars throughout the ages, from philosophers to poets and, more recently, developmental psychologists and educators. More specifically, researchers have raised questions about whether adults can change their thinking patterns, and if so what might these changing patterns of thinking look like over the adult life span.

The study of the pathways of adult cognitive development, that is, how thinking patterns change over time, is often linked to a combination of factors, primarily the interaction of maturational and environmental variables. As in other research traditions on learning, the major studies on cognitive development have been predominantly carried out with children and adolescents. When this research is extended to adulthood, the underlying assumption has often been that adults move toward a final stage of cognitive development, however that is defined, or if that stage has been attained, work at maintaining that stage. Still other theorists have posited models of cognitive development that may be unique to adulthood.

Explored here is the foundational work of Piaget and how scholars have used and extended this work. We then discuss alternative conceptualizations of cognitive development that are linear or categorical in nature (for example, Belenky, Clinchy, Goldberger, and Tarule, 1986; Perry, 1981). This discussion is followed by an exploration of dialectic thinking and models that are representative of this form of thinking. The contextual perspective on cognitive development and key theorists who represent this perspective are presented next. We conclude with an overview on the concept of wisdom, which is often posited as the pinnacle of cognitive development.

FOUNDATIONAL WORK

When we speak of cognitive development, Jean Piaget immediately comes to mind. Although Piaget's work is entirely focused on childhood cognitive development, his theory has provided the foundation for work completed with adults. Piaget proposed four invariant stages of cognitive development that are age related. These stages represent "qualitatively different ways of making sense, understanding, and constructing a knowledge of the world" (Tennant, 1988, p. 68). In Piaget's view, children's thought processes move from innate reflex actions (sensory-motor stage), to being able to represent concrete objects in symbols and words (preoperational stage), to an understanding of concepts and relationships of ideas (concrete operational stage), to an ability to reason hypothetically, logically, and systematically (formal operational stage). Piaget contended that normal children have the capacity to reach this final stage of formal operations between the ages of twelve and fifteen, which he later revised upward to ages fifteen to twenty (Piaget, 1972). It is this final stage, characterized by the ability to think abstractly, that characterized the apex of mature adult thought for Piaget.

Tennant (1988, p. 77) has noted a number of ways in which Piaget's work laid the foundation for our understanding of cognitive development in adulthood. Piaget's most salient contributions in this respect are as follows:

- The emphasis on qualitative rather than quantitative developmental changes in cognition (and his related "structuralist" approach to cognitive development)
- The importance attached to the active role of the person in constructing his or her knowledge (with the implication that learning through activity is more meaningful [than passive learning])
- A conception of mature adult thought (that is, formal operations)

In extending Piaget's theory to the study of adult learners, research has mainly focused on studies of concrete tasks (the concrete operational stage), with only a few studies of formal operational thought (Blackburn and Papalia, 1992). Another line of research has explored why many adults never reach (or perhaps never seem to use) the formal operations stage. For example, it is estimated that "in Western culture, virtually all adults think easily at the concrete operational level, and perhaps half of adults think at the formal operations level at least some of the time" (Bee, 1996, p. 168). Summaries of the application of Piaget's theory to adulthood have been completed by a number of authors (Papalia and Bielby, 1974; Long, McCrary, and Ackerman, 1979; Denney, 1982; Blackburn and Papalia, 1992). The essence of these summaries is threefold. First, within the Piagetian framework, there are diverse explanations for how adult cognition develops and possibly regresses over the life span. Second, there appears to be sufficient evidence to question the traditional view that cognitive development ends with the formal operations stage. Rather, a number of scholars have proposed stages beyond or different from formal operations. And third, "although formal operations generates solutions using logical analysis …, Piaget's model provides few useful insights into how adults solve 'real life' personal problems" (Blackburn and Papalia, 1992, p. 157).

In line with the second observation, that cognitive development does not end with the formal operations stage, a number of scholars have proposed new structures or patterns of thinking that are seen as developmentally beyond Piaget's stage of formal operations (for example, Arlin, 1975, 1984; Benack and Basseches, 1989; Kegan, 1994; Labouvie-Vief, 1992; Richards and Commons, 1990; Sinnott, 1984, 1994). The emphasis in this work is that changes in cognition extend beyond or differ from the level of formal operations he proposed. We discuss Arlin's work as representative of theorists who have hypothesized stages beyond Piaget's formal operations.

Arlin (1975, 1984), drawing on the work of Gruber (1973) on the development of creative thought in adults, has sought to identify a fifth stage of development, beyond that of Piaget's formal operations. She contends that formal thought actually consists of two distinct stages, not one, as Piaget proposed. In her framework, Piaget's formal operations stage is renamed the problem-solving stage; the focus of this stage is on "the process of seeking a solution of a specific presented task" (Arlin, 1975, p. 603). Arlin then hypothesizes a new fifth stage, the problem-finding stage, characterized by "creative thought vis-à-vis 'discovered' problems" (p. 603) and the ability to generate and respond to important new questions and problems. In postulating these newly organized stages of development, she fully accepts the commonly recognized criteria for a stage model of development with the notions of sequential and hierarchical ordering of development. Therefore, "the relationship between formal operational thinking in the Piagetian sense (problem-solving stage) and the new stage of problem finding should also be characterized as formal operational thinkers in the Piagetian sense" (p. 603).

Arlin (1975) tested her proposed framework by studying the problem-solving and problem-finding behavior of sixty female college seniors. Although her findings generally support the existence of a distinct fifth stage (at least for some people), the study produced more questions than answers. For example, in further conceptualizing these fourth and fifth stages, it is not clear how the patterns of thinking within each stage relate to one another. Nor is it clear what operations in the problem-solving stage might assist a person in moving into the fifth state of problem finding.

LINEAR AND CATEGORICAL MODELS OF ADULT COGNITIVE DEVELOPMENT

There are other models of cognitive development that differ from Piaget's, and yet are also linear or categorical in nature. These writers come from a variety of disciplines and interests (for example, college student development, women's development, psychology), but all have the same interest in exploring how adult thinking changes over time. Although some of these writers have used Piaget's work as part of their foundational thinking (for example, King and Kitchener, 1994; Perry, 1970), others have moved "beyond the boundaries of Piagetian formality" (Kincheloe and Steinberg, 1993, p. 297) and posed very different assumptions on which to base the research on adult cognitive development (Miller and Cook-Greuter, 1994). A discussion of a range of these linear or categorical models of cognitive development follows.

Perry's Developmental Scheme

Perry's (1970, 1981) map of cognitive development is perhaps the best known and has been used the most often in the study of young adults, most of whom have been college students. Based on a study of the thinking patterns of male college students, Perry proposed a model of cognitive development consisting of nine positions, each position representing a qualitatively different way of interpreting learning experiences. Perry purposely chose the word *position* over *stage* for several reasons, one being that he "considers 'position' to be consistent with the image of a point of view with which one looks at the world" (Evans, Forney, and Guido-DiBrito, 1998, p. 228). As in Piaget's work, each position is conceptualized as hierarchical and sequential and moves from relatively simple thinking patterns to highly complex ways of perceiving and evaluating knowledge. People move from viewing knowledge in "dualistic" terms, as either right or wrong, to an acceptance of knowledge and values as "relativistic"—that is, the context of the knowledge is as important as the knowledge itself. Perry places as much emphasis on the transitions between each position as on the positions themselves and observes: "Perhaps development is all transitions and 'stages' [are] only resting points along the way" (1981, p. 78). Some examples of Perry's proposed positions and the transitions between them are outlined below (see Perry, 1970, 1981, for a complete description):

> *Position 1:* Authorities know, and if we work hard, read every word, and learn Right answers, all will be well.
> *Transition* between positions 1 and 2: But what about those Others I hear about? And different opinions? And uncertainties? Some of our own Authorities disagree with each other or don't seem to know, and some give us problems instead of answers.
> *Position 2:* True Authorities must be Right, the Others are frauds. We remain Right. Others must be different and wrong....
> *Transition* between positions 5 and 6: But if everything is relative, am I relative too? How can I know I'm making the Right Choice?
> *Position 6:* I see I'm going to have to make my own decisions in an uncertain world with no one to tell me I'm Right....
> *Transition* between positions 8 and 9: Things are getting contradictory. I can't make logical sense out of life's dilemmas.
> *Position 9:* This is how life will be. I must be wholehearted while tentative, fight for my values, yet respect others, believe my deepest values right yet be ready to learn. I see that I shall be retracing this whole journey over and over—but, I hope, more wisely. [Perry, 1981, p. 79]

Within this schema one can see shades of the conceptually complex notions of dialectic thinking, which is discussed later in this section, as well as the major theme of becoming more relativistic in one's thought patterns as one matures.

Not only is each position descriptive of individual cognitive growth, but Perry's positions have also been used to describe how people view instructors' roles and their own roles as learners. Learners at the lowest positions, for example, tend to view instructors as authority figures; their job as learners is to filter out the right answers from the material presented. Those at the higher end of the continuum view knowledge in a contextual sense and search for relationships between ideas; they see instructors more as guides.

Although most of the work using Perry's schema has been completed with young college students, a few studies have been constructed with nontraditional or older adult students (Cameron, 1983; Lavallee, Gourde, and Rodier, 1990) or with adults who are not students (for example, Wilson, 1996). The findings from these three studies on adult learners were contradictory at best. Lavallee, Gourde, and Rodier (1990) and Wilson (1996) found that the majority of their respondents were at positions three or four (multiplicity) on Perry's scheme, while Cameron's subjects were primarily at position two (dualist). In addition, the findings of Wilson and Lavallee, Gourde, and Rodier (1990) differed on the importance of the level of education in terms of reaching higher levels of cognitive development. Wilson (1996) found that those with "master's degrees scored significantly higher in intellectual development than did those … either with a baccalaureate or less than a baccalaureate degree" (p. 1), while Lavallee, Gourde, and Rodier (1990) concluded that level of education had little effect on the cognitive development of their subjects.

Another use of this work has been an attempt to integrate Perry's work into other areas of study, as Kasworm (1983) has done on self-directed learning. Kasworm, using Perry's framework among others, proposes that self-directed learning "represents a qualitative evolvement of a person's sense of cognitive definition and developmental readiness for ambiguous and nondefined actions" (p. 8). From Kasworm's work and observations made by Perry (1970, 1981) and others, it appears that Perry's work could have implications across a wider spectrum of learners, but this line of thinking has yet to be extended to adults in any systematic or concerted fashion.

The Reflective Judgment Model

King and Kitchener, like Perry, have also constructed a stage model; they term theirs the development of "epistemic cognition" (Kitchener and King, 1981; King and others, 1983; King and Kitchener, 1994). Also like Perry, the majority of the research subjects in their original ten-year longitudinal study were college students, although both male and female students were included, as well as undergraduate and graduate students. Following this group of academically bright white adults (a fourth of whom were seventeen years old when the study began), King and Kitchener (1994) found that "to think reflectively does not emerge fully formed but develops in a sequential fashion, with earlier stages building on prior stages and laying the foundation for subsequent stages" (p. 152). Based on their findings, and also influenced primarily by the work of Piaget (1972) and Dewey (1933), they constructed the reflective judgment model. This model outlines a "developmental progression that occurs between childhood and adulthood in the way people understand the process of knowing and in the corresponding ways that they justify their beliefs about ill-structured problems" (King and Kitchener, 1994, p. 13).

According to this model, people move through seven stages, with the final two stages encompassing the more mature thinking patterns of what King and Kitchener term *reflective thinking*. In Stages One, Two, and Three (termed *prereflective thinking*), people assume that knowledge comes from authority figures or is gained through personal experience. Individuals in these stages do not see problems as ill structured, but rather view all problems as having complete and right answers. In Stages Four and Five, the middle stages, people define knowledge in terms of uncertainty and are more subjective in their thinking. Although they understand that ill-defined problems exist, they have trouble dealing with the ambiguity of those problems and tend to respond in very individualistic ways. In the final two stages of thinking (Stages Seven and Eight), knowledge is no longer a given. Rather, knowledge, especially knowledge used to solve life's ill-structured problems, may have to be constructed by the person, and this knowledge must be understood within the context in which it was generated. Decisions and judgments people make, although they must be grounded in relevant data, should remain open to evaluation and reevaluation. As we shall see under the title Experience and Learning, King and Kitchener's work is similar to authors who discuss reflective practice in terms of the importance of the context of that practice.

There appear to be many similarities between the Perry scheme and that developed by King and Kitchener. For example, both start with the assumption that people at earlier levels of thinking are more absolute in their thinking and depend primarily on outside authority for their knowledge, while later in the thinking hierarchy, the ideas of relativistic thinking becomes predominant. What is different about the King and Kitchener model is that in their final higher stages of development, they describe a further development of cognitive thinking, that of knowledge construction, while Perry focuses on expanding his ideas of using relativistic thinking in a responsible way. Although a great deal of research has been completed using the reflective judgment model (see King and Kitchener, 1994), few studies, as with the Perry schema, have been completed with adults outside the higher education setting. As with the Perry model, this model holds promise in discovering more about adult cognitive development, provided that the populations are expanded to include adults from all walks of life.

Women's Ways of Knowing

In reaction to the work of Perry (1970) and Kohlberg (1973), among others, in which only male samples were used, researchers have become more interested in hearing the voices of women on developmental issues. The most prominent and often quoted study on cognitive development using a sample of women is the work of Belenky, Clinchy, Goldberger, and Tarule, *Women's Ways of Knowing* (1986). These researchers interviewed women from diverse social and ethnic backgrounds from two major settings: different types of academic institutions and parenting classes. From their in-depth interviews of 135 women, "based on the theoretical and empirical work of Perry, Kohlberg, and Gilligan" (p. 14), Belenky, Clinchy, Goldberger, and Tarule (1986, p. 15) grouped women's perspectives on knowing into five major categories:

1. Silence—a position in which women experience themselves as mindless and voiceless and subject to the whims of external authority. [They are passive, feel incompetent, and are defined by others.]
2. Received knowledge—a perspective from which women conceive of themselves as capable of receiving, even reproducing, knowledge from the all-knowing external authorities but not capable of creating knowledge on their own. [They listen to the voices of others; their world is literal and concrete, good or bad.]
3. Subjective knowledge—a perspective from which truth and knowledge are conceived of as personal, private, and subjectively known or intuited. [The locus of truth shifts to the self; intuition is valued over logic and abstraction; here women begin to gain a voice. Half the women in the study were in this category.]
4. Procedural knowledge—a position in which women are invested in learning and applying objective procedures for obtaining and communicating knowledge. [This position takes two forms: *separate knowing,* the self is separate from the object of discourse, making it possible to doubt and reason; and *connected knowing,* there is intimacy and equality between the self and the object of discourse, based on empathetic understanding.]
5. Constructed knowledge—a position in which women view all knowledge as contextual, experience themselves as creators of knowledge, and value both subjective and objective strategies for knowing. [This stage is characterized by the development of an authentic voice.]

These categories, which are not necessarily fixed or universal, move from the simple to the complex–from having no voice, to being able to value and create different ways of knowing, which are contextual in nature. Although these authors do not assert that the categories constitute specific stages of cognitive development, they appear to present them as such (Clark, 1990), and some people continue to interpret them in this way (Goldberger, 1996b).

Clark (1990, pp. 22–23) also noted significant parallels between the findings of Belenky, Clinchy, Goldberger, and Tarule and those of Perry: "Received knowledge parallels the dualistic position; subjective knowledge correlates with multiplicity; and procedural and constructed knowledge has elements of relativism." In addition, the final category of constructed knowing seems comparable with the more recent findings of King and Kitchener (1994) and Baxter Magolda (1992) (Baxter Magolda's work is reviewed later.) For example, King and Kitchener (1994) speak to the importance of contextual knowing and constructing one's own knowledge as characteristic of their final two stages, and Baxter Magolda (1992) stresses the integration of relational (subjective) and impersonal (objective) knowing as key to what she terms *contextual knowing*. These apparent similarities add confirmation to the work of Belenky and her colleagues and are in line with their original interpretations about their research. Although all of the subjects in their 1986 study were women, Belenky, Clinchy, Goldberger, and Tarule have never claimed that these ways of knowing are distinctively female, even though their work has often been interpreted as such. Rather, they believe that these categories "might be expanded or modified with the inclusion of a more culturally and socioeconomically diverse sample of women and men" (Goldberger, 1996b, p. 7). However, their work, which has provided a significant contribution to understanding adult cognitive development, did uncover salient themes that were either missing or deemphasized in earlier work on cognitive development, themes "related to the experience of silencing and disempowerment, lack of voice, the importance of personal experience in knowing, connected strategies in knowing, and resistance to disempassioned knowing" (Goldberger, 1996b, p. 7).

The work of Belenky, Clinchy, Goldberger, and Tarule has provided both lively debate about their findings and new ways of thinking about how to design educational programs for both women and men (for example, Caffarella, 1996; Taylor and Marienau, 1995; Goldberger, Tarule, Clinchy, and Belenky, 1996; Belenky, Bond, and Weinstock, 1997). Goldberger, Tarule, Clinchy, and Belenky (1996) have compiled the most comprehensive set of materials on how their women's ways of knowing scheme "was taken up, used, evaluated and criticized, extended and elaborated, to accommodate new data and new thinking" (Goldberger, 1996b, p. 2). Criticisms of their theory range from their theory being a women-only model, and more specifically a white women's scheme, to the mistaken argument by some that they are endorsing the superiority of antirational ways of thinking. In their most recent work, however, they have "listened to and learned from women of color and other culture theorists …, [and] have become much more alert to the situational and cultural determinants of knowing and to the relationship of power and knowledge" (Goldberger, 1996a, p. 8). The work of Goldberger, Tarule, Clinchy, and Belenky (1996) related to the cultural or contextual significance in cognitive development is reviewed in more depth later.

Epistemological Reflection Model

Baxter Magolda (1992) originally developed the epistemological reflection model as a model of knowing and reasoning in college. She has recently extended her work to young adults beyond their college experience. Like others who have studied cognitive development, Baxter Magolda's work is grounded in the assumption that ways of knowing are socially constructed and context bound.

Baxter Magolda (1992, p. 29) followed a group of seventy predominantly white male and female college students over five years, interviewing them yearly, and discovered "four qualitatively different ways of knowing, each characterized by a core set of epistemic assumptions": absolute knowing, transitional knowing, independent knowing, and contextual knowing. Student voices told stories of moving from being certain about what they knew, to uncertainty, and finally to being able to integrate information from diverse points of views in order to apply that knowledge within a particular context. Baxter Magolda noted that only a small percentage of students used contextual knowing while in college. Like Perry's (1981) and King and Kitchener's (1994) work, Baxter Magolda provides excellent descriptions of what this work means for practice in higher education.

Unlike the work on the Perry (1981) and King and Kitchener (1994) schemes, Baxter Magolda found patterns of thinking within each of the ways of knowing that were gender related, that is, "related to, but not dictated by, gender"(p. 22). For example, in the independent knowing category, two patterns emerged: interindividual and individual. Those exhibiting the interindividual pattern, which women used more than men did, were characterized by their "dual focus on thinking for themselves and engaging the views of others" (Baxter Magolda, 1992, p. 56). The individual-pattern students, although also valuing interchange of ideas, still had their primary focus on their own independent thinking and also expected peers to think in the same way. More men than women exhibited this individual pattern. Magolda notes that none of the patterns was employed exclusively by men or women and that these differing patterns "led to equally complex ways of viewing the world" (p. 13). Baxter Magolda's gender-related patterns of how women know bear some similarity to those discovered by Belenky, Clinchy, Goldberger, and Tarule (1986) in their study of just women.

Baxter Magolda (1995) extended her study to follow these students for another two years, after they graduated from college. What she found was that when her subjects exhibited her fourth category of knowing (contextual knowing), their ways of knowing were no longer gender related. Rather, as they took on different adult roles, their patterns of thinking within this contextual framework became more integrated. More specifically, the patterns of relational and impersonal modes of knowing, which characterize contextual knowing, were used in an integrative fashion: "Participants recognized that connecting to their emotions was essential in deciding what to believe, yet they were aware that this had to be balanced with rational reflection. Contextual knowers emphasized that dialogue, or access to other's perspectives and experiences, was required for developing beliefs" (Baxter Magolda, 1995, p. 66). Her more recent descriptions of contextual knowing echo somewhat the descriptions of "constructed knowledge" described by Belenky, Clinchy, Goldberger, and Tarule (1986).

The Transcendence View

A very different view of cognitive development has emerged from scholars writing from the perspective of transpersonal psychology. Wilber (1982, 1983, 1990) and Thomas (1994) are among those researchers who have extended models of cognitive development beyond the rational level by identifying deeper structures in the mind that undergird higher or transpersonal levels of consciousness. An important component of these theories is Consciousness of human beings with a capital C, which denotes "the unlimited reservoir from which we draw personal, ego-centered awareness. Our individual Consciousness is an infinitesimal spark within the eternal flame of Universal Consciousness" (Nuernberger, 1994, p. 96). When we allow ourselves to move beyond our own individual limits of time and space, our individual Consciousness, a whole new world of expanded Consciousness with limitless boundaries, almost mystical in nature, is open to us. "The great spiritual leaders and mystics of all cultures and time ... all speak of the power of direct knowledge, of reality beyond the capacity of the logic and rationality of the mind" (Nuernberger, 1994, p. 96).

Wilber's (1982, 1983, 1990) model of transpersonal cognitive development allows these spiritual and mystical dimensions to emerge, and it recognizes "cross-cultural differences in values and assumptions that are glossed over by much of our Western psychological theory" (Thomas, 1994, p. 72). To move to these transpersonal levels of development, one must move beyond "the conventional levels of culture and hence beyond normal societal support and structures" (Thomas, 1994, p. 74). More specifically, Wilber has posited eight levels of movement toward the highest level of transpersonal cognitive development. The last two levels illustrate well the transpersonal nature of Wilber's theory. The *subtle* level, level seven, is based on "a truly trans-rational structure ... not emotionalism or merely felt meaning ... or hunch" (Wilber, 1982, p. 30). Rather, phrases such as illumination of the spirit, intuition as an elemental sense, and mystical awareness characterize the thinking of this developmental level. The eighth level, the *causal* state, indisputably moves individuals beyond themselves. As described by Wilber (1983, p. 97): "This is total and utter transcendence and release into Formless Consciousness, Boundless Radiance. There is here no self, no God, no final-God, no subjects, no thingness, apart or other than consciousness as such." This final developmental state closely resembles Nuernberger's (1994) notion of the Universal Consciousness.

In reviewing these and other theoretical models of adult cognitive development, what becomes apparent is there are two themes that many of these theories address: that higher stages of cognitive development in some models suggest the presence of dialectical thinking in adulthood, that is, the acceptance of the inherent contradictions and alternative truths; and that context, including the acceptance of cultural differences, is critical in determining what thinking patterns in adulthood really mean. The discussions of dialectical thinking have a long history in adult cognitive development, beginning with the work of Riegel (1973) and others. In contrast, viewing the contextual dimensions of development is more recent. Each of these themes and representative work illustrating the themes is discussed next.

DIALECTICAL THINKING

Our modern world is rife with contradictions and paradoxes. We have the capability to clone cells, with the possibility for great advances in medicine and many other areas, yet we fear what might be constructed with this technology. We eradicate one dreaded disease (such as smallpox), and other vicious diseases take its place. We can replace most body parts at will, but ethically cannot decide who should get the limited supply of these parts. We downsize workforces to respond to short-term demands, only to find out that the cost of doing business for some groups actually rises in the long run. And the list keeps expanding to the point where Kegan (1994), among others, views us literally "in over our heads" in responding to a world of continuous change and disparities.

A number of writers point to the fact that conflict and contradictions in adult life are not new phenomena (Phelan and Garrison, 1994); rather, they may just be more apparent now in that we can often see and hear them up close through television and other technological formats. In addition, what used to be intensely personal, such as the beginning and the end of life, has also become public knowledge. How many babies should a women be allowed to carry? Should we continue to support the children of welfare mothers? Who has the right to end someone's life? These are just a few of the questions debated in the public forum. In responding to life's inherent contradictions and complexities, a number of authors have posited that dialectical ways of thinking must become part of the ways adults think. In essence, thinking in a dialectic sense allows for the acceptance of alternative truths or ways of thinking about similar phenomena that abound in everyday adult life. One might abhor killing, for example, and yet silently applaud the gentle person who switches off the life-support system of her spouse who is suffering beyond relief from a terminal illness.

One of the earliest and most thoughtful theorists to describe dialectic thinking was Riegel (1973, 1975, 1976). According to Riegel (1973, p. 350), "dialectic conceptualization characterizes the origin of thought in the individual and in society [and] represents a necessary synthesis in the development of thought toward maturity." In describing the dialectic thought process, Riegel (1973, 1975) proposed a corresponding mode of dialectic operations to stand beside Piaget's formal system (see Figure 1-3). The key to this alternative system is the inclusion of the dialectic, or the acceptance of inherent contradictions and ambiguities in thought processes, at all developmental levels and not just as part of the more mature thought of adulthood. "The skills and competence in one area of concern, for instance in sciences, might be of the type of formal dialectic operations, while in everyday business transactions, might be of the type of concrete dialectic operations," and so on (Riegel, 1973, p. 365). Riegel's basic assumptions are that people do not have to pass through any of the Piagetian levels to reach the higher levels of thinking within the dialectic framework and that people can operate simultaneously on all levels. In proposing this system, Riegel (1973, p. 366)

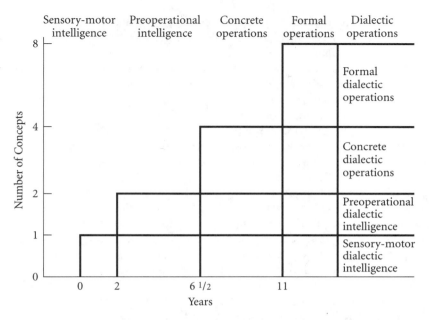

Figure 1-3. Schematic Representation of Piaget's Extended Theory of Cognitive Development.
Source: Riegel, 1973, p. 365. Reprinted with permission of S. Karger AG, Basel.

argued that people are not only ready to live with life's inherent contradictions and ambiguities but will accept "these contradictions as a basic property of thought and creativity."

A number of other writers have incorporated the notion of dialectic thinking into their work on adult cognitive development. Kramer (1983, 1989) is representative of theorists who appear to follow the thinking of Riegel (1973) in that she postulates a series of cognitive developmental stages separate from those of Piaget. Kramer's theory is grounded in the assumption that adult thought centers on both relativistic and dialectical operations, with the acceptance of contradiction and different worldviews as hallmarks of adult thinking. She posits a sequence of seven levels of development, with the last four stages representing adolescent and adult thought processes. (See Kramer, 1989, for a complete description of these stages.)

Like Riegel, Kramer (1989, p. 151) observes that rudimentary dialectic thinking begins in childhood, but she hypothesizes that mature dialectic thought (termed the *stage of dynamic dialecticism*) "rarely appears before middle age." This mature dialectic thought is characterized by an awareness that all thought processes are culturally and historically bound and therefore dynamic and constantly evolving. An acceptance of this premise allows people to categorize ways of thinking and yet also accept the inherent contradictions that these different ways of thinking represent. Ways of thinking then become neither inherently good nor bad but rather are seen as unique for different groups of people at specified points in time. Although Kramer's model of cognitive development is not built on Piaget's stages, she does see each adult stage of the model as "characterized by some degree of abstract thought" (1989, p. 155). Thus "a minimal Piagetian competence of formal operativity" (p. 157) is necessary for fully developed adult thinking. Continuing work is being done on this model, such as the effects of the role of gender and role conflict on the development of dialectical thinking (Kramer and Melchior, 1990) and how dialectic thinking can be incorporated into the teaching and learning process in higher education (Kramer and Bacelar, 1994).

Unlike Riegel and Kramer, however, some writers view dialectical thought as evolving from the formal stages Piaget proposed (Pascual-Leone, 1983; Benack and Basseches, 1989). Benack and Basseches (1989, p. 98), for example, in exploring dialectical thinking as a postformal stage of thought, have developed a "dialectical schemata framework" consisting of twenty-four schemata representing different "moves in thought that dialectical thinkers tend to make." These schemata were abstracted from "writings reflecting dialectic world-outlooks" (Basseches, 1984, p. 72) and interviews with college students and professors about the nature of education. Basseches claims that "some of the dialectical schemata describe ways of introducing dialectical perspectives on existence and knowledge into processes of inquiry. Others describe ways of maintaining dialectical movement within one's own thought" (p. 73). Based on his research, Basseches has suggested that there are actually four phases to the development of mature dialectic thinking. (See Basseches, 1984, and Benack and Basseches, 1989, for a full description of these phases.)

Kegan (1994), framing his work from both a psychological and contextual approach, proposes a level-of-consciousness model that incorporates dialectical thinking as part of the highest level of consciousness. His assumption in proposing this model is that the "hidden curriculum" of modern life necessitates different ways of thinking and "a new conception of *consciousness thresholds* individuals may have to reach in order to satisfy contemporary expectations of love and work". Through examples of real-world demands on our private lives (parenting and partnering) and our public lives (work, dealing with differences, healing, and learning), Kegan (1994) explains how our thinking must continue to evolve through five levels of consciousness in order to navigate our complex lives. First, adults need to discern how to use their mental capacities inherent in social situations. This form of thinking moves adults from the concrete world (having a point of view) to abstractions (being able to build inferences and hypotheses), to abstract systems (conceiving relations between abstractions), and finally to dialectical thinking (testing of paradoxical and contradictory formulations). Dialectical thinking thus becomes the hallmark of mature adult thinking.

Kegan argues that this pressing demand for dialectic thinking comes from our need as adults to respond to what he terms "culture's curriculum"—that is, the mental demands the postmodern world places on us. Kegan, like Riegel and Kramer, also views contradictions and paradoxes as inevitable and at the heart of the dialectical process. He then adds a new framework to this process: trans-systems thinking. What is key in this trans-systems way of thinking is that the parties or systems in conflict move beyond trying to "win" for their position, even the most desired of outcomes—the "win-win" position. Rather what is needed is the recognition that "the other side will not go away, [and] probably *should* not.... The conflict is potentially a reminder of our tendency to pretend to completeness when we are in fact incomplete" (Kegan, 1994, p. 319). Therefore, we must acknowledge and value the thought processes that brought about these conflictual relationships, knowing they are often based in fundamental ideological differences. We need to work within these relationships, miserable as that might be, to advance our ways of thinking and working.

In working together, the parties or systems in these conflictual relationships must then focus on transforming who they are versus trying to solve the conflict. As Kegan goes on to observe:

> This view does not mean that the challengers are coopted into the status quo. It means that the old status quo is replaced by a new status quo. It does not mean that blacks can come into the office only if they act white. It does not mean that women's experience is included in the curriculum simply by changing pronouns and making a "Michael" example into a "Mary" example. It means that formally marginalized people will come into the office, and they will have their own distinctive way of seeing things, setting the agenda, getting the goals accomplished; and it means that these ways will be recognized, acknowledged, and respected, provided that some common ground can be found where all contending "cultures" in their wholeness and distinctness can stand. This common ground becomes, in effect, a new status quo and a new ideology, but a much more wholesome one.

From his longitudinal work, Kegan has found that most people do not even enter the fourth level of consciousness until their forties. Kegan sees our expanded life span as a wonderful opportunity to expand our consciousness to this fifth level. From Kegan's perspective, "Highly evolved people do not mate and create highly evolved children. The evolution of human consciousness requires long preparation. We may gradually become ever more ready to engage the curriculum of the fifth order because we have found ways to increase the number of years we live" (p. 352). In some ways Kegan's thesis is similar to that of Kramer, in that both acknowledge the importance of culture and time in developing truly mature ways of adult thinking.

CONTEXTUAL PERSPECTIVE ON COGNITIVE DEVELOPMENT

When we read through the many theories of cognitive development, some of us might resonate better than other people with many of these theories. Those of us who are white, college educated, and middle class may even have memories of how our thinking has changed over time, which matches at least in part some of these theories. For example, when we introduce the work of Belenky, Clinchy, Goldberger, and Tarule (1986) on women's ways of knowing to graduate students, the white women students latch onto this work, while some of our male students are puzzled, especially about the notions of connected knowing. Inevitably a number of students, both male and female, wonder about the "silence category." Or when we introduce writers like Bell Hooks (1989, 1994) or P. Collins (1990) to a group of predominantly white middle-class students, or even black males, the material often first makes them angry, as these authors vividly display their emotions and thoughts about how people are racist, demonstrate gender bias, and ignore issues of class. They do not want to be spoken to in this way; they do not deserve this treatment. In essence, they neither want to admit these voices are legitimate, nor do they want to deal with them. As these same students wrestle with this material more and come to grips with its message, most reflect later in the course as to how powerful "being forced" to hear different ways of thinking has been. Acknowledging the contextual factors of cognitive development, that is, taking into account how social, cultural, economic, and political forces shape the development of adult thinking, completes the picture. Our theories and models need to be altered and perhaps totally revamped when these contextual aspects are seriously considered by scholars studying adult cognitive development (Goldberger, Tarule, Clinchy, and Belenky, 1996; Goldberger, 1996a; Hurtado, 1996; Kegan, 1994; Kincheloe and Steinberg, 1993; Labouvie-Vief, 1980, 1984, 1990, 1992, 1994). The work of Labouvie-Vief and Goldberger is used to illustrate the work of scholars who consider context as central to cognitive development.

Labouvie-Vief (1980, 1984) was one of the earlier scholars to acknowledge the importance of contextual factors in cognitive development. Observing that "one feature of development which has become so bothersome to life-span psychologists [is] the contextual embeddedness" (1980, p. 142) of the developmental process, Labouvie-Vief challenged the more accepted notion at that time that the perfection of formal logic was the ultimate goal of adult thinking. Rather, Labouvie-Vief contends that a different form of thinking must be integrated into one's model of adult cognitive development: "While the theme of youth is flexibility, the hallmark of adulthood is commitment and responsibility. Careers must be started, intimacy bonds formed, children raised. In short, in a world of a multitude of logical possibilities, one course of action must be adopted. This conscious commitment to one pathway and the deliberate disregard of other logical choices may mark the onset of adult maturity" (1980, p. 153). In essence, this new form of thinking is "characterized by the ability to fit abstract thinking into the concrete limitations of life" (Tennant, 1988, p. 79). Therefore, what may have been conceived of as a regression in later life to Piaget's notion of concrete thought patterns is, rather, a positive adaptation to the realities of adult life. One key factor in being able to adapt to these new ways of thinking is the ability to accept and even thrive on contradiction. This in turns leads to acceptance of the notion of inherent relativity of knowledge and the ability to be self-regulating in choosing one's worldview.

Labouvie-Vief (1990, p. 256), expanding on her earlier work, postulates that "it may be variables related [more] to one's social context than to one's age that account for particular developmental gradients" in cognition. Therefore, if one wishes to discover changes and patterns in cognitive development, it might be more fruitful to examine groups of people who share pertinent life events and experiences versus people of a certain chronological age group. For example, age has been most often cited as the marker by which cognitive declines are measured. Labouvie-Vief (1990) instead asks the question of whether a major life event, such as retirement, "could be the cause of the ubiquitous decline in cognitive functioning" (p. 263). In posing this framework, Labouvie-Vief is echoing the sentiments of those studying personal and intellectual development from a sociocultural or contextual perspective.

More recently, Labouvie-Vief (1994) has explored the role of the mind and gender in the life course. In a fascinating book, *Psyche and Eros,* she brings together her empirical work and her exploration into mythology. Using the classical Greek myth of Psyche and Eros, she examines both historical and current concepts of what is viewed as masculine and feminine qualities. Labouvie-Vief suggests that we need to confront the traditional polarity of masculine and feminine, and thus "restructure the traditional imagery of gender. Such a restructuring involves deidealizing the traditional notion of the masculine and grounding it in the material and concrete [versus the abstract and logical], while elevating the feminine [that of emotion and imagination] and enriching it with mind and spirit" (p. 217). Her work in this arena echoes other scholars, like Bem (1993), who are interested in reconstructing what we mean by gender.

Goldberger (1996a), from interviews with approximately sixty bicultural individuals, primarily women, living in the United States, has added different dimensions of meanings to all of the original categories of knowing that she and Belenky, Clinchy, Goldberger, and Tarule (1986) had described. Goldberger found that the position of "not knowing," that of silence, for example, is a much more complicated phenomenon than was described in *Women's Ways of Knowing.* Rather, how silence is defined can be culturally determined and is actually a positive way of knowing for some. In American Indian cultures, "silence is taught [as something to be respected] within their tribal groups.... Allaq [a member of the Inuit nation] remembers the 'nice silence' of many children in a room, listening as the elders told stories.... Hard Rider [a member of the Canadian West Coast Dtidahy band], struggling to learn from his grandfather how to be a tribal leader, had already recognized the advantages of silent and respectful listening" (Goldberger, 1996a, p. 343). Goldberger also highlights the importance of silence for others, such as African American women, as a tactical strategy for "negotiating life in white communities or workplaces" (p. 345). This distinction of types of silence has led Goldberger to differentiate between those who are truly silenced "by oppressive and demeaning life conditions who feel powerless, mindless, and truly without words ... from individuals who resort to strategic or culturally and ritually endorsed silence, but who may have other well-developed ways of acquiring, even constructing knowledge" (p. 346). In reframing the original categories from a contextual perspective, Goldberger views them more as strategies for knowing than as "person types" to which individuals are assigned based on their response patterns. In conceptualizing these categories as knowing strategies, one can then explore how contextual factors limit or expand our ways of knowing and allow us to speak of different uses or even meanings of each of the ways of knowing.

In this review of the work of Labouvie-Vief, Goldberger, and others on the contextual perspective of cognitive development, two major points become apparent. First, the majority of the mainstream theory in adult cognitive development is "based largely on the findings from a mainly white, well educated U.S. population" (Hofer and Pintrich, 1997, p. 89). There is a paucity of studies that incorporate people of color or different social classes or that examine cross-cultural differences. It appears from studies where the contextual aspect is acknowledged that people from varying backgrounds may define and value knowledge quite differently. Goldberger (1996a), for example, shares three stories from bicultural women living in the United States: Kat, a South American–born woman from a mestize background who is a counselor; Allaq, a Native Alaskan of the Inuit people and a health worker; and Toshi, an African American professor recently granted tenure:

KAT: My grandmother [who is a shaman] would teach me the difference between thinking that you know something and knowing it. She would take me out into the woods and have me sense becoming things. Not just looking and describing what I saw. I had to be the tree, I had to be the rock, I was the bird. Some of that [kind of knowing] is helped with the sacred medicine plants. They allow one to open up many different channels and get all the information possible. Whereas [simply] thinking about something feels like it is a very narrow band, a very narrow channel.

ALLAQ: As a child, I learned a lot just listening to the elders. They talked about the way of living of the Yupik people.... Knowledge is part of the soul. You have to learn it spiritually in every aspect of life spiritually, mentally, emotionally, physically, socially, as a whole person. Yugarag is passed through generations.... In my world everything is interrelated. Everything interrelates.

TOSHI: Black people have a different way of relating to the world. Even intellectually active black people. And that way is more experientially related than cognitively related. We think less about something but react more. I like being able to go from my experience, rather than having to think about it. As a black person, I don't have to hold it in. I can express it. [pp. 336–337]

What is evident in these stories, and those from other writers (for example, Goldberger, Tarule, Clinchy, and Belenky, 1996; Reybold, 1997), is that culture and personal experience shape what and how people develop their distinctive ways of knowing.

The second point regarding the contextual perspective, as observed by Goodnow (1990, p. 82), is that social context is not, as it is often presented, "a relatively benign, neutral, or free market" commodity. Rather, the social world in which we live "takes an active and managing interest in the ideas people acquire" (p. 93). This active and managing interest manifests itself in two ways related to adult cognitive development. The first is that the dominant culture may subvert ways of knowing it does not value. We return to the stories of Kat, the South American–born woman; Allaq, the Native Alaskan Inuit; and Toshi, the African American woman (Goldberger, 1996a):

KAT: When I came to [the United States], I became very quiet. The silence became almost like this cage that I could not get out of.... In this culture, there are certain ways of knowing that are much more valued than others. So unless one can quantify, qualify, and prove and have backup and example, then any knowledge that doesn't fit is just not valid—or society doesn't see it as valid.

ALLAQ: The white society has tried to assimilate and acculturate us through education. We had to hang up our nativeness outside the door and come in and think like white people in the classroom ... I became very, very angry. And when I was real angry I couldn't listen and I couldn't learn.... You know in the Caucasian world, everything is systematic, everything is categorized. Where in my world, everything is interrelated.

TOSHI: But if you want to be successful in this country, the United States of America, you have to be able to function in a white world. You have to give up a lot of who you are [and how you think] to make it through the system. It makes you crazy to do it in a way that's not natural to you. You do it "their way," which is not a bad way, it's just a different way.

Because these ways of knowing may not be valued by the dominant culture, they may be hidden or lost and, worse, viewed as illegitimate or not needed in our modern world. And second, scholars themselves may choose to study only the development of the ways of knowing that they are familiar with and value. This bias will continue to block the construction of alternative models and theories that acknowledge contextual factors as a critical aspect of adult cognitive development.

WISDOM: THE HALLMARK OF ADULT THINKING

Wisdom is often seen as the pinnacle or hallmark of adult thinking. It is something we all speak about and sometimes yearn for as we face the many challenges of adult life. Should we tell our teenage grandchildren they are making horrendous decisions? Should we make a major career change, especially if it means losing our financial security? Can we take a chance on building new relationships when old ones fade? What ethical stands are we willing to "lay down our keys for" (that is, resign) at work? Questions like these haunt many of us, and we wish we had the wisdom of the elders to make the "right" decisions. Yet this wisdom of the ages continues to be a fluid and elusive idea, which is most often characterized by the acceptance of ambiguity, as one of its many virtues.

Wisdom is not a new concept; it has been discussed through the ages by great philosophers and theologians of all backgrounds and persuasions. As Joan Erikson (1988) has observed:

> Throughout time and everywhere on the globe, people have earnestly and with great labor undertaken to pass on, to store, to preserve their nugget of truth, of wisdom. They remain embedded in myth, legend, song, and poetry, carved in hieroglyphs and in cave paintings. In some written form they have been enshrined as "sacred writ" and "relic" housed in such edifices as tombs, temples, mosques, monasteries, cathe drals, and churches.... We can find documentation of these records in our great libraries and now in smaller ones, too, as all the verbal knowledge becomes translated and disseminated. Computers and microfilm also increase our capacities to store and make available great riches previously unavailable. [pp. 156–157]

Erikson goes on to point out that "wisdom remains an elusive word because it encompasses an attitude, a disposition toward life, past, present, and future, only occasionally recognized in rare individuals" (p. 177).

Psychologists and educators have defined and studied wisdom from a variety of perspectives. Robinson (1990) noted that the definition of wisdom has changed over time, differing in ancient Greek, traditional Christian, and contemporary conceptions. Sternberg (1990a) defines wisdom as a metacognitive style and Baltes and Smith (1990) as expertise in everyday life. Kramer and Bacelar (1994) link wisdom to being able to think in a dialectic way, while Macdonald (1996, p. 1) states that wisdom is "a whole array of better-than-ordinary ways of being, and living and dealing with the world." And Sternberg (1996b, p. 276) has noted the importance of the social-interaction nature of wisdom, which stresses "that wisdom by definition will hardly ever be found in an individual, but rather in cultural or social interactive products." These and other definitions point to the complexity of the concept. Most researchers do agree, however, that wisdom is the province of adulthood, although older is not always equated with wiser.

Researchers and writers on wisdom have attempted to delineate its major components and its relationship to the aging process. Holliday and Chandler (1986), for example, have sought to provide empirical parameters for the term *wisdom* in three interlocking studies. They first collected general descriptions of wise people from which they formulated the basic description of wisdom in a second study. In the third phase of their research, they "examined the influence of the wise prototype on people's information processing strategies" (p. 44). The 458 subjects in their study represented all age cohorts of adults: young, middle aged, and older. They concluded that wisdom is a multidimensional construct consisting of more than objective and context-free aspects of thought. Using Habermas's (1970) framework, Holiday and Chandler propose a tripartite model of wisdom that consists of technical, practical, and emancipatory elements. In their view, "Wise people must be able to solve problems but not in an abstract sense. The type of problems that wise people presumably deal with appear to have strong practical and emancipatory components.

That is, wisdom problems are problems endemic to life and to the human condition.... Consequently, the problems typically involve or center on values"

In a somewhat different way, Sternberg (1986b, pp. 177–178) sought to discover people's conceptions or implicit theories of wisdom by exploring "the nature and the interrelationships of intelligence, wisdom, and creativity." Through a series of studies with both laypersons (community volunteers and students) and specialists (college professors from a variety of disciplines), Sternberg found that people not only have implicit theories about intelligence, wisdom, and creativity, but use them to evaluate others. Moreover, he found differences in the way laypersons and specialists perceived each of the three constructs, including the notion of wisdom.

Laypersons perceived the wise individual to have much the same analytic reasoning ability one finds in the intelligent person. "But the wise person has a certain sagacity that is not necessarily found in the intelligent person. He or she listens to others, knows how to weigh advice, and can deal with a variety of different kinds of people.... The wise individual is especially well able to make clear, sensible, and fair judgments and is perceived to profit from the experiences of others and ... learn from others' mistakes, as well as from his or her own" (p. 186). The specialists, on the other hand, tend to emphasize certain aspects of wisdom as more critical than others. The art professors, for example, "emphasize insight, knowing how to balance logic and instinct ... and sensitivity," while the business professors emphasize such things as "maturity of judgment, understanding of the limitations of one's own actions ... and appreciation of the ideologies of others" (pp. 186–187). Sternberg concludes that the three major constructs of intelligence, wisdom, and creativity are indeed distinct and yet interrelated and, moreover, that we must pay as much attention to wisdom and creativity as we do to intelligence.

Joan Erikson (1988), also connecting creativity to wisdom, delineated ten attributes of wisdom, including the following:

- *Interdependence and interrelatedness.* In her mind, the "wise elder has learned to understand *interdependence,* the ecology of living with others. Early training and much of adult life stress independence, which if pressed to absurdity leads one to isolation and emotional stagnation. Human beings need one another, and their vital involvement in relationships nourishes and sustains the whole cycle of life" (p. 178).
- *Humor.* It is humor—"healing, enlivening laughter that keeps human feet firmly on the ground (humus). The world being full of incongruities, perplexity would surely be overwhelming if humor abandoned us.... When we can even see ourselves as funny, it eases this daily living in such close proximity with ourselves" (p. 182).
- *A sense of the complexity of living.* A wise person embraces the "sense *of the complexity of living,* of relationships, of all negotiations. There is certainly no immediate, discernible, and absolute right and wrong, just as light and dark are separated by innumerable shadings.... [The] interweaving of time and space, light and dark, and the complexity of human nature suggests that ... this wholeness of perception to be even partially realized, must of necessity be made up of a *merging* of the *sensual,* the *logical,* and the *aesthetic* perceptions of the individual" (p. 184).
- *Caritas.* There is "an attitude of wisdom that seems of great importance which can be described as nonpossessive attachment. It is possible to care for and about things, and of course individuals as well as this green earth, without dominating anything. 'Let it be,' the [Beatles] song repeats. 'Let it be'. The wise old man or woman learns to go lightly, receive gratefully, release easily, in order to feel as unfettered as possible. Loss is inevitable, so holding on is defeating" (p. 186).

In discussing each of the ten attributes, Erikson places them within the framework of life cycle development and speaks to how they are nurtured throughout the life span. Erikson closes her discussion by observing that all of these attributes of wisdom should be considered "universal age-old survival skills" (p. 188).

In contrast to the work of Sternberg and Erikson, other writers have framed their work from the perspective that wisdom is a part of intelligence, that is, the "pragmatics of intelligence" (Smith, Dixon, and Baltes, 1989; Dittmann-Kohli and Baltes, 1990). Smith, Dixon, and Baltes, for example (1989, p. 311), view wisdom as cognitive expertise in the fundamental pragmatics of life that are "visible in situations related to life planning, life management, and life review. This expertise is reflected in individuals' definition of, judgments about, and solutions to life problems" and is built on a person's store of factual knowledge and experience. In the most global sense, they see wisdom as "good judgment about important but uncertain matters" (p. 312). The basis of this wise judgment "is both specialized knowledge about life in general and a repertoire of efficient strategies for applying and adapting that knowledge to many contexts, interpersonal situations, and life tasks" (p. 326).

Macdonald (1996) reflects a few of the same sentiments of the scholars we have just reviewed. Writing from a lay-oriented exploration of wisdom, Macdonald, like Erikson, has outlined attributes of people who are wise, although these attributes are mostly different from Erikson's. These attributes include "seeing things clearly; seeing things as they are; acting in prudent and effective ways; acting with the well-being of the whole in mind; deeply understanding the human/cosmos situation; knowing when to act and when not to act; being able to handle whatever arises with peace of mind and an effective, compassionate, holistic response; and being able to anticipate potential problems and avoid them" (p. 1). In addition, Macdonald connects his foundation for wisdom to Maslow's concept of self-actualization and the values espoused as part of that concept: "wholeness, perfection, completion, justice, aliveness, richness, simplicity, beauty, goodness, uniqueness, effortlessness, playfulness, truth, honesty, reality, self-sufficiency" (p. 2). Although Macdonald uses values like reality and playfulness as part of the foundation of wisdom, his sense of wisdom seems very rationalistic and almost otherworldly.

Despite the different perspectives from which wisdom has been studied and the lack of consensus on its precise dimensions, several points of agreement have emerged (Holliday and Chandler, 1986; Erikson, 1988; Sternberg, 1990b; Jarvis, 1992; Kramer and Bacelar, 1994; Bennett-Woods, 1997). Wisdom is grounded in life's rich experiences and therefore is developed though the process of aging. Although book learning may be a part of developing wisdom, it is not a requirement. Rather, being able to respond well to the pragmatics of life seems to form the core of being wise. Moreover, wisdom seems to consist of the ability to move away from absolute truths, to be reflective, and to make sound judgments related to our daily existence, whatever our circumstances.

In reflecting on this study of wisdom and how it might enrich learning in adulthood, we are struck by observations made by Dychtwald and Flower (1989) about "the third age"—that part of life beyond age sixty, a time of life that more and more people are experiencing as healthy and vital individuals. Dychtwald and Flower contend that this third age allows for the "further development of the interior life of the intellect, memory, and imagination, of emotional maturity, and of one's personal sense of spiritual identity" (p. 53). It is a time for people to give back to society through their wisdom, power, and spirituality "the lessons, resources, and experiences accumulated over a lifetime" (p. 53). They then quote Monsignor Fahey, the director of Fordham University's Third Age Center: "People in the third age should be the glue of society, not its ashes" (p. 53). Their conclusion is clear and dramatic: "Think about it. We know even with the best care overall fitness will decline gradually over the years. While the strength of the senses is weakening, what if the powers of the mind, heart, and the spirit are rising? If life offers the on-going opportunity for increased awareness and personal growth, think how far we could evolve, given the advantage of extra decades of life!" (p. 52). Their observations of using our later years to develop our cognitive thinking abilities further are similar to Kegan's (1994), discussed earlier. In incorporating the concept of wisdom in our thinking about cognitive development, mature adult cognition is more than just abstract logic, complex reasoning, and dialectical thinking; it also encompasses the ability to think, feel, and act "wisely" in life.

SUMMARY

Cognitive development refers to the change in thinking patterns as one grows older. Much of the earlier work on cognitive development in adulthood has been grounded primarily in the work of Piaget. One line of research has focused on how Piaget's stages play out in adulthood. A more fruitful research tradition, grounded in Piaget's work, has been the conceptualization of adult stages of cognition beyond that of formal operations, such as the work of Arlin (1975). Other researchers have posited entirely new schemes of adult cognitive development. These alternative theories range from the traditional stage theories of development, such as the work of Perry (1970, 1981) and King and Kitchener (1994), to those theories that bring in new voices (Belenky, Clinchy, Goldberger, and Tarule, 1986; Goldberger, Tarule, Clinchy, and Belenky, 1996) and different ways of framing development, represented by Baxter Magolda (1992) and Labouvie-Vief, 1980, 1990).

In the review of the many theories of adult cognitive development, two major themes became apparent: the importance of dialectical thinking and that contextual factors are critical in determining how we develop our thinking patterns as adults. Dialectical thinking, as represented by the work of Riegel (1973), Kramer (1983, 1989), and Kegan (1994), allows for the acceptance of alternative truths or ways of thinking about the many contradictions and paradoxes that we face in everyday life. To be able to engage in dialectic thinking is viewed by some as the only way to navigate our postmodern world successfully. Bringing in the contextual perspective on adult cognitive development acknowledges that the world around the thinker makes a difference in how adults develop their thinking patterns. Social, cultural, economic, and political forces help shape both how we think and what kind of knowledge we value. The contextual perspective was illustrated by later work of Labouvie-Vief (1990, 1992, 1994) and Goldberger (1996a).

The section concluded with a brief overview of the concept of wisdom, often regarded as the hallmark of mature adult thinking. Although it has been discussed over the ages by the great philosophers and theologians, this area of study has received little attention in the literature on cognitive development and learning in general. Representative conceptions of wisdom, such as those of Holliday and Chandler (1986), Sternberg (1986b), Erikson (1988), and Macdonald (1996), were reviewed. Despite the different perspectives from which wisdom is viewed, scholars seem to agree that wisdom involves special types of experience-based knowledge and is characterized by the ability to move away from absolute truth, to be reflective, and to make sound judgments related to everyday life.

INTELLIGENCE AND AGING

SHARAN B. MERRIAM
ROSEMARY S. CAFFARELLA

The adage that "you can't teach an old dog new tricks" haunts both instructors of adults and adult learners themselves as they set forth on new learning ventures. The image of staff members who refuse to use the office e-mail system because "it just takes too long to learn" is still a reality. So too is the existence of the young trainer, fresh out of graduate school, who secretly believes she will never be able to teach her entrenched training staff anything, let alone to work as a team. This powerful myth—that adults lose their ability to learn as they age—prevails, although for the most part it has not been substantiated in the literature.

Intelligence is defined in a number of ways. From the perspective of the casual observer, intelligence is often equated with "being smart"—that is, being able to act intelligently when dealing with every day life. But there is another definition of intelligence that many adults have carried with them since their elementary school days: intelligence is a specific measurement of their ability to learn. While not actually knowing their IQ scores, many adults have vague recollections of being labeled an "average," "above-average," or "below-average" student. Worse still are the memories of using IQ tests to be placed in a "slow" reading or math group or of watching one's best friend be put in the "high group." Beginning with the early work of Spearman (1904), Binet (1916), Thorndike, Bregman, Tilton, and Woodyard (1928), and others, researchers have sought to understand the nature of intelligence and whether it changes with age.

In this section, we first explore the concept of intelligence and how it has been measured. Next, we present several theories of intelligence developed since the 1960s that inform our practice as educators of adults. We follow with a review of how age affects intellectual abilities. The section concludes with an exploration of three ideas about intellectual functioning in adulthood that are particularly intriguing and useful for educators of adults.

CONCEPT OF INTELLIGENCE AND ITS MEASUREMENT

The concept of intelligence has become much more complex and multifaceted over the last two decades, often causing confusion to casual readers. Different words describing the same concept have been interchanged or slightly modified, adding to the complexity of understanding the vast array of work on adult intelligence. For example, some authors use the terms *intellectual development* and *cognitive development* interchangeably, whereas other authors using these terms are exploring very different phenomena. Schaie (1996) and Berg (1992) have sought to add clarity to discussions of what the term *intelligence* means. Berg (1992) highlights several perspectives that dominate current research in intelligence. Among these are the psychometric tradition, the process orientation of Piagetian and neo-Piagetian thought, information processing, and the contextual perspective. Schaie (1996) agrees that at least two of these theoretical perspectives—those of information processing and the psychometric tradition—have driven the study of intelligence, but adds a third, that of practical intelligence. More specifically, Schaie purports that "there is a natural hierarchy in the study of intelligence leading from information processing, through the products measured in tests of intelligence, to practical and everyday intelligence" (p. 266). The Piagetian and neo-Piagetian traditions were discussed earlier under the title Cognitive Development in Adulthood and the information processing perspective is discussed earlier under the title Memory, Cognition, and the Brain. In this section we use work from the psychometric tradition, practical intelligence, and the contextual perspective to illustrate important ideas related to intelligence and aging.

Intelligence has been most often studied from the psychometric tradition (J. Anderson, 1996; Schaie and Willis, 1986; Sternberg, 1996b), which assumes that it is a measurable construct. Those who have studied intelligence from this perspective, as echoed in the words of Schaie (1996, p. 267), assert that "the products or intellectual skills that characterize psychometric intelligence are likely to represent the most appropriate label for the direct prediction of many socially desirable outcomes." Some who have studied intelligence from the psychometric perspective, such as Binet and Spearman (Schaie and Willis, 1986; Schaie, 1996), describe it as a single factor termed the "general ability" or "g" factor. This means that a person's "performance on many different types of tests (vocabulary, arithmetic, object assembly, block design) can be explained in terms of a *single* underlying ability" (Hayslip and Panek, 1989, p. 197). Therefore, scores from diverse tests or subscales can be combined to form an overall general score or index of intelligence quotient (IQ). The g factor is most often viewed as an innate capacity that is genetically determined.

Schaie (1996) views this single concept of intelligence as appropriate for childhood but not as useful beyond adolescence "because of the lack of a unidimensional criterion in adults and because convincing empirical evidence supports the presence of multiple dimensions of intelligence displaying a different life course" (p. 267). "The 'purest' tests of these multiple dimensions [grounded in the psychometric tradition] are sometimes administered as tests of the 'primary mental abilities'" (Schaie and Willis, 1986, p. 290) consisting of spatial ability, perceptual speed, numerical ability, verbal relations, words, memory, and induction.

Intelligence Testing with Adults

The first widespread use of intelligence testing with adults was by the army in World War I, with the administration of the Army Alpha Tests of Intelligence. Thorndike, Bregman, Tilton, and Woodyard (1928) followed closely behind with their pioneering work that challenged the fundamental notion that learning ability peaks very early in life. Using primarily laboratory or schoolroom tasks, Thorndike measured the speed of the performance of people from ages fourteen to fifty on a variety of tasks, from memorizing poetry to acquiring an artificial language (Kidd, 1973). Thorndike, Bregman, Tilton, and Woodyard (1928, pp. 178–179) concluded from their many studies that, "in general, teachers of adults of age twenty-five to forty-five should expect them to learn at nearly the same rate and in nearly the same manner as they would have learned the same thing at twenty." In reflecting on Thorndike's work, Kidd (1973) noted two major contributions. The first was to raise the age of onset of the downhill slide of a person's ability to learn from twenty years of age to forty-five. Second, and even more important, Thorndike "helped to stimulate colleagues to reject traditional views and formulas" (Kidd, 1973, p. 79) about learning in adulthood. Other noted studies of intelligence (Jones and Conrad, 1933; Miles and Miles, 1932) of that same era reached similar conclusions, "although they found that the decline begins at a later age and the rate of that decline is not as sharp as in 'Thorndike's curve'" (Cross, 1981, p. 158).

Overall, the use of psychometric intelligence tests with adults has not been as prevalent as the testing of children. The predominant uses of intelligence tests with adults include assessing people in the workplace for job placement and in clinical settings for appropriate treatment plans. In addition, intelligence tests have been used in research to determine how intellectual abilities change as people age. The two tests of adult intelligence most often used in both research and practice are the Wechsler Adult Intelligence Scale–Revised (WAIS-R) (Thomas, 1992; Sternberg, 1996b) and the Primary Mental Abilities (PMA) test. The most recent version of the PMA is the Schaie-Thurston Adult Mental Abilities Test (STAMAT) (Schaie, 1985, 1987).

The WAIS-R (and its predecessor, the WAIS) consists of eleven subtests grouped into verbal and performance scales. This test provides three scores: a verbal, a performance, and an overall score. The verbal portion of the test relies heavily on language skills, such as word definitions and general information items, although two subtests of this scale also address basic numerical abilities. Responses to the performance scales are primarily based on nonverbal skills such as locating missing parts of a picture or reconstructing block designs. The majority of the verbal tests are not timed; all those in the performance category are timed. Several of the WAIS-R and WAIS subtests are often grouped together for measuring Cattell's (1987) constructs of fluid and crystallized intelligence, which are discussed later in this section. Wechsler himself believed early on in his career that mental ability as a whole declines with age in a similar fashion to the rest of one's body (Kidd, 1973; Schaie and Willis, 1986).

On closer examination on both earlier and later WAIS test results, however, it became apparent to both Wechsler and others that the decline in intellectual functions was not equal for all tasks: "In general, scores on performance tests [did] show a loss, but not on the verbal tests" (Kidd, 1973, p. 81). "One key was that the subtests in which older subjects do poorly are all 'speeded' tests" (Schaie and Willis, 1986, pp. 294–295). These conflicting results raised numerous questions about the true nature of adult intelligence that are still being debated (Goleman, 1995; Sternberg, 1996a, 1996b). For example, are verbal tests more appropriate measures of intelligence in adulthood than performance tests? Is a timed task as valid as an untimed task? Is adult intelligence more than what can be measured by conventional measures of intelligence?

The second test of adult intelligence, the PMA test, is often associated with the work of Schaie and colleagues on intelligence and aging (Schaie, 1979, 1994, 1996). The underlying assumption of the PMA, grounded in the work of Thurstone and Thurstone (1941), is that intelligence is actually several distinct abilities and not a single general trait. Purported to measure five relatively independent factors, the PMA test battery consists of five subtests: (1) verbal meaning, which is the ability to understand ideas expressed in words; (2) space, describing the ability to think about an object in two or three dimensions; (3) reasoning, involving the ability to solve logical problems; (4) number, the ability to handle arithmetic problems; and (5) word fluency, concerning the speed and ease with which words are used (Schaie, 1979). The PMA subtests, all of them timed, can be reported as a composite score that constitutes an overall index of intellectual ability. Like the WAIS-R, the PMA appears to assess academic abilities (such as verbal and reasoning ability) related to formal schooling. In a challenge to this idea, Schaie and others (Schaie, 1996; Willis and Schaie, 1986) found that at least in later adulthood, certain primary mental abilities do predict competent behavior in specific situations—for example, "competence in active situations was predicted by spatial ability and inductive reasoning, and competence in passive situations was predicted by verbal abilities" (Schaie and Willis, 1986, p. 290). Active situations included traveling around a city looking for a new residence or preparing large meals for friends, while more passive ones were attending an art exhibit or worrying about the ability to pay a debt. To these researchers, the findings suggest "a strong relationship between the 'building blocks' of intelligence and abilities on real life tasks" (p. 290). Only further research will tell whether the PMA and other intelligence tests of this nature can actually be used as adequate predictors of everyday intelligence.

Major Issues and Future Concerns in Assessing Adult Intelligence

In using the traditional psychometric measures of intelligence with adults, there are two cogent issues: the tests themselves and the social and policy implications of IQ scores. As Tennant and Pogson (1995) have observed, these tests "are too culture-specific; ... [and] they are constructed from problems and tasks derived from the context or 'culture' of schooling rather than everyday life" (p. 17). In other words, in using these tests, we perpetuate the notion of intelligence as being more "academic" in nature and culture free. In addition, Thomas (1992) has pointed out that the timed nature of some of these tests is biased against older adults, in that the reaction time of many older adults is slower.

The second issue, that of how scholars have used the results from IQ tests to make statements about groups of people in society and then propose policy initiatives related to the statements, has been the most controversial and possibly the most perilous of the two problems cited. *The Bell Curve,* by Herrnstein and Murray (1994), represents the most recent iteration of this problem. These authors assert that intelligence, as measured by traditional IQ tests, "has a powerful bearing on how people do in life ... [and] that people differ in intelligence for reasons that are not their fault" (p. 535), meaning that intelligence is substantially inheritable. They recommend sweeping and often repressive policy changes grounded in simplification of the rules for living so that persons of "low cognitive ability" (who are most often poor and/or of color) can function better in society. Rebuttals and challenges to Herrnstein and Murray's work have come from many quarters, from scholars who study intelligence to historians and social scientists (Fraser, 1995; Jacoby and Glauberman, 1995; Kincheloe, Steinberg, and Gresson, 1996). As Jacoby and Glauberman (1995, p. xi) have observed, "The extraordinary response to *The Bell Curve* suggests it touches an open nerve. The book bespeaks to a society that is losing confidence in its own egalitarian and democratic process."

In thinking about future means of assessing intelligence in adulthood, two major concerns have surfaced. First, we must develop assessment tools that can measure both academic and practical notions of intelligence, including emotional intelligence. This effort would include further study of existing measures, such as that undertaken by Willis and Schaie (1985), as well as the development of new assessment tools (Baltes, Dittmann-Kohli, and Dixon, 1984; Gardner, 1995). Second, we must pay more attention to revising and designing assessments that are "age fair." These measures would take into account "tests of adult intelligence relevant to competence at different points in the lifespan" (Schaie and Willis, 1986, p. 292), unlike current measures, which assess primarily competencies needed for academic activities. Research in this arena has just begun. The development of alternative assessments of intelligence suitable for adult learners will require much time and effort.

REPRESENTATIVE THEORIES OF INTELLIGENCE

Two theories of intelligence grounded in the psychometric tradition of measurement, those of Horn and Cattell and of Guilford, which are useful in helping us understand more clearly the connection between intelligence and aging, are described first in this section. These descriptions are followed by a review of the work of scholars who have challenged traditional theories, such as Gardner and Sternberg, who believe that these traditional models have little, if any, relationship to what they term "real-world" or "practical" intelligence. Theorists who advocate practical intelligence most often view intelligence as a combination of biological and environmental factors and stress genetic and environmental interactions.

Although this interactionist perspective of intelligence is not a new idea (for example, Piaget, 1952, and Vygotsky, 1978, were interactionists), only relatively recently have theories of intelligence emphasized the importance of this interaction to both the continued development and assessment of adult intelligence. Tennant and Pogson (1995) have provided a thoughtful treatise on why practical intelligence has been overlooked for so long, especially by scholars representing Western culture. They assert that "historically, Western culture has taken a lower view of manual work than of cognitive activity [which has led to] the exaltation of the theoretical or contemplative over the practical" (pp. 37, 39). More specifically, they cite the attributes of verbal, abstract, and complex thinking as being far more valued than either those of concrete and sensual thought or the active use of knowledge.

Theory of Fluid and Crystallized Intelligence

One of the major conceptualizations of adult intelligence was popularized by the work of Cattell (1963, 1987) and Horn (Horn 1976, 1982, 1985). They viewed intelligence as consisting of two primary factors: fluid intelligence (Gf) and crystallized intelligence (Gc). Fluid intelligence, or the ability to perceive complex relations and engage in short-term memory, concept formation, reasoning, and abstraction, is measured by tests for rote memory, basic reasoning, figural relations, and memory span. In contrast, crystallized intelligence is normally associated with acculturated information—those "sets of skills and bits of knowledge that we each learn as part of growing up in any given culture, such as verbal comprehension, vocabulary, [and] the ability to evaluate experience" (Bee, 1996, pp. 155–156). Examples of measures of crystallized intelligence include vocabulary and verbal comprehension, numerical reasoning, and an individual's ability to extract information from the environment. Tests of fluid intelligence are primarily speeded and are viewed as "culture fair," while crystallized intelligence is more likely to be assessed by nonspeeded measures. There is no single test that researchers can use to measure both factors of intelligence;

rather, researchers often label tests as measures of either fluid or crystallized intelligence (see, for example, Christensen, 1994; Kaufman, Kaufman, Chen, and Kaufman, 1996).

Although the popular understanding is that fluid intelligence is more innate and therefore dependent on a neurophysiological base, Horn (1985, p. 289) now does not hold to this notion: "There are good reasons to believe that Gf is learned as much as Gc, and that Gc is inherited as much as Gf." Rather, he believes that both types of intelligence can be nurtured, at least until very old age. This has led researchers to study whether fluid intelligence, which was thought to be primarily innate, can be either restored (if loss has been shown) or strengthened as people age (Baltes and Willis, 1982; Lohman and Scheurman, 1992; Schaie and Willis, 1986; Willis and Schaie, 1994). Schaie (1996) provides a concise summary of this work.

Overall, even with studies showing that the loss of fluid intelligence is remediable, there is still consensus that fluid intelligence begins to decline much earlier, perhaps at age thirty-five or forty (Horn and Donaldson, 1980), than crystallized intelligence. Again, challenges to the exact time frame of decline and what that decline means have been made on a number of fronts, including the ways in which fluid intelligence has conventionally been measured. Some researchers (for example, Lohman, 1989; Schaie, 1996) would like to see more useful and realistic tests of fluid intelligence for adults based on the underlying premise that "fluid and crystallized general abilities can be placed along a continuum" throughout the life span (Lohman and Scheurman, 1992, p. 78). Lohman and Scheurman go on to argue that educators must "encourage fluidization, not merely crystallization of knowledge and skills" (p. 81), because both types of intelligences are needed as we grow older.

Guilford's Structure of Intellect Model

In contrast to the two-factor model of fluid and crystallized intelligence proposed by Cattell, Guilford's model (1967, 1985) consists of 120 theoretical factors clustered into three major categories that are independent of each other: (1) contents, referring to the type of verbal, numerical, or behavioral material being tested; (2) operations, which are the basic mental processes such as memory, reasoning, and creative thinking; and (3) product, referring to the form of information that results from the interactions of the other two categories (from a single unit to complex patterns of information). A key assumption underlying the model is that the mental operations used on a particular task area are as important as the nature of the task itself. Guilford's model offers researchers an alternative frame of reference about the human intellect on which hypotheses about new factors of intelligence can be generated (Guilford, 1967, 1985; Huyck and Hoyer, 1982). Therefore, the model continues to provide a major building block for expanding our thinking about the fundamental nature of human intelligence.

Some have expressed reservations about the theory's utility: "While Guilford's theory of intelligence has generated a great deal of research, the structure of intellect model has for the most part yet to be integrated into adult developmental research on intelligence" (Hayslip and Panek, 1989, p. 198). The noted exception has been the studies on divergent thinking: the ability to produce alternative ideas or solutions. For example, in cross-sectional comparisons of the creative process and products of younger versus older women, Alpaugh, Parham, Cole, and Birren (1982) found a decline in divergent thinking abilities with age. They hypothesized that the older creative person may rely "more on previous experience than on present divergent thinking abilities, whereas younger creators draw more heavily on divergent thinking" (p. 112). Although Guilford's model has not been used often by researchers of intelligence in adulthood, we believe his model, especially the notion of both multiple and interacting factors of intelligence, may prove useful in future research and theory building on adult learning.

Gardner's Theory of Multiple Intelligences

Gardner is representative of theorists who broke away from the psychometric tradition of intelligence during the early 1980s. From Gardner's perspective, the concept of intelligence has been too narrowly limited to the realm of logical and linguistic abilities, primarily by the way intelligence has been measured. Rather, he argues, "there is persuasive evidence for the existence of several relatively autonomous human intellectual competencies ... that can be fashioned and combined in a multiplicity of adaptive ways by individuals and cultures" (Gardner, 1983, pp. 8–9). From a number of unrelated sources, such as studies of prodigies, brain-damaged patients, and normal children and adults, Gardner originally identified seven different forms of intelligence, with an eighth recently added. His first seven forms include "not only the standard academic ones of linguistic, logical-mathematical, and spatial (the visual skills exhibited by a painter or architect) but also musical, 'bodily-kinesthetic,' and two 'personal' intelligences involving a fine-tuned understanding of oneself and others" (Levine, 1987, p. 54). (See Gardner, 1983, for a complete description of his seven original intelligences.) Gardner calls his newest form of intelligence the "naturalist" intelligence: "The intelligence of the naturalist involves the ability to recognize important distinctions in the natural world (among flora, fauna). It can also be applied to man-made objects in our consumer society (cars, sneakers). Obviously this skill is crucial in hunting or farming cultures, and it is at a premium among biologists and others who work with nature in our own society" (Shores, 1995, p. 5).

In introducing this new theory, Gardner (1983, p. 280) stressed that "the idea of multiple intelligences is an old one" recognized even in early Greek times. In Gardner's framework, our tendency to label people as being generally bright, average, or dull just does not seem to fit. Rather, a person may exhibit high intelligence in one or two areas, such as music and math, and yet demonstrate only average intelligence in other respects. In other words, you can be very talented in one or two areas and have little or no capacity in other areas. Gardner views his theory of multiple intelligences as presenting a critique of the predominant model of "psychometrics-as-usual" in measuring intelligence. Therefore, although scholars have made some attempts to develop and use traditional paper-and-pencil tests to measure multiple intelligences (for example, Shearer and Jones, 1994; Rosnow, Skleder, Jaeger, and Rind, 1994), Gardner (1995) himself argues that any assessments of multiple intelligences must be "intelligent fair"; that is, the assessments must "examine the intelligence directly rather than through the lens of linguistic or logical intelligence (as ordinary paper-and-pencil tests do)" (p. 202).

When Gardner proposed his theory of multiple intelligences, he was interested in both promoting theory building on the nature of intelligence with his fellow psychologists and having scholars examine the educational implications of his theory. His work has stirred a great deal of theoretical debate among scholars, but what Gardner was unprepared for was the almost overwhelming positive response among educators of preschool and school-age children (Gardner and Hatch 1989; Gardner, 1993, 1995). The theory of multiple intelligences was almost immediately put into practice, and whole curricula have been developed using this conceptualization of intelligence. We even found one article that described using his theory as the basis for graduate study (Brougher, 1997). Although almost all of the published work we could locate described applications with children, as in the case of Guilford's theory, we see significant value in integrating Gardner's ideas into our study and practice of learning in adulthood. We recommend paying heed to Gardner's (1995, p. 206) position that there is no "single educational approach based on the MI [multiple intelligences] theory ..., [and] that educators are in the best position to determine the uses to which MI theory can and should be used."

Sternberg's Theories of Intelligence

Sternberg too has broken from the tradition of framing intelligence as primarily a measure of formal testlike problem solving to one that includes problem solving for everyday life. Unlike the "schooling world," where problems are usually highly definitive and structured, real-world issues tend to be both ill defined and contexualized. Therefore, Sternberg contends that most theories, especially the measures of intelligence, address only the "schooling" kind of intelligence and almost totally ignore the notion of practical intelligence. Sternberg has proposed an important theory of human intelligence, the triarchic theory, and a layperson's version of theory that he terms "successful intelligence."

According to Sternberg (1985, 1986a, 1988), the triarchic theory is composed of three subtheories: a componential subtheory, describing the internal analytical mental mechanisms and processes involved in intelligence; an experiential subtheory focusing on how a person's experience combined with insight and creativity affects how she thinks; and a contextual subtheory, emphasizing the role of the external environment in determining what constitutes intelligent behavior in a situation. The first part of the subtheory, the mental mechanisms of intelligence, is posited as universal: "Although individuals may differ in what mental mechanisms they apply to a given task or situation, the potential set of mental mechanisms underlying intelligence is claimed to be the same across all individuals, social classes, and cultural groups" (Sternberg, 1986a, pp. 23–24). The other two parts of Sternberg's theory, which emphasize the experience of the learner and the real-world context, are seen as having both universal and relativistic components. The universal aspect has to do with areas being studied within each of these subparts of the theory (such as the processes of automation, environmental adaption, and shaping). These processes are seen as important no matter what the cultural milieu or the person's experience with the tasks or situations chosen to measure these aspects. The relativistic nature of these parts of the theory comes from the recognition that what constitutes intelligent behavior is not the same for all groups of people. As Sternberg puts it, "Parts of the theory are culturally universal, and parts are culturally relative" (1986a, p. 24).

Sisco (1989) offers an excellent overview of how Sternberg's triarchic theory may apply to adult learning. From Sisco's perspective, "one of the most significant implications would appear to be something that many adult educators have believed, at least implicitly, for a long time now: that human intelligence is much more than performance on standardized tests and achievement in schools" (p. 287). In taking this view, Sternberg (1985, 1988) and Gardner (1983) offer similar observations: that intelligence consists of not only the academic abilities, such as verbal and logical-mathematical skills, but also the capacity to perform in the everyday world. Sternberg's notion of practical intelligence—"intelligence as it operates in real-world contexts" (1986a, p. 301)—seems especially useful in gaining a clearer picture of adult intelligence.

A second major application from Sternberg's work, cited by Sisco (1989), is the notion that intelligence can be taught. Although others have investigated this idea (for example, Schaie, 1996), Sternberg has offered a comprehensive blueprint of a practical training program for enhancing intellectual skills (see Sternberg, 1986a, 1988). In this program Sternberg offers applied examples of each subtheory along with practical exercises. According to Sisco, the main strengths of this program are that "it is based on a theory that has been subjected to fairly extensive and rigorous empirical testing … , focusing on academic as well as practical intelligence … , [and] has assessment tools for measuring training effects" (p. 287).

Sternberg (1996b) has carried his work further into what he calls "successful intelligence." His view of successful intelligence is grounded in the same basic components as those in his triarchic theory: "To be successfully intelligent is to think well in three different ways: analytically [componential subtheory], creatively [experiential subtheory], and practically [contextual subtheory].... Analytical thinking is required to solve problems and to judge the quality of ideas. Creative intelligence is required to formulate good problems and ideas in the first place. Practical intelligence is needed to use the ideas and their analysis in an effective way in one's everyday life" (Sternberg, 1996b, pp. 127–128). All three intelligences are interrelated and therefore are needed in adult life. Sternberg stresses that it is not enough just to have these three abilities; rather, people are successfully intelligent when they are able to choose how and when to use these abilities effectively. For example, students in graduate programs often develop research studies that meet the test of being highly analytical in nature. Nonetheless, the problems they choose to study may not be important to their fields (lack of creative intelligence) or have little practical significance (something valued in educational research). Sternberg goes on to outline twenty characteristics and attributes of people who are successfully intelligent, with the assertion that "their presence can serve as self-activators and can lead, ultimately, to success … , [while] their absence [results in] self-sabotage and failure"

(p. 251). Successfully intelligent people motivate themselves, know how to make the most of their abilities, translate thought into action, have a product orientation, complete tasks and follow through, and are not afraid to risk failure. In summary, Sternberg's work on intelligence, like that of Gardner, is very useful in informing both the theory and practice of learning in adulthood.

Goleman's Theory of Emotional Intelligence

Goleman (1995) too has challenged our traditional views of intelligence. By expanding what we mean by intelligence, Goleman (1995, p. 9), grounding his work in the new discoveries of the emotional architecture of the brain, asserts that we have two very different ways of knowing—the rational and the emotional—which are, for the most part, intertwined and "exquisitely coordinated; feelings are essential to thought, thought to feelings." Yet, in Goleman's beliefs, it is the emotional mind—in his terms, emotional intelligence—that is the major determiner of success in life. Building on the work of Salovey and Mayer (1990), Goleman describes five major domains of emotional intelligence: knowing one's emotions, managing emotions, motivating oneself, recognizing emotions in others, and handling relationships. He believes self-awareness of one's feelings is the key to emotional intelligence, but one must also be attuned to the emotions of others. His descriptions of how adults might display their emotional intelligences are similar to Gardner's concepts of personal intelligences. For example, both authors speak to the need for people to make personal connections and be empathetic as well as to have access to their own internal feelings. In addition, Goleman's ideas about emotional intelligence are echoed in Sternberg's list of the characteristics and attributes of people who display successful intelligence.

As with Gardner's theory of multiple intelligences, educators of children have gravitated to Goleman's ideas. And Goleman himself has outlined a number of ways that schools could change their practices to encourage the development of emotional intelligence. In addition, Goleman has addressed how emotional intelligence can assist in our lives as adults, in both home and work situations. Other authors too have addressed the concept of emotional intelligence in adulthood (Simmons and Simmons, 1997; Weisinger, 1998). Weisinger (1998), for example, has explored the application of emotional intelligence in the workplace. Based on his work with a variety of businesses and other organizations, he gives helpful practical examples and exercises on how to develop one's own emotional intelligence and then use that intelligence in relating to others effectively in work situations. Weisinger's hope is that people who have developed their own emotional intelligence can build emotionally intelligent organizations.

We move next in the section to a discussion of the contextual perspective of intelligence. As will become apparent, there is some overlap among researchers who highlight the importance of context as a critical component of adult intelligence and those who stress the concepts of practical and emotional intelligence.

THE CONTEXTUAL PERSPECTIVE OF INTELLIGENCE

Acknowledging the contextual dimension of intelligence in adulthood has moved thinking about intelligence beyond individual learners. Within the broad framework of the contextual perspective, two major threads are important in gaining a clearer understanding of adult intelligence: intellectual abilities lie at the intersection between mind and context, and intelligence is defined differently by different social classes and cultural groups.

We all have wondered why some people can be successful in more than one setting, even when those settings are radically different, while others fail miserably when they move, even when they are doing the same job. One explanation is that people who succeed across settings have the internal capacity and are able to scan and adapt to new environments. Without the ability to understand and actively participate in new situations, a contextual theorist would observe that being cognitively competent internally makes little, if any, difference. In essence, the contextual perspective captures the adaptive functions of intelligence—being able to act intellectually within a number of different contexts, based on accumulation of both generalized and specialized knowledge and abilities (Baltes, Dittmann-Kohli, and Dixon, 1984; Dixon, 1992; Sternberg, 1985, 1994b, 1996b).

Also within the contextual framework, we have come to understand that intelligence is not defined the same way by different cultural groups and social classes (Berry, 1996; Keats, 1995; Kohl de Oliveira, 1995; Luttrell, 1989; Sternberg, 1996b). As Kohl de Oliveira (1995, p. 245) has observed, "Individuals, growing up in their cultural settings, develop their own conceptions about intellectual competence, acquisition and use of cognitive abilities, and organization of these abilities within different situations." For example, respondents in Luttrell's study (1989, p. 37) of working-class black and white women judged people as intelligent by their ability "to cope with everyday problems in an everyday world." In other words, they saw using common sense as an important intellectual skill. But even in their definitions of common sense, each group described the formulation and value of this commonsense know-how very differently. White women valued working-class men's commonsense knowledge, such as manual and craft knowledge, more highly than their own intuitive knowledge springing from their domestic responsibilities. In contrast, black women viewed as important the knowledge and abilities they gained through caretaking and domestic work. In addition, working-class black women also considered their racial identity and relationships with "extended kin" and the black community as critical to both what they know and how they used this knowledge.

Kohl de Oliveira (1995, p. 262), in her longitudinal study of how adults in a *favela* (squatter settlement) in the city of São Paulo, Brazil, understand intelligence, found that her respondents "characterized intelligent people as those who are able, basically, to 'make things,' to create concrete products with their own hands: build houses, do woodwork, do mechanical work, paint, make objects in straw, ceramics, and so on." These people, who were living in a squatter settlement, defined intelligence as the ability to cope with their everyday lives, which in essence meant possessing the skills to make things with their own hands and having the ability to learn easily and quickly things that could assist them in their daily survival.

Although the concept of practical intelligence could be used to describe how both the Luttrell and Kohl de Oliveira respondents characterized intelligence, the concrete descriptions their subjects used are different from those given by the populations often used in studies of intelligence: those with middle-class backgrounds. For example, in a study by Berg and Sternberg (1992), subjects from membership lists of large Protestant churches in the New Haven, Connecticut, and Salt Lake City, Utah, areas used phrases like "is able to analyze topics in new and original ways," "is open-minded to new ideas and trends," "displays good common sense," "acts in a mature manner," "acts responsibly," and "is interested in home and family life" as important behaviors characterizing adults with practical intelligence.

AGE AND INTELLECTUAL ABILITIES

Does intelligence decline with age? Responses to this question are mixed and often controversial. The classic school of thought contends that intelligence enters a process of irreversible decline in the adult years, although the hypothesized onset of that decline has been extended from the early twenties to at least the age of fifty or sixty. Others say that intelligence is relatively stable through the adult years, with substantial intellectual changes occurring only very late in life, and then primarily "in abilities that were less central to the individual's life experience and thus perhaps less practiced" (Schaie, 1996, p. 2). In essence, we have enough brain capacity to do almost anything we choose, until serious illness sets in. Still others argue that intelligence declines in some respects, remains stable in others, and may even increase in some functions (Baltes, Dittmann-Kohli, and Dixon, 1984; Kaufman, Kaufman, Chen, and Kaufman, 1996; Raykov, 1995).

What creates this confusing picture of adult intellectual abilities? Botwinick (1977) has provided a helpful framework, citing four key factors on which the controversies rest: definitions of age or aging, definitions of intelligence, types of tests used to measure intelligence, and research methods and their pitfalls. All of these factors are discussed in this section, using current ideas from research and practice. Underlying most of this discussion is that we are addressing the issue of age and intellectual abilities primarily from the perspective of the psychometric framework.

What Is Meant by Age and Aging

Whether or not one believes intelligence declines with age depends on "where in the age spectrum one chooses to look" (Botwinick, 1977, p. 580). Are we talking about adults in early, middle, or later adulthood? In reviewing data on early and middle adulthood, our response would be that intelligence does not decline with age. (See Baltes, Dittmann-Kohli, and Dixon, 1984; Schaie, 1994, 1996; Schaie and Hertzog, 1983.) In fact, some intellectual functions, no matter what testing procedures are employed, seem to increase over the course of the years. Our response to whether intelligence declines in later adulthood is not as clear-cut. (See Baltes, 1993; Baltes, Dittmann-Kohli, and Dixon, 1984; Horn and Donaldson, 1976; Schaie, 1996.) Most agree that some decline in functioning occurs between age sixty and the early seventies, but the precise nature of decline and, more important, its practical effect on learning ability are still unknown. For example, intelligence does appear to drop within a few years of death. This phenomenon, labeled the *terminal drop,* might account at least in part for the decrease in the intellectual functioning of older adults. This explanation contrasts with the traditional view that intellectual impairment is a universal condition of advancing age (Labouvie-Vief, 1990; Troll, 1982). In line with this observation, only a few studies have addressed the intellectual abilities of healthy adults beyond the age of seventy. In one longitudinal comparison of subjects ranging in age from seventy-three to ninety-nine, researchers found that although many of the subjects showed some decline in abilities, more than half displayed no such changes, even at the older ages (Field, Schaie, and Leino, 1988). In a more recent study of eighteen people between the ages of 100 and 106, these "centenarians reported rich late-life learning experiences, ... the majority of [which] occurred through social interactions" (Fenimore, 1997, p. 57).

Definitions of Intelligence

There is no universal agreement as to what constitutes intelligence. Therefore, when we speak about changes in intellectual ability as we age, a key question must be answered: What do we mean by intelligence? When intelligence is defined as a unitary property, the research tends to confirm that intelligence does indeed decline with age, although again the point of the departure for that decline often varies (Schaie and Willis, 1986). Yet when intelligence is defined as a multifaceted entity, the response tends to be that some of our abilities decline, while others remain stable or even increase (Baltes, 1993; Baltes, Dittmann-Kohli, and Dixon, 1984; Schaie, 1979, 1987, 1996; Sternberg and Berg, 1987).

The best example of this kind of thinking is seen in the study of fluid and crystallized intelligence, where it is hypothesized that fluid intelligence decreases with age whereas crystallized intelligence first increases and then remains relatively stable (Horn, 1982). Intertwined with this idea of multidimensional intelligence is an even more fundamental question: Are the primary factors that have been identified as the building blocks of intelligence, such as verbal and numerical abilities, the foundations on which all intellectual skills are developed for a lifetime? Or are different kinds of intellectual abilities, such as those needed for everyday learning, of greater importance for learning in adulthood? (See Gardner, 1983, 1995; Labouvie-Vief, 1990; Schaie, 1987, 1996; Scribner, 1984; Sternberg, 1986b, 1996b; Sternberg and Wagner, 1986.) These are questions for which no clear answers are yet forthcoming, but common sense would tell us must be addressed more fully.

Types of Tests

Behind every intelligence test is a definition of intelligence, whether given directly or implied by the test's author. Thus, it is apparent that generalizations about intelligence and about the aging process are also affected by the tests used.

Most research on the effects of intelligence and aging has been conducted using either the WAIS-R or the PMA. The question then arises as to whether either of these two measures captures a holistic picture of adult intelligence. Some would say that they do (for example, Schaie, 1979, 1987), while others have raised serious questions about their validity for adult learners (Sternberg, 1986a, 1996b; Sternberg and Wagner, 1986). Another criticism of both of these tests, and others like them, has been their inclusion of timed items. All of the PMA subtests are timed, and about half of the subtests in the WAIS-R are timed. Is a timed test, particularly one involving perceptual motor function, a valid measure of intelligence, especially for older adults? Some would choose to eliminate this factor of speed in assessing intelligence. Moreover, questions have been raised about the language of the test items, which may be biased toward a younger age cohort.

Research Methods

The research designs employed in investigations of changes in intelligence over the life span have also generated much discussion in the literature. Results of cross-sectional studies, those that compare one-time test scores of different age groups (twenty, forty, and sixty years old, for example), have been misinterpreted to show that as we age, our intelligence declines. (See Botwinick, 1977; Knox, 1977; Schaie and Willis, 1986.) Findings from longitudinal studies, however, usually support a very different conclusion. Based primarily on readministration of intelligence tests over time and to the same group of people, various longitudinal investigations demonstrate that intellectual abilities of groups of older people are remarkably stable over time (Ivnik and others, 1995; Rabbitt and others, 1993; Schaie, 1994, 1996). However, the group data appear to mask individual changes within each of the cohort groups. Botwinick (1977, p. 582), reflecting on this problem of research designs, has observed that "the cross-sectional method may spuriously magnify age decline, and the longitudinal method may minimize it." In cross-sectional investigations, the background and experiences of the different cohorts being studied may cloud the results due to such factors as formal educational attainment and health. Moreover younger cohorts, especially those of college students in their twenties, may be more "testwise" than those comprising people in their sixties and seventies. In longitudinal studies, on the other hand, there are problems of selective attrition and dropout.

In response to this problem, researchers have adopted alternative designs to control some of the biases inherent when only a simple cross-sectional or longitudinal design is used. (See Bee, 1996, and Schaie and Willis, 1986, for a description of these designs). Schaie and his associates, as part of the Seattle Longitudinal Study, provide the best example of the work using these alternative designs (Schaie, 1979, 1994, 1996; Schaie and Hertzog, 1983; Schaie and Labouvie-Vief, 1974; Schaie and Parham, 1977; Schaie, Willis, and O'Hanlon, 1994). The primary variables for this study were the five measures of psychological competence from the PMA tests described in the previous section. The data for the study were collected from more than five thousand subjects over a thirty-five-year period in six testing cycles. With six cross-sectional studies, in addition to longitudinal data, the researchers were able to do a number of different forms of analysis, such as cross-sequential and cohort sequential. In essence, the cross-sectional data showed a typical pattern of intellectual decline, while the longitudinal data suggested little if any decline of any practical consequence until after the mid- to late sixties. Even "this decrement is modest until the 80s are reached, and for most individuals it is not a linear phenomenon but occurs in stair-step fashion" (Schaie, 1994, p. 308). Schaie and others attributed the differences in findings between the two research designs to cohort variation—differences between the generations versus differences in the ages of subjects. These cohort variations are, in turn, attributed to higher educational levels of succeeding generations and overall better nutrition and health care that may have resulted in superior physiological brain functioning.

Schaie's (1996) overarching conclusion from this vast array of data is that any significant reductions in intelligence do not occur in most persons until their eighties or nineties and then not in all abilities or for all individuals. "Even at such advanced ages, competent behavior can be expected by many persons in familiar circumstances. Much of the observed loss occurs in highly challenging, complex, or stressful situations" (Schaie, 1996, p. 273), versus the everyday tasks of life. Schaie (1994) and his colleagues have also isolated variables that reduce the risk of cognitive decline in old age, among them, absence of cardiovascular and other chronic diseases, living in favorable environmental circumstances, substantial involvement in activities, maintenance of high levels of perceptual processing speed into old age, being married to a spouse of high cognitive status, and rating one's self as satisfied with one's life.

INTELLIGENCE, AGING, AND ADULT LEARNING

Among the many new ideas about intellectual functioning in adulthood, three ideas surface as the most intriguing and useful to educators. The first is the framing of more holistic conceptions of adult intelligence that are grounded in the real lives of adults of all colors, races, and ethnic backgrounds. Theorists such as Gardner (1983, 1995) and Sternberg (1996a, 1996b) have moved the boundaries of intelligence beyond just the minds of individuals and have challenged researchers and practitioners to consider how the individual and the context interact to shape intellectual functioning in adulthood. They have also moved intelligence out of the hallowed hallways of schools and universities, which have always placed more value on academic skills and abilities, into how people function in all aspects of life. Sternberg (1994b) has added a further idea to understanding of the mind in context: that of the "luck" or "whoops" factor. Each of us is born with different gifts and into different circumstances. Some of us are lucky enough to find places where our gifts have been prized and nurtured (luck factor), while others, no matter what the individual effort, are never recognized or are blocked by circumstances beyond their control (whoops factor).

Second, researchers such as Schaie (1994, 1996) are creating a greater understanding of the internal and external factors that can strengthen intellectual abilities. This is especially important as life expectancy has increased dramatically, especially in developed nations. We may not have control over all of these factors, such as disease or high levels of perceptual processing speed; however, individuals can control other variables such as maintaining activity levels and effecting public policy decisions benefiting older adults (Peterson and Masunaga, 1998). With further exploration of both mainstream and alternative theories of intelligence, our sense is that other controllable factors will be isolated as well.

Third, educators of adults have tremendous opportunities to help ensure that adult learners, especially older adults, are provided a variety of educational opportunities to inhibit decline and expand our intellectual capacity. This assertion is premised on the assumptions that adult intelligence encompasses far more than results on traditional IQ tests and that researchers have identified, and will continue to isolate, numerous other factors on which intelligence depends (for example, Herasymowych, 1997; Schaie, 1996; Schaie and Willis, 1986; Sternberg, 1996a). We need to think through carefully what intellectual abilities and skills are the most useful for adults, both young and old, and could be amenable to educational interventions. Good models of such materials are Perkins's (1995) book on the science of the learnable intelligence, Weisinger's (1998) work on emotional intelligence at work, and Herasymowych's (1997) ideas on increasing intelligence through action learning. Herasymowych (1997), for example, developed and successfully tested a practical model for increasing managers' capacity for reflecting on their experience critically, using the literature on the learning cycle, action learning, and learnable intelligence. And Perkins (1995) describes a number of programs in which the teaching of intelligence, and more specifically what he terms reflective intelligence, was effectively taught. Perkins views reflective intelligence in adults as being particularly supportive of "coping with novelty … [and] thinking contrary to certain natural trends" (pp. 112–113).

SUMMARY

In this section we discussed the concept of intelligence and how different ways of viewing intelligence can better help us understand learning in adulthood. The most often used paradigm of intelligence is the psychometric tradition, which assumes that intelligence is a measurable quantity. First conceptualized from this tradition as a single factor of general ability, the construct has broadened to include the notion that there are multiple forms of intellectual ability, such as those proposed by Horn (1976), Cattell (1963), and Guilford (1967). Commonly used tests of adult intelligence that fit within this psychometric tradition include the Wechsler Adult Intelligence Scale–Revised and the Primary Mental Abilities Test. Two issues that have surfaced with the use of these types of tests are the test items and the social and policy implications of IQ scores.

Challenges to the psychometric tradition have come primarily from scholars who question whether what is measured as intelligence through this tradition has any relationship to what these scholars have termed real-world or practical intelligence and how context affects development. Three of the most prominent theorists who represent this alternative view of intelligence are Gardner (1983), Sternberg (1985, 1996b), and Goleman (1995). The contextual perspective of intelligence, which often includes the notion of practical and emotional intelligence, acknowledges the importance of the intersection of the mind and the outside world as critical in gaining a clearer understanding of intelligence. What this acknowledgment means is that intelligence has been defined differently by people of varying cultural backgrounds and social classes.

The question of whether adults retain their intellectual abilities as they age has not been definitively answered. Four key factors on which the age and intelligence controversies center are the definition of age or aging, definitions of intelligence, types of tests used to measure intelligence, and research methods and their pitfalls. The consensus is that significant reductions in intelligence do not occur in most people until their eighties or nineties, and then not in all abilities or for all individuals. In addition, a number of variables reducing the risk of intellectual decline in old age have been isolated, such as living in favorable circumstances and maintaining substantial involvement in activities. What this means is that we need to replace the stereotype of the old dog and new tricks with a somewhat different adage: "And so we come to the general conclusion the old dog can learn new tricks, but the answer is not a direct and simple one.... He is less likely to gamble on the results, particularly when he is not convinced that the new trick is any better than the old tricks which served him so well in the past. He may not learn the new trick as rapidly as he did in the past, but learn it he does. Further, the best evidence seems to indicate that, if he starts out as a clever young pup, he is very likely to end up as a wise old hound" (Bischof, 1969, p. 224).

The section concludes with an exploration of three ideas about intellectual functioning in adulthood that are particularly intriguing and useful for educators of adults: alternative conceptions of adult intelligence that do not rely on psychometric measurement as their foundation, factors that have been isolated as either halting any decrement or even increasing adults' intellectual capacities, and the tremendous potential that educators of adults have for providing learning opportunities that can strengthen adults' intellectual abilities.

SECTION TWO

EXPERIENCE AND LEARNING

Sharan B. Merriam
Rosemary S. Caffarella

We vividly remember attending a professional development program where the program presenters spent quite a bit of time at the start gathering information from participants concerning what they already knew about the subject and what they wanted to know. This collection of data was spread out on newsprint on most available wall space. Ah yes, we all thought. These presenters really know how to tune into us as adult learners. They are getting a good sense of our prior knowledge and experience and what our needs as learners are. We assumed they would use the material we had generated, which represented both our individual and collective selves, as both a starting point for our learning and a way to help us connect our new learning to what we already knew. Were we ever wrong! Instead the presenters went on to do their own "show and tell," and never again referred to the materials on the wall. Once again our experiences were seen as inconsequential in the learning process, and as a result the majority of the participants either tuned themselves out or left before the session was over.

Numerous adult educators have underscored the fundamental role that experience plays in learning in adulthood (for example, Boud and Miller, 1996b; Freire, 1970b; Jackson and Caffarella, 1994; Knowles, 1980; Lindeman, 1961; Mezirow, 1981; Usher, Bryant, and Johnston, 1997). For example, one of Lindeman's (1961, p. 6) four major assumptions about adult learning was that "the resource of highest value in adult education is the learner's experience." Experience then becomes "the adult learner's living textbook ... already there waiting to be appropriated" (p. 7). Similarly, one of the major assumptions underlying Knowles's (1980, p. 44) work on andragogy is that adults "accumulate an increasing reservoir of experience that becomes an increasingly rich resource for learning." As adults live longer they accumulate both a greater volume and range of experiences. Knowles also observes that adults tend to define themselves by their experiences, describing themselves as parents, spouses, workers, volunteers, community activists, and so on. Boud and Miller (1996b) and Usher, Bryant, and Johnston (1997), also acknowledging that experience is foundational to adult learning, advocate that adults use their experience, but with a clear understanding that this form of knowledge is highly influenced by sociocultural and historical factors.

Although adult educators have accepted for some time the connection between experience and learning, we are still learning about this connection and how to use it most effectively in both formal and nonformal learning situations. A number of questions puzzle us: What leads to learning from experience? Is the context in which the experience happens important? Are there ways we can design learning episodes to capture this experiential component best? In this section we explore responses to these and other important questions related to experience and learning. Discussed first are representative scholars who have addressed how we learn from life's experiences. Next is an exploration of how in general we can assist each other in learning from experience. We then describe reflective practice, one of the major ways educators have structured learning from experience. An overview of situated cognition, stressing how authentic experiences are viewed as one of the key assumptions in operationalizing this concept, is then provided. As part of this overview, we also examine how the individual learner and the context of the learning cannot be separated within the situated frame of learning. We conclude the section by discussing instructional practices that are grounded in the concept of situated cognition.

LEARNING FROM LIFE EXPERIENCES

John Dewey (1938), in his classic volume *Experience and Education,* made some of the most thoughtful observations about the connections between life experiences and learning. More specifically, Dewey postulates that "all genuine education comes about through experience" (p. 13), although "he is careful to note that *not all experience educates,* by which he means that not all experiences lead to the growth of ever-widening and deeper experiences" (Merriam, 1994, p. 81). In fact, some experiences "mis-educate," in that they actually "distort growth … , narrow the field of further experiences … , [and land people] in a groove or rut" (Dewey, 1938, p. 13). Judging whether experiences actually produce learning can be difficult because "every experience is a moving force. Its value can be judged only on the ground of what it moves toward and into" (p. 31). For example, being diagnosed as HIV positive may make some people so bitter and angry that any positive or growth-enhancing learning from that life change is almost impossible. On the other hand, others become highly active inquirers and participants in maintaining their health as well as involved in caring for those with full-blown AIDS.

For learning to happen through experience, Dewey (1938, p. 27) argues that the experience must exhibit the two major principles of continuity and interaction: "The principle of the continuity of experience means that every experience both takes up something from those which have gone before and modifies in some way the quality of those which come after." In other words, experiences that provide learning are never just isolated events in time. Rather, learners must connect what they have learned from current experiences to those in the past as well as see possible future implications. For example, we can assume that people who are enjoying their retirement have been able to connect their past experiences to those of the present. Glennie, a retired salesperson, who may have always traveled vicariously through the Sunday paper's travel section, has bought a small travel trailer and now spends six months of the year exploring new places.

The second principle, that of interaction, posits that "an experience is always what it is because of a transaction taking place between an individual and what, at the time, constitutes his environment" (Dewey, 1938, p. 41). Going back to the example of Glennie, she is learning about new places firsthand because she now has the time and means to visit them. Through her travels, she has developed an interest in Native American culture and so seeks out new tribal groups to explore. As illustrated through Glennie's interest in Native American culture, the two principles of continuity and interaction are always interconnected and work together to provide the basis for experiential learning. What Glennie has learned in visiting one reservation "becomes an instrument of understanding" for attending the next tribal celebration with a different group of Native Americans. In translating Dewey's ideas into educational practice, what is key is how important the situation becomes in promoting learning. Developing a welcoming and comfortable atmosphere, providing the right materials, and linking these materials to learners' past and future experiences is critical in assisting adults to learn from their experiences.

A number of other writers have also examined how we learn from experience (Bateson, 1994; Boud and Walker, 1990, 1992; Kolb, 1984; Jarvis, 1987a, 1987b; Usher, 1992; Usher, Bryant, and Johnston, 1997). Kolb (1984), building primarily on the work of Dewey, Piaget, and Lewin, conceptualized that learning from experience requires four different kinds of abilities: (1) an openness and willingness to involve oneself in new experiences (concrete experience); (2) observational and reflective skills so these new experiences can be viewed from a variety of perspectives (reflective observation); (3) analytical abilities so integrative ideas and concepts can be created from their observations (abstract conceptualization); and (4) decision-making and problem-solving skills so these new ideas and concepts can be used in actual practice (active experimentation). Kolb pictured these capabilities as interrelated phases within a cyclical process, starting with the concrete experience and then moving through reflective observation and abstract conceptualization to active experimentation. Whatever action is taken in the final phase becomes another set of concrete experiences, which in turn can begin the experiential learning cycle again. "Thus, in the process of learning, one moves in varying degrees from actor to observer, and from specific involvement to general analytic detachment" (Kolb, 1984, p. 31).

In thinking through how to make Kolb's learning cycle more usable by practitioners, Barnett (1989) has added a fifth component to Kolb's model, that of "planning for implementation," which he has inserted between the abstract conceptualization and active experimentation phase

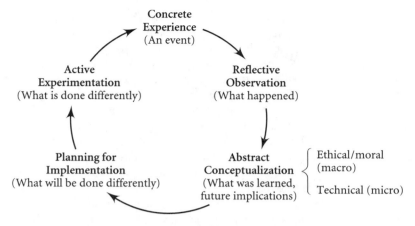

Figure 2-1.   A Model of Reflective Thought and Action.
Source: Barnett, 1989, p. 4.

(see Figure 2-1). Planning for implementation, which also assumes the ability to problem-solve and make decisions, allows time for people to develop a specific plan for action, which they then carry out in the active experimentation phase. At the very least this plan should include "a rationale for undertaking the plan, specific activities that will occur, other people who will be involved, a time line of events and activities, and types of data to be collected to determine how the plan is working" (Barnett, 1989, p. 6). The active experimentation phase then becomes the time when this plan is actually carried through. Barnett sees this planning phase as important in operationalizing Kolb's cycle for two reasons: it moves people in a concrete way toward a commitment to action, and it provides a mechanism for further learning and subsequent action. Through reflecting on what happened as a result of the plan (which becomes a concrete experience), the experiential learning cycle begins again.

Jarvis (1987a, 1987b) expands on the work of Kolb, seeing Kolb's model as too simplistic for explaining the complex phenomenon of learning from experience. Jarvis (1987a, p. 16) premises his theory on the assumption that "all learning begins with experience." "Like Kolb, he believes that learning involves transforming these experiences into knowledge, and he would add skills and attitudes. Like Dewey, he emphasized the *potential* of learning from experience; not all experience leads to learning" (Merriam, 1994, p. 82).

Jarvis's (1987a) model of the learning process begins with the person's moving into a social situation in which a potential learning experience might occur. From an experience there are nine different routes that a person might choose to take, some of which result in learning and some of which do not (see Key Theories of Learning in this section for a complete explanation of Jarvis's theory). Jarvis includes both experimental learning (the result of a person experimenting on the environment) and reflective practice (thinking about and monitoring one's practice as it is happening) with what he conceives as the highest forms of learning. Both experiential learning and reflective practice call for fairly intense involvement of the learner.

Capturing many of the elements proposed by Dewey, Kolb, and Jarvis, Boud and his colleagues (Boud, Keogh, and Walker, 1985, 1996; Boud and Walker, 1990, 1992; Boud and Miller, 1996b) also describe how adults can learn from experience. These scholars, like those we have discussed previously, believe "that learning can only occur if the experience of the learner is engaged at some level" (Miller and Boud, 1996, p. 9). In promoting learning from experience, Boud and his colleagues see a strong link between using the reflective process and actually learning from experience. Boud, Keogh and Walker's (1985, 1996) original model consisted of three stages:

(1) returning to and replaying the experience, (2) attending to the feelings that the experience provoked, and (3) reevaluating the experience. In recollecting what took place during the experience, these authors assert that exploring "the feelings evoked during the experience" (Boud, Keogh, and Walker, 1996, p. 43) is of particular importance. More specifically, we need to work through any negative feelings that have arisen and eventually set those aside, while retaining and enhancing the positive feelings. If the negative feelings are not addressed, what commonly happens is that learning becomes blocked. In the reevaluation stage, our aim is to use this experience as a way of getting us ready for new experiences, and thus new learning. Four processes may contribute to this reevaluation stage: "*association,* that is, relating of new data to that which is already known; *integration,* which is seeking relationships among the data; *validation* to determine the authenticity of the ideas and feelings which have resulted; and *appropriation,* that is, making knowledge one's own" (Boud, Keogh, and Walker, 1996, pp. 45–46).

In response to some criticism of this initial model, Boud and Walker (1990, 1992) have recently revised their model to include the totality of life experiences, in which they acknowledge that "each experience is influenced by the unique past of the learner as well as the current context" (Miller and Boud, 1996, p. 9). "Thus their most recent model of learning through experience accounts for the preparation the learner brings to the experience, the experience itself (during which the learner can both 'notice' and 'intervene'), and the two-way process of reflecting back and forward during and subsequent to the experience" (Tennant and Pogson, 1995, p. 161). In revising their model, their current stance is more aligned with the original thinking of Dewey and that of Schön.

Like the more recent work of Boud and Walker (1990, 1992) and the earlier work of Dewey (1938), Bateson (1994) and Usher, Bryant, and Johnston (1997) speak to the importance of the situated nature of experience in learning, although in very different ways. Bateson (1994, p. 30), using the metaphor of the double helix, asserts "that lessons too complex to grasp in a single occurrence spiral past again and again, small examples gradually revealing greater and greater implications." In other words, we continually recycle our past experiences, especially those "events that were ambiguous, mysterious, incomplete…. What was once barely intelligible may be deeply meaningful a second time. And a third" (pp. 30–31). Bateson goes on to observe that one way to encourage this spiral learning is to encounter familiar issues within an unfamiliar environment. More specifically, she believes that examining our life experiences through the framework of other cultures can provide powerful learning experiences. One example Bateson gives is to look at parenting practices within totally different cultural frames. Through these observations, we learn that parenting and childhood experiences are very much bound by culture. As a result, we can have the opportunity to rethink our own worlds as children, as well as our actions as parents or perhaps grandparents. Our earlier or current experiences about being a child and a parent or grandparent become more accessible to awareness through this spiral learning process, and therefore we may be more open to changing our beliefs and actions related to these experiences.

Usher, Bryant, and Johnston (1997) approach the situated or contextual nature of experience in a very different way from most other scholars who discuss experience as foundational to learning. Although they acknowledge that Jarvis (1987a) and Boud and Walker (1990), among others, use a contextual or sociological frame for learning from experience, they still view the work of these authors as centered on an individualized self who uses experiences as "*raw material*" to be acted upon by the mind through the controlled and self-conscious use of the senses (observations) and the application of reason (reflection)" (Usher, Bryant, and Johnston, 1997, p. 101). Rather, grounded in the assumption that "the self is a culturally and historically variable category," Usher, Bryant, and Johnston (1997, p. 102) view experience as a text to be used in learning—as "something to be 'read' or interpreted, possibly with great effort, and certainly with no final, definitive meaning" (p. 104). Like Bateson (1994), these authors assert that "the meaning of experience is never permanently fixed; thus, the text of experience is always open to reinterpretation" (p. 105). Usher, Bryant, and Johnston have proposed a "map" of experiential learning within the framework of postmodern thought. With this model, "learning does not

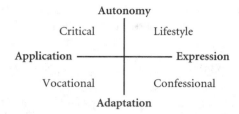

Figure 2-2. **Map of Experiential Learning in the Social Practices of Modernity.**
Source: Usher, Bryant, and Johnston, 1997, p. 106.

simplistically derive from experience; rather, experience and learning are mutually positioned in an interactive dynamic" (p. 107). In posing this model, these authors view the use of experience as part of the learning process as "inherently neither emancipatory nor oppressive, neither domesticating nor transformative. Rather, ... it is perhaps most usefully seen as having a potential for emancipation *and* oppression, domestication *and* transformation, where at any one time and according to context both tendencies can be present and in conflict with one another" (p. 105).

Usher, Bryant, and Johnston's model, shown in Figure 2-2, is structured around two intersecting continua—*Autonomy-Adaptation* (empowerment of individuals to act independently to being able to adapt one's actions in relation to the context) and *Expression-Application* (being able to apply what one knows within real-world contexts)—and four quadrants, referred to as Lifestyle, Confessional, Vocational, and Critical. Learning from experience happens both between and within the quadrants, which represent different types of learning venues.

Lifestyle practices center on the achievement of autonomy through individuality and self-expression, particularly in taste and style (for example, ways of speaking, clothes, leisure pursuits, vacations). Experience is used as a means of defining a lifestyle that is both actively sought by people, but also influenced by socially and culturally defined norms. Instructors become facilitators who assist learners in interpreting their own knowledge and opening up different experiences so these learners can view alternative ways of thinking about lifestyle.

Vocational practices are conveyed through the market. Learners need to be highly motivated in the direction of a personal change linked to the needs of the socioeconomic environment. Vocationalism then is designed to produce flexible competencies and a predisposition to change. As a result of learning adaptive skills through experiential means, learners become more empowered to respond to their changing vocational environments.

In *confessional practices* our private, self-regulating capacities become public. In other words, to realize oneself, to find out the truth about oneself, to accept responsibility for oneself, becomes both personally desirable and economically functional. The emphasis within this process is on self-improvement, self-development, and self-regulation. Experience is used as enabling access to knowledge and the innermost truths about self, which in turn creates productive and empowered people in a number of roles (for example, as active citizen, ardent consumer, enthusiastic employee).

In *critical practices* there is a recognition that experience is never a basic given. The focus is on changing particular contexts rather than adapting to them, and therefore working with learners becomes a political practice. Experiential learning becomes a strategy designed to find and exercise one's voice in the service of self and social empowerment and transformation and is not regarded as something that leads to knowledge, but as knowledge itself.

In constructing this model, Usher, Bryant, and Johnston suggest that "educators need to help [learners] to problematise and interrogate experience as much as to access and validate it" (p. 118). In this way, the model could be used as a heuristic device for learners to "triangulate experience through an investigation of personal meanings alongside the meanings of others and the presence and influence of different contexts" (p. 120). For example, in conducting a workshop on effective ways of relating to a diverse customer base, the workshop facilitators might choose to use the experience of the participants as one of the major content areas for the workshop. They could first ask the participants to reflect individually and then in small groups on times when they have been treated differently as customers because of their gender, race, disability, or ethnic background. In doing this they would use what Usher, Bryant, and Johnston have called the lifestyle experiences of the learners. Participants could then generate lists in their small groups of how their experiences have been the same or different and share those with the large group. The facilitators could then ask people to reflect critically on what they had learned from each other's experiences, and how they might use this knowledge to improve their own customer service practices (thereby integrating their experiential knowledge from the lifestyle, vocational, and confessional practices arenas). Hopefully by having the participants reflect on their own and others' experiences, the end result might be a positive change in how they think and act with customers from diverse backgrounds or perhaps reinforce the positive methods they were already using.

The end product might be quite different if the instructors or learners also chose to view the issue from a critical practices perspective. By using the lens of critical practices to reflect on their individual and collective experiences, they could, for example, come to the realization that the only way to serve a diverse group of customers effectively would be to change the culture of the organization, and not just their individual practices.

Clearly the role of experience in learning is a highly complex process. Although it is important that individual learners are able to reflect on and revisit their own experiences and learn from them, the importance of assisting learners to recognize the contextual factors and how experiences are defined by those factors can not be left to chance.

ASSISTING OTHERS IN LEARNING FROM EXPERIENCE

Boud and Miller (1996b, 1998) and their colleagues (Miller and others, 1997) have provided one of the most eloquent and useful descriptions of the general roles that adults can play in helping others learn from their experiences, no matter what form this learning takes. Miller and Boud (1996, p. 7) term "the function of working with the experience of others as 'animation' and refer to the person who works to promote others' learning as an 'animator.'" They describe "the function of animators to be that of acting with learners, or others, in situations where learning is an aspect of what is occurring.... While teaching or instruction may be an aspect of animation, it is a secondary one which is subordinate to that of fostering learning from experience" (p. 7). Therefore, although animators may be someone with a teaching or instructional role, they also may be friends, co-learners, or supervisors. Key to the influence of animators is the relationship they build with learners. This relationship is influenced by a number of factors, including the political and economic context of their working together. One of the central tasks of animators then becomes to establish "an appropriate micro-culture, climate, and space within which to work" (Boud and Miller, 1996a). This includes acknowledging the power relations in this relationship as well as the broader constraints that are present in most learning settings. Animators also need to take into consideration the feelings and emotions of the learner and construct what they are doing so that the experiences of the learners are the primary source of learning.

Included in the work of Boud and Miller (1996b) are detailed depictions of how instructors and community workers have carried through their role of animator in a variety of settings. Tisdell (1996b), for example, describes how she uses the life experiences of her graduate students and her own developing sense of feminist consciousness to teach feminist theory. Tisdell uses stories to work with her students' individual and collective experiences as a way to "problematise gender relations [and] to demystify [feminist] theory" (p. 120). "Some of the things that typically come up ... are the significance of gender socialization, of mothers' primary influence in the home and family, of religion, and of a growing awareness in each of our lives over time of the patriarchal nature of most societal institutions" (p. 120). She is also able to bridge to what her students do not know through their experiences to broaden their knowledge of feminist theory. Because most of her students are white and middle class, they typically have little experience with thinking about race and class as a fundamental part of understanding feminist theory. By acknowledging their lack of experience in these areas through their sharing of stories, those students in her class who have experienced poverty or an understanding of themselves as racial beings begin to fill in some of the missing pieces of what it is like to be poor or a person of color.

Ireland (1996) reflects back on his role over twenty-five years as an animator with a group of male construction workers in Brazil. In this role, he worked with these workers to help them get elected to the directorship of their local union chapter. Once they were elected, which took a number of years, his role changed to that of assisting the directors in learning how to administer a complex bureaucracy, which included supervision of staff and the overseeing of work actions, such as strikes. More recently, he has concentrated on formal literacy and postliteracy programs for the rank-and-file members. In thinking back on these learning experiences, Ireland points to three fundamental lessons he has learned. First, "the bonds of friendship and shared political ideals are both necessary ingredients of the learning process" (p. 139). Second, in educational processes of a long-term nature, the context in which that learning process takes place profoundly affects what happens in that process, and the needs of both animators and learners continually evolve and are altered. And third, "the permanent interplay between experiential learning and more systematic learning processes within the perspective of popular education is particularly pertinent for workers with low levels of formal schooling.... Experience is an invaluable dimension of informal and formal learning processes in the same way that theory and practice are two sides of the same coin" (pp. 139–140).

Other authors have described very specific processes of how adults learn from experience. In the remaining sections of this section we explore two concepts that have influenced greatly how adult educators use learners' experience as a central part of the learning process: reflective practice and situated cognition.

REFLECTIVE PRACTICE

Reflective practice allows one to make judgments in complex and murky situations—judgments based on experience and prior knowledge. Although reflective practice is most often associated with professional practice, this process can be applied to other types of learning situations, both formal and informal. Practice knowledge, the cornerstone of reflective practice, consists of much more than abstract theoretical or technical knowledge (Schön, 1983; Cervero, 1988; Peters, 1991). The knowledge we gain through experience and the way we practice our craft is just as important. The initiation of reflective practice involves using data in some form, which almost always includes our past and current experiences. Our tacit knowledge about practice, that is, knowledge that we use every day, almost without thinking about it, is an important part of these data.

Three major assumptions undergird the process of reflective practice (Cervero, 1988; Osterman and Kottcamp, 1993; Peters, 1991; Schön, 1983, 1987):

Assumption One. Those involved in reflective practice are committed to both problem finding and problem solving as part of that process. In problem finding, the assumption is that often the problems we are presented with in practice are murky and ill defined. Therefore, we need to be open to discovering new problems or different ways of looking at old problems.

Assumption Two. Reflective practice means making judgments about what actions will be taken in a particular situation. Because these actions usually involve seeking changes in ourselves, other people, or in systems, there is an ethical dimension to reflective practice.

Assumption Three. Reflective practice results in some form of action, even if that action is a deliberate choice not to change practice. Without this action phase, the reflective practice process is incomplete. The lack of attention to this phase as a critical part of reflective practice often frustrates practitioners who are committed to reflection, but see it as a dead-end endeavor when nothing tangible results.

Although reflective practice theoretically should result in the most thoughtful and useful solutions to practice problems, this may not be the case depending on the beliefs educators have about this practice. Wellington and Austin (1996) have argued that depending on their beliefs and values, practitioners have very different orientations toward reflective practice. These differing orientations influence both how reflective practice is used, and therefore the possible outcomes of this practice. For example, do those involved believe that education should be a liberating or "domesticating" form of practice? And what is more important to them: system or human concerns? Wellington and Austin have depicted a way of thinking about reflective practice that acknowledges how it could be filtered through the belief and value systems of practitioners, which in their view results in five orientations toward reflective practice: the immediate, the technical, the deliberative, the dialectic, and the transpersonal (see Figure 2-3).

Practitioners who use the immediate orientation, focusing basically on survival, rarely use any form of reflective practice. Those who view practice as more of a domesticating activity, that is, they see societal needs as taking precedence over individual needs, lean toward the technical and deliberative orientations. The technical mode "uses reflection as an instrument to direct practice" (Wellington and Austin, 1996, p. 308), usually within predetermined guidelines and standards. The deliberative orientation "places emphasis on the discovery, assignment and assessment of personal meaning within an educational setting" (p. 310). Those operating from this orientation are typically humanistic, stress communication, and believe that the attitudes and values of learners are important. Although people who use the deliberative orientation sometimes are uncomfortable with the organization in which they work, they nevertheless tend to work within that system. And finally, those who view educational practice as liberating primarily use the dialectic and transpersonal orientation. Practitioners using the dialectical orientation toward reflective

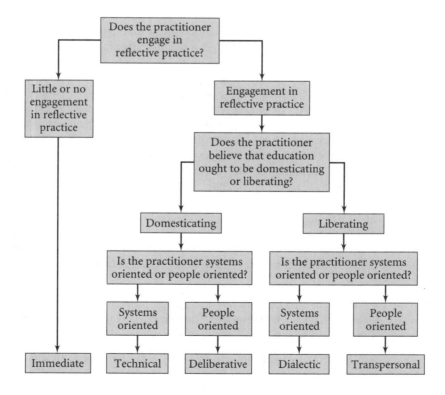

Figure 2-3. Orientations to Reflective Practice.
Source: Wellington and Austin, 1996, p. 312.

practice "reject the limitations of authorized organizational structures and parameters and are uncomfortable working within them.... They tend to ... focus on political and social issues ... [and] advocate political awareness and activism" (p. 310). On the other hand, the transpersonal orientation "centers on universal personal liberation.... They question educational ends, content and means from a personal, inner perspective" (p. 311).

Wellington and Austin cast these orientations not as competing views of what reflective practice should encompass, but as different ways of going about reflective practice. They believe that practitioners need to recognize their own predominant modes, as well as respect the preferred orientations of others. "When practitioners become aware of their own preferences and prejudices across models, they can begin to reflect upon a wider range of questions and develop a wider range of responses" (p. 314). No matter what orientation people have, two basic processes have been identified as central to reflective practice: reflection-on-action and reflection-in-action.

Reflection-on-Action

Reflection-on-action involves thinking through a situation after it has happened. This mode of reflection is presented by most authors as primarily an analytical exercise, which results in new perspectives on experiences, changes in behavior, and commitments to action. In reflection-on-action, we consciously return to the experiences we have had, reevaluate these experiences, decide what we could do differently, and then try out whatever we decided to do differently. Different authors have offered various models of carrying out this reflective cycle. Kolb's (1984) model, or adaptations of his model, is the one most often used in practice. The cyclical nature of the model allows for a process of continued change and growth. Boud, Keogh, and Walker (1985, 1996) have added to Kolb's work on reflection-on-action by stressing we must attend to the feelings created by our experiences in order for the reflective process to be truly effective. In addition, they have added more in-depth descriptions of four cognitive processes (association, integration, validation, and appropriation) that can contribute to the reflective process. And Osterman and Kottkamp (1993), borrowing from the work of Argyris and Schön (1978), set reflective practice within the framework of espoused theories (beliefs) and theories-in-use (actions). Within this frame, they view the reflective practice cycle as helping practitioners become aware of and act on the discrepancies between their beliefs (their espoused theories) and what they actually do.

Descriptions are plentiful on how to put into practice reflection-on-action (for example, Brookfield, 1996b, Jackson and Caffarella, 1994; Smyth, 1996; Osterman and Kottkamp, 1993). Some of the most popular methods used in education and other fields are portfolio development, journal writing, and critical reflection. Key to all of these methods is the framing of critical observations and questions as part of the reflection-on-action process. For example, Smyth (1996), in assisting teachers to uncover the social constraints in which they practice, asks them to respond to four stem questions: (1) Describe (What do I do?), (2) Inform (What does this mean?), (3) Confront (How did I come to be like this?) and (4) Reconstruct (How might I do things differently?). Through this process "teachers begin to link consciousness about the processes that inform the day-to-day aspects of their teaching with the wider political and social realities within which it occurs ... [and] they are able to challenge the ... way schools are conceived, organised and enacted" (Smyth, 1996, p. 54).

Reflection-in-Action

In contrast, reflection-in-action reshapes "what we are doing while we are doing it" (Schön, 1987, p. 26). "Thinking on your feet" and "keeping your wits about you" are commonly used phases that describe reflection-in-action. Schön (1983, 1987, 1991, 1996) is perhaps the best-known author who has challenged professionals to incorporate this form of reflective process as an integral part of professional development. In Schön's view, reflection-in-action is triggered by surprise. What we have been thinking and doing all along as professionals no longer works. "We think critically about the thinking that got us into this fix or this opportunity; and we may, in the process, restructure strategies of action, understanding of phenomena, or ways of framing problems…. Reflection gives rise to [the] on-the-spot experiment" (Schön, 1987, p. 28).

For example, in running an institute for professionals, the institute staff sense that the sessions on a particular day have not gone well. Over coffee, they ask for feedback from participants, and the general observation is that they are finding the material too esoteric and are tired of being "talked at." The next presenter, who is listening to these conversations, has also planned to lecture. Although Ron knows he is an excellent lecturer, he decides that unless he changes the way he presents the material, he will totally lose the audience. Knowing that many of the people in the audience have experience related to his content area, he asks for volunteers to join him in a panel discussion on the topic, explaining that he is changing his format to respond to their needs as learners. While Ron works with the panel members on their roles, he asks the rest of the participants to generate questions they would like to ask panel members. Although he has never used this format in quite this way before, he believes it might work and is willing to take a chance to recapture the interest of the participants. In this way, Ron is using his expertise as an instructor to change on the spot what he is doing as a presenter as he goes along. Schön goes on to observe that competent and experienced professionals use reflection-in-action as a regular part of their practice, although they may not verbalize they are doing this. This form of reflective practice allows professionals to go beyond the routine application of rules, facts, and procedures and gives them the freedom to practice their craft more as a professional artistry where they create new ways of thinking and acting about problems of practice.

Recently there have been both validation of and criticisms to Schön's model of reflection-in-action. Ferry and Ross-Gordon (1998), for example, in exploring the links between experience and practice, support Schön's theory that "reflection-in-action goes beyond 'stable rules' by devising new methods of reasoning" (p. 107) and fostering new ways of framing and responding to problems. Educators who were reflective in their practice used both reflection-on-action and reflection-in-action to build their expertise. They did not find, however, that the amount of experience a person possessed necessarily had anything to do with that person using reflective practice.

On the other hand, Usher, Bryant, and Johnston (1997) assert that although Schön adequately describes the reflection-in-action process, in his own work he did not use "his own practice as a producer of text … [and they view that as] a problem of the *absence of reflexivity* in his own work" (p. 143). By this, Usher, Bryant, and Johnston meant that Schön did not question how the context of his work, being academic in nature, could get in the way of the message. They would have liked to have seen a text that included both the conventional academic type of writing as well as more informal commentary on what was written, including critical comments on what Schön had proposed. Overall Usher, Bryant, and Johnston believe that despite Schön's clear message that reflection-in-action should be implemented in a critical manner, the way in which he conveyed that message makes it easy for practitioners to co-opt the process into one of a technical and rationalistic dialogue.

Boud and Walker (1990, 1992) also have revised their earlier framework of reflective practice to include Schön's idea of reflection-in-action. As pictured in Figure 2-4, Boud and Walker, like Schön, believe that "we experience as we reflect and we reflect as we experience" (Boud and Walker, 1992, p. 168). In other words we cannot, nor should we, separate our past experiences from our current ones. In capturing the reflective element while the experience is happening, Boud and Walker believe it is necessary to use the interaction between the milieu and the learners. They suggest two ways of doing this. The first is "*noticing*, by which the person becomes aware of the milieu, or particular things within it, and uses this for the focus of reflection" (Boud and Walker, 1990, p. 68). The second is "*intervening*, in which the person takes an initiative in the event" (p. 68). Learners may intervene by asking for clarification of what is happening and may even attempt to change the event in some minor or major way. In formal and nonformal settings, learners can often benefit from assistance by facilitators in helping them in the noticing and intervening processes.

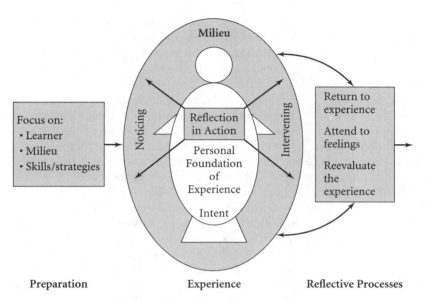

Figure 2-4. Framework for Reflective Practice.
Source: Boud and Walker, 1990, p. 67.

Tremmel (1993) also argues that reflection-in-action is critical to professional practice, but from a very different perspective. Grounding his thinking in the Zen Buddhist tradition of "mindfulness," he, like Schön, believes that reflection can best be accomplished in the midst of everyday practice. Mindfulness, a specific Zen practice, "is 'to return,' [that is] … to 'return' to mindful awareness of the present moment" (p. 443). Being mindful is to pay attention to the here and now, not in an analytical or evaluative way, but rather to invest oneself in "the present moment with full awareness and concentration" (p. 443). It is to move away from the endless parade of thoughts that go through our minds in any one situation, and instead pay attention to what we are thinking and feeling at that moment; it becomes in essence the study of the self at any one point in time. For example, rather than thinking about what I have written about reflective practice, or how I will edit what I have written, being mindful makes me aware of how my shoulders ache right now sitting at the computer, how difficult mindfulness is for me to explain with my Western ways of thinking, and how I hope that at least a few people will be able to grab this idea and help others understand it. The concept of mindfulness seems important to me, even if I cannot explain it well. Tremmel goes on to suggest that "freewriting," that is, writing everything down that comes to mind without editorializing, might be one way for professionals to pay more attention to the here and now in their work. We have used "stem writing" in this way, where we ask learners to respond to a specific stem (such as "What I am feeling right now is …" or "What I wish would happen is …") with the first thing that comes to their mind as one way to enter this realm of the present.

Writing in a similar vein to Tremmel, but coming from a very different cultural tradition, Nuernberger (1994) also speaks of the importance of using our powers of attention in reflective practice. Grounded in Tantric thought as expressed through the work of Shankara, "considered to be India's greatest logician and philosopher" (Nuernberger, 1994, p. 90), Nuernberger reminds us that our powers of attention and concentration are crucial to the reflective life. As he observes: "Typically, our mind is scattered. When we pay attention, we focus the mind's energy. The more focused we become, the greater our concentration, the more powerful our mind [and therefore our reflective processes] become" (Nuernberger, 1994, p. 112–113).

Nuernberger asks us to draw on four types of knowledge in our reflective practice: spiritual knowledge, intuitive knowledge, instinctual knowledge, and analytic or sensory knowledge. Spiritual knowledge is almost mystical in quality and allows for what he terms transformational experiences, which alter "the identity of the individual and eventually [lead] to wisdom" (Nuernberger, 1994, p. 109). Intuitive knowledge is what we gain when we have what he terms "insight into the real consequences of our actions ... [and gives us] the power to discern cause/effect relationships and subtle movements of change" (Nuernberger, 1994, p. 109). Instinctual knowledge is based on subliminal perception, related to the very essence of our own personas or beings. It is the knowledge that we respond to long before we are even aware of any specific sensory information, such as what we see or hear. For example, using our instinctual knowledge is knowing that there is something wrong with a loved one or that we are in danger, but having no specific signs we can point to that tell us that. Nuernberger cautions us that "we can be misled by our instincts when we confuse them with emotional needs, wants, and fears, or through lack of awareness" (p. 110). The knowledge that is most familiar to us is our analytical or sensory knowledge, the knowledge we gain through hearing, seeing, and feeling. "Distorted emotions, poor memory, even faulty sensory mechanisms may limit sensory knowledge" (Nuernberger, 1994, p. 110). In addition, our sensory knowledge is influenced by the conventions of the world around us; it is contextual in nature. Practical consequences of using our attention and concentration skills effectively in reflective practice range from strengthening our perceptual and visionary skills to enhancing our health and well-being.

SITUATED COGNITION

Although reflective practice and situated cognition both involve learning from real-world experiences, how these experiences are interpreted is often vastly different. In most models of reflective practice, learning from experience is still viewed as something that goes on in someone's head. Individuals, whether by themselves or in groups, think through problems presented to them and then act on those problems by changing their practice on the spot or as they encounter similar situations at a later date. Experience provides the catalyst for learning in reflective practice, but most often it is seen as separate from the learning process itself.

In situated cognition, one cannot separate the learning process from the situation in which the learning is presented. Knowledge and the process of learning within this framework are viewed as "a product of the activity, context, and culture in which it is developed and used" (Brown, Collins, and Duguid, 1989, p. 32). The proponents of the situated view of learning argue that learning for everyday living (which includes our practice as professionals) happens only "among people acting in culturally organized settings" (Wilson, 1993c, p. 76). In other words the physical and social experiences and situations in which learners find themselves and the tools they use in that experience are integral to the entire learning process.

Hansman and Wilson (1998), through their study of the teaching of computer-based writing to community college students, provide us with an excellent example of how the major components of situated cognition translate into practice. The students in this study perceived computers to be their major tools for learning. Using computers as tools "gave them 'power' over their writing" (p. 30), and this "power" made writing easier for them than just using pen and paper. "Thus, computers used as tools shaped how students wrote, or at least their perceptions of how they wrote" (p. 30). Students also perceived that using computers allowed them "to construct their own processes for writing, which typically meant that they did not follow prescribed 'how to' methods" (p. 30). And finally, the interactive and relaxed social environment of the class gave students the opportunity to talk with one another about the writing process, which included having students critique each other's work. In essence, the learning experience for these students became a complex social phenomenon, "situated [and] structured by people interacting with each other in tool-dependent environments" (p. 36).

In viewing learning from a situated perspective, two other ideas are key. The first is the emphasis in the learning process changes from being concerned about memory and how we process information internally to that of perception and the settings in which those perceptions are made (Young, 1993). In essence, according to Clancey (1997), "every human thought and action is adapted to the environment, that is, *situated,* because what people *perceive,* and how they *conceive of their activity,* and what they *physically do* develop together" (pp. 1–2). This situated nature of cognition makes the transfer process from using learning gained from one situation to the next more problematic, which has led some theorists to question whether knowledge, especially practical knowledge, can really transfer across situations (Anderson, Reder, and Simon, 1996; Lave, 1988). Context, then, and how this influences the perceptions learners make, is "the element that makes sense of cognition" (Wilson, 1993a, p. 338) versus a nuisance variable that muddies the waters and gets in the way of "real learning." Of course, not everyone shares this view that the situational aspects of learning are the key to understanding cognition (for example, see Anderson, Reder, and Simon, 1996, 1997).

Second, making the assumption that learning and knowing are primarily a cultural phenomenon moves the study of cognition (and, therefore, learning from experience) into the social and political realm and raises the issue of knowledge and power as a legitimate part of the study of cognition (Kirshner and Whitson, 1997; Wilson, 1993c). Although this issue of power and knowledge is fundamental to the theory of situated cognition, it has often been downplayed or overlooked in favor of how to apply the concept practically. This has also been true until recently in much of the work on learning and experience and reflective practice (Usher, Bryant, and Johnston, 1997; Wellington and Austin, 1996). In acknowledging cognition and learning from experience as a cultural phenomenon, the perspectives of critical, feminist, and postmodern thinkers become crucial. A major result of thinking about cognition from a cultural frame is the critiques that have been fostered about traditional educational theory and practice (Brown, Collins, and Duguid, 1989; Lave, 1988; Wilson, 1993c). Foremost among these critiques is a challenge to the fundamental notion that learning is something that occurs within the individual. Rather, learning encompasses the interaction of learners and the social environments in which they function.

In using experience within the framework of situated cognition, the emphasis is on "providing enabling experiences in authentic versus decontextualized contexts" (Choi and Hannafin, 1995, p. 53). As Greeno (1997) has thoughtfully observed, "When we recognize that all learning involves socially organized activity, the question is not *whether* to give instruction in a 'complex, social environment' but *what kinds* of complex, social activities to arrange, for which aspects of participation, and in what sequence to use them" (p. 10). In this perspective education and training by just abstraction is of little use. Rather, "to meet the test of 'authenticity,' situations must at least have some of the important attributes of real-life problem solving, including ill-structured complex goals, an opportunity for the detection of relevant versus irrelevant information, active/generative engagement in finding and defining problems as well as in solving them, involvement in the student's beliefs and values, and an opportunity to engage in collaborative interpersonal activities" (Young, 1993, p. 45). Cognitive apprenticeships and anchored instruction are two ways in which the concept of authentic experiences has been put into practice by educators.

Cognitive Apprenticeships

Cognitive apprenticeships have received the most attention in the literature. "Cognitive apprenticeship methods try to enculturate [learners] into authentic practices through activity and social interaction in a way similar to that evident—and evidently successful—in craft apprenticeship" (Brown, Collins, and Duguid, 1989, p. 37). The cognitive nature of the apprenticeship places emphasis on teaching learners different ways of thinking about whatever they are learning, as well as any skills associated with the apprenticeship.

Based on a study of different forms of cognitive apprenticeship used in several professions, such as engineering, medicine, and educational administration, Brandt, Farmer, and Buckmaster (1993) have offered one of the clearest descriptions of cognitive apprenticeships as an instructional process. (Also see Farmer, Buckmaster, and LeGrand, 1992; Prestine and LeGrand, 1991.) Their

Table 2-1.   Cognitive Apprenticeship Phases.

	Role of Model	Role of Learner	Key Concepts
Phase 1: Modeling	Model real-life activity that learner wants to perform satisfactorily. Model states aloud the essence of the activity. He or she can include tricks of the trade.	Observe performance of total activity, not merely the individual steps. Develop a mental model of what the real thing looks like.	Articulation Domain-specific heuristics
Phase 2: Approximating	Provide coaching to the learner. Provide support when needed.	Approximate doing the real thing and articulate its essence. Reflect on the model's performance. Use self-monitoring and self-correction.	Scaffolding Coaching
Phase 3: Fading	Decrease coaching and scaffolding.	Continue to approximate the real thing. Operate in increasingly complex, risky, or ill-defined situations. Work individually or in groups.	Fading
Phase 4: Self-directed learning	Provide assistance only when requested.	Practice doing the real thing alone. Do so within specified limits acceptable to profession and society.	Self-directed learning
Phase 5: Generalizing	Discuss the generalizability of what has been learned.	Discuss the generalizability of what has been learned.	Generalizability

Source: Brandt, Farmer, and Buckmaster, 1993, p. 71.

five-phase model (see Table 2-1) "starts with deliberate instruction by someone who acts as a model; it then proceeds to model-guided trials by practitioners who progressively assume more responsibility for their learning" (Farmer, Buckmaster, and LeGrand, 1992, p. 42).

Crucial aspects of implementing successful cognitive apprenticeships are selecting appropriate real-world situations or tasks that are grounded in learner needs, finding the right person or persons to do the modeling, and facilitating the learning process. (See Choi and Hannafin, 1995, for clear and concise descriptions of facilitating skills.) In facilitating this process, models "must express the essence of their thoughts, which may otherwise be unspoken, while they demonstrate how to do a particular aspect of the task" or solve a specific problem (Brandt, Farmer, and Buckmaster, 1993, p. 76). Through this articulation, learners are given access not only to what they see, but to what the model is seeing and sensing, plus the model can give further explanations about what she is doing. Coaching learners as they work through the situations or tasks is also a helpful facilitating process, as well as regulating the task difficulty and providing support (scaffolding). The outcomes of cognitive apprenticeships are twofold: (1) internalizing what has been learned so learners can do the task or solve the problem on their own, and (2) generalizing what they have learned as both a way to apply this learning to similar situations and as a starting point for further learning.

Anchored Instruction

Anchored instruction "provides a way to recreate some of the advantages of apprenticeship training in formal educational settings" (Cognition and Technology Group at Vanderbilt, 1990, p. 2). More specifically, the purpose of anchored instruction is to create situations in which learners, through sustained experiences, can grapple with the problems and opportunities that experts encounter. To do this, the instructional process is anchored in what the Cognition and Technology group calls macrocontexts, which are complex problems explored over extended periods of time and through multiple lenses (Cognition and Technology Group at Vanderbilt, 1990, 1992, 1993). These macrocontexts, which in essence become the tools of learning, can take many forms. For example, instructors could provide videodisks containing the problems to be explored, or they could ask learners to prepare problem-based case studies. We have found building macrocontexts to be an especially effective instructional technique with graduate students and professional groups we have worked with over an extended period of time. The goal of anchored instruction is to have learners "experience what it is like to grow from novices who have only rudimentary knowledge ... to relatively sophisticated experts who have explored an environment from multiple points of view" (Cognition and Technology Group at Vanderbilt, 1990, p. 9).

SUMMARY

The experiences of adults have always been viewed as a critical component of learning in adulthood. Although exploring the role of experience in learning has a long history, we continue to discover more about the connections between learning and experience and how to assist adults in formal and nonformal settings to capture the richness of learning from experience. Discussed in this section were the theories of Dewey (1938), Kolb (1984), Jarvis (1987a) Boud and Walker (1990), Bateson (1994), and Usher, Bryant, and Johnston (1997), which offer varying conceptual views of the process of learning from experience. Central to all of these writers is the notion that learning from experience involves adults' connecting what they have learned from current experiences to those in the past as well to possible future situations. Therefore, learning from experience is cyclical in nature; whatever we learn from one experience is then applied to new experiences. Although the focus of the study of the role of experience in learning has been on the individual learner, there has been a shift to understanding how the context of that learning influences both the learning process and the outcomes.

Assisting each other in learning from experience is a critical role adults play as educators in formal settings and as friends, supervisors, and colleagues. Key to this role, which Miller and Boud (1996) have termed being an animator, is the relationships we build with learners. In building these relationships, Miller and Boud point to the importance of understanding the power dynamics in these relationships and emphasize creating supportive climates for learning that acknowledge the contextual nature of knowledge, including the political and social dimensions of that knowledge.

Reflective practice, one of the major ways educators have structured learning from experience, focuses on helping learners make judgments based on experience related to primarily complex and murky problems. One of the fundamental premises underlying reflective practice is that practice knowledge is much more than theoretical and technical knowledge, which is primarily rational in nature. In addition, the knowledge gained through solving the ill-defined problems of practice is just as critical, if not more so. There are many orientations to reflective practice depending on the beliefs and values of the person using this practice. A range of orientations (such as the technical, the deliberate, the dialectical, and the transpersonal) and both reflection-on-action and reflection-in-action should be a regular part of reflective practice.

Experience also plays a critical role in the practice of situated cognition, which acknowledges the importance of the social and cultural context of learning. In other words, the physical and social experiences and situations in which learners find themselves and the tools they use are integral to the learning process. The importance of the authenticity of the experience in which adults learn is stressed within the situated framework. Two ways educators have put this concept of authentic experiences into formal practice are cognitive apprenticeships and anchored instruction. The primary focus of each of these forms of instruction is to help learners develop specific skills and competencies in a particular context of practice.

KEY THEORIES OF LEARNING

SHARAN B. MERRIAM
ROSEMARY S. CAFFARELLA

Learning, so central to human behavior yet so elusive to understanding, has fascinated thinkers as far back as Plato and Aristotle. Indeed, the views of these two philosophers underpin much modern research on learning conducted by psychologists and educators. The fact that so many people have thought about, investigated, and written about the process of learning over the years suggests the complexity of the topic. Learning defies easy definition and simple theorizing. This section reviews some of the major ways that learning has been studied and delineates the contributions these orientations have made to our understanding of learning in adulthood.

Originally, learning was within the purview of philosophical investigations into the nature of knowledge, the human mind, and what it means to know. Plato believed that the physical objects in our everyday world have corresponding abstract forms that we can come to know "by reflecting on the contents of one's mind" (Hergenhahn, 1988, p. 31). Aristotle, on the other hand, believed that all knowledge comes through the senses; these sense impressions can be pondered "to discover the lawfulness that runs through them" (p. 33). Plato's "rationalism" can be seen in Gestalt and cognitive psychology; Aristotle's "empiricism" is particularly evident in early behavioral psychology. Later philosophers presented variations on these two basic positions, ranging from Descartes's separation of mind and body to Kant's notion of innate mental faculties.

It was not until the nineteenth century that the study of the mind, of how people know, and, by extension, of behavior became "scientifically" investigated. Hergenhahn (1988, p. 42) writes that Hermann Ebbinghaus "emancipated psychology from philosophy by demonstrating that the 'higher mental processes' of learning and memory could be studied experimentally" and that many of his findings on learning and memory published in 1885 are still valid. Another pioneer, Wilhelm Wundt, set up the first psychological laboratory in Leipzig in 1879 and investigated how experience is assimilated "into the knowledge structures one already had" (Di Vesta, 1987, p. 206). By the turn of the century, systematic investigations into human learning were well under way in Europe and North America.

In this section we first present a brief discussion of learning and learning theories in general, and then we focus on five different learning theories: behaviorist, cognitivist, humanist, social learning, and constructivist.

LEARNING AND LEARNING THEORIES

Although learning has been defined in a variety of ways, most definitions include the concepts of behavioral change and experience. A common definition from psychologists, especially those who were investigating the phenomenon until the 1950s, is that learning is a change in behavior. This definition, however, fails to capture some of the complexities involved—such as whether one needs to perform in order for learning to have occurred or whether all human behavior is learned. The notion of change still underlies most definitions of learning, although it has been modified to include the potential for change. And the idea that having an experience of some sort, rather than learning as a function of maturation, is important. Thus a reasonable definition of learning would be: "Learning is a relatively permanent change in behavior or in behavioral potentiality that results from experience and cannot be attributed to temporary body states such as those induced by illness, fatigue, or drugs" (Hergenhahn, 1988, p. 7). Or as Maples and Webster (1980, p. 1) stated more simply, "Learning can be thought of as a process by which behavior changes as a result of experiences."

Learning as a process (rather than an end product) focuses on what happens when the learning takes place. Explanations of what happens are called learning theories, and it is these theories that are the subject of this section. There are, however, many explanations of learning, some more comprehensive than others, that are called theories. How the knowledge base in this area is divided and labeled depends on the writer. Hilgard and Bower (1966), for example, review eleven learning theories and then note that they fall into two major families: stimulus-response theories and cognitive theories. Knowles (1984) uses Reese and Overton's (1970) organization in which learning theories are grouped according to two different worldviews: mechanistic and organismic.

Since there is little consensus on how many learning theories there are or how they should be grouped for discussion, we have organized this section according to orientations that present very different assumptions about learning and offer helpful insights into adult learning. With these criteria in mind, five basic orientations have been selected for discussion: behaviorist, cognitivist, humanist, social learning, and constructivist. As Hill (1977, p. 261) has observed, "For most of us, the various learning theories have two chief values. One is in providing us with a vocabulary and a conceptual framework for interpreting the examples of learning that we observe. These are valuable for anyone who is alert to the world. The other, closely related, is in suggesting where to look for solutions to practical problems. The theories do not give us solutions, but they do direct our attention to those variables that are crucial in finding solutions."

For the five orientations examined in this section, the following topics are covered: the major proponents, the view of the learning process itself, the purpose of education, the role of the teacher, and the ways in which these theories are manifested in adult learning. A summary of this information can be found in Table 2-2 in this section.

BEHAVIORIST ORIENTATION

Behaviorism is a well-known orientation to learning that encompasses a number of individual theories. Developed by John B. Watson in the early decades of the twentieth century, behaviorism loosely encompasses the work of such people as Thorndike, Tolman, Guthrie, Hull, and Skinner (Ormrod, 1995). What characterizes these investigators is their underlying assumptions about the process of learning. In essence, three basic assumptions are held to be true. First, observable behavior rather than internal thought processes is the focus of study; in particular, learning is manifested by a change in behavior. Second, the environment shapes behavior; what one learns is determined by the elements in the environment, not by the individual learner. And third, the principles of contiguity (how close in time two events must be for a bond to be formed) and reinforcement (any means of increasing the likelihood that an event will be repeated) are central to explaining the learning process (Grippin and Peters, 1984).

Edward L. Thorndike, a contemporary of Watson, is "perhaps the greatest learning theorist of all time" (Hergenhahn, 1988, p. 55). A prolific researcher and writer, "he did pioneer work not only in learning theory but also in the areas of educational practices, verbal behavior, comparative psychology, intelligence testing, the nature-nurture problem, transfer of training, and the application of quantitative measures to sociopsychological problems" (p. 55). His major contribution to understanding learning has come to be called connectionism, or the S-R theory of learning. Using animals in controlled experiments, Thorndike noted that through repeated trial-and-error learning, certain connections between sensory impressions, or stimuli (S), and subsequent behavior, or responses (R), are strengthened or weakened by the consequences of behavior. Thorndike formulated three laws of learning to explain his findings: the Law of Effect, which states that learners will acquire and remember responses that lead to satisfying after-effects; the Law of Exercise, which asserts that the repetition of a meaningful connection results in substantial learning; and the Law of Readiness, which notes that if the organism is ready for the connection, learning is enhanced; otherwise learning is inhibited (Ormrod, 1995). Although Thorndike himself and later researchers modified these laws, they are nevertheless still applied widely in educational settings.

Thorndike's connectionism became refined and expanded on by his contemporaries and by those who followed. Pavlov, for example, working in Russia, added concepts of reinforcement, conditioned stimulus, and extinction to the basic notion of the stimulus-response connection. Guthrie stated that one law of learning based on contiguity is all that is needed to make learning comprehensible: "Whatever you do in the presence of a stimulus, you do again when that stimulus is re-presented" (Grippin and Peters, 1984, p. 61). Tolman (1959) introduced the notion that learning occurs in relation to purpose and that there are intervening variables between a stimulus and a response. Hull (1951) expanded Tolman's concept of intervening variables and proposed that a response depends on such factors as habit, strength, drive, and motivation. Important as the work of these researchers was (for a detailed discussion, see Hergenhahn, 1988; Ormrod, 1995; Sahakian, 1984), behaviorism was most developed as a theory of learning by B. F. Skinner.

Skinner's major contribution to understanding learning is known as operant conditioning. Simply stated, operant conditioning means "reinforce what you want the individual to do again; ignore what you want the individual to stop doing" (Grippin and Peters, 1984, p. 65). Reinforcement is essential to understanding operant conditioning. If behavior is reinforced or rewarded, the response is more likely to occur again under similar conditions. Behavior that is not reinforced is likely to become less frequent and may even disappear. Within this framework, even something as complex as personality can be explained by operant conditioning. Personality, according to Skinner (1974, p. 149), is a "repertoire of behavior imported by an organized set of contingencies"—in effect, a personal history of reinforcements. Skinner's research concentrated on positive and negative reinforcement schedules, the timing of reinforcements, and avoidance behavior. In essence, his work indicates that since all behavior is learned, it can be determined by arranging the contingencies of reinforcement in the learner's immediate environment. Behaviorists since Skinner have taken into account certain aspects of the human organism but still emphasize that it is environment that controls behavior, "not some mechanism within the individual" (Grippin and Peters, 1984, p. 71).

The behaviorist orientation has been foundational to much educational practice, including adult learning. Skinner in particular has addressed the application of his theory to educational issues. As he sees it, the ultimate goal of education is to bring about behavior that will ensure survival of the human species, societies, and individuals (Skinner, 1971). The teacher's role is to design an environment that elicits desired behavior toward meeting these goals and to extinguish undesirable behavior.

Several educational practices can be traced to this type of learning. The systematic design of instruction, behavioral objectives, notions of the instructor's accountability, programmed instruction, computer-assisted instruction, competency-based education, and so on are solidly grounded in behavioral learning theory. Adult vocational and skills training—in which the learning task is broken into segments or tasks—in particular draws from behaviorism, as does technical and skills training within human resource development (HRD). The relatively new field of HRD focuses on adult learning in organizational settings, especially business and industry. Employees attend training sessions to improve performance, with performance usually being objectively and quantitatively measured (Swanson and Arnold, 1996). Some have even conceptualized HRD as human performance technology designed "to change the outcomes of behavior" (Jacobs, 1987, p. 19). Thus, the behavioral orientation to learning has had a profound effect on our educational system. It has also been challenged by theorists from two radically different perspectives: cognitivism and humanism.

COGNITIVE ORIENTATION

The earliest challenge to the behaviorists came in a publication in 1929 by Bode, a Gestalt psychologist. He criticized behaviorists for being too particularistic, too concerned with single events and actions, and too dependent on overt behavior to explain learning. Gestalt (a German word meaning "pattern or shape") psychologists proposed looking at the whole rather than its parts, at patterns rather than isolated events. Through the research of Gestaltists Wertheimer, Kohler, Koffka, and later Lewin (Hergenhahn, 1988; Ormrod, 1995), Gestalt views of learning rivaled behaviorism by the mid-twentieth century. These views have been incorporated into what have come to be labeled as cognitive or information processing learning theories.

Perception, insight, and meaning are key contributions to cognitivism from Gestalt learning theorists. According to cognitivists, "The human mind is not simply a passive exchange-terminal system where the stimuli arrive and the appropriate response leaves. Rather, the thinking person interprets sensations and gives meaning to the events that impinge upon his consciousness" (Grippin and Peters, 1984, p. 76). Learning involves the reorganization of experiences in order to make sense of stimuli from the environment. Sometimes this sense comes through flashes of insight. Hergenhahn (1988, p. 252) summarizes the learning process according to Gestalt psychology: "Learning, to the Gestaltist, is a cognitive phenomenon. The organism 'comes to see' the solution after pondering a problem. The learner thinks about all the ingredients necessary to solve a problem and puts them together (cognitively) first one way and then another until the problem is solved. When the solution comes, it comes suddenly, that is, the organism gains an *insight* into the solution of a problem. The problem can exist in only two states: (1) unsolved and (2) solved; there is no state of partial solution in between." A major difference between Gestaltists and behaviorists, therefore, is the locus of control over the learning activity. For Gestaltists it lies with the individual learner; for behaviorists it lies with the environment. This shift to the individual—and in particular to the learner's mental processes—is characteristic of cognitivist-oriented learning theories.

A cognitive psychologist who clarified the focus on internal cognitive processes was Jean Piaget (1966). Influenced by both the behaviorist and Gestalt schools of thought, Piaget proposed that one's internal cognitive structure changes partly as a result of maturational changes in the nervous system and partly as a result of the organism's interacting with the environment and being exposed to an increasing number of experiences. His four-stage theory of cognitive development and its implications for adult learning were discussed more fully under the title Cognitive Development in Adulthood (Section One).

Currently, a number of research and theory-building efforts take as their starting point the mental processes involved in learning. These efforts include information processing theories, work on memory and metacognition, theories of transfer, mathematical learning theory models, the study of expertise, computer simulations, and artificial intelligence. Converging with cognitive learning theory are theories of instruction that attempt to unite what is known about learning with the best way to facilitate its occurrence. Ausubel, Bruner, and Gagne provide good examples of how the understanding of mental processes can be linked to instruction.

Ausubel (1967) distinguishes between meaningful learning and rote learning. He suggests that learning is meaningful only when it can be related to concepts that already exist in a person's cognitive structure. Rote learning, on the other hand, does not become linked to a person's cognitive structure and hence is easily forgotten. Also unique is Ausubel's notion of "reception" learning. New knowledge is processed by the learner "only to the extent that more inclusive and appropriately relevant concepts are already available in the cognitive structure to serve a subsuming role or to provide definitional anchorage" (1967, p. 222). He suggests the use of "advance organizers" to prepare a person for new learning (1968). Ausubel's work can be seen as an antecedent to current research on schema theory whereby schemata—structures that organize the learner's worldview—determine how people process new experiences (J. Anderson, 1996; Di Vesta, 1987; Ormrod, 1995).

Ausubel emphasizes the importance of the learner's cognitive structure in new learning. Bruner, whose views are often contrasted with Ausubel's, emphasizes learning through discovery. Discovery is "in its essence a matter of rearranging or transforming evidence in such a way that one is enabled to go beyond the evidence so reassembled to additional new insights" (Bruner, 1965, pp. 607–608). According to Knowles (1984), Bruner's instructional theory is based on a theory about the act of learning that involves "three almost simultaneous processes: (1) acquisition of new information ...; (2) transformation, or the process of manipulating knowledge to make it fit new tasks; and (3) evaluation, or checking whether the way we have manipulated information is adequate to the task" (p. 25).

Linking the acquisition and processing of knowledge to instruction has probably been most thoroughly developed by Gagne, Briggs, and Wager (1992). They contend that there are eight different types of knowledge—signal learning, stimulus-response, motor training, verbal association, discrimination learning, concept learning, rule learning, and problem solving—each with appropriate instructional procedures. Kidd (1973, p. 182) points out that the work of Gagne and others has been an important influence on the "learning how to learn" concept, which has been explored in some depth by Smith, who has been particularly interested in applying it to adult learning (Smith, 1982, 1987; Smith and Associates, 1990). According to Smith (1982, p. 19), "Learning how to learn involves possessing, or acquiring, the knowledge and skill to learn effectively in whatever learning situation one encounters." Three subconcepts are involved: the learner's needs, a person's learning style, and training, which is organized activity, or instruction, to increase competence in learning. In addition to Smith's work on learning how to learn, the cognitive orientation can be seen in two other areas that have particular relevance for adult learning. First, interest in cognitive development in adulthood has been the subject of recent research; second, the study of learning processes as a function of age draws from the cognitive focus on learning. (See also Tennant and Pogson, 1995.)

In summary, cognitively oriented explanations of learning encompass a wide range of topics with a common focus on internal mental processes that are within the learner's control. Di Vesta (1987, p. 229) has summarized recent directions in cognitive learning: "It is apparent that the current cognitive movement, rather than seeking the general all-encompassing laws for controlling and predicting behavior, as did the earlier grand theories of learning, is directed toward miniature models of specific facets of cognition, such as models of discourse analysis, models of comprehension, ways of aiding understanding and meaningful learning, the nature of the schemata, the memory system, the development of cognitive skills, and the like."

HUMANIST ORIENTATION

Humanist theories consider learning from the perspective of the human potential for growth. This shift to the study of the affective as well as cognitive dimensions of learning was informed in part by Freud's psychoanalytic approach to human behavior. Although most would not label Freud a learning theorist, aspects of his psychology, such as the influence of the subconscious mind on behavior, as well as the concepts of anxiety, repression, defense mechanism, drives, and transference, have found their way into some learning theories. Sahakian (1984), in fact, makes the case for psychoanalytic therapy as a type of learning theory.

Despite Freud's focus on personality, humanists reject the view of human nature implied by both behaviorists and Freudian psychologists. Identifying their orientation as a "third force," humanists refuse to accept the notion that behavior is predetermined by either the environment or one's subconscious. Rather, human beings can control their own destiny; people are inherently good and will strive for a better world; people are free to act, and behavior is the consequence of human choice; people possess unlimited potential for growth and development (Rogers, 1983; Maslow, 1970). From a learning theory perspective, humanism emphasizes that perceptions are centered in experience, as well as the freedom and responsibility to become what one is capable of becoming. These tenets underlie much of adult learning theory that stresses the self-directedness of adults and the value of experience in the learning process. Two psychologists who have contributed the most to our understanding of learning from this perspective are Abraham Maslow and Carl Rogers.

Maslow (1970), considered the founder of humanistic psychology, proposed a theory of human motivation based on a hierarchy of needs. At the lowest level of the hierarchy are physiological needs such as hunger and thirst, which must be attended to before one can deal with safety needs—those dealing with security and protection. The remaining levels are belonging and love, self-esteem, and, finally, the need for self-actualization. This final need can be seen in a person's desire to become all that he or she is capable of becoming. The motivation to learn is intrinsic; it emanates from the learner.

For Maslow self-actualization is the goal of learning, and educators should strive to bring this about. As Sahakian (1984) notes, learning from Maslow's point of view is itself "a form of self-actualization. Among the growth motivations was found the need for cognition, the desire to know and to understand. Learning is not only a form of psychotherapy …, but learning contributes to psychological health" (p. 438). Although self-actualization is the primary goal of learning, there are other goals (p. 439):

1. The discovery of a vocation or destiny
2. The knowledge or acquisition of a set of values
3. The realization of life as precious
4. The acquisition of peak experiences
5. A sense of accomplishment
6. The satisfaction of psychological needs
7. The refreshing of consciousness to an awareness of the beauty and wonder of life
8. The control of impulses
9. The grappling with the critical existential problems of life
10. Learning to choose discriminatively

Another major figure writing from a humanist orientation is Carl Rogers. His book *Freedom to Learn for the 80s* (1983) lays out his theory of learning, which he sees as a similar process in both therapy and education. In fact, his "client-centered therapy" is often equated with student-centered learning. In both education and therapy, Rogers is concerned with significant learning that leads to personal growth and development. Such learning, according to Rogers, has the following characteristics (p. 20):

1. *Personal involvement:* the affective and cognitive aspects of a person should be involved in the learning event.
2. *Self-initiated:* a sense of discovery must come from within.
3. *Pervasive:* the learning "makes a difference in the behavior, the attitudes, perhaps even the personality of the learner."
4. *Evaluated by the learner:* the learner can best determine whether the experience is meeting a need.
5. *Essence is meaning:* when experiential learning takes place, its meaning to the learner becomes incorporated into the total experience.

Quite clearly, Rogers's principles of significant learning and Maslow's views have been integrated into much of adult learning. Knowles's theory of andragogy, with its assumptions about the adult learner, and much of the research and writing on self-directed learning are grounded in humanistic learning theories. As Caffarella (1993b, p. 26) observes about self-directed learning, "The focus of learning is on the individual and self-development, with learners expected to assume primary responsibility for their own learning. The process of learning, which is centered on learner need, is seen as more important than the content; therefore, when educators are involved in the learning process, their most important role is to act as facilitators, or guides." Moreover, humanistic theories have the potential for designing a true learning society, since "there is a natural tendency for people to learn and that learning will flourish if nourishing, encouraging environments are provided" (Cross, 1981, p. 228).

SOCIAL LEARNING ORIENTATION

This learning theory, which combines elements from both behaviorist and cognitivist orientations, posits that people learn from observing others. By definition, such observations take place in a social setting—hence the label "observational" or "social" learning (Lefrancois, 1996). Just *how* the learning occurs has been the subject of several investigations.

Miller and Dollard in the 1940s were the first to explore how people learn through observation. Drawing from stimulus-response and reinforcement theory, they argued that people do not learn from observation alone; rather, they must imitate and reinforce what they have observed. "If imitative responses were not made and reinforced, no learning would take place. For them, imitative learning was the result of observation, overt responding, and reinforcement" (Hergenhahn, 1988, p. 321). These ideas are totally congruent with the behaviorist orientation to learning. Miller and Dollard's main contribution was to demonstrate that "social-personality phenomena could be described and explained with the more objective and reliable concepts of a learning theory" (Phares, 1980, p. 412). Not until the 1960s, however, with the work of Bandura, did social learning theory break from a purely behaviorist orientation.

Bandura focused more on the cognitive processes involved in the observation than on the subsequent behavior. Central to his theory is the separation of observation from the act of imitation. One can learn from observation, he maintains, without having to imitate what was observed (Lefrancois, 1996). In fact, the learning can be vicarious: "Virtually all learning phenomena resulting from direct experiences can occur on a vicarious basis through observation of other people's behavior and its consequences for the observer" (Bandura, 1976, p. 392). In addition to being cognitive and vicarious, Bandura's observational learning is characterized by the concept of self-regulation. He contends that "persons can regulate their own behavior to some extent by visualizing self-generated consequences" (p. 392).

Observational learning is influenced by the four processes of attention, retention or memory, behavioral rehearsal, and motivation (Hergenhahn, 1988). Before something can be learned, the model must be attended to; some models are more likely than others to be attended to, such as those thought to be competent, powerful, attractive, and so on. Information from an observation then needs to be retained or stored for future use: "Symbols retained from a modeling experience act as a template with which one's actions are compared. During this rehearsal process individuals observe their own behavior and compare it to their cognitive representation of the modeled experience" (Hergenhahn, 1988, p. 327). Finally, the modeled behavior is stored until a person is motivated to act on it. More recently, Bandura has focused on self-efficacy, that is, our own estimate of how competent we feel we are likely to be in a particular environment. This self-assessment influences how effective we are in interactions with others and with our environment (Lefrancois, 1996).

Bandura's theory has particular relevance to adult learning in that it accounts for both the learner and the environment in which he or she operates. Behavior is a function of the interaction of the person with the environment. This is a reciprocal concept in that people influence their environment, which in turn influences the way they behave. This three-way interactive model is pictured by Bandura as a triangle (Bandura, 1986; Staddon, 1984). Learning is set solidly within a social context.

The importance of the social situation is central to Rotter's (1954) theory, which includes strands from behaviorism, cognitivism, and personality theory. Rotter's theory is framed by seven propositions and attendant corollaries that delineate relationships among the concepts of behavior, personality, experience, and environment. Rotter's theory assumes "that much of human behavior takes place in a meaningful environment and is acquired through social interactions with other people" (Phares, 1980, p. 406). Key to understanding "which behavior (once acquired) in the individual's repertoire will occur in a given situation" (p. 407) are the concepts of expectancy and reinforcement. Expectancy is the likelihood that a particular reinforcement will occur as the result of specific behavior: "The way in which the person construes or psychologically defines the situation will affect the values of both reinforcement and expectancy thereby influencing the potential for any given behavior to occur" (p. 408). Phares notes that research on the ways in which expectancies "generalize and change" has been a major contribution to our understanding of the learning process (p. 426).

Several useful concepts emerge from social learning theory. For example, the motivation to engage in adult learning activities might be partly explained by Rotter's (1954) notion of locus of control. Some people attribute their successes and failures to factors over which they feel they have no control—they exhibit an external locus of control—versus those who attribute successes and failures to personal, internal factors. An example of how this might relate to motivation and participation in adult education would be the case of someone out of work. He might blame his unemployment on factors over which he feels he has no control such as "the economy," or lack of public transportation, or his age, gender, or skin color. Another person, whose locus of control is more internal, might decide that his being unemployed is more due to his inability to get along with coworkers, his lack of computer skills, and so forth. This person is much more likely to engage in learning activities to make himself more employable. Another connection to adult learning is the importance of context and the learner's interaction with the environment to explain behavior. That is, explanations of learning may need to focus on more than overt behavior, mental processes, or personality. Studying the interaction of all these factors may result in a more comprehensive explanation of how adults learn. Moreover, Bandura's work on observational learning and modeling provides insights into social role acquisition and the nature of mentoring, a topic explored in depth by several adult educators (see Cohen, 1995; Daloz, 1986; Galbraith and Cohen, 1995).

CONSTRUCTIVISM

Like some of the other theories already reviewed, constructivism encompasses a number of related perspectives. Basically, a constructivist stance maintains that learning is a process of constructing meaning; it is how people make sense of their experience. Beyond that basic assumption, constructivists differ as to the nature of reality, the role of experience, what knowledge is of interest, and whether the process of meaning making is primarily individual or social (Steffe and Gale, 1995).

In an essay underscoring the variety of perspectives that are labeled constructivist, Phillips (1995) identifies six major strands: von Glaserfeld's work in math and science education, Kant's notions of knowledge and experience, feminist theorists' views on knowledge construction, Kuhn's work on scientific paradigms and revolutions, Piaget's theory of cognitive development, and Dewey's assumptions about knowledge and experience. Where these strands seem to converge is in the debate over the individual versus the social. Driver and her colleagues (1994) frame the issue as one of personal versus social constructivism. Drawing heavily from Piaget, learning as an individual or personal activity involves a "progressive adaptation of [an] individual's cognitive schemes to the physical environment" (Driver and others, 1994, p. 6). Meaning is made by the individual and is dependent on the individual's previous and current knowledge structure. Learning is thus an internal cognitive activity. Teaching from the personal constructivism perspective involves providing "experiences that induce cognitive conflict and hence encourage learners to develop new knowledge schemes that are better adapted to experience. Practical activities supported by group discussions form the core of such pedagogical practices" (Driver and others, 1994, p. 6).

The social constructivist view, on the other hand, posits that knowledge is "constructed when individuals engage socially in talk and activity about shared problems or tasks. Making meaning is thus a dialogic process involving persons-in-conversation, and learning is seen as the process by which individuals are introduced to a culture by more skilled members" (Driver and others, 1994, p. 7). This approach involves learning the culturally shared ways of understanding and talking about the world and reality.

Phillips (1995) points out that a continuum actually exists between the personal or individual orientation of Piaget and Vygotsky and the social perspective of feminist epistemologists. Some constructivists "believe that their theories throw light on both the question of how individuals build up bodies of knowledge and how human communities have constructed the public bodies of knowledge known as the various disciplines" (p. 7). Cobb (1994, p. 13), for example, suggests viewing mathematical learning as "both a process of active individual construction and a process of enculturation into the mathematical practices of wider society." However, regardless of one's position on the continuum, there are important pedagogical implications to be derived, "each of which has a degree of credibility that is independent of the fate of the respective epistemologies"

(p. 10). Candy (1991, p. 275), writing from a predominantly social constructivist perspective, discusses how this view translates to adult education: "Becoming knowledgeable involves acquiring the symbolic meaning structures appropriate to one's society, and, since knowledge is socially constructed, individual members of society may be able to add to or change the general pool of knowledge. Teaching and learning, *especially for adults,* is a process of negotiation, involving the construction and exchange of personally relevant and viable meanings" (emphasis added).

A constructivist perspective is congruent with much of adult learning theory. Candy (1991, p. 278) points out that "the constructivist view of learning is particularly compatible with the notion of self-direction, since it emphasizes the combined characteristics of active inquiry, independence, and individuality in a learning task." Transformational learning theory, especially as presented by Mezirow, focuses on both the individual and social construction of meaning. Perspective transformation is a highly cognitive process in which one's meaning schemes and meaning perspectives undergo radical change (Mezirow, 1991). The central role of experience in adult learning is another point of connection. Andragogy and other models of adult learning see life experience as both a resource and a stimulus for learning; so constructivism too begins with the learner's interaction with experience. Finally, much of what the field of adult learning draws from situated cognition is constructivist in nature. Concepts such as cognitive apprenticeship, situated learning, reflective practice, and communities of practice are found in both adult learning and constructivist literature. Two adult education practice arenas in particular where constructivist and situated cognition concepts are having an impact are in continuing professional education (Ferry and Ross-Gordon, 1998) and human resource development (Stamps, 1997). As Wegner (cited by Stamps, 1997, pp. 38–39) explains, "What is shared by a community of practice—what makes it a community—is its practice. The concept of practice connotes doing, but not just doing in and of itself. It is doing in a historical and social context that give structure and meaning to what we do.... Learning is the engine of practice, and practice is the history of that learning.... Indeed, practice is ultimately produced by its members through the negotiation of meaning."

SUMMARY

Learning, a process central to human behavior, has been of interest to philosophers, psychologists, educators, and politicians for centuries. Since the late nineteenth century, the systematic investigation of this phenomenon has resulted in many explanations of how people learn. This section has reviewed some of these theories. Because there are dozens of learning theories and volumes written describing them, we have explored different orientations to learning, any of which might include numerous learning theories. The behaviorist, cognitivist, humanist, social learning, and constructivist orientations were chosen for their diversity and for their insights into learning in adulthood. Table 2-2 summarizes these five orientations. Since each is based on different assumptions about the nature of learning, the strategies one might use to enhance learning will depend on one's orientation. Instructors and program developers can use this review of major learning theories to identify their own theory of learning and discover the strategies for facilitating learning that are most congruent with their theory.

In brief, behaviorists define learning as a change in behavior. The focus of their research is overt behavior, which is a measurable response to stimuli in the environment. The role of the teacher is to arrange the contingencies of reinforcement in the learning environment so that the desired behavior will occur. Findings from behavioral learning theories can be seen in training and vocational adult education.

In contrast to behaviorists, researchers working from a cognitivist perspective focus not on external behavior but on internal mental processes. Cognitivists are interested in how the mind makes sense out of stimuli in the environment—how information is processed, stored, and retrieved. This orientation is especially evident in the study of adult learning from a developmental perspective. The major concerns are how aging affects an adult's ability to process and retrieve information and how it affects an adult's internal mental structures.

Table 2-2.   Five Orientations to Learning.

Aspect	Behaviorist	Cognitivist	Humanist	Social Learning	Constructivist
Learning theorists	Guthrie, Hull, Pavlov, Skinner, Thorndike, Tolman, Watson	Ausubel, Bruner, Gagne, Koffka, Kohler, Lewin, Piaget	Maslow, Rogers	Bandura, Rotter	Candy, Dewey, Lave, Piaget, Rogoff, von Glasersfeld, Vygotsky
View of the learning process	Change in behavior	Internal mental process (including insight, information processing, memory, perception)	A personal act to fulfill potential	Interaction with and observation of others in a social context	Construction of meaning from experience
Locus of learning	Stimuli in external environment	Internal cognitive structuring	Affective and cognitive needs	Interaction of person, behavior, and environment	Internal construction of reality by individual
Purpose of education	Produce behavioral change in desired direction	Develop capacity and skills to learn better	Become self-actualized, autonomous	Model new roles and behavior	Construct knowledge
Teacher's role	Arranges environment to elicit desired response	Structures content of learning activity	Facilitates development of whole person	Models and guides new roles and behavior	Facilitates and negotiates meaning with learner
Manifestation in adult learning	• Behavioral objectives • Competency-based education • Skill development and training	• Cognitive development • Intelligence, learning, and memory as function of age • Learning how to learn	• Andragogy • Self-directed learning	• Socialization • Social roles • Mentoring • Locus of control	• Experiential learning • Self-directed learning • Perspective transformation • Reflective practice

Also in contrast to behaviorism is the humanistic orientation to learning. Here the emphasis is on human nature, human potential, human emotions, and affect. Theorists in this tradition believe that learning involves more than cognitive processes and overt behavior. It is a function of motivation and involves choice and responsibility. Much of adult learning theory, especially the concepts of andragogy and many of the models of self-directed learning, are grounded in humanistic assumptions.

The fourth orientation discussed here is social learning. This perspective differs from the other three in its focus on the social setting in which learning occurs. From this perspective, learning occurs through the observation of people in one's immediate environment. Furthermore, learning is a function of the interaction of the person, the environment, and the behavior. Variations in behavior under the same circumstances can be explained by idiosyncratic personality traits and their unique interaction with environmental stimuli. Social learning theories contribute to adult learning by highlighting the importance of social context and explicating the processes of modeling and mentoring.

Finally, constructivism, representing an array of perspectives, posits that learners construct their own knowledge from their experiences. The cognitive process of meaning making is emphasized as both an individual mental activity and a socially interactive interchange. Aspects of constructivism can be found in self-directed learning, transformational learning, experiential learning, situated cognition, and reflective practice.

ANDRAGOGY AND OTHER MODELS
OF ADULT LEARNING

Sharan B. Merriam
Rosemary S. Caffarella

Do adults learn differently from children? What distinguishes adult learning and adult education from other areas of education? What particular characteristics about the learning transaction with adults can be identified to maximize their learning? Prior to the 1970s, adult educators relied primarily on psychologists' understandings of learning in general to inform their practice. With the publication of Houle's *The Design of Education* (1972), Kidd's *How Adults Learn* (1973), and Knowles's *The Adult Learner: A Neglected Species* (1973) and *The Modern Practice of Adult Education* (1970), attention turned to research and theory-building efforts in adult learning. Attempts at codifying differences between adults and children as a set of principles, a model, or even a theory of adult learning have been, and continue to be, pursued by adult educators. However, just as there is no single theory that explains all of human learning, there is no single theory of adult learning. What we do have are a number of frameworks or models, each of which contributes something to our understanding of adults as learners. The best known of these efforts is andragogy, a concept Knowles introduced from Europe in a 1968 article. Andragogy focuses on the adult learner and his or her life situation, as do a number of other models presented here.

The first part of this material is devoted to describing and critiquing andragogy. In the second half of the material we review four other models of the adult learning transaction: Cross's CAL model, McCluskey's theory of margin, Knox's proficiency theory, and Jarvis's learning process.

ANDRAGOGY

Over thirty years ago Malcolm Knowles (1968, p. 351) proposed "a new label and a new technology" of adult learning to distinguish it from preadult schooling. The European concept of *andragogy,* meaning "the art and science of helping adults learn," was contrasted with pedagogy, the art and science of helping children learn (Knowles, 1980, p. 43). Andragogy is based on five assumptions about the adult learner:

1. As a person matures, his or her self-concept moves from that of a dependent personality toward one of a self-directing human being.
2. An adult accumulates a growing reservoir of experience, which is a rich resource for learning.
3. The readiness of an adult to learn is closely related to the developmental tasks of his or her social role.
4. There is a change in time perspective as people mature—from future application of knowledge to immediacy of application. Thus an adult is more problem centered than subject centered in learning (Knowles, 1980, pp. 44–45).
5. Adults are motivated to learn by internal factors rather than external ones (Knowles and Associates, 1984, pp. 9–12).

From each of these assumptions (the fifth was added after the original four), Knowles drew numerous implications for the design, implementation, and evaluation of learning activities with adults. For example, with regard to the first assumption that as adults mature they become more independent and self-directing, Knowles suggested that the classroom climate should be one of "adultness," both physically and psychologically. The climate should cause "adults to feel accepted, respected, and supported"; further, there should exist "a spirit of mutuality between teachers and students as joint inquirers" (1980, p. 47). Being self-directing also means that adult students can participate in the diagnosis of their learning needs, the planning and implementation of the learning experiences, and the evaluation of those experiences.

This theory, "model of assumptions" (Knowles, 1980, p. 43), or "system of concepts" (Knowles, 1984, p. 8) as Knowles has also called it, has given adult educators "a badge of identity" that distinguishes the field from other areas of education, especially childhood schooling (Brookfield, 1986, p. 90). Andragogy became a rallying point for those trying to define the field of adult education as separate from other areas of education. However, it also stimulated more controversy, philosophical debate, and critical analysis matched only, perhaps, by the recent discussions on transformational learning.

At first the main point of contention was whether andragogy could be considered a "theory" of adult learning (Elias, 1979). Davenport and Davenport (1985, p. 157) chronicle the history of the debate and note that andragogy has been classified "as a theory of adult education, theory of adult learning, theory of technology of adult learning, method of adult education, technique of adult education, and a set of assumptions." They are a bit more optimistic than other critics for andragogy's chances of possessing "the explanatory and predictive functions generally associated with a fully developed theory" (p. 158). For them, the issue can be resolved through empirical studies that test the underlying assumptions.

Hartree (1984) observed that it was not clear whether Knowles had presented a theory of learning or a theory of teaching, whether adult learning was different from child learning, and whether there was a theory at all—perhaps these were just principles of good practice. The assumptions, she noted, "can be read as descriptions of the adult learner ... or as prescriptive statements about what the adult learner *should* be like" (p. 205). Because the assumptions are "unclear and shaky" on several counts, Hartree (1984) concludes that while "many adult educators might accept that the principles of adult teaching and conditions of learning which he [Knowles] evolves have much to offer, and are in a sense descriptive of what is already recognized as good practice by those in the field, conceptually Knowles has not presented a good case for the validity of such practice.... Although he appears to approach his model of teaching from the point of view of a theory of adult learning, he does not establish a unified theory of learning in a systematic way" (pp. 206–207).

Brookfield (1986, p. 98), who also raises the question of whether andragogy is a "proven theory," assesses to what extent a "set of well-grounded principles of good practice" can be derived from andragogy. He argues that three of the assumptions are problematic when drawing inferences for practice: self-direction is more a desired outcome than a given condition, and being problem centered and desiring immediate application can lead to a narrow, reductionist view of learning. Brookfield finds only the experience assumption to be well grounded. However, even it can be questioned. The fact that adults have lived longer than children and thus have a quantity of experience greater than children have does not necessarily translate into quality experience that can become a resource for learning; indeed, certain life experiences can function as barriers to learning (Merriam, Mott, and Lee, 1996). Further, children in certain situations may have a range of experiences qualitatively richer than some adults (Hanson, 1996). As for the more recently added fifth assumption, although adults may be more internally than externally motivated to learn, in much of workplace learning and continuing professional education, not to mention governmental or socially mandated learning (as in the case of driving school, job preparation, and prison education, for example), participation is required.

On the issue of whether andragogy can be considered a theory of adult learning, perhaps Knowles himself put the issue to rest. In his autobiographical work, *The Making of an Adult Educator* (1989, p. 112), he wrote that he "prefers to think of [andragogy] as a model of assumptions about learning or a conceptual framework that serves as a *basis* for an emergent theory" (emphasis added).

A second point of criticism was Knowles's original inference that andragogy, with all its technological implications for instruction, characterized adult learning, while pedagogy, with another set of implications, characterized childhood learning. Close scrutiny of the five assumptions and their implications for practice by educators in and out of adult education led Knowles to back off his original stance that andragogy characterized only adult learning. The clearest indication of this rethinking was the change in the subtitles of the 1970 and 1980 editions of *The Modern Practice of Adult Education.* The 1970 subtitle is *Andragogy Versus Pedagogy,* whereas the 1980 subtitle is *From Pedagogy to Andragogy.* Knowles's later position, as reflected in the 1980 subtitle, is that pedagogy-andragogy represents a continuum ranging from teacher-directed to student-directed learning and that both approaches are appropriate with children and adults, depending on the situation. For example, an adult who knows little or nothing about a topic will be more dependent on the teacher for direction; at the other extreme, children who are naturally curious and who are "very self-directing in their learning *outside of school* ... could also be more self-directed in school" (Knowles, 1984, p. 13). Andragogy now appears to be situation specific and not unique to adults.

There are also some inconsistencies in Knowles's reconstruction of andragogy-pedagogy into a continuum. As Brookfield (1986) points out, his reformulation from a dichotomy to a continuum only added to the conceptual confusion, for, as Cross (1981, p. 225) observes, "a continuum from pedagogy to andragogy really does not exist. Although some andragogical assumptions (such as experience) lie on a continuum, others (such as problem-centered versus subject-centered learning) appear more dichotomous in nature." In support of Cross's critique, a study by Delahaye, Limerick, and Hearn (1994) testing the notion of a continuum between andragogy and pedagogy found the relationship to be more complex than the one-dimensional line of a continuum: "An individual can be located within a two dimensional space that is bounded on one side by andragogy and on the adjoining side by pedagogy. For example, a learner could be considered to be high on pedagogy and high on andragogy, or low on pedagogy and low on andragogy" (p. 195).

More recent critiques of andragogy have pointed out that in its slavish focus on the individual learner, the sociohistorical context in which learning takes place is virtually ignored (Grace, 1996b; Little, 1994; Pearson and Podeschi, 1997; Pratt, 1993). Knowles's reliance on humanistic psychology results in a picture of the individual learner as one who is autonomous, free, and growth oriented. There is little or no awareness that the person is socially situated and, to some extent, the product of the sociohistorical and cultural context of the times; nor is there any awareness that social institutions and structures may be defining the learning transaction irrespective of the individual participant. Pratt (1993, p. 22) summarizes these two tensions as "likely to characterize further debate about andragogy. First, there is a tension between freedom and authority, especially regarding the management and evaluation of learning. Andragogy leans heavily toward learner freedom (versus teacher authority) on this issue, promoting self-direction and personal autonomy. Second, there is a tension between human agency and social structures as the most potent influences on adult learning. Here, andragogy is unconditionally on the side of human agency and the power of the individual to shed the shackles of history and circumstance in pursuit of learning."

Grace (1996b, p. 383) points out how Knowles himself and his theory of andragogy were logical products of the 1960s, "a period of rapid change; action-oriented curricula that valued individual experience were advocated. The individual had to keep up and self-improvement was in *vogue.* The andragogical model in the face of pedagogy was welcomed by many adult educators as revolutionary" (p. 383). But although its influence on adult learning has been substantial over the past thirty years, "Knowles never proceeded to an in-depth consideration of the organizational and social impediments to adult learning; he never painted the 'big picture.' He chose the mechanistic over the meaningful" (Grace, 1996b, p. 386). Pratt (1993), Grace (1986b), and others (Collins, 1992; Jarvis, 1987a) see andragogy's hold on the field subsiding as more sophisticated analyses of the adult learner as a social being living and learning in a social context take center stage. In the words of Grace (1996b, p. 391), because "Knowles has reduced the adult learner to a technically proficient droid, operating in a world where formulaic social planning and self-directed learning mantras are the order of the day," he "is in danger of being left behind. The adult learning pendulum is slowly swinging away from him."

Considering that andragogy has been the primary model of adult learning for nearly thirty years, relatively little empirical work has been done to test the validity of its assumptions or its usefulness in predicting adult learning behavior. A few studies have focused on the relationship between andragogical assumptions and instruction. Beder and Darkenwald (1982) asked teachers who taught both adults and preadults if their teaching behavior differed according to the age of the students. Teachers reported viewing adult students differently and using more andragogical techniques. Gorham (1985), however, actually observed teachers of adults and preadults. She found no differences in how a particular teacher instructed adults or preadults, although teachers claimed that they did treat the two age groups differently. Beder and Carrea (1988) found that training teachers in andragogical methods had a positive and significant effect on attendance but no effect on how teachers were evaluated by the students. Yet another study draws from Knowles's assumption that adults are self-directing and thus like to plan their own learning experiences. Rosenblum and Darkenwald (1983) compared achievement and satisfaction measures between groups who had planned their course and those who had it planned for them. No differences were found in either achievement or satisfaction. Courtenay, Arnold, and Kim (1994) reviewed all previous literature and research *and* conducted their own quasi-experimental study of learner involvement in planning. They found previous research results to be inconclusive (indeed, "capricious"); from their own study, which attempted to address some of the shortcomings of previous studies, they found that "participation in planning does not appear to affect learning gain or satisfaction, even when the amount of participant input in planning is increased; the relationship between classroom environment and achievement or satisfaction is inconsequential; and classroom environment … may simply be a function of the satisfaction of the learner" (p. 297). They recommend more thought be given to both the independent variable (that is, just what constitutes learner participation in planning) and the dependent variables (for example, perhaps unintended learning is as important as achievement).

Although there has not been much direct testing of the validity of andragogy, one could consider the extent to which a broader range of research in adult learning may or may not support the assumptions underlying andragogy. For example, some of the research on self-directed learning would tend to support the assumption that as adults mature, they move toward self-direction. Many studies on participation indicate that participation is clearly linked to adult roles of worker, family member, and so on, lending support to the assumption that the readiness of an adult to learn is closely linked to the developmental tasks of his or her social roles. That the developmental issues of adulthood lead to learning was also underscored in Aslanian and Brickell's (1980) findings that 83 percent of adult learners were engaged in learning activities because of some transition in their lives. On the other hand, the growing prevalence of mandated continuing education could be cited to argue against the assumption that adults are internally motivated.

Despite these rather grim predictions of andragogy's demise, practitioners who work with adult learners continue to find Knowles's andragogy, with its characteristics of adult learners, to be a helpful rubric for better understanding adults as learners. The implications for practice that Knowles draws for each of the assumptions are also considered to be good instructional practice for all ages, especially adults. Thus, we see andragogy as an enduring model for understanding certain aspects of adult learning. It does not give us the total picture, nor is it a panacea for fixing adult learning practices. Rather, it constitutes one piece of the rich mosaic of adult learning.

OTHER MODELS OF ADULT LEARNING

Although andragogy remains the best-known model of adult learning, there are a number of other models that offer us some insights into adult learning. The following four models will be discussed: Cross's CAL model, McClusky's theory of margin, Knox's proficiency model, and Jarvis's learning process. Like andragogy, these models have a common focus on the characteristics and life situation of the adult learner.

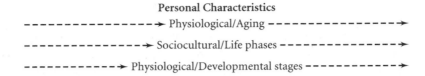

Personal Characteristics

$- - - - - - - - - - - - - - \rightarrow$ Physiological/Aging $- - - - - - - - - - - - - - - \rightarrow$

$- - - - - - - - - - - - - \rightarrow$ Sociocultural/Life phases $- - - - - - - - - - - - - - \rightarrow$

$- - - - - - - - - - - \rightarrow$ Physiological/Developmental stages $- - - - - - - - - - - \rightarrow$

Situational Characteristics
Part-time learning versus full-time learning
Voluntary learning versus compulsory learning

Figure 2-5.   Characteristics of Adults as Learners: A Conceptual Framework.
Source: Cross, 1981, p. 235.

Cross's CAL Model

The characteristics of adults as learners (CAL) model offered by Cross (1981, p. 234) is "a tentative framework to accommodate current knowledge about what we know about adults as learners in the hope that it may suggest ideas for further research and for implementation." Cross points out that some of the assumptions of andragogy such as readiness and self-concept can be readily "incorporated into [the] CAL construct" (p. 238).

Based on differences between children and adults, the model consists of two classes of variables: personal characteristics and situational characteristics (see Figure 2-5). Personal characteristics comprise physical, psychological, and sociocultural dimensions. These are continua and reflect growth and development from childhood into adult life. Situational characteristics focus on variables unique to adult participants—for example, part-time versus full-time learning and voluntary versus compulsory participation.

Cross (1981) believes her model incorporates completed research on aging, stage and phase developmental studies, participation, learning projects, motivation, and so on. The model can also be used to stimulate research by thinking across and between categories. It might be asked, for example, whether there is a "relationship between stage of ego development and voluntary participation in learning" or whether transition points in development "generate extra amounts of volunteer learning" (p. 248). Rather than suggesting implications for practice, as Knowles's andragogy does, Cross's model offers a "framework for thinking about *what* and *how* adults learn" (p. 248).

Although the CAL model is intended to be a comprehensive explanation of adult learning, the variables may be too broadly defined. What situational characteristics when combined with which personal characteristics lead to explaining different types of learning, for example? Probably a more serious problem with the model is its focus on the characteristics of adults, which tells us little about how adults actually learn or if they learn differently than children do. Furthermore, the personal characteristics can apply to children as well as adults since they are on continua reflective of growth from childhood into adulthood. Nor do the situational characteristics neatly divide between children and adults. Some adult learners are full time, and some participate because of mandatory continuing education requirements; some preadults are part-time learners, and some learning is done on a voluntary basis. Perhaps because of some of these weaknesses, the CAL model has yet to be empirically tested.

McClusky's Theory of Margin

McClusky first presented his theory of margin in a 1963 publication, followed by discussions of application in 1970 and 1971. His theory is grounded in the notion that adulthood is a time of growth, change, and integration in which one constantly seeks balance between the amount of energy needed and the amount available. This balance is conceptualized as a ratio between the "load" (L) of life, which dissipates energy, and the "power" (P) of life, which allows one to deal with the load. The energy left over when one divides load by power McClusky called "margin in life" (M = L/P).

Both load and power comprise external and internal factors. Hiemstra (1993, p. 42) explains: "The external load consists of tasks involved in normal life requirements (such as family, work, and community responsibilities). Internal load consists of life expectancies developed by people (such as aspirations, desires, and future expectations). Power consists of a combination of such external resources ... as family support, social abilities, and economic abilities. It also includes various internally acquired or accumulated skills and experiences contributing to effective performance, such as resilience, coping skills, and personality."

Taking both power and load into consideration, McClusky (1970a) explains how the theory works:

> Margin may be increased by reducing Load or increasing Power, or it may be decreased by increasing Load and/or reducing Power. We can control both by modifying either Power or Load. When Load continually matches or exceeds Power and if both are fixed and/or out of control, or irreversible, the situation becomes highly vulnerable and susceptible to breakdown. If, however, Load and Power can be controlled, and, better yet, if a person is able to lay hold of a reserve (Margin) of Power, he [sic] is better equipped to meet unforeseen emergencies, is better positioned to take risks, can engage in exploratory, creative activities, is more likely to learn, etc. [p. 83]

To engage in learning, then, an adult must have some margin of power "available for application to the processes which the learning situation requires" (McClusky, 1970a, p. 84). Adult students in particular have to be adept at juggling multiple responsibilities and demands on their time. McClusky gives two examples of how his theory might be applied to an adult's situation:

> First, I have an image of Mrs. A, a mother and the only adult in a poorly furnished home with four children at school and two at home, barely holding the line against family breakdown. Fighting a continual battle for survival, she has *no margin* for the P.T.A., night school ..., or the inner-city neighborhood committee organized to cooperate with local programs of urban renewal.
>
> For our second example let us sketch a more optimistic picture. Mr. C is in the prime of his middle years. In good physical condition, with competence in his profession, with substantial influence in the community, and with access to ample financial resources, Mr. C carries a large *load* which is a reflection of his *powers*. If his load is just a notch under his capacity, it might appear that his margin is small, but at any time and at his own discretion, Mr. C can reduce his *load* and hence his *margin* may be regarded as ample. [p. 28]

Maintaining some margin of power in order to engage in learning is a concept adults readily relate to. As Hiemstra (1993, p. 42) observes, an adult student's first encounter with McClusky's theory is often "an epiphany in terms of their own life circumstances."

McClusky (1970a) also saw his theory as helpful in explaining the developmental changes characteristic of adult life. Changes adults undergo as they age could be translated into adjustments of load and power. These adjustments are made "as a person accumulates and later relinquishes adult responsibilities and modifies the varying roles which the successive stages of the life cycle require" (p. 84). Since learning in adulthood is often a function of changing roles and responsibilities and physical and mental development, McClusky's theory can be used in understanding this link between development and learning. Several studies have in fact investigated this link. Baum (1980) used the theory as a framework for exploring the power and load of one hundred randomly selected widows. Self-identified problems encountered in widowhood were viewed as load factors, and services and resources available to widows were categorized as power factors. She found that negative attitudes toward widowhood predicted more problems (load), but that it also led to finding more resources (power). As load increased, power increased, resulting in a fairly stable margin in life. Using an instrument developed to measure margin in life, Stevenson (1980) compared the load, power, and margin patterns of independent older adults, nursing home residents, and young and middle-aged adults. She found that the two groups of older adults perceived themselves as having slightly more power (and less load) than the young and middle-aged adults. Finally, a number of studies have used McClusky's theory to study adult student needs, performance, and participation in continuing education (Demko, 1982; Garrison, 1986; Hansen, 1988; James, 1986; Mikolaj, 1983; Walker, 1996; Weiman, 1987). The findings of all of these studies were mixed, so no clear-cut generalizations can be drawn regarding the validity of McClusky's theory.

McClusky's theory has appeal in that it speaks to the everyday events and life transitions that all adults encounter. It is perhaps a better counseling tool than it is an explanation of adult learning, however. In fact, there is a striking similarity between McClusky's power, load, and margin concepts and the components of Schlossberg's model for counseling adults in transition. In her model, one determines the ability to work through a transition by assessing the relative strength of four factors: the situation, the self (internal strengths), external supports, and strategies one has developed to handle stress (Schlossberg, 1984, 1987). Although life events and transitions certainly precipitate many (and some would say the most potent) learning experiences, McClusky's model does not directly address learning itself but rather *when* it is most likely to occur. One might also question whether a reserve of energy or margin of power is necessary for learning to occur. Learning can occur under conditions of stress or, in McClusky's terms, when load is greater than power. In addition, the fact that learning itself has the potential to increase one's power is not addressed by McClusky.

Knox's Proficiency Theory

Knox's (1980) proficiency theory also speaks to an adult's life situation. Adult learning, he writes, is distinctive on at least two counts: "the centrality of concurrent adult role performance" (p. 383) and the "close correspondence between learning and action beyond the educational program" (p. 384). Proficiency, as defined by Knox, is "the capability to perform satisfactorily if given the opportunity" (p. 378), and this performance involves some combination of attitude, knowledge, and skill. At the core of his theory is the notion of a discrepancy between the current and the desired level of proficiency. This concept of proficiency helps explain "adult motivation and achievement in both learning activities and life roles. Adults and society expect that individual adults will be proficient in major life roles and as persons generally" (1985, p. 252). A model representation of the theory contains the following interactive components: the general environment, past and current characteristics, performance, aspiration, self, discrepancies, specific environments, learning activity, and the teacher's role.

This set of interrelated concepts hinges on what Knox (1980, p. 99) defines as being the purpose of adult learning (whether self-directed or in organized programs): "to enhance proficiency to improve performance." Both teachers and learners can benefit from an analysis of the discrepancy between current and desired levels of proficiency: "An understanding of discrepancies between current and desired proficiencies helps to explain motives of adult learners and enables those who help adults learn to do so responsively and effectively" (Knox, 1986, p. 16). Knox (1986, p. 16) is careful to distinguish between his notion of proficiency and competency-based learning: "Whereas competency-based preparatory education emphasizes the achievement of minimal standards of performance in educational tasks, proficiency-oriented continuing education emphasizes achievement of optimal standards of proficiency related to adult life roles."

Knox's theory is not well known by adult educators, perhaps because its publication has been in sources outside the field. Its emphasis on performance would also appear to limit its application to learning that can be demonstrated by better performance. More problematic is the model's mixture of learning, teaching, and motivation. Knox (1985, p. 252) writes that the theory "suggests fundamental relationships among essential aspects of adult learning and teaching which constitute an interrelated set of guidelines for helping adults learn, with an emphasis on motivation." How one tracks the interaction of numerous components (or "essential aspects of adult learning and teaching") to arrive at an explanation of how adults learn is far from clear. And perhaps because of the complexity of the model and difficulty operationalizing the interrelationships of the variables, no reports of empirical use of the model could be found.

Jarvis's Learning Process

Jarvis's (1987a, p. 16) model begins with an adult's life situation or, more correctly, an adult's experience: "Even miseducative experiences may be regarded as learning experiences.... *All* learning begins with experience." Some experiences, however, are repeated with such frequency that they are taken for granted and do not lead to learning, such as driving a car or household routines. At the start of the learning process are experiences that "call for a response" (p. 63). Like Knox's and McClusky's theories, Jarvis's model is based on a discrepancy between biography (all that a person is at a particular point in time) and experience—an incident that a person is unprepared to handle. This "inability to cope with the situation unthinkingly, instinctively, is at the heart of all learning" (1987a, p. 35).

For Jarvis (1987a, p. 64), all experience occurs within a social situation, a kind of objective context within which one experiences life: "Life may be conceptualized as an ongoing phenomenon located within a sociocultural milieu which is bounded by the temporality of birth and death. Throughout life, people are moving from social situation to social situation; sometimes in conscious awareness but in other occasions in a taken-for-granted manner." Jarvis's model of the learning process begins with a person moving into a social situation in which a potential learning experience occurs. From an experience, there are nine different routes that a person might take, some of which result in learning and some of which do not. Presumption, nonconsideration, and rejection do not result in learning. The six other responses (preconscious, practice, memorization, contemplation, reflective practice, and experimental learning) represent six different types of learning. The nine responses form a hierarchy. The first three are nonlearning responses, the second three are nonreflective learning, and the final three are reflective learning. These last three, Jarvis (1987a, p. 27) says, are the "higher forms of learning." Of the nonlearning responses, one can respond in a mechanical way (that is, presume that what has worked before will work again), one can be too preoccupied to consider a response, or one can reject the opportunity to learn. The nonreflective learning responses can be preconscious (that is, a person unconsciously internalizes something); one can practice a new skill until it is learned; or learners can acquire information "with which they have been presented and learn it, so that they can reproduce it at a later stage" (p. 33). The three higher forms of learning call for more involvement. Contemplation is thinking about what is being learned and does not require a behavioral outcome; reflective practice is akin to problem solving; experimental learning is the result of a person's experimenting on the environment.

In his book on the model, Jarvis (1987a) explains how each of the nine responses coincides with the visual representation of the learning process (see Figure 2-6). A person enters a social situation, has an experience, and can exit (box 4) unchanged because he or she ignored the event or took it for granted. One might also go from the experience (box 3) to memorization (box 6) and exit either unchanged (box 4) or changed (box 9). For a higher type of learning, a person might go from the experience to reasoning and reflecting (box 7) to practice and experimentation (box 5) to evaluation (box 8) to memorization (box 6) and to being changed (box 9).

More than the other theories discussed in this section, Jarvis's model does deal with learning itself. The thoroughness of his discussion, which concentrates on explaining the responses one can have to an experience, is a strength of the model. These responses encompass multiple types of

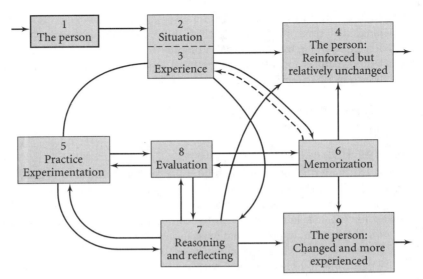

Figure 2-6.   A Model of the Learning Process.
Source: Jarvis, 1987a, p. 25. Reprinted by permission.

learning and their different outcomes, a refreshingly comprehensive view of learning. Furthermore, his model situates learning within a social context; learning is an interactive phenomenon, not an isolated internal process. There is some question, however, as to whether his model is unique to adults. Although it was constructed from research with adult learners and has been used by Jarvis with adults in various settings, he himself suspects that "it is as valid for children as it is with adults.... There may be a relationship between the frequency of use of these different types of learning and the age of the learner, [but] no evidence exists at present that might verify this" (Jarvis, 1987a, pp. 35–36).

SUMMARY

Although there was sporadic attention given to adult learning in the early decades of the twentieth century, it was not until the 1970s that adult educators themselves began to focus systematically on some of the distinguishing characteristics of adult learning as separate from the body of information from psychologists' and educational psychologists' investigations of learning in general. This shift in focus was part of the field's efforts to differentiate itself from other areas of education. It also led to the search for a single theory of adult learning, one that would differentiate adults from children, include all types of learning, and was at once elegant and simple. But just as there is no single theory that explains human learning in general, no single theory of adult learning has emerged to unify the field. Rather, there are a number of theories, models, and frameworks, each of which illuminates some aspect of adult learning. The ones reviewed in this section all focus on adult learner characteristics of the adult's life situation, or both.

The best-known theory of adult learning is Knowles's andragogy. Nevertheless, it is less of a theory and more of a set of assumptions about adult learners that learners and educators alike can use to strengthen the learning transaction. The assumptions regarding an adult's self-concept, experience, readiness to learn, problem-centered focus, and internal motivation all have some intuitive validity, making andragogy popular with practitioners in many fields. These assumptions were critiqued in this section, as was Knowles's isolation of the individual learner from the learning context.

The section then turned to reviewing other less well-known models of adult learning. Like andragogy, Cross's characteristics of adults as learners (CAL) model is more about personal characteristics of adults than learning per se. McClusky's theory of margin emphasizes both personal characteristics (internal load and power factors) and situational characteristics (external load and power factors). His model has more to say about adult development and the timing of learning, though, than about the actual learning transaction. Knox's proficiency theory centers on the gap between what adults currently know and what they want to know or be able to do. Once this gap is identified, instruction can be planned accordingly. The last model discussed is Jarvis's model of the learning process. All life experiences hold the potential for learning to occur. Some experiences result in learning, and some do not. Jarvis's model distinguishes among nine responses, six of which involve learning (three nonreflective learning and three reflective learning). Although the model is derived from research with adult learners, Jarvis does not claim that it is limited to adults.

All of the models discussed in this section contribute in their own ways to advancing our understanding of adult learners, but with the possible exception of Jarvis's, none tells us much about the learning process itself. Furthermore, there has been little research testing the power of the models to explain or predict adult learning behavior. The process of model and theory building does, however, stimulate inquiry and reflection, all of which may eventually provide some of the answers to our questions about adult learning.

SECTION THREE

PARTICIPATION IN ADULT EDUCATION

SHARAN B. MERRIAM
ROSEMARY S. CAFFARELLA

Adult education is a large and amorphous field of practice, with no neat boundaries such as age, as in the case of elementary and secondary education, or mission, as in the case of higher education. Adult education with its myriad content areas, delivery systems, goals, and clienteles defies simple categorization. One way to grasp something of the field is to find out who is involved in the activity itself—hence, studies of participation.

Historically, participation in adult education is largely a voluntary activity. Not only is there curiosity about who volunteers to participate, but without volunteer learners, there would be a much smaller enterprise of adult education. Providers of adult education therefore need to know who is participating, why they are participating, and what conditions are likely to promote greater participation. Conversely, knowing who is *not* involved can be important information for providers who wish to attract new learners. Interestingly, the report of the first national study of participation is titled *Volunteers for Learning* (Johnstone and Rivera, 1965).

Knowledge about participation is useful to policymakers in terms of funding and to those who plan and implement programs. At the federal level, for example, funding for literacy and other programs is a function of who is now participating, in conjunction with the perceived needs of nonparticipants. Along with current numbers and rates of participation of various segments of the adult population, other sociopolitical and economic factors play important parts in federal policy formation, not the least of which is the desire to maintain a stable democratic and globally competitive society. For those who plan learning activities and instruct adults, it is certainly helpful to know as much as possible about the clientele being served.

This section offers a descriptive profile of who participates in adult learning activities. The emphasis is on formal, institutionally based programs, because that is where the bulk of information lies. There are no national studies of participation in nonformal adult education activities that we could find; as for participation in self-directed learning, only one national study has been conducted. There are, however, many studies on what motivates adults to participate *or not* in adult education. Why an adult might choose to participate is also discussed in this section. Finally, we review attempts to build models that explain and predict participation.

WHO PARTICIPATES?

In 1962 an "inquiry into the nature of adult education in America" was funded by the Carnegie Corporation and carried out by researchers Johnstone and Rivera (1965) at the National Opinion Research Center (NORC) in Chicago. The study sought to describe participation in formal and informal educational activities, assess attitudes and opinions held by adults concerning education, describe the organizations delivering adult education in a typical urban community, and focus on the educational and work experiences of young adults aged seventeen to twenty-four. The findings of this first national study have provided a baseline against which the findings of subsequent studies have been compared.

Since comparisons are made, it is important to know how *adult education* and *adult* are defined in this study. Realizing the import of this function, Johnstone and Rivera (1965, p. 26) struggled to come up with a definition of an adult educational activity that was broad enough to capture systematic efforts at learning but not so broad as to include "a host of activities ... which would fall beyond the range of any reasonable or workable definition of adult education." They decided that an adult education activity would have as its main purpose the desire to acquire some type of knowledge, information, or skill and that it would include some form of instruction (including self-instruction). They thus measured involvement as a full-time adult student, as a part-time participant in adult education activities, and as a participant in independent self-education. An adult was defined as anyone either age twenty-one or over, married, or the head of a household. Interviews with a random national sample of nearly twelve thousand households formed the data set.

Using the above definitions, Johnstone and Rivera estimated that 22 percent of American adults participated in "one or more forms of learning" between June 1961 and June 1962 (p. 1). They also discovered that what adults were learning was largely practical and skill oriented rather than academic: "Subject matter directly useful in the performance of everyday tasks and obligations accounted for the most significant block of the total activities recorded. Together, the vocational and home and family life categories alone represented 44 percent of all formal courses studied and 47 percent of the subjects people studied on their own" (p. 3).

This landmark study also identified the major demographic and socioeconomic variables characteristic of participants. Age and formal schooling were delineated as the major correlates of participation in adult education. Johnstone and Rivera's often-quoted profile of the typical adult learner has held up, with minor deviations, in all subsequent national studies of participation. Their profile is as follows: "The adult education participant is just as often a woman as a man, is typically under forty, has completed high school or more, enjoys an above-average income, works full-time and most often in a white-collar occupation, is married and has children, lives in an urbanized area but more likely in a suburb than large city, and is found in all parts of the country, but more frequently in the West than in other regions" (p. 8).

Beginning in 1969, the National Center for Education Statistics (NCES) in the U.S. Department of Education undertook a set of triennial surveys of participation of adults in education. The results of the first six surveys (1969, 1972, 1975, 1978, 1981, 1984) and two studies in 1991 and 1995 can be loosely compared with each other to reveal participation trends. In these surveys, adult education is equated with organized instruction: "Adult education is defined as any course or educational activity taken part-time and reported as adult education by respondents seventeen years old and over" (U.S. Department of Education, 1986). Changes in methodology and sample design over the years warrant caution in making comparisons (Collins, Brick, and Kim, 1997). Nevertheless, certain trends emerge.

The first trend is that the numbers of adults participating part time in organized instruction has increased from a low of 10 percent in the 1969 survey, to 14 percent in 1984, to 38 percent in 1991, and to 40 percent in 1995. The 40 percent figure obtained in 1995 is congruent with a subsequent study of participation by the United Nations Educational, Scientific, and Cultural Organization (UNESCO) that found that 41 percent of the American adults in the study sample participated in some form of education (Valentine, 1997). In a recent report comparing the NCES study findings with the UNESCO study, Valentine summarizes the following trends:

- In 1969 and the years immediately following, men were disproportionately represented among participants. By 1984, participation rates had equalized, with women participants outnumbering men in both job-related and non-job-related activities. In the 1991 and 1995 NCES reports—and in the present [UNESCO] study—there is no significant difference in men and women's participation rates.
- In 1969, adult education courses were nearly evenly split between job-related and non-job-related. In the late seventies, job-related courses began to gain ascendancy, and by 1984, job-related courses dominated 2 to 1. This trend continued through June 1993 (Kopka and Peng), though the 1995 study places this ratio closer to 1 to 1. In the current UNESCO study, fully 90.6 percent of adults cited career or job-related reasons for educational participation. Clearly, there is a marked increase in the employment-orientation of adult education in the United States. Also clear, however, is the fact that methodological differences must be blamed for a large proportion of the observed differences in percentage.
- Since 1969, whites were overrepresented among participants. This trend continues through the 1990–91 report. (Comparable figures have not yet been released for the 1994–95 data.) The

current UNESCO survey, unfortunately, does not include analyses based on race and ethnicity. Even without current data, it is safe to assume that "minority" groups in the United States are underrepresented in most types of adult education endeavors. [1997, pp. 6–7]

Johnstone and Rivera's profile of the typical adult learner has changed little over the past thirty years. Compared to those who do not participate, participants in adult education are better educated, younger, have higher incomes, and are most likely to be white and employed full time. Except for race, which was not a variable, the most recent UNESCO study findings are congruent with this profile. As can be seen in Table 3-1, better-educated, younger, married or single (never married), American-born versus immigrants, and adults employed full-time in professional and technical occupations are most likely to participate in adult education.

Table 3-1. Personal Attributes of Participants.

Attribute	Participation Rate (percent)
Level of Education	
Did not complete secondary school	15.3 percent
Secondary school diploma	31.7
Postsecondary degree	62.3
Age	
17–24 years	47.6 percent
25–34 years	44.1
35–44 years	44.3
45–54 years	42.1
55–64 years	26.3
Marital Status	
Single	43.6 percent
Married	41.7
Widowed, divorced, or separated	33.9
Country of Origin	
United States	42.8 percent
Other	29.1
Type of Community	
Nonurban	43.9 percent
Urban	33.8
Employment Status	
Employed	47.8 percent
Unemployed, looking for work	27.5
Homemaker	13.5
Retired	12.5
Student	91.8
Other	16.3
Size of Company	
Fewer than 200 employees	36.0 percent
200 or more employees	58.0
Occupation	
Government	57.7 percent
Professional and technical	70.0
Clerical	52.6
Service	39.4
Crafts, manufacturing, and skilled agriculture	25.2
Nature of Job	
Employee with no supervisory responsibilities	40.0 percent
Employee with supervisory responsibilities	61.5
Self-employed	33.0

Source: Valentine, 1997. Reprinted from Paul Belanger and Sofia Valdivielso (eds.), *The Emergence of Learning Societies: Who Participates in Adult Learning?* Copyright 1997, Chapter 6, with permission from Elsevier Science.

Among the other national studies, two are worth mentioning for their somewhat different emphases. Aslanian and Brickell (1980) sampled 1,519 adults over age twenty-five, of whom 744, or 49 percent, reported having learned something formally or informally in the year prior to the study. Although the focus of this study was on reasons that adults gave for their participation, the authors present a profile of learners compared to nonlearners. In contrasting the 744 learners with the 775 nonlearners, learners were found to be younger and better educated; they also had higher incomes, were employed, lived in urbanized areas, were white, were engaged in professional and technical work, and were single or divorced.

The second study, by Penland (1979), had a considerably different focus from the other work reviewed here. Penland was interested in corroborating Tough's (1979) findings that more than 90 percent of adults are engaged in independent learning projects. Briefly, Tough felt that adults were engaged in learning as part of their everyday lives—learning that was not necessarily institutionally based and not easily recognized by the learners themselves due to the association of learning with formal instruction. Consequently, Tough and Penland asked adults to think about major learning activities that were clearly focused efforts to gain and retain knowledge or skill. A learning project had to have occurred over at least a two-day period, totaling at least seven hours of learning. Respondents in both studies were given a list of things people learn about—a foreign language, gardening, raising children, and so on. Penland's 1,501 respondents were selected from the U.S. population by means of a modified probability sample. He found that "almost 80 percent (78.9) of the population of eighteen years and over perceive themselves as continuing learners whether in self-planned or formal courses" and "over three-quarters (76.1 percent) of the U.S. population had planned one or more learning projects on their own" (p. 173). Furthermore, of the nine areas of study, personal development and home and family ranked highest in popularity, followed by hobbies and recreation, general education, job, religion, voluntary activity, public affairs, and agriculture/technology.

In summary, although participation rates vary depending on how adult and adult education are defined, the profile of the typical adult learner has remained remarkably consistent across studies. Next we discuss why adults do or do not choose to participate in learning activities.

WHY ADULTS DO OR DO NOT PARTICIPATE

Adults are busy people. Most spend at least eight hours a day working and often as many hours attending to family, household, and community concerns. Why do as many as 79 million of these adults (Valentine, 1997) enroll in adult education classes, seek private instruction, or engage in independent learning projects? Teachers, counselors, administrators, and policymakers all have a keen interest in understanding why people do or do not participate in learning activities. One approach to answering this question is to ask people their reasons for participating, and this has been done as part of the national survey studies already cited. Another approach is to try to determine the underlying motivational orientations or barriers to participation of certain groups of learners. These approaches are discussed here.

Survey Studies

Hundreds of local, state, and national studies have asked adults their reasons for engaging in educational pursuits. In most of these studies, respondents are presented with a list of reasons that people might participate and asked to indicate which ones apply to them. Most respondents report multiple reasons. If asked to indicate the main reason (as they were in the NCES surveys), however, they most commonly cite job-related motives.

The strength of employment-related motives was first uncovered by Johnstone and Rivera (1965). Thirty-six percent of respondents indicated that they were "preparing for a new job or occupation" (p. 144), and 32 percent said they participated in education "for the job I held at that time." The authors concluded that "vocational goals most frequently direct adults into

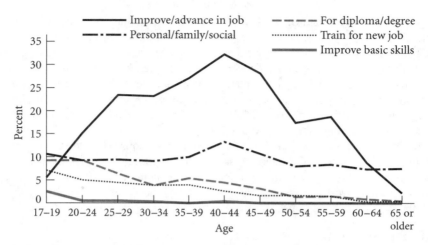

Figure 3-1.   Participation Rates in Adult Education and Main Reasons for Participating, by Age, 1991.

Source: U. S. Department of Education, National Center for Education Statistics. *National Household Education Survey, Adult Education Component,* cited in Kopka and Peng, 1993, p. 4.

continuing education" (p. 144). The eight surveys of participation conducted by the NCES have consistently revealed job-related reasons as the most frequently cited, with personal development courses a close second in the most recent study, from 1995 (Kim, Collins, Stowe, and Chandler, 1995). Figure 3-1, which is drawn from the 1991 NCES study (cited by Kopka and Peng, 1993), shows the relative importance of work-related reasons by age group. In the most recent UNESCO survey, fully 90.6 percent cited career- or job-related reasons for participation, and 9.4 percent cited "personal interest" (Valentine, 1997). When asked about the goal of the learning activity, the largest percentage (58 percent) said it was professional or career upgrading, 18.3 percent "other," 17.6 percent to earn a college or university degree, 3.8 percent to earn a vocational or apprenticeship certificate, and 2.3 percent to complete secondary school (Valentine, 1997). Clearly, there is a strong linkage between one's work life and participation in adult education. Cross (1981) explains this relationship as quite logical given most adults' life situations:

> People who do not have good jobs are interested in further education to get better jobs, and those who have good jobs would like to advance them. Women, factory workers, and the poorly educated, for example, are more likely to be pursuing education in order to prepare for new jobs, whereas men, professionals, and college graduates are more likely to be seeking advancement in present jobs. Men are more interested in job-related learning than women are, and young people are far more interested in it than older people are. Interest in job-related goals begins to decline at age 50 and drops off sharply after age 60. Those who are not currently participating in learning activities (most often the economically disadvantaged and poorly educated) are even more likely to express an interest in job-related education than are their more advantaged peers, who can afford the luxury of education for recreation and personal satisfaction. [1981, pp. 91–92]

Approaching people's reasons for participating in adult education from a somewhat different angle, Aslanian and Brickell (1980) sought to test the hypothesis that life transitions motivate adults to seek out learning experiences. They found that 83 percent of the learners in their sample could describe some past, present, or future change in their lives as reasons for learning. The other 17 percent were engaged in learning for its own sake—that is, to stay mentally alert—or for the social aspects or because learning is a satisfying activity. Those going through transitions, such as marriage, retirement, job changes, birth of children, and so on, were able to identify specific events, such as getting fired or promoted, that triggered their transition. The authors noted seven kinds of transitions. Those relating to career and family accounted for 56 percent and 16 percent of the transitions, respectively. The other transitions, in descending importance, concerned leisure (13 percent), art (5 percent), health (5 percent), religion (4 percent), and citizenship (1 percent). "To know an adult's life schedule," the authors conclude, "is to know an adult's learning schedule" (pp. 60–61).

The survey studies have been helpful in identifying reasons adults give for participating in learning activities. Since most adult learners are employed and derive much of their identity from their work, it is not surprising to find that at least half of them are involved in education for job-related reasons. Other investigations have sought to go beyond these self-reported data in trying to understand the why of participation.

Motivational Orientations of Learners

Interest in categorizing the various reasons given for participating in adult learning has spurred a line of inquiry in addition to the survey studies. This area of investigation was initiated with the publication by Houle in *The Inquiring Mind* in 1961. Choosing a small, select sample of twenty-two adults "conspicuously engaged in various forms of continuing learning" (p. 13), Houle conducted in-depth interviews that explored his subjects' history of learning, factors that led them to be continuing learners, and their views of themselves as learners. An analysis of the interview data revealed three separate learning orientations held by the adults. The now-famous typology consists of *goal-oriented* learners, who use education as a means of achieving some other goal; *activity-oriented* learners, who participate for the sake of the activity itself and the social interaction; and *learning-oriented* participants, who seek knowledge for its own sake.

Houle's research stimulated a number of studies attempting to affirm or refine the original typology. Sheffield (1964), for example, used Houle's interview transcriptions to develop an instrument to measure adults' learning orientations. Through factor analysis, he came up with five orientations, two of which could be subsumed under two of Houle's categories. Burgess (1971) and Boshier (1971) also developed scales in which the items have been shown to cluster into between five and eight factors.

By far the most extensive work has been done with Boshier's forty-eight item Education Participation Scale (EPS), later refined to forty items. Used first by Boshier in New Zealand, it was subsequently used by Morstain and Smart (1974) with 611 adults in evening credit courses at a college in New Jersey. Their six-factor solution extended Houle's typology somewhat:

1. *Social Relationships.* This factor reflects participation in order to make new friends or meet members of the opposite sex.
2. *External Expectations.* These participants are complying with the wishes or directives of someone else with authority.
3. *Social Welfare.* This factor reflects an altruistic orientation; learners are involved because they want to serve others or their community.
4. *Professional Advancement.* This factor is strongly associated with participation for job enhancement or professional advancement.
5. *Escape/Stimulation.* This factor is indicative of learners who are involved as a way of alleviating boredom or escaping home or work routine.
6. *Cognitive Interest.* These participants, identical to Houle's learning-oriented adults, are engaged for the sake of learning itself.

Boshier himself conducted an extensive test of Houle's typology using his EPS scale (Boshier and Collins, 1985). Using cluster analysis instead of factor analysis, because the technique is more congruent with Houle's original conceptualization of three separate but overlapping orientations, he analyzed the responses of 13,442 learners from Africa, Asia, New Zealand, Canada, and the United States. Boshier and Collins were able to effect a three-cluster solution "loosely isomorphic with Houle's topology" (p. 125). They found that "Cluster I consisted of the Cognitive Interest items and was congruent with his learning orientation." Cluster II, the activity orientation, "was multifaceted and composed of items normally labeled Social Stimulation, Social Contact, External Expectations, and Community Service" (p. 125). Cluster III consisted of the Professional Advancement items and thus resembled Houle's goal orientation. The authors note that although their three-cluster solution is "loosely isomorphic," the grouping of items to make up the activity cluster that matches Houle's typology is "overly generous." They conclude that "Houle's intuition has been partly collaborated; two of the six clusters were as he described them" (p. 127).

A more recent study using Boshier's EPS analyzed responses from 1,142 students in programs at a large state university (Fujita-Starck, 1996). Results confirmed the seven-factor typology proposed by Boshier in 1991 (communication improvement, social contact, educational preparation, professional advancement, family togetherness, social stimulation, and cognitive interest). The author also found the scale to be reliable "in differentiating among a diverse group of students with varying reasons for participating in continuing education" (p. 38).

Despite the limitations of this line of research (Courtney, 1992; Long, 1983), it has become evident that learners' motivations for participating in adult education are many, complex, and subject to change. The search for an underlying motivational structure related to participation is likely to continue, however, for such knowledge "can assist educators and administrators in identifying and meeting the needs of a wide spectrum of learners relative to program content, as well as the time, duration, and location of related activities" (Fujita-Starck, 1996, p. 39).

Barriers to Participation

Knowing why adults participate in adult education does not tell us why many do not. That is, we cannot assume that those who are not participating are happily employed and satisfied with their family, community, and leisure activities. In fact, one of the field's biggest mysteries is why more adults, especially those who might benefit the most, are not involved in adult education. This question has prompted research into why adults do not participate in adult education.

The two most often cited reasons for nonparticipation are lack of time and lack of money. These are socially acceptable reasons for not doing something, of course, and probably very legitimate reasons for adults who are busy people trying to become or stay economically solvent and take care of their families and themselves. Johnstone and Rivera (1965) in their national study of participation found that 43 percent cited cost as a reason for not attending adult education courses and 39 percent said they were too busy. These were also the two major reasons for nonparticipation cited in the UNESCO study (Valentine, 1997). Forty-five percent of respondents said lack of time was a barrier for job-related education; this figure climbs to 60.1 percent for non-job-related education. Interestingly, 33.4 percent gave cost as a barrier for job-related education, but 25.4 percent reported cost as a barrier for non-job-related education (Valentine, 1997). For both types of education, "family responsibilities" was cited as the next most salient barrier.

Reasons that adults do not participate have been clustered by several researchers into types of barriers. Johnstone and Rivera (1965) clustered ten potential barriers into two categories: external, or situational, and internal, or dispositional, barriers. External barriers are "influences more or less external to the individual or at least beyond the individual's control" (p. 214), such as cost of the program. Internal barriers reflect personal attitudes, such as thinking one is too old to learn. Older adults, for example, cited more dispositional barriers, and younger people and women were more constrained by situational barriers. On the other hand, Valentine's (1997) analysis of the UNESCO data revealed that situational barriers affected both men and women: "Women were more likely than men to report that family responsibilities interfered with both job-related and non-job-related education. Men were more likely than women to report that work demands interfered with non-job-related education."

To situational and dispositional barriers, Cross (1981, p. 98) added a third cluster: institutional barriers, consisting of "all those practices and procedures that exclude or discourage working adults from participating in educational activities." Darkenwald and Merriam (1982) also cite institutional and situational barriers but divide the dispositional barrier into psychosocial obstacles (beliefs, values, attitudes, and perceptions about education or about oneself as a learner) and informational, which reflects the lack of awareness as to what educational opportunities are available.

Darkenwald and colleagues have gone beyond the three-part or four-part barrier typologies in developing a scale of deterrents to participation that can be factor analyzed to reveal the structure of reasons underlying nonparticipation (in much the same way the EPS does for participation). A form of the Deterrents to Participation Scale (DPS) used with the general adult public revealed six factors of nonparticipation: lack of confidence, lack of course relevance, time constraints, low personal priority, cost, and personal problems (such as child care, family problems, and personal health) (Darkenwald and Valentine, 1985). In a later analysis of the same data, Valentine and Darkenwald (1990) derived a typology of adult nonparticipants. According to their analysis, the adult nonparticipants in the general public cluster into five distinct groups. People are deterred from participating by personal problems, lack of confidence, educational costs, lack of interest in organized education generally, or lack of interest in available courses.

Viewing participation from the perspective of barriers lends another dimension to the field's attempt to understand why some adults participate in adult education and others do not. But this perspective tells only part of the story. The bulk of research in North America on nonparticipation has been from the perspective of the *individual's* motivation, attitudes, beliefs, behaviors, position in the life cycle, and so on. This has not always been the case, however, as Courtney (1992) points out in his historical analysis of participation research. Prior to the 1960s, a popular topic among researchers was social participation. General social participation refers to the extent to which a person is an active participant in family and community life; participating in adult education activities was considered just one component of social participation. Benn (1997) has recently revisited this notion of social participation in a survey study of 259 adults in a range of educational programs. She concludes that the extent of one's general social activity affects learning activity, a finding that has implications for marketing and recruitment: "Rather than blanket publicity, a more effective approach might be to advertise through social groups and organizations.... Adult education does not choose its students, they choose (or do not choose) adult education" (p. 34).

For some, a combination of psychological and social factors acts as a barrier to participation. Rubenson (1998, p. 259) points out that "only when we include structural factors and analyze the interaction between them and the individual conceptual apparatus does an interpretation become possible. Adults' readiness to learn and barriers preventing it ... can be understood in terms of societal processes and structure, institutional processes and structure and individual consciousness and activity." Hall and Donaldson's (1997) study of why women without a high school diploma chose *not* to participate provides examples of how the social and the psychological interact. Pre-adult factors such as parents' education, early pregnancies, and economic status formed part of the picture. Lack of a support system was a second factor. Conventional barriers such as lack of time, information, and child care were also operative. The fourth dynamic Hall and Donaldson termed "lack of voice": "At the heart of nonparticipation lies a 'deterrent' so deeply embedded in some women that no theory can fully capture its meaning. The way a woman feels about herself, her self-esteem and self confidence, and the way she can express herself are significant elements in her decision about whether to participate in adult education" (p. 98).

The question of why some adults participate and others do not can also be addressed from a strictly sociological perspective (Bagnall, 1989; Courtney, 1992; Jarvis, 1985; Nordhaug, 1990; Quigley, 1990; Rubenson, 1998; Sissel, 1997). Rubenson (1998, p. 261) characterizes this approach to participation as consisting of two dimensions—"the long arm of the family as reflected in the relationship between social background, educational attainment and participation ... and the long arm of the job: the increased importance of adult education and training as investment." Nordhaug

(1990) examined participation in Norwegian adult education not from the individual participant's perspective, but from variables such as material resources and population density related to the structure of municipalities. Sissel's (1997) study of parent involvement in Head Start programs found that "power relations were expressed in the withholding or allocation of programmatic resources, and functioned to either impede or promote participation" (p. 123). She recommends that more research be conducted on "specific structural factors" (such as race and gender) that "enhance or impede participation" (p. 135). Davis-Harrison (1996) also found race and class to be important variables in investigating the nonparticipation of blue-collar male workers. Finally, in raising the interesting question of just how "voluntary" voluntary participation in continuing education was for government workers in British Columbia, Stalker (1993b) found the concept to be something of a myth. The notion of voluntary participation did not adequately account for issues of power, authority, and control.

Working from this same critical perspective, Jarvis (1985) makes the case for a class analysis in that the middle-class bias found in all studies of participation can be explained by the idea that adult education is organized by the middle class, and the presentation of knowledge is middle class in both language and content. Furthermore, previous school experiences select out "those who were labeled as successful in education" (p. 204), and those who will be labeled successful is pretty much predetermined by one's class, age, sex, and educational background. In a similar vein, Keddie (1980, p. 63) makes the point that what we consider to be "problems" in adult education—attracting more participants from the lower socioeconomic classes, for example—are really society's problems: "That is, change will depend on seeing that the 'problems' lie within the nature of the provision adult education makes and not in those who do not avail themselves of the resources it offers."

In summary, looking at social structure rather than individual needs and interests reveals some very different explanations as to why adults do or do not participate in adult learning activities. These competing perspectives imply different strategies for increasing participation. If individual interests and motivation account for participation, then recruitment efforts would center on responding to an adult's perceived learning needs and stimulating motivation. If, on the other hand, participation or nonparticipation is seen as a function of the social structure, then one would work toward changing society in ways that would facilitate participation. The most robust explanation of participation is likely to be found in considering *both* the psychological and sociological perspectives.

EXPLAINING AND PREDICTING PARTICIPATION

When one considers the myriad of psychological and sociological variables and the relationships between them that affect participation, it is not surprising that there is as yet no single theory or model to explain or predict participation in adult education. What we have are a number of models, some emphasizing the psychological and some linking the individual with social and environmental forces. Some focus on the decision to participate (Henry and Basile, 1994), others on persistence in the adult education activity (Boshier, 1973). A recent model connects participation, learning, and noninvolvement (Sissel, 1997). Most of the models apply to participation in formal learning activities rather than informal or self-directed learning, and only a few have been tested. Some models are borrowed from other fields and applied to adult students. Tinto's (1993) model of student departure from higher education, for example, has been applied to nontraditional students in higher education (Ashar and Skenes, 1993) and to doctoral graduate students (Lees, 1996). In this material of the section we offer a brief overview of a number of models from adult education and then step back and assess model-building efforts generally.

Models of Participation

Models are visual representations of how concepts related to participation interact to explain who participates and perhaps even predict who will participate in the future. Following are summaries of seven such models.

Miller's Force-Field Analysis.

One of the earliest efforts to explain participation was presented by Harry Miller in 1967. Miller attempted to link the motivational needs hierarchy of Maslow (1954) with Lewin's (1947) force-field theory. From Maslow, Miller hypothesized that adults from lower socioeconomic classes would participate for job-related and basic skills reasons, whereas participants from higher social classes would seek education to satisfy achievement and self-realization needs. This tendency was also related to one's place in the life cycle: younger people would be more interested than older people in achieving economic security, for example. From Lewin, Miller drew the idea that both negative and positive forces act on the individual, and the direction and sum total of these forces determine an adult's motivation to participate. Miller's model consists of figures depicting forces by arrows, with wider arrows signifying a stronger force at work. There are figures for four social classes (lower lower, working, lower middle, and upper middle) and four content areas (vocational, family, citizenship, and self-development). Figure 3-2 displays the strength of positive and negative forces for education for vocational competence for the lower-lower-class level. Five arrows represent negative forces (such as "hostility to education") and four arrows represent positive forces (such as "survival needs"). The summative level of motivation for this group is relatively low, as indicated by the bar's being below the midpoint of the figure.

Boshier's Congruency Model.

Like Miller, Boshier (1973) explains participation in terms of the interaction between personal factors and social factors. According to Boshier, "the model asserts that 'congruence' both within the participant and between the participant and his educational environment determine participation/nonparticipation and dropout/persistence" (p. 256). Drawing from Maslow, Boshier posits that people are either primarily growth motivated or deficiency motivated, with deficiency-oriented people "more at the mercy of social and environmental forces" (p. 256). The model is based on the assumptions that participation and persistence in adult education are determined by how people feel about themselves and the match between the self and the educational environment. As can be seen in Figure 3-3, the cumulative effect of these discrepancies is mediated by social and psychological variables such as age, sex, and social class and subenvironmental variables such as transportation and class size. The arrows in the model suggest that these two groups of mediating variables have had an effect on the person's orientation to learning in the first place.

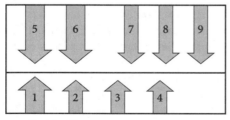

Negative Forces

5. Action-excitement orientation of male culture

6. Hostility to education and to middle-class object orientation

7. Relative absence of specific, immediate job opportunities at end of training

8. Limited access through organizational ties

9. Weak family structure

Positive Forces

1. Survival needs

2. Changing technology

3. Safety needs of female culture

4. Governmental attempts to change opportunity structure

Figure 3-2.   Education for Vocational Competence: Lower-Lower-Class Level.
Source: Miller, 1967, p. 21.

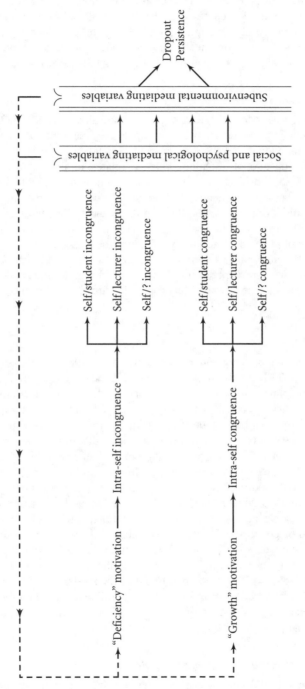

Figure 3-3. Boshier's Model to Explain Dropout from Adult Education Institutions.
Source: Boshier, 1977, p. 91.

Moderate testing of the model by the author (Boshier, 1973, 1977) and by Garrison (1987) suggests that it is at least a promising beginning. With a sample of 1,372 university continuing education students, Boshier (1973) confirmed his hypothesis that those with high incongruence scores are more likely to drop out. Garrison (1987), on the other hand, was better able to predict persisters (93 percent) than dropouts (20.8 percent). Boshier (1986) himself has proposed another model drawing on some of the same assumptions underlying the congruency model, as well as taking into account learners' motivation, need, and orientation to future-centeredness. (For a discussion of Boshier's as yet untested revised model, see Bagnall, 1990.)

Rubenson's Expectancy-Valence Model.

Rubenson's Expectancy-Valence model (1977) addresses both socialization and structural dimensions, as well as individual orientation. The decision to participate is a combination of the negative and positive forces within the individual and the environment. Expectancy consists of the anticipation of being successful in an educational situation. Valence relates to the value a person puts on being successful; one could be positive, negative, or indifferent. The individual is the center of Rubenson's model because everything depends on a person's perception of the environment and the value of participating in adult education. People develop these perceptions through being socialized by family, school, and work. Structural factors in the environment—such as the values of people important to one's self-definition and accessibility of educational programs—directly affect how one sees the environment. Running parallel with socialization and structural factors are the person's current needs. Again, it is how one experiences these needs that determines whether one has a positive, negative, or neutral valence toward the proposed education. This model has yet to be systematically tested.

Cookson's Isstal Model.

Based on Smith's (1980) social participation model, Cookson's (1986) model stresses the social dimension of participation. ISSTAL stands for "interdisciplinary, sequential specificity, time allocation, and life span." It is interdisciplinary in that it includes concepts from several disciplines; sequential specificity relates to the causal interconnectedness of variables leading to participation; and time allocation and life span assumptions have to do with viewing participation in adult education as but one form of an adult's overall social participation. Cookson asserts that social participation is a lifelong pattern: "People who exhibit higher levels of [participation in adult education] in their thirties may be expected to display similarly higher levels in their forties, fifties, and sixties" (p. 132).

The model begins with the external context, which includes climate, topography, culture, and social structures. Sociodemographic factors such as age, education, and occupation follow. Midway in the model are four interactive components: personality traits, intellectual capacities, retained information, and attitudinal dispositions. The final component of the model are situational variables that reflect the person's immediate situation and have the most specific influence on the decision to participate. Cookson (1987) tested his model in two studies conducted in British Columbia. Fifty-eight independent variables were used to operationalize the model with fifty male low-income heads of household and four hundred men and women in public evening school classes. None of the variables proved significant with the male-only group, and only three were significantly related to participation in the other study.

Darkenwald and Merriam's Psychosocial Interaction Model.

Darkenwald and Merriam's (1982, p. 142) model emphasizes "social-environmental forces, particularly socioeconomic status, not because individual traits or attitudes are unimportant but because less is known about their influence on participation." This model, shown in Figure 3-4, has two major divisions: preadulthood and adulthood. In the preadulthood phase, individual and

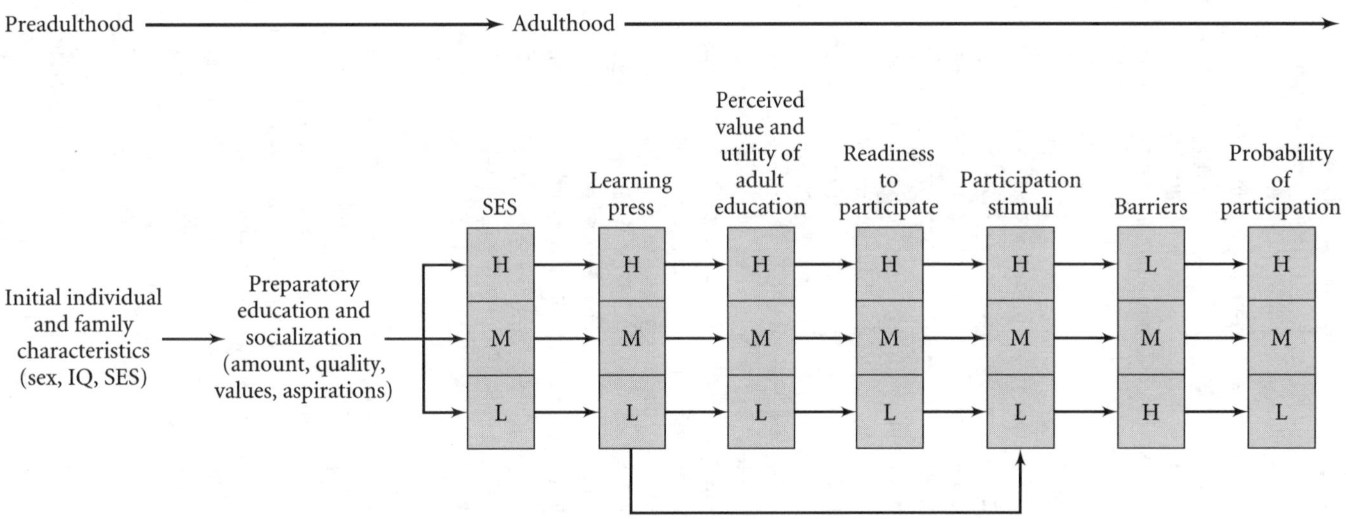

Figure 3-4. Psychosocial Interaction Model of Participation in Organized Adult Education.

Note: H = high, M = moderate, L = low.

Source: From *Adult Education: Foundations of Practice,* by Gordon Darkenwald and Sharan B. Merriam. Copyright © 1982 by Harper & Row, Publishers, Inc. Reprinted by permission of Addison-Wesley Educational Publishers Inc.

family characteristics, particularly intelligence and socioeconomic status, determine the type of preparatory education and socialization a person undergoes in becoming an adult. The adult's socioeconomic status is the direct result of these preadulthood experiences. The adulthood phase consists of six components, each of which can have a high, moderate, or low value. Socioeconomic status (SES) is followed by learning press, defined as "the extent to which one's total current environment requires or encourages further learning" (p. 142) and directly related to SES. The other components of the model are perceived value and utility of adult education, readiness to participate, participation stimuli, and barriers. Participation stimuli are specific events that prod adults into considering an educational activity.

Cervero and Kirkpatrick's (1990) test of the model found that the preadulthood variables, especially father's level of education, explained a significant amount of participation for both credit and noncredit activities.

Henry and Basile's Decision Model.

Henry and Basile's (1994) model is unique in its incorporation of *both* motivational factors and deterrents to participation to help explain adults' decision to participate in formal adult education. The starting point for the model is the target population and its characteristics, such as age, sex, race, education, and occupation. Reasons for enrolling, such as improving one's work situation, meeting new people, or dealing with major life changes, are related to sources of information about learning opportunities. This leads to three more factors—course attributes, deterrents, and institutional reputation—all of which are taken into account in the decision to take the course or not. The authors explain that "in some cases, a strong motivation may be overcome by the lack of a specific course offering, or by some negative impressions of the program or institution. In other cases, a strong institutional reputation and availability of a convenient course may induce participation despite a weak motivational interest. The conceptual framework allows the empirical investigation of these complex relationships" (p. 70). They tested their model with a group of 138 learners who enrolled in a continuing education course and 180 nonparticipants who had sought information about a course but had failed to enroll. The findings of their study confirmed the complexity involved in "a simple decision to participate in a course ... that both motivations and deterrents influence the decision to participate" (p. 80). The authors note that vocational reasons were a particularly strong motivator with these adults: "According to our data, work-related factors pile up in favor of participation: typical is a person who has a job-related interest, received a course brochure at work, and has an employer who is willing to pay the course fees" (p. 80).

Cross's Chain-of-Respose Model.

Drawing on a synthesis of the common elements in Miller's (1967), Boshier's (1973), and Rubenson's (1977) models, Cross (1981, p. 124) proposed "a conceptual framework designed to identify the relevant variables and hypothesize their interrelationships." She assumes that participation in a learning activity is the result of a chain of responses to both psychological and environmental factors.

The chain of responses (COR) begins with the individual, as depicted in Figure 3-5. Self-evaluation (A) is one's assessment as to whether achievement in an educational situation is possible. This evaluation combines with attitudes about education (B). Echoing Boshier's notion of growth-motivated or deficiency-motivated learners, Cross comments on the linking of points A and B: "There is a relatively stable and characteristic stance toward learning that makes some people eager to seek out new experiences with a potential for growth while others avoid challenges to their accustomed ways of thinking or behaving" (p. 126). Point C—the importance of goals and the expectation that participation will meet them—is equivalent to Rubenson's notions of expectancy and valence. Expectancy is closely related to points A and B "in that individuals with high self-esteem 'expect' to be successful" (p. 126). Positive attitudes and self-evaluation usually result in an expectation to succeed, thus making motivation to participate relatively high at this juncture in the model.

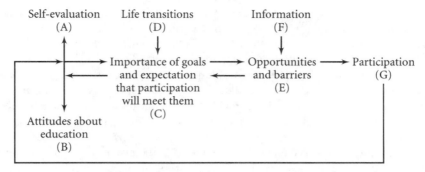

Figure 3-5. Cross's Chain-of-Response Model for Participation in Adult Education.
Source: Cross, 1981, p. 124.

Cross's COR model is the first to incorporate life events and transitions. Life transitions (D) are those events and changes that all adults encounter as they move through the life cycle. Graduation, marriage, retirement, and so on precipitate transitions that, according to one study, account for 83 percent of the motivation to participate in adult education (Aslanian and Brickell, 1980).

Points E and F are environmental factors that may decide whether one participates in education. Barriers can be overcome and opportunities taken advantage of if one has the information needed to proceed (point F). "Without accurate information, point E in the model is weak because opportunities are not discovered and barriers loom large" (p. 127). If responses all along the chain are positive, the result will be participation (point G).

Cross says that the model is not really as linear as these steps might suggest. It is also a reciprocal model, in that participation in adult education (G) can affect how one feels about education (B) and oneself as a learner (A).

Although this model does have environmental components, it is primarily a psychological model with its focus on the individual progressing through the chain of response. For Cross, the psychological factors are most important: "If adult educators wish to understand why some adults fail to participate in learning opportunities, they need to begin at the beginning of the COR model—with an understanding of attitudes toward self and education" (p. 130). Gooderham (1993), however, feels that antecedent sociological factors are what shape the factors in Cross's model. In his framework for understanding adults' pursuit of higher education, for example, he proposes that one's attitude to formal learning (point B in Cross's model) is actually determined by the antecedent factors of "social origin" and "degree of success at school" (p. 37).

Assessment of Model-Building Efforts

All these models of participation point to the complexity of the topic of explaining and predicting participation in adult education. Each model is an attempt to account for who participates and why, as well as stimulate new research directions. All the models posit an "interaction between the individual and his or her environment" (Cross, 1981, p. 123). The relative weight of these two factors varies from model to model—from the emphasis on the individual's orientation in Boshier's model to the external context and social background stressed in the ISSTAL model. Moreover, most of these models attempt to explain participation in institutionally sponsored learning activities—that is, after all, what most educators are interested in. Of the seven models reviewed here, only Cross's seems capable of explaining participation in self-directed learning activities. Bagnall (1989, p. 256) points out that these models assume the learner's physical presence, which is only one way to think of participation. Participation can also be thought of as involvement (the extent to which the learner is actively engaged in the learning event) and control (the extent to which the learner controls the content, goals, or outcomes of the event).

There are some unique features in the different models. Rubenson, for example, makes use of member and reference groups whose norms determine one's perceptions of the usefulness of education. Fingeret's (1983) research on illiterate adults, in which she explores the effects of their membership in a social network, lends support to the validity of this concept for explaining participation. That is, many illiterates may fail to join literacy classes because their literacy needs are met through an exchange of goods and services and the groups with whom they identify do not promote education as a means of dealing with their literacy needs. Cross includes life transitions as an important determinant of participation. This component takes into account the research on adult development, in particular the potential of periods of change in the adult life cycle for precipitating learning needs. Aslanian and Brickell (1980), discovering that 83 percent of the learners were participating in adult education because of some past, present, or anticipated change in their lives, provide strong support for the life transition component of Cross's model. Unique to Darkenwald and Merriam's model is learning press, which includes general social participation, occupational complexity, and lifestyle—all of which, in combination, press one in varying intensity toward further learning. Henry and Basile are the first to combine motivational factors along with deterrents to help predict the decision to participate. Finally, Cookson's ISSTAL model includes an intellectual capacity factor. He notes that when the intellectual capacity factor is operationalized in terms of intelligence test scores, there is a relationship to persistence in adult basic education programs. The practical and ethical considerations involved in obtaining such a score, however, may mitigate against its use in predicting persistence.

It might be asked to what extent these isolated attempts to explain and predict participation have moved the field toward a comprehensive explanation of this phenomenon. On the other hand, a comprehensive theory may not be possible given the number of variables that might be needed to cover the topic adequately. As of this writing, there has been relatively little testing of the models reviewed here, partly because of the difficulty in operationalizing complex variables such as personality traits, structural factors in the environment, and learning press and their interrelationships with each other. Several recent efforts to map these interactions in combination with sophisticated measurement techniques seem promising (Dirkx and Jha, 1994; Yang, 1995; Yang, Blunt, and Butler, 1994). Yang's (1995) work in particular is the first longitudinal study to address how participation affects, and is affected by, personal and social factors across the life span. Continued work in this direction might yet result in a good explanatory model of participation that will be of use to researchers and educators alike.

SUMMARY

Participation is one of the more thoroughly studied areas in adult education. We have a sense of who participates, what is studied, and what motivates some adults and not others to enroll in a course or undertake an independent learning project. This accumulation of descriptive information about participation has led to efforts to fit the pieces together in the form of models that try to convey the complexity of the phenomenon.

Although there were numerous studies of participation in the forty years between the inauguration of the field of adult education and the 1960s, it was not until 1965 that the first national study of participation was published. Johnstone and Rivera's study, with its care in defining participation and selecting methods of data collection and analysis, remains a benchmark contribution to this literature. Subsequent surveys by the National Center for Education Statistics (NCES), Aslanian and Brickell (1980), Penland (1979), and UNESCO (Valentine, 1997) have contributed to this database. Regardless of the study, the profile of the typical adult learner remains remarkably consistent: white, middle class, employed, younger, and better educated than the nonparticipant. Further, employment-related reasons account for the majority of participant interest in continuing education.

Why adults do or do not participate in adult education is an important question, having implications for both theory and practice. Surveys have uncovered both reasons for and barriers to participation. The work on determining an underlying structure of motivational orientations begun by Houle (1961) has been carried on most notably by Boshier's research using the Education Participation Scale (EPS). Between three and seven factors have been delineated to explain why adults participate. In a similar approach, barriers to participation have been investigated using various forms of the Deterrents to Participation Scale (DPS), developed by Darkenwald and colleagues. Further, explanations of participation have been advanced from a sociological rather than a psychological perspective. In these analyses, people's decisions to participate have less to do with their needs and motives than with their position in society and the social experiences that have shaped their lives.

Finally, seven models of participation were reviewed in this section. The value of these models in explaining and predicting participation has yet to be determined through research and testing. Nevertheless, they constitute a contribution to the literature on participation in that they attempt to map the interaction of variables that have been shown to influence a person's decision to participate and subsequent perseverance in the activity.

SECTION FOUR

ADULT LEARNING AND CONTEMPORARY SOCIETY

SHARAN B. MERRIAM
ROSEMARY S. CAFFARELLA

Learning, even self-directed learning, rarely occurs "in splendid isolation from the world in which the learner lives; ... it is intimately related to that world and affected by it" (Jarvis, 1987a, p. 11). What one wants to learn, what is offered, and the ways in which one learns are determined to a large extent by the nature of the society at any particular time. Contrast the young male apprentice of colonial times learning to be a blacksmith with today's middle-aged woman learning data processing, for example, or the preparation needed to become a medical doctor at the turn of the century—less than a high school diploma—with today's long and specialized training.

It can also be argued that the nature of society at any particular point in time determines the relative emphasis placed on *adult* learning. In preindustrial societies, the rate of change was such that what a person needed to know to function as an adult could be learned in childhood (Jarvis, 1983). In societies hurrying to catch up, however, and in our own society with its accelerated rate of change, the urgency of dealing with social realities lies with adults. Society no longer has the luxury of waiting for its youth. As Belanger (1996, p. 21) notes, "The question is no longer whether adult learning is needed, and how important it is. The issue today is how to respond to this increasing and diversified demand, how to manage this explosion." Youth, in fact, "who are sent out into life with a dwindling sackful of values, ... face a situation in which they have to keep filling up their sack. This leads adult education to take 'lifelong learning' as its motto. The duty to be free (with the pressure to realize oneself) is the duty to go on learning.... The hole in the ozone layer provides the stimulus for courses to which people turn for advice, mad cow disease pushes up the numbers attending vegetarian cooking courses, and backache creates a need for posture classes" (Geissler, 1996, pp. 35–36). Ironically, to some observers, adult education finds itself in the position of being "both a victim and a perpetrator of the modernization process" (Geissler, 1996, p. 37).

To some extent, the learning that goes on in adulthood can be understood through an examination of the social context in which it occurs. How is learning in adulthood shaped by the society in which it takes place? How does the sociocultural context determine what is learned and by whom? What is it about the American context in particular that promotes learning in adulthood?

This section explores three dimensions of the current sociocultural context that are shaping the nature of adult learning in today's world: demographics, the global economy, and technology. Although we present each of these separately at first, these three factors are very much interrelated, and thus their convergence and subsequent impact on learning in adulthood are discussed in the final section of this material.

DEMOGRAPHICS

Changing demographics is a social reality shaping the provision of learning in contemporary American society. Demographics is about people, groups of people, and their respective characteristics. For the first time in our society, adults outnumber youth, there are more older adults, the population is better educated than ever before, and there is more cultural and ethnic diversity. For various reasons, individuals and groups of people seek out learning experiences; for other reasons, society targets learning activities for certain segments of the population. Thus, certain learning activities are learner initiated and others are society initiated in response to the changing demographics. The field is concerned with the growth and development of adult learners, while at the same time, there are emerging groups of learners with special needs.

To begin, there are simply more adults in our society than ever before, and the population will continue to age. In comparison to colonial times when half the population was under age sixteen, in 1990, fewer than one in four Americans were under age 16 and half were age 33 or older (U.S. Bureau of the Census, 1992). The median age of the American population of 34.0 years in 1994 is expected to increase to 35.5 in 2000, and 39.1 in 2035 (U.S. Bureau of the Census, 1995). The so-called baby boomers—the seventy million people born between 1946 and 1964—are a contributing factor to this change in the population. Cross (1981, p. 6) notes that such a large cohort, "because of its political and economic strength, manages to gain the attention of the society throughout the life span of the cohort. Because of its sheer size, it has commanded the attention of education, industry, and government." Although we might hear more about youth, they have less of an impact on the economy than the boomers. "People over fifty represent 26 percent of the population, are owners of 80 percent of all money in banks and S&Ls, holders of 77 percent of the nation's financial assets, and buyers of 48 percent of all luxury cars" (Wagschal, 1997, p. 25).

The shift from a youth-oriented to an adult-oriented society is solidified by the increasing numbers of older adults in the population. In 1987, for the first time ever, Americans over the age of sixty-five outnumbered those under twenty-five (Spear and Mocker, 1989). Furthermore, the oldest old, those over eighty-five years old, are the fastest-growing segment of the older population. As of January 1, 1995, there were over three and one half million adults over eighty-five years old, an increase of 18.5 percent from the 1990 census (U.S. Bureau of the Census, 1995). Older adults are also increasingly better educated, in better health, and economically better off than previous cohorts. Society is already heeding their learning needs with policies like tuition waivers for higher and continuing education programs and specially designed programs, such as the popular Elderhostel program and learning-in-retirement institutes. There has also been a subtle change in the philosophical rationale—at least among those working in the fields of gerontology and educational gerontology—underlying the provision of education for this group. Along with an economic rationale (the better educated need fewer social services) and social stability rationale (millions of healthy retired people need something to do) is an awareness that older adults as well as younger ones have an unending potential for development. Williamson (1997, p. 175) suggests that our culturally endorsed notion about what represents "appropriate" learning over the course of the life span tends to "reinforce prevailing myths about retirement and aging as processes of withdrawal and decline." This mind-set ignores the exciting possibilities for personal growth and societal contributions among older members of the population. A more inclusive educational model would promote lifelong learning as a process to make young and old alike "'connoisseurs of the past, implementers of the present and visionaries of the future'" (Berman cited by Williamson, 1997, p. 174).

Thus, more adults and an increase in the number of older adults are two demographic factors influencing the provision of learning activities in our society. So, too, is the rising level of education characteristic of our population. This is dramatically illustrated by the fact that over 80 percent of today's twenty year olds have completed four years of high school compared with less than half (49 percent) of those in their grandparents' generation (Mercer and Garner, 1989). Since previous education is the single best predictor of participation in adult education, the rising educational level of the adult population is a contextual factor of considerable import. Participation data from the Center for Education Statistics show, for example, that 16 percent of adults with fewer than four years of high school participate in organized adult education, while 31 percent of high school graduates and 58 percent of college graduates participate (Kim, Collins, Stowe, and Chandler, 1995). Nevertheless, even as the educational attainment level of the population as a whole continues to rise, an alarming number of high school students drop out before graduating. And "as a high school education becomes the minimum educational standard, those who drop out are more likely to become members of an educational underclass, from which adult education (especially in the form of adult basic and secondary education) may be the only hope of escape" (Rachal, 1989, pp. 10–11). Unfortunately, 1995 data from the National Center for Education Statistics "show that adults with less than a high school diploma were least likely to participate in adult education activities overall, in credential programs, and in work-related courses, and only 5 percent of these adults participated in adult basic education or GED preparation" (Kim, Collins, Stowe, and Chandler, 1995, p. 3). The recent change in government welfare policies limiting time on welfare combined with better education and training opportunities may have a positive effect on raising the level of participation by this population.

Another demographic characteristic of the social context is the growing cultural and ethnic diversity of America's population. Briscoe and Ross (1989, p. 584) point out that "not only is America graying, the skin color of America is also changing." In contrast to the influx of European immigrants at the end of the nineteenth century, today's immigrants are more likely to come from Asia and Latin America. If current trends in immigration and birthrates persist, it is projected that between the years 2000 and 2005, the Hispanic population will account for 37.7 percent of the total population growth, Asian–Pacific Islanders about 19.5 percent, and African Americans 17 percent (Gardner, 1996a). By the year 2000, Hispanics will be the largest minority group in America, with African Americans the second largest (Briscoe and Ross, 1989). Furthermore, the average age of minority populations is decreasing, while the majority population is growing older. For example, "Hispanics will be the youngest population with one-half under 26 years of age while the white population will remain the oldest" (Gardner, 1996a, p. 59). Briscoe and Ross (1989, p. 584) report that "minorities also tend to be clustered in metropolitan areas, and, in the future, fifty-three major U.S. cities will have minority populations that outnumber the present majority population." Not only is the composition of the minority population changing, but so too are the overall numbers. By the year 2000, minorities are expected to compose 29 percent of the population; by 2050, minorities will account for nearly 47 percent of the overall population (U.S. Bureau of the Census, 1995).

The implications of these population trends for society in general and adult education in particular are staggering. Although changing demographics offer a tremendous opportunity for capitalizing anew on the merits of many peoples from many lands, there are also risks (Henry, 1990, p. 29). Minority adults, for example, are disproportionately represented among the unemployed, the low-income stratum, and the less educated. These characteristics are correlated with low rates of participation in organized adult education. The nation's minorities constitute a sizable resource. Briscoe and Ross (1989, p. 586) stress the urgency of the problem: "The consequences to North American society of leaving this resource undeveloped are great. It is likely that young people who leave school early will never participate fully in society or in the decision-making processes of government, and that they will neither enjoy the benefits of good health, nor experience the upward mobility needed as adults to make them full contributors and partners in shaping and participating in the larger society. One cause of the problem is educational institutions not responding quickly enough to change, even though educators are aware of the impact they can have on societal systems."

The growing ethnic and cultural diversity of our population has been identified by Naisbitt and Aburdene (1990) as one of the megatrends for the twenty-first century. They have observed that "even as our lifestyles grow more similar, there are unmistakable signs of a powerful countertrend: a backlash against uniformity, a desire to assert the uniqueness of one's culture and language.... Outbreaks of cultural nationalism are happening in every corner of the globe" (p. 119). Adult educators are slowly becoming aware of the instructional implications of the fact that "as our outer worlds grow more similar, we will increasingly treasure the traditions that spring from within" (Naisbitt and Aburdene, 1990, p. 120).

In summary, the composition of society is an important factor in the provision of learning opportunities for citizens of all ages. In the United States, there are more adults than youth, there is a growing number of older adults, the population as a whole is better educated than ever before, and there is a large minority population. The field of adult education with its orientation to the learners themselves is especially sensitive to these demographic trends—whether by focusing on individual growth or by diagnosing and addressing the needs of special groups.

THE GLOBAL ECONOMY

A second dimension of the social context that has a direct bearing on learning in adulthood is the economic structure. Clearly the American economy is changing and with it the learning needs of adults. In particular there is a recognition of global interdependence, a shift to a service economy, and a change in composition of the labor force.

Americans have become increasingly conscious of the interrelatedness of their lives with the rest of the world. Naisbitt and Aburdene (1990, p. 19) identify the global economy as one of the megatrends for the twenty-first century: "We are in an unprecedented period of accelerated change, perhaps the most breathtaking of which is the swiftness of our rush to all the world's becoming a single economy. Already it may be said that there is no such thing as a U.S. economy, as enmeshed is it in all the other economies of the world." The globalization of economies worldwide is creating a competitive atmosphere that has dramatic implications for adult learning. Petrella (1997) paints a vivid picture of this relationship:

> The globalisation of economies is therefore launching every company, every town, every region, every country into an open confrontation with other companies, towns, regions and countries in arenas from which will emerge triumphant, or at least as survivors, only the strongest, the most competitive, those with the oldest battle scars and those who were astute enough to prepare themselves in good time for the new scuffles associated with globalising markets. Competition, everyone competing against everyone else across the globe, is thus now considered as being the major "must" for every economic agent, whether private-sector or public-sector.
>
> To be competitive in a liberalised, deregulated, privatised and globalising market, every company is obliged, so the theory goes, to adopt a strategy of reducing production costs and improving the quality and range of its goods and services.... One of the most efficient options open to companies for achieving this goal is that of making "aggressive" and intelligent use of human resources, especially those segments thereof which are at the various extremes: the best and the worst qualified, the best and worst paid, the oldest and the youngest. [p. 25]

What does all this mean for adult learning? For one thing, "it does a worker very little good to train specifically for a job with a company that outsources the position, downsizes, or sells to a foreign owner who reorganizes or 'reengineers' the company, selling off pieces, leaving the worker trained and unemployed" (Tomlin, 1997, p. 20). Global economics has led to changing work practices, which require different kinds of preparation and training. This has resulted in the control of education shifting to business. Business is "almost unintentionally evolving new meanings for learning and new methods of delivering education. And it is doing so in ways that are consistent with its fundamental role as business, competitively filling unmet needs in the marketplace. All business visions are anchored in this fundamental belief" (Davis and Botkin, 1994, p. 34). The emphasis now is on improved product and service quality, greater worker responsibility, and teamwork approaches. Adult education and human resource development, in particular, have responded with broad-based workplace literacy programs and training and development packages designed to address a wide range of economy-driven needs. Participation rates also reflect the increasingly job-oriented nature of adult education in America. While in 1969, "adult education courses were nearly evenly split between job-related and non-job-related," in the most current study of participation, "fully 90.6 percent of adults cited career or job-related reasons for educational participation. Clearly, there is a marked increase in the employment orientation of adult education in the United States" (Valentine, 1997, p. 5).

The global economy is having an impact on learning in broader ways too. We have become, in the words of Usher, Bryant, and Johnston (1997, p. 4), "a culture of consumption.... The factory, the assembly line, large-scale manufacturing—are being increasingly displaced by centres of consumption—financial services, small-scale specialised enterprises, shopping malls and superstores, entertainment complexes, heritage and theme parks." This shift is evidenced in a changing relationship between educator and learner to one of a "market relationship between producer and consumer. Knowledge is exchanged on the basis of the performative value it has for the consumer" (p. 14). Educational institutions themselves "become part of the market, selling knowledge as a commodity and increasingly reconstructing themselves as enterprises dedicated to marketing their commodities and to competing in the knowledge 'business'" (p. 14). In a recent article on a community college in Arizona, for example, "its booming enrollment and low overhead" were attributed to the college's "treat[ing] students like customers" and a philosophy whereby education is seen as "a commodity that can be adapted to what the market demands" (Healy, 1998, p. A32).

A second economic shift has been from a society employed in producing goods to one employed in providing services. The decline in industrial labor stems from automation and competition from other countries with low labor costs. Dislocated workers from both the industrial and agricultural sectors, with few if any transferable skills, find themselves in low-skill, low-paying service jobs. Ironically, "the ready supply of displaced workers with limited employable skills will lead to low wages in parts of the service sector and thus will promote the general growth of service-related business" (Charner and Rolzinski, 1987, p. 8). Tomlin (1997, p. 20) cites research that estimates "that the U.S. alone will create 10,000 new jobs a day, every day for the next ten years" and that "many of these jobs will be in the service sector, many more will be in careers that have yet to be invented. These new workers do not yet know what or how they will need to learn."

Concurrent with the shift to a service economy is the shift to what has been called the information society. Our economy increasingly is based on information rather than heavy industry: "Already more workers are engaged in generating, processing, analyzing, and distributing information than are engaged in agriculture, mining, and manufacturing combined" (Hart, 1983, p. 10). Fay, McCune, and Begin (1987, p. 20) estimate that by the year 2000, "80 percent of all workers in the United States will be employed in the information industry.... This will have a major impact on workers as economic units. In an industrial age, workers are expendable cogs in the machine; in an information age (and to a lesser extent, in a service age), human capital is the most valuable capital an organization has." The implications for learning—and in particular for work-related training—are enormous. Already the amount spent annually by business, industry, and government agencies on job-related training is in the billions of dollars and exceeds that spent on public higher education (Rowden, 1996b). Furthermore, since skills learned in preparation for a job or career cannot keep pace with the demands of the world of work, the ability to learn becomes a valuable skill in and of itself.

Developing simultaneously with the emphasis on learning to learn is the notion of the learning organization. To survive in the global economy, an "organization needs to evolve into 'a learning organization' whereby new and expansive patterns are permitted, allowing employees to learn individually and collectively (continually learning how to learn)" (Gardner, 1996b, p. 43). The growing body of literature on the learning organization positions learning, information processing, and problem-solving skills as central to the survival of both the individual worker and the organization. Ulrich (1998) underscores how globalization necessitates the creation of learning organizations. Globalization requires companies "to move people, ideas, products, and information around the world to meet local needs. They [companies] must add new and important ingredients to the mix when making strategy: volatile political situations, contentious global trade issues, fluctuating exchange rates, and unfamiliar cultures. They must be more literate in the ways of international customers, commerce, and competition than ever before. In short, globalization requires that organizations *increase their ability to learn* and collaborate and to manage diversity, complexity, and ambiguity" (p. 126, emphasis added).

Closely related to shifts to a service and information economy are changes in America's labor force. The largest job-growth categories are jobs related to service—cashiers, orderlies, fast food workers—and to information and technology—computer programmers and operators, engineers, teachers, and so on (Rachal, 1989). Not surprisingly, women, minorities, and the elderly are overrepresented in the lower-paying service jobs. Since the middle of this century, however, the labor force has changed from one dominated by blue-collar occupations to one where the majority of jobs are considered white collar. Significant changes in the composition of the workforce are also occurring along racial and ethnic lines. Although white non-Hispanic workers account for the vast majority of workers (73 percent in 1996), "their rate of growth is considerably below that for the black, Asian, and Hispanic groups. Continued rapid growth of the Hispanic population makes it likely that this group will become the second largest ethnic grouping, replacing blacks, by 2006" (Bowman, 1997, p. 4). Perhaps the greatest change of all has been the steady increase of women in the workforce. In 1960, 37.7 percent of women in the population were members of the workforce; in 1994, 58.8 percent participated; and the rate is estimated to be 61.6 percent by the year 2000 (U.S. Bureau of the Census, 1995). Economic necessity and the freeing of occupations traditionally assigned to men have contributed to this change. Cross (1981) observes that "the revolution in women's roles is the result of two complementary forces. On the one hand, social and technological changes push women out of the home; on the other hand, new opportunities in education and the labor market pull women into the new worlds of work and education" (p. 26).

In summary, economic factors are shaping the nature of our society and, by extension, the nature of learning that adults are most likely to undertake. A global economy, the shift to a service and information society, and consequent changes in the configuration of the labor force are determining to a large extent where learning takes place, what is offered, and who participates.

TECHNOLOGY

There is no more apt metaphor for reflecting the rate of technological change than the computer. Itself a major component of our highly technological age, computer language has invaded the ways in which we talk of adult learning. We process students and information; we plan learning activities with an eye to inputs, flow, and outputs; we provide feedback to individual learners and to programs. Indeed, we program learning experiences and ourselves. Technology has had an enormous impact on society and adult learning. It has been instrumental in bringing about the so-called information society, which has created new jobs and eliminated others. The technology-driven information society has also affected adult education.

The move to an information society has been a function of technological developments associated with an information explosion. Within a short span of time, electronic, communication, and information technologies have changed society as a whole and affected how people go about their daily lives. From ordering pizza by computer, to making telephone calls from one's car, to faxing a request to the local radio station, everyday life has been irrevocably influenced by technology.

Concurrent with these technological advances has been an information explosion. It has been estimated that the amount of information in the world doubles every seven years (Apps, 1988, p. 23), and some have projected that information will "soon double every 20 months" (Whitson and Amstutz, 1997, p. 1). Others have speculated that half of what most professionals know when they finish their formal training will be outdated in less than five years, perhaps even months for those in technology-related careers. Thus, the need for continuing education has dramatically escalated with the increase in knowledge production. Not only is there considerably more information than ever before, but links with technology have made its storage, transmission, and access more feasible than ever before. Laser technology in particular is revolutionizing the dissemination of information, as well as its storage and retrieval. A compact disk using laser technology makes it possible to store huge amounts of information in a very small space, and the Internet and World Wide Web have become repositories for more information than any one person could access in a lifetime. Further, the merging of the three technologies of communications, computer, and video-image handling promises to have a significant impact on teaching and learning. "Communications provides the ability to transfer information; computers offer interactivity, control, and storage of information; and video uses images and sound as well as text to enhance information. General-purpose microcomputer workstations have become available that integrate all three technologies.... Workstations integrating the three technologies will be the fundamental, conceptual prototypes for much of the hardware designed and developed for use in all organizations, including schools" (Picciano, 1998, p. 254).

Boucouvalas (1987) and others make the case that a major societal shift, such as moving from an industrial to an information society, results in profound changes in the society's structure. In an industrial society, machine technology extends physical ability; in an information society, computer technology extends mental ability. Material wealth has major value in an industrial society; knowledge and information are key assets in an information society. The social structure changes from hierarchies and bureaucracies to multicentered and horizontal networks; labor movements versus citizen movements are the locus for social change (Boucouvalas, 1987). These changes in society's underlying structure can be seen most dramatically in changes in the workforce. As noted earlier, the shift is eliminating certain classifications of work while creating others not yet dreamed of.

In addition to the creation and elimination of jobs, technological changes are affecting workers in other ways, such as where work is done. As Gardner (1996b, p. 48) observes, "Computer technology frees labor from a particular location.... Knowledge workers can work anywhere; they simply have to have access to a computer connection. Even within the team framework, workers can stay engaged in their mutual tasks even if not in close proximity to each other. Delocalizing work has been touted as one of the more appealing aspects of technological advances in the workplace." Telecommuting, or "home work," some predict, has increased because of the new technologies, and it is considered desirable because it fits in with alternative family patterns (such as more single-parent families), worker concerns for control of time and worksite, and organizational efforts to cut costs and remain flexible by contracting out for services rather than hiring more workers. Estimates of the number of people who currently telecommute vary because of different interpretations of this new work structure. However, estimates for the mid-1990s range from 7 million (Piskurich, 1996) to 8.4 million (Hill, Hawkins, and Miller, 1996).

Yet others have cautioned against the unquestioning adoption of technology in the workplace. Attewell (1996, p. A56) points out that information technologies have created a "productivity paradox" in the workplace. Designed to get more work done more efficiently by fewer employees, information technologies have instead offered more ways to communicate, increased the demand for information, and raised the level of expectations with regard to the print and graphic presentation of material. One result has been a displacement of clerical workers with higher-skill-level professional and managerial workers.

Clearly, technology and the information age that it spawned are changing the nature of adult learning. Professionals whose knowledge becomes outdated in a few years, auto mechanics who must now master sophisticated electronic diagnostic systems, adults who must learn new ways to bank or shop from home computers: all must be able to function in a fast-changing society, and this necessitates continued learning. Technology is not only making learning mandatory, it is providing many of the mechanisms for it to occur. Computer-assisted instruction, teleconferencing, interactive videodisk, the Internet, and the World Wide Web are expanding the possibilities of meeting the growing learning needs of adults.

Simultaneous with the development of technologically sophisticated delivery systems is the development of new roles for educators and trainers. Having access to unlimited information is not the same as being able to search efficiently for the most significant information, or to even know what is most significant. Heclo (1994, p. B2) states that "in the long run, excesses of technology mean that the comparative advantage shifts from those with information glut to those with ordered knowledge, from those who can process vast amounts of blab to those who can explain what is worth knowing and why." Ratinoff (1995, p. 163) points out that the information explosion has had both positive and negative effects: "On the positive side, the myths and riddles of power are more exposed to public scrutiny. To fool all people is very difficult under the present circumstances." On the downside, "information has been growing faster than the individual and institutional capacities required to make sense of the new diversity of signals and messages" (p. 164). The result of this information overload has been "a social craving for simplifications, a popular demand for translating simplicity into action and a preference to reduce action to means" (p. 165). The need for order among information chaos has led to "closing the alternatives. Pre-conceived beliefs, analytical parsimony and political correctness" take the place of grappling with too many alternatives and information overload (p. 173). What is needed, Ratinoff (1995, p. 165) suggests, is to consider "the interaction between the quantity and quality of knowledge."

Whitson and Amstutz (1997) suggest a number of strategies for dealing with the information and technology overload. First, adult educators should "build more and better connections with those who directly teach information access skills," especially librarians, but also computer specialists (p. 133). Educators can also focus on developing students' "higher level thinking skills" such that judgments can be made about the credibility and usefulness of information (p. 137). Since much information is available electronically through the Internet and the World Wide Web, the authors underscore the need for educators themselves to become comfortable in this environment, to the point that they can help learners take advantage of technology. Finally, "we have an obligation to consider the ethical implications of our information access processes.... The rights of poor people to have access to information and the ways in which information should be made accessible to them are important concerns. We need to resist the growing tendency for business, industry, and government to control access to information" (p. 141).

With regard to the ethical questions of access and equity, Winner (1991, p. 164) alerts us to the myth that "a widespread adoption of computers and communications systems, along with broad access to electronic information, will automatically produce a better world for humanity." The more affluent and better-educated adults with home computers have access to information and instructional packages that make them even more informed. On a global level, the "have" nations can communicate and exchange information in ways that will never be a reality to the majority of the world's people. Even job training necessitated by technological change tends to favor the haves. Levison (1995, p. B5) warns against fostering a technology-based social elite where knowledge workers become insulated "from disturbing news and contrary opinions, isolating them from the concerns and problems of the nation's have-nots."

On the other hand, technology's potential for increasing access to learning for people of all ages and possibly all economic levels is unlimited. In more and more communities, computers can be found in libraries, restaurants, laundromats, and other public places. In addition, what is known as WebTV—where for a few hundred dollars one can access the World Wide Web through the television—holds the potential for bringing most of society onto the information superhighway. Naisbitt and Aburdene (1990) argue that technology is "empowering." In their opinion, "there are fewer dictators on the planet today because they can no longer control information.... Computers, cellular phones, and fax machines empower individuals, rather than oppress them, as previously feared" (pp. 303–304).

THE CONVERGENCE OF DEMOGRAPHICS, ECONOMICS, AND TECHNOLOGY

Demographics, economics, and technology forces are closely entwined with each other. Advances in technology, for example, are interrelated with changes in the economic structure. Automation and robotics displace production workers but create other jobs. Technology creates alternative work structures. The need to be competitive in the world market leads to further technological sophistication. Demographics and economics are clearly related. The baby boom cohort that is now in the labor force, for example, is saturating middle and upper management career levels, forcing younger people to consider career alternatives. As another example, the growing number of older adults in our society is having several effects on the economy. Some older adults are being asked to retire early to make room for younger workers; with increased longevity and good health, others are pursuing second or third careers; and some employers, especially those in the service sector, are recognizing the human resource potential of this group and are actively recruiting older workers.

Embedded in this convergence of demographics, economics, and technology is a value system based on the political and economic structure of capitalism. More than a decade ago, Beder (1987, p. 107) explained how these three forces are linked within the value system: "The beliefs undergirding the capitalist system emphasize material values. The health of the system is gauged in terms of national wealth as embodied in the gross national product, and social equality is assessed in terms of economic opportunity—the potential of members of the underclasses to amass more income. Hence, the political and social systems become directed toward ... economic productivity, and economic productivity under the rationale of human capital theory becomes the predominant rationale for all publicly funded social interventions including adult education." This value system directly shapes adult education in the United States in several ways. First, economic productivity becomes "the dominant rationale for all public subsidy of adult education" (p. 109). Second, social justice becomes equated with economic opportunity in that "the just society is a society that provides opportunity for members of the underclasses to amass more income and material goods" and adult education "helps learners acquire the skills and knowledge" to do so (p. 109). The emphasis is on productivity and efficiency, both of which benefit from advances in technology. Thus technology, in the service of economic productivity, converges with changing demographics in shaping the adult learning enterprise.

The global economy in particular seems to be shaping adult learning and the face of adult education worldwide. Youngman (1996, p. 9) points out that the collapse of the Soviet Union and the Eastern bloc has resulted in a "'new world order' and the dominance of a small group of advanced capitalist countries led by the USA.... This new stage [of imperialism] is distinguished by changes taking place in the world economy, driven by the technological revolution and the internationalization of production and trade by the multinational corporations." The implications for adult education reside in the cultural dimension of the new global economy: "Ideologies, language, social values, patterns of behavior, modes of consumption, and cultural institutions in the South are powerfully influenced from the North through the media, advertising, tourism, and other means which shape the way people think and act. Education as an agency of the legitimation and reproduction of the capitalist order is a crucial element of cultural imperialism" (Youngman, 1996, p. 11).

A number of writers would like to see the values and purposes of adult education reexamined in the wake of the wide-scale social and economic changes taking place. In a postmodern world characterized by large-scale changes in global activity resulting in economic, social, and political uncertainty, adult education tends to be an entrepreneurial instrument of the so-called new world order. Adult education is particularly sensitive to a restructured workplace, reliance on technology to produce knowledge, and a market demand for multiskilled workers. Petrella (1997) emphasizes the decreased importance placed on individuals in the new market economy in observing that humans as "resources" take precedence over humans as human beings. As well, knowledge has become an important business commodity that is readily marketed, due, in part, to the explosion of the Internet and other information technologies (Gardner, 1996b; Usher, Bryant, and Johnston, 1997). Finger (1995) and Youngman (1996) believe that adult education is in danger of losing its social action orientation as it focuses on helping "individuals face up to the overwhelming economic and other challenges that threaten their identities and survival in the increasingly dense jungle of a postmodern society" (Finger, 1995, p. 115).

While globalization has extended economic and cultural boundaries, it has also served to fragment society in many ways. For example, although minorities and other ethnic groups may be perceived as valuable contributors within society, conflict results when scarce educational and other resources are allocated. Minority groups may become more isolated from mainstream society. In other ways, too, individuals within society may experience fragmentation as they struggle to make sense of their disordered and sometimes disrupted lives. In a time when nations, companies, and families are splintering, there is little sense of security. As Gardner (1996b, p. 53) points out, "not even in the entrepreneurial world will security be held out as a term of employment. College graduates place their highest priority on finding a secure job. Their challenge, however, has become one of redefining their expectations and finding security in their skills and experiences; a process few have taken seriously nor know how to do."

If the postmodern world is characterized by fragmentation and diversity, it is also characterized by new alliances and interactions. Demographics, the global economy, and technology have come together in adult education in the blurring of the field's content and delivery mechanisms. For example, adult education has been variously divided into formal, nonformal, and informal learning activities (Coombs, Prosser, and Ahmed, 1973). Formal learning takes place in educational institutions and often leads to degrees or credit of some sort. Nonformal learning refers to organized activities outside educational institutions, such as those found in learning networks, churches, and voluntary associations. Informal learning refers to the experiences of everyday living from which we learn something. Today, many formal providers offer learning experiences that are noncredit, leisure oriented, and short term. Similarly, nonformal learning and informal life experiences can be turned into formal, credit-earning activities.

Another blurring can be noted in higher education (Apps, 1989). Once composed of learners eighteen to twenty-two years old, the student body has grayed along with the population. In fact, students twenty-five years of age and older now make up close to 50 percent of all college enrollments in the United States (The College Board, in press). Similar subjects may be taught at the local community college for credit and at the public adult school for noncredit. The part-time adult student taking a course during the day at a college is an adult learner as much as the sixteen year old studying for a high school diploma in a local evening class. There is also a blurring between higher education and business and industry. Many postsecondary institutions have business institutes that provide training and development services to business. Conversely, a growing number of private companies, such as McDonald's Hamburger University and the Rand Graduate Institute, are offering accredited degrees (Eurich, 1985, 1990).

Finally, a blurring of content and delivery is found in such popular slogans as "workplace literacy," "learning to learn," "critical thinking," and "media literacy." Educators, employers, and society at large are focusing attention on developing the skills needed to be productive and informed members of a fast-changing and highly technical society. With the erosion of boundaries in the content and provision of adult learning, we may be witnessing the emergence of what has been called the learning society. Taking human beings rather than educational institutions as its beginning point, the learning society is a response to the social context. Jarvis (1983, p. 51) concludes that "it may be possible to detect its emergence as rapidly changing levels of technology provide people with the social conditions necessary for, and make people aware of, the opportunities to extend their learning throughout the whole of their lives."

SUMMARY

Adult learning does not occur in a vacuum. What one needs or wants to learn, what opportunities are available, the manner in which one learns—all are to a large extent determined by the society in which one lives. This section has discussed several characteristics of American society today that are shaping the nature of learning in adulthood.

Demographics, the global economy, and technology are three forces affecting all of society's endeavors, including adult learning. With regard to the American population, adults outnumber youth, there are more older adults, adults are better educated, and there is more cultural and ethnic diversity among the population than ever before. We have entered a world economy in which "individuals become 'linked' into an international order … by virtue of economic and material interdependence" (Beder, 1987, p. 106). Technology has contributed to, if not caused, the shift to an information society, which is creating dramatic changes in the workforce. Although we have treated them separately, these three forces are interactive and firmly embedded in the American capitalist value system. Adult education both reflects and responds to the forces prevalent in the sociocultural context. Among the implications discussed in the section are the field's responsiveness to special groups of people, the economic productivity rationale behind much of adult education, the potential of technology for enhancing or impeding learning, and the blurring of content and delivery in current adult education.

MEMORY, COGNITION, AND
THE BRAIN

Sharan B. Merriam
Rosemary S. Caffarella

One of the predominant views about adult learning is that learning is an internal process; it involves something happening inside our heads. Cognitive scientists, primarily from the discipline of psychology, have had the longest history of research in this arena. What cognitive scientists do is "attempt to discover the mental functions and processes that underlie observed behavior" (Bruer, 1997, p. 10). These mental functions and processes include, but are not limited to, the study of how people receive, store, retrieve, transform, and transmit information. Neurobiologists, on the other hand, "study the anatomy, physiology, and pathology of the nervous system" (Taylor, 1996, p. 301), including the brain and related systems. They are primarily interested in the structures of the brain and how the brain actually works, including its electrical and chemical systems. With more recent technological advances, like magnetic resonance imaging (MRI) and positron emission tomography (PET), neurobiologists have begun to generate actual pictures of how the brain operates.

In using work from both the cognitive and neurobiological sciences to talk about learning in adulthood, care must be taken because the majority of studies in these two areas have been done with children (for the cognitive sciences) or with animals (in the neurosciences). Still, there are some intriguing ideas that have informed the study of adult learning from both perspectives. The work with adult populations related to cognition has been primarily in the area of memory and aging. This section first highlights that work, presenting an overview of the information processing framework. Next, we explore the concept of knowledge structures or schemas, the effect of prior knowledge and experience on learning, and cognitive and learning styles. These three topics, which are grounded in the cognitive sciences, are important for educators of adults to understand. Key ideas relating to neurobiology and learning are then reviewed. These include how the brain is organized and functions, and the limitations we currently have in connecting this knowledge about the brain to learning and education. The section concludes with a short discussion of the promises of merging the current research in the cognitive and neurobiological sciences for gaining a clearer picture of adult learning.

HUMAN MEMORY

Fear of memory loss is a common concern of people as they age. Parents often observe how much more easily their children can remember such simple things as telephone numbers and computer access codes, while many older adults seem to remember childhood events vividly but sometimes have difficulty remembering the names of people they just met. These observations and images foster the idea that memory loss is a normal result of aging and thus is something we all must accept. Are these perceptions of memory loss accurate, and, if so, what effects do they have on learning in adulthood? Often memory functions are equated with learning or are seen as one of the primary mental processes associated with learning (Huber, 1993). If adults do suffer major changes, especially decline, in their memory functions, it follows that the learning process may also be impaired. To understand how memory can be affected by the aging process, we first need to examine how the process of memory from the cognitive framework is conceptualized.

Since the 1960s, human memory has been studied primarily from the information processing approach (J. Anderson, 1996; Kausler, 1994; Ormrod, 1995; Salthouse, 1992b). The mind is visualized as a computer, with information being entered, stored, and then retrieved as needed. Conceptualizing where people store or file what they learn, termed the *structural aspect of memory,* was the first major focus of study from this perspective. Three categories have been traditionally used to describe the different structures of memory: sensory memory, short-term memory, and long-term memory. More recently there has been a movement away from dividing up the structure of memory in such a definitive manner. This change in thinking has stemmed primarily from the study of working memory, which has been conceptualized in three different ways: as part of long-term memory, as part of or the same as short-term memory, or as the mediator between sensory memory and either long- or short-term memory (J. Anderson, 1996; Kausler, 1994; Ormrod, 1995). For the purposes of our discussion, we discuss human memory within the framework of sensory, working, and long-term memory.

Sensory memory, also called the sensory register, "holds incoming information long enough that it can undergo preliminary cognitive processes" (Ormrod, 1995, p. 218). Primarily through the senses of vision, hearing, and touch, images, sounds, and vibrations are entered into our memory systems. Sensory memory has a very brief storage time of only milliseconds before it either enters our working memory system or is lost. "Working memory is a hypothesized 'entity' or 'process' (the vagueness is deliberate), responsible for preserving information while simultaneously processing the same or other information.... The most salient characteristic of working memory is that it has definite limits, a fact made very apparent when one tries to perform a task containing many steps, none of which are difficult to perform in isolation" (Salthouse, 1992a, p. 39). The storage capacity of working memory is estimated to be from 5 to 30 seconds. Long-term memory has an enormous capacity for storage and is that part of the memory structure that retains information for long periods of time. "It includes memory for specific events and general knowledge that has been gleaned from those events over the years" (Ormrod, 1995, p. 225). Long-term memory has been conceptualized as the most complicated component of the memory system, and therefore has received the most attention in the research literature.

In recent years our understanding of long-term memory has moved from viewing it as one monolithic system "to one that is less hierarchical, involving several different kinds of memory, each playing a significant role" (Taylor, 1997b, p. 293). Most of the research on long-term memory has involved explicit (or declarative) memory, "the term used for things which we can consciously recall" (J. Anderson, 1996, p. 229). "This form of memory is more sensitive and prone to interference, but it is also invaluable, providing the ability for personal autobiography and cultural evolution" (Taylor, 1997b, p. 263). Implicit (or nondeclarative) memory, on the other hand, "concerns itself with memories that we are not conscious we have" (J. Anderson, 1996, p. 229). Although these memories are developed unconsciously and thus form a hidden world we know little about, "people are influenced by [these types of memories] without any awareness they are remembering" (Schacter, 1996, p. 161). Several authors have provided useful descriptions of several forms of implicit memory, including procedural knowledge (skills and habits), category-level knowledge, conditioning, and priming, and they describe practical examples of how these types of implicit memory are used (J. Anderson, 1996; Schacter, 1996; Squire, Knowlton, and Musen, 1993; Taylor, 1997b). Classic examples of implicit memories are riding a bike, which is procedural knowledge, and the "acquisition of rules often found in grammar [involving categorical knowledge]. Grammar is a particularly good example of implicit memory, where people have acquired abstract rules, but are unable to articulate what guides their speech and writing" (Taylor, 1997b, p. 264).

The second major focus of study within the information processing framework has been how we process information. The processing aspect consists of "the mental activities that we perform when we try to put information into memory (learn), or make use of it at some later date (remember)" (Schulz and Ewen, 1988, p. 134). Usually the memory process is divided into three phases (J. Anderson, 1996; Ormrod, 1995; Schacter, 1996). The encoding or acquisition phase is the initial process in which the information is entered into the system. Filing this material for future use is termed the storage or retention phase. The final phase, retrieval, describes how you get material out of storage when needed. Two of the most common methods of retrieval are recall, or bringing forth "to-be-remembered" information, and recognition, which involves choosing from a group of possible answers. As we well remember from our school testing days of essay versus multiple-choice exams, "recall is considered to be a more demanding test of retrieval than is recognition" (Schulz and Ewen, 1988, p. 138).

A number of alternatives have been proposed for how the structural components fit within the process model (J. Anderson, 1996; Ormrod, 1995; Salthouse, 1992a). The most common explanation is that information from our environment is registered within sensory memory through our visual, auditory, and tactile senses. Material is then selectively transferred or encoded into working memory. The control system of selective attention determines what is important enough to be moved into working memory. There is considerable flexibility with what can be done with the information in working memory. It "can be used as a cue to retrieve other information from long-term memory, it can be elaborated, it can be used to form images, it is used in thinking, it can be structured to be placed in long-term or secondary memory, or if nothing is done with it, it can be discarded" (Di Vesta, 1987, p. 211).

Because the functions of working memory are complex and its time and capacity are limited, two major control processes are used to sort and file the data: chunking and automatization. Chunking essentially is organizing the information in groups or patterns (a phone number in three chunks—970–351–2119, for example), while automatization allows for a chunk of information to become so familiar that a person can handle it without recall thinking (Kausler, 1994; Ormrod, 1995). The material structured in working memory for long-term memory is then encoded into that memory bank for permanent storage. The information "is rarely stored in long-term memory exactly as it was received. Individuals tend to remember the 'gist' of what they see and hear rather than word-for-word sentences or precise mental images" (Ormrod, 1995, p. 226). The material is organized "so that related pieces of information tend to be associated together" (Ormrod, 1995, p. 226) by highly organized episodes (by time and place) or by meaningful relations to earlier stored material. This type of processing is sometimes referred to as deep processing versus the shallow processing done at the working memory level. The information is then retrieved as needed from this long-term storage.

MEMORY AND AGING

A great deal of research from the information processing framework has been conducted on the topic of memory and aging (J. Anderson, 1996; Kausler, 1994; Rybash, Hoyer, and Roodin, 1986; Salthouse, 1985, 1992a; Siegler, Poon, Madden, and Welsh, 1996; A. D. Smith, 1996). The general consensus from that work is that certain memory functions do decline with age. Nevertheless, a number of authors have cautioned that because of methodological considerations and the variables being studied, this work must be interpreted with care. The vast majority of it has focused on comparing young adults (usually college students) with older adults by using cross-sectional designs (Bee, 1996). These two factors combined make it difficult to generalize across age groups because of subject and cohort bias. Subject bias comes from using people in a study who do not necessarily represent the general population (such as college students versus the broad population of young adults). Cohort bias or effect "is any difference between groups of adults of varying ages that is due not to age or aging, or to any other developmental process, but simply to the fact that the different age groups have grown up under different historical and cultural circumstances" (Bee, 1996, p. 11). Moreover, most of this research has been conducted primarily in laboratory settings using memory tasks and activities, such as repeating back nonsense words and lists of random numbers. The primary criticism leveled against this type of research on memory is that these tasks and skills are generally artificial and taken out of the context of everyday life. A response to this criticism in recent years has been to design "ecologically valid" research that takes into account the everyday learning demands of adults (Agrawal and Kumar, 1992; N. Anderson, 1996; Knopf, 1995; Langer, 1997; Rybash, Hoyer, and Roodin, 1986). With these limitations in mind, we offer a summary of this research on memory in adulthood.

Sensory and Working Memory

In general, few clearly defined changes have been found in sensory memory as people age. Because there are fairly major changes with age in both vision and hearing, one would expect to see these changes reflected in sensory memory. Yet only minor deficits have been found, although it is often difficult with testing procedures to distinguish between age-related physiological decline in the senses themselves, especially hearing, and actual decrements in the process of sensory memory.

Working memory, on the other hand, with its definite limits, "is considered by many researchers to be a potentially important mediator of the relations between age and cognition" (Salthouse, 1992a, p. 39). More specifically, the processing speed within working memory has been shown to be very important in accounting for differences in the memory performances of older adults (Bors and Forrin, 1995; Salthouse, 1992a, 1992b, 1995; A. D. Smith, 1996). Older adults appear to process materials more slowly, especially ones that are more complex in nature. One of the explanations for this slowing of the processing of information seems to be the "older adults' capacity to simultaneously perform a cognitive task while trying to remember some of the information for a later memory task" (Smith, 1996, p. 241). In other words, it appears to be more difficult for older adults to both respond immediately to whatever stimulus triggered working memory and store pertinent information in long-term memory. Salthouse (1995, p. 124) does caution, however, that this "processing speed interpretation is still at the speculative stage," and much more research needs to be completed on working memory.

Long-Term Memory

As with working memory, age deficits are also more commonly found in long-term memory (Bee, 1996; Rybash, Hoyer, and Roodin, 1986; Smith, 1996). Three major differences have surfaced in long-term memory for older versus younger learners: changes in the encoding or acquisition of material, the retrieval of information, and the speed of processing. Few changes have been noted in the storage or retention capacity of long-term memory over the life span.

The question that often surfaces in reviewing the process related to long-term memory is whether it is more difficult for adults as they age to get information into the system (to encode it) or get it out (to retrieve it). The response to this question appears to be both. It is not yet clear which part of the process creates more difficulty (Bee, 1996; Smith, 1996). Encoding problems are most often associated with the organization of information. Specifically, older adults appear to be less efficient at organizing new material. Possible explanations of why organization is a problem relates to the amount and type of prior knowledge they already possess. According to Ormrod (1995, p. 261), "Storage processes such as meaningful learning and elaboration can occur only to the extent that learners have existing knowledge to which they can connect new material." In addition, "if this new information is clearly viewed by the person as 'wrong' within the context of what they believe about the world, they may sometimes ignore the information altogether" (p. 266). In other words, this type of information may never enter long-term memory because it is incompatible with what the person already knows.

On the retrieval side, changes are most often noted in the recall versus recognition of information. In tests of recall, for example, major differences have been demonstrated for older and younger people, whereas in recognition activities, the differences are small or nonexistent, although the retrieval time may be slower (Bee, 1996). Many older adults do "know" things, but "they can not readily or quickly bring [them] to mind. If they are given a hint, or reminded of the item at some later time, the memory [may] come back" (Bee, 1996, p. 162). Another aspect of retrieval that is often taken as a given is that older persons can retrieve "ancient memories" better than younger people, along with the accompanying myth that older people can clearly remember events in their distant past but have trouble recalling recent events. Rather, it appears that this reversal of memory strengths—remote memories are stronger than recent memories—may be a natural phenomenon that occurs at all ages, not just with older people. We all seem better able to recall occurrences that happened to us in the distant or far past than in very recent past.

In terms of the speed of processing, adults do seem to have more difficulty with speeded tasks, especially ones that are complex (as was also noted with working memory). When tests for memory tasks are paced—meaning that the time given per item or between items is fixed—age deficits definitely show an increase (Salthouse, 1985; Smith, 1996). Salthouse (1995) and Smith (1996) account for at least part of these differences in speeded tasks as a slowing of both the encoding and retrieval processes in both long-term and working memory.

In summary, in relation to long-term memory it appears that older adults may not acquire or retrieve information as well as do younger adults, nor do they organize information as effectively. This line of research may have limited generalizability because of the research designs, the subjects, the memory activities tested, and the separation of the research from the real world of the adult learner.

Real-Life Memories

In response to some of the criticisms of memory research just cited, a different approach has been taken by placing memory tasks in the context of everyday adult lives, called functional memory by some researchers (N. Anderson, 1996). This strand of research, which fosters what has been termed ecological validity, has received little attention, primarily because it is affected by so many different variables and is still considered controversial by some researchers (J. Anderson, 1996). The term *ecological validity* assumes that the tasks being studied are meaningful to the person and accurately reflect real-life adult experiences. These studies use a variety of memory tests, from "memory for text" formats, which include reviews of sentences, paragraphs, and stories versus single words and symbols, to memory skills for everyday activities, such as keeping appointments and remembering what items to buy at the grocery store (N. Anderson, 1996; Knopf, 1995; Luszcz, 1992). These studies also address some of the other concerns voiced by scholars of the contextual approach, such as the person's needs and motivation, the specificity of the task, and situational variables. The evidence is mixed as to whether there is less decline when using memories that are grounded in actual situations versus the more artificial tasks used in laboratory studies (Smith, 1996).

Fostering Memory Capacity and Skills

The assumption underlying the research on memory is that memory capacity and skills form one of the keys to how adults learn. Formal memory training, the most structured approach to building memory skills, has been shown to be useful in helping older adults cope with memory deficits (Bee, 1996; Rybash, Hoyer, and Roodin, 1986). This training has most often focused on the teaching of encoding strategies, such as practicing rehearsal information or fostering the use of mnemonics (devices for helping people improve their memory). For example, Yesavage (1983) taught older adults to improve their name and face recall using visual imagery as a mnemonic. Moreover, Perlmutter and Hall (1985) have suggested teaching adults about metamemory—the understanding of the way the memory system works. A number of authors have suggested ways to integrate training in memory skills into formal learning programs for adults: providing both verbal and written cues, such as advance organizers and overheads, when introducing new material to learners; using mnemonics and rehearsal strategies; and giving opportunities to apply the new material as soon after the presentation as possible. (For a thorough discussion of these ideas, see Knox, 1986; Di Vesta, 1987; Ormrod, 1995; West, Farmer, and Wolff, 1991.)

Adults learning on their own may also find it helpful to use memory aids in their learning activities (Rybash, Hoyer, and Roodin, 1986). These can come in many forms, from structured checklists for learning a new skill to personal note taking on items of interest. For example, someone might jot down in a pocket notebook interesting new words she encountered each day. She could then practice using these words until they became a natural part of her vocabulary.

Cognitive psychologists, in addition to their work on memory and aging, have provided us with a number of other important concepts related to learning in adulthood. Three of those concepts—knowledge structures, the role of prior knowledge and experience, and learning and cognitive styles—are discussed next in the section.

KNOWLEDGE STRUCTURES

Within the cognitive framework, the emphasis is on what learners know versus how they behave. This knowing involves both the acquisition of knowledge, discussed in the section on human memory, and the actual structure of that knowledge (J. Anderson, 1996; Bruer, 1993; Cervero, 1988; Shuell, 1986). In this perspective, considerable importance is placed on prior knowledge as well as new knowledge being accumulated. Since it is assumed that most adults have a greater store of prior knowledge than children, understanding the role that this knowledge plays in learning is critical. In thinking through the possible connections of prior knowledge to learning in adulthood, the concept of schemas provides a useful framework. (See J. Anderson, 1996; Di Vesta, 1987; Ormrod, 1995; Rumelhart and Norman, 1978.)

Schemas "represent categorical knowledge ..., [that is] concepts in terms of supersets, parts, and other attribute value pairs" (J. Anderson, 1996, pp. 155–156). "People often form schemas about events as well as objects; such event schemas are often called scripts" (Ormrod, 1995, p. 264). These schemas, which may be embedded within other schemas or may stand alone, are filled with descriptive materials and are seen as the building blocks of the cognitive process. Schemas are not just passive storehouses of experience, however; they are also active processes whose primary function is to facilitate the use of knowledge. "It seems that schemas are a major mechanism for elaborating material ..., and are also a major mechanism for reconstructing memories" (J. Anderson, 1996, p. 216).

We all carry around with us our own individualized set of schemata that reflect both our experiences and our worldview. Therefore, as adult learners, each of us comes to a learning situation with a somewhat different configuration of knowledge and how it can be used. For example, some participants in a workshop on diversity in the workplace may bring to that experience firm beliefs that diversity is a worthwhile goal based on their positive experiences with women and people of color. Others may not believe in diversity at all, and view it as an easy way for "some people" to get hired. And still others may be downright angry, either because they believe they have been discriminated against or passed over for a promotion because they were of the "wrong color" or gender. Therefore, each learner in the workshop not only comes with different schema sets but also departs having learned very different things—even though all were exposed to basically the same material.

In categorizing schema types, two kinds of knowledge are most often distinguished: declarative knowledge and procedural knowledge. Anderson (1993) describes declarative knowledge as "factual knowledge that people can report or describe"; procedural knowledge, by contrast, "is knowledge people can only manifest in performance" (p. 18). We may be able to describe two or three different models for instruction (declarative knowledge), for example, but when we try to put these models into action (procedural knowledge), we may fail miserably. Because the question is open whether learning facts or knowing how to perform comes first, the scenario just described could also be reversed: a person may be an excellent instructor and yet have no specific knowledge of instructional models.

According to Rumelhart and Norman (1978), three different modes of learning fit the schema framework: *accretion,* meaning the daily accumulation of information that is usually equated with learning facts; *tuning,* which includes slow and gradual changes in current schema; and *restructuring,* involving both the creation of new schema and reorganization of those already stored. Many current models of memory reflect only learning by the accretion or fact-gathering process. Educators, however, are well aware that most learning in adulthood goes far beyond the simple memorization of facts. The expectation is that adults will be able to put those facts to good use in their everyday living, whether as workers, parents, spouses, friends, and so on. Therefore, the processes of tuning and restructuring of information, as well as both declarative and procedural knowledge, become vital in adult learning. The general processes of problem solving and critical thinking are good examples of the importance of these constructs. Specifically, in most problem-solving situations, we are trying to fit new ideas (declarative knowledge) and ways of acting (procedural knowledge) into earlier patterns of thinking and doing (our current schemas). If we are unable to change our earlier thought patterns (that is, fine-tune or restructure them), our chances of being able to frame and act on problems from a different perspective are remote, if not impossible.

In addition to these three different modes of learning (accretion, tuning, and restructuring) cognitive scientists also cite the importance of a fourth process, metacognition, defined as "the ability to think about thinking, to be consciously aware of oneself as a problem solver, and to monitor and control one's mental processing" (Bruer, 1993, p. 67). Metacognition is often viewed as the highest level of mental activity and is especially needed for complex problem solving.

PRIOR KNOWLEDGE AND EXPERIENCE

One key assumption underlying the concept of schemas is that "learning is cumulative in nature—nothing has meaning or is learned in isolation from prior experience. This assumption has a pedigree dating back to Dewey, who said, 'no one can think about anything without experience and information about it'" (Cervero, 1988, p. 41). In addition, many adult educators, such as Knowles (1980), Caffarella (1994), MacKeracher (1996), and Daley (1998), have also spoken to the importance of acknowledging adults' prior knowledge and experience as integral to the learning process. In exploring the role of prior knowledge and experience in learning, two ideas are important: the amount of prior knowledge and experience and its nature.

In terms of the amount of prior knowledge and experience one possesses, the difference between those who know a great deal about what they are experiencing (termed experts) and those who know very little (novices) is key. A person can be an expert in a variety of areas from growing tomatoes to skiing. According to Sternberg (1995, p. 10), "Perhaps the most fundamental difference between experts and novices is that experts bring more knowledge to solving problems ... and do so more effectively than novices." In addition, experts are able to solve problems faster and in a more economical way, have stronger self-monitoring skills, and are able to view and solve problems at a deeper level than novices (Ferry and Ross-Gordon, 1998; Sternberg, 1995; Tennant and Pogson, 1995). J. Anderson (1996, pp. 283, 292, 294) has observed that experts appear to solve problems more effectively and more quickly because of the following processing changes:

- They switch from explicit use of declarative [factual] knowledge to direct application of procedural [performance] knowledge.
- They learn the sequences of actions required to solve the problem or portions of the problem [known as tactical learning].
- They develop new constructs for representing key aspects of a problem.
- They can recognize chunks in problems which are patterns of elements that repeat over problems.

J. Anderson (1996, p. 273) contends that "no one develops expertise without a great deal of hard work ... [and] the difference between ... novices and ... experts increases as we look at more difficult problems."

In further examination of the issue of a novice versus expert learner, many authors (for example, J. Anderson, 1996; Glaser, 1984, 1987; Glaser and Chi, 1988; Tennant and Pogson, 1995) have noted that being an expert is related to certain domains or subject matter areas. More specifically, experts acquire ways of organizing problems that are "optimally suited to problems in a [specific] domain" (J. Anderson, 1996, p. 289). And "as people become more expert in a domain, they develop a better ability to store problem information in long-term memory and to retrieve it" (p. 296). Educators have often observed that being an expert in one area does not necessarily translate into being an expert in another, no matter what the learner's motivation or background.

Many graduate students, for example, although very perceptive and advanced in their own fields of study, may have a great deal of trouble completing statistical and advanced research design courses that are quantitatively based. This is especially true of students who are not mathematically inclined. Moreover, some people become experts in carpentry or tracing genealogy, while others view these tasks as beyond their capabilities.

Therefore, in helping adults connect their current experience to their prior knowledge and experience, we need to be knowledgeable about the amount of prior knowledge they possess in a particular area and design our learning activities accordingly. For example, in teaching a group of expert instructors of adults, it probably does little good to outline just one instructional model, even when this model is the newest and supposedly the most complete model. They can probably think of every exception under the sun as to why this model will not work with all of their students. It would make more sense to ask these instructors to look at alternative models, including this new model, then have them problem-solve which of these models or parts of these models have worked best for them in what type of situations. By following this plan, the participants' level of expertise would be acknowledged, they would be asked to think more deeply about the many situations they have faced in teaching, and they would need to use their problem-solving abilities related to their prior knowledge and experience as instructors.

It would be helpful, in addition, to know how the transition between being a novice and being an expert takes place in order to facilitate learning from prior knowledge and experience. To this end, J. Anderson (1996), Glaser (1987), Chi, Glaser, and Farr (1988), and Sternberg (1995), among others, have provided comprehensive descriptions of the development of expertise that are useful in designing learning activities to assist adults in moving along the continuum from novice to expert.

COGNITIVE STYLE AND LEARNING STYLE

Another important aspect of cognition related to learning in adulthood is the notion of cognitive style. Cognitive styles are characterized as consistencies in information processing that develop in concert with underlying personality traits. They are reflected in "how individuals typically receive and process information" (Joughin, 1992, p. 4) and encompass the ways people see and make sense of their world and attend to different parts of their environment. Some people tend to look at problems from a global perspective, while others are more interested in taking in the detail (Flannery, 1993c). The latter types, which Flannery labels analytical information processors, want information in a step-by-step manner and tend to perceive information in an abstract and objective manner. In contrast "the global learners process information in a simultaneous manner. The ideas or experiences are seen all at once, not in any observable order" (Flannery, 1993c, p. 16). In addition, global learners perceive information in a concrete and subjective manner.

A number of cognitive-style dimensions, including the concepts of global and analytical processing styles, have been identified through research (Bonham, 1987; Joughin, 1992; Kolb, 1984; Messick, 1976, 1984, 1996). The outstanding feature of these varying dimensions is their tendency to be bipolar. In contrasting people's cognitive styles, we tend to label people as being at either end of the continuum, which is "probably not complex enough to capture the essence of individual differences among human beings" (Bonham, 1988, p. 15). For the most part, cognitive styles are considered relatively stable.

Although a great deal of research has been conducted on cognitive styles, much of the research has been done with children, and "no style has led to clear implications with respect to adult learning" (Joughin, 1992, p. 4). Therefore it is still unclear how this work may relate to helping adults learn more effectively. Hiemstra and Sisco (1990) have conjectured that knowledge about cognitive styles might assist instructors in predicting how learners are "likely to form typical learning tasks such as remembering, selecting, comparing, focusing, reflecting, and analyzing" information (p. 241). In addition, Flannery (1993c) has asserted that "teaching, texts and structures can be adapted to teach to different" cognitive styles (p. 19).

A related yet somewhat different phenomenon is the concept of learning style. The literature describing cognitive and learning style is rather confusing; some authors use the two terms interchangeably (see Tennant, 1988; Toye, 1989), others view *cognitive style* as the more encompassing term (Kirby, 1979), and still others see *learning style* as the more inclusive term (Hiemstra and Sisco, 1990; James and others, 1996). Clearly there is no common definition of learning style, nor is there a unified theory on which this work is based (Bonham, 1987, 1988; Claxton and Murrell, 1987; Flannery, 1993a; Sternberg, 1990b). Learning style "attempts to explain learning variation between individuals in the way they approach learning tasks" (Toye, 1989, pp. 226–227). More specifically, James and Blank (1993, pp. 47–48) "define *learning style* as the complex manner in which, and conditions under which, learners most efficiently and most effectively perceive, process, store and recall what they are attempting to learn." Although this definition and other parallel definitions of learning style (for example, Smith, 1982) are quite similar to cognitive style, it appears that the real difference between these two concepts lies in the emphasis placed by learning style researchers on the learning situation versus the more general notion of how people perceive, organize, and process information. Therefore, those who study learning style usually place the emphasis on both the learner and the learning environment (Hiemstra and Sisco, 1990; James and Blank, 1993).

It is also important to acknowledge that learning styles may be in part culturally based (Anderson, 1988; Bell, 1994; Brookfield, 1990; Macias, 1989). Anderson (1988, p. 4), for example, asserts that "it would seem feasible that different ethnic groups, with different cultural histories, different adaptive approaches to reality, and different socialization practices, would differ concerning their respective learning styles." He goes on to observe that "there is no such thing as one style being 'better than another,' although in our country [the United States] the Euro-American style is projected by most institutions as the one which is most valued" (p. 6). Anderson characterizes the Euro-American style as primarily field independent, analytic, and nonaffective, which to him reflects primarily male and acculturated minority views. In contrast, he views a non-Western style (meaning such groups as American Indians, African Americans, and many Euro-American females) as field dependent, relational and holistic, and affective. Bell's (1994) research with African Americans confirms some of Anderson's thinking on learning styles. Bell's findings support "a holistic African American learning style ... which consistently reflects a relational style.... The relational style has been defined as a preference for a whole-to-parts (rather than parts-to-whole) analysis of information, a perceptual vigilance for person social cues over object cues, and a preference for contextually 'rich' over contextually 'sterile' (abstract) learning/problem-solving structures" (p. 57).

Despite the lack of uniform agreement about which elements constitute a learning style, it seems apparent that learning-style inventories, unlike most cognitive-style instruments, have proved useful in helping both learners and instructors alike become aware of their personal learning styles and their strengths and weaknesses as learners and teachers. What must be remembered in using these instruments, however, is that each inventory measures different things, depending on how the instrument's author has defined learning style. In using the variety of learning-style inventories available, it is therefore important to help learners understand how the author of the instrument has conceptualized learning style. (For a review of these instruments see Smith, 1982; Bonham, 1987; James and Blank, 1993.) Some of the most popular instruments used with adults have been Kolb's Learning Style Inventory (1984) and Grasha-Riechmann's Student Learning Style Scales (Hruska, Riechmann, and Grasha, 1982). It is also important to remember that "learning style instruments are best used as tools to create awareness that learners differ and as starting points for individual learners' continued investigation of themselves as learners" (Hiemstra and Sisco, 1990, p. 240). This careful use of learning-style inventories, especially in making programming decisions about learners, is especially crucial; James and Blank (1993, p. 55) have observed that "although various authors claim strong reliability and validity for their instruments, a solid research base for many of these claims does not exist."

More recently Sternberg (1994a, 1996c) has proposed a new term, *thinking styles,* which seems very similar, if not identical, to *learning styles.* Sternberg (1994a) defines a thinking style as "a preferred way of using one's abilities. It is not in itself an ability but rather a preference. Hence, various styles are not good or bad" (p. 36). Although Sternberg has described his theory of thinking styles primarily in the context of children, and more specifically childhood education, many components of his theory would also be useful in understanding the thinking patterns of adults. His work on thinking styles is grounded in ten general characteristics of styles, such as "styles can vary across tasks and situations, people differ in strengths of stylistic preferences, styles are socialized, and styles can vary across the life span—they are not fixed" (Sternberg, 1996c, pp. 349–350). Sternberg uses the concept of mental self-government, patterned after the kind of governments and government branches that exist worldwide, to describe his theory of thinking styles. "According to this theory, people can be understood in terms of the functions, forms, levels, scope, and leanings of government" (Sternberg, 1996c, p. 351). Table 4-1 sets out the styles. Sternberg (1994a, p. 39) emphasizes the importance of taking into account people's thinking styles in designing learning programs and cautions that most instructors are best at teaching people "who match their own styles of thinking and learning … and tend to overestimate the extent to which their students share their own styles."

In summary, scholars studying learning from a cognitive perspective have added a great deal to our knowledge about learning in adulthood. Some of the major contributions described thus far in this section are our understanding of memory and how aging may affect memory processes, how our knowledge is organized in schemas, what effect prior knowledge and experience have on learning, and the concepts of cognitive and learning style. We now turn to a discussion of one of the newest research arenas related to adult learning, the neurobiology of learning.

Table 4-1. Styles of Mental Self-Government.

Style	Characterization
Functions	
Legislative	Likes to create, invent, design, do things his or her own way, have little assigned structure
Executive	Likes to follow directions, do what he or she is told, be given structure
Judicial	Likes to judge and evaluate people and things
Forms	
Monarchic	Likes to do one thing at a time, devoting to it almost all energy and resources
Hierarchic	Likes to do many things at once, setting priorities for which to do when and how much time and energy to devote to each
Oligarchic	Likes to do many things at once, but has trouble setting priorities
Anarchic	Likes to take a random approach to problems; dislikes systems, guidelines, and practically all constraints
Levels	
Global	Likes to deal with big picture, generalities, abstractions
Local	Likes to deal with details, specifics, concrete examples
Scope	
Internal	Likes to work alone, focus inward, be self-sufficient
External	Likes to work with others, focus outward, be interdependent
Leaning	
Liberal	Likes to do things in new ways, defy conventions
Conservative	Likes to do things in tried-and-true ways, follow conventions

Source: Adapted from Sternberg, Robert J. "Allowing for Thinking Styles." *Educational Leadership,* Volume 52, Number 3, pages 36–40. (Figure 1, page 38). Alexandria, VA: Association for Supervision and Curriculum Development. Copyright © 1994 ASCD. Reprinted by permission. All rights reserved.

NEUROBIOLOGY AND LEARNING

Although the cognitive sciences have contributed a great deal to our knowledge about learning in adulthood, one of the most fascinating frontiers in the study of learning is that of the neurobiological basis of learning. This work is grounded in the study of neurobiology: "the life sciences that involve the anatomy, physiology, and the pathology of the nervous system" (Taylor, 1996). Although most of our knowledge about the linkage of our brains to our minds is currently only in the form of working hypotheses, what we might learn from scientists who study the physical functions of the brain and its related systems has the possibility of moving our understanding of learning significantly forward. Viewing the devastation of the memory and learning capacity of a person with advanced Alzheimer's disease or a massive stroke brings home to each of us the innate and yet almost mystical ways in which the brain functions.

The image of the computer has been the primary way we have pictured how the brain works. But more recently scholars have argued that the computer is "an inappropriate model because a computer is developed, programmed, and run by an external force, and our brain isn't" (Sylwester, 1995, p. 18). Edelman (as cited by Sylwester, 1995) has suggested a better model:

That the electrochemical dynamics of our brain's development and operation resemble the rich, layered ecology of a jungle environment. A jungle has no external developer, no predetermined goals. Indeed, it's a messy place characterized more by organic excess than by goal-directed economy and efficiency. No one organism or group runs the jungle.... So it is with our brain, Edelman argues. Think of the vast number of highly connected neural networks that make up our brains as the neural equivalent of the complex set of jungle organisms that respond variously to environmental challenges. The natural selection processes that shape a jungle over long periods of time also have shaped our brain over an extensive period, and they shape our brain's neural networks over our lifetime. [Sylwester, 1995, pp. 18–19]

Thus, from Sylwester's perspective, "learning becomes a delicate but powerful dialogue between genetics and the environment.... Our brain is powerfully shaped by genetics, development, and experience—but it also then actively shapes the nature of our own experiences and the culture in which we live" (p. 21). This image of the brain as a jungle raises in Sylwester's mind, among others (for example, *Scientific American,* 1992), many questions about how we conceptualize learning and what the implications might be in the future for the teaching and learning process. What becomes very clear is that the connections between what we know about how the brain functions and learning are very complex, and therefore the majority of work is still in its infancy in terms of having practical relevance to adult learning.

The way the brain is organized and functions has captured the notice of the general public as well as continued study by the scientific community (Bissette, 1996; Boucouvalas, 1988b; De Beauport, 1996; Lemonick, 1995; Pert, 1997; Restak, 1995; *Scientific American,* 1992; Sylwester, 1995). "For good reason, the brain is sometimes hailed as the most complex object in the universe. It comprises a trillion cells, 100 billion of them neurons linked in networks that give rise to intelligence, creativity, emotion, consciousness and memory" (Fischback, 1992, p. 51). One of the most striking features of the brain "are the large, seemingly symmetric cerebral hemispheres" (p. 48) that sit on a central core or base. The two hemispheres are connected by the corpus callosum, a large band of nerve fibers that provides interactions between the two sides and allows the two hemispheres to collaborate on many tasks. The largest part of the brain, which consists of these two hemispheres, "contains an outer layer of gray matter called the cerebral cortex and underlying white matter that relays information to the cortex" (Lemonick, 1995, p. 46). The cerebral cortex (or cortex), about the size of an office desk when spread out, is made up of "the most evolutionary ancient part of the cortex [the limbic system] ... and the larger, younger neocortex [which] is divided into frontal, temporal, parietal and occipital lobes" (Fischback, 1992, p. 51).

The limbic system is "our brain's principal regulator of emotions. It also influences the selection and classification of experiences that our brain stores as long-term memory.... Because the limbic system plays important roles in processing both emotion and memory, emotion is an important ingredient in processing many memories" (Sylwester, 1995, p. 44). The amygdala appears to be the main structure within the limbic system for processing emotion, while the hippocampus, also part of the limbic system, appears to play an important role in converting short-term memories into long-term ones. Also embedded within the limbic system are other structures, such as the thalamus and hypothalamus, which also assist in regulating our emotional life and physical safety. The thalamus is an especially important part of the system because it is a major relay center for information coming into the brain. The other four lobes have been found to have very specific, but not exclusive, functions, such as the occipital lobe for vision and the frontal lobe for planning, language expression, and speech. The central core or base of the brain on which the major parts of the brain rest consists of "structures such as the medulla, which regulates the autonomic functions (including respiration, circulation, and digestion), and the cerebellum, which coordinates movement (Fischback, 1992, p. 51).

How information is exchanged within the structures of the brain has fascinated neurobiologists and laypeople alike. Although we have a number of newer technologies, such as magnetic resonance imaging and positron-emission tomography, that give us clearer pictures of the way the brain operates, we still do not know for sure how the system truly functions. One of the most popular visions is that "most messages involve neuron-to-neuron communication ... [whereby] a neuron constantly receives messages from and sends messages to other cells" (Sylwester, 1995, p. 29). "A typical neuron collects signals from others through a host of fine structures called dendrites. The neuron sends out spikes of electrical activity through a long thin strand known as an axon, which splits into thousands of branches" (Hinton, 1992, p. 145). The communication among neurons is mediated by chemical molecules, called neurotransmitters, "that are released at specialized contacts called synapses" (Fischback, 1992, p. 50). These neurotransmitters can be classified into three types, with the peptides, such as endorphin, being the largest and most complex form. It is at these synapses that "the electrical and chemical brain seemed to merge" (Pert, 1997). The neurotransmitters send either "excitatory or inhibitory messages to the receiving neurons.... Neural activity in our brain is fortunately much more inhibitory than excitatory. At any moment, we focus our attention, limit our activity, and ignore most of our memories. Imagine life with a principally excitatory brain that continually attended to everything, carried out all possible actions, and had continual open access to all prior experiences!" (Sylwester, 1995, p. 36).

What is critical about this internal transmission process is that "information in our brain flows in multiplex patterns" (Sylwester, 1995, p. 39) and involves parallel processing. "Parallel processing means that many conscious and unconscious actions occur simultaneously within circuitry that includes all sorts of interconnections and feedback loops.... At some level, everything seems connected to everything else" (Sylwester, 1995, pp. 39–40). These multiple connections and patterns mean that information moves not in a linear fashion but in highly complex and multilayered ways. In addition, despite the fact that we continue to lose brain cells as we age, it appears that there is also an inherent "plasticity (i.e., modifiability and regenerative capacity) of the neuronal structures" (Boucouvalas, 1988b, p. 16). In fact, "many structures of the brain appear to be modified by enriching *experiences* (particularly exposure to a variety of experiences).... In other words, the brain appears to be a plastic organ responding to shaping and modifiability by interaction with the external culture and environment" (Boucouvalas, 1988b, p. 16).

More recently, Pert (1997) has challenged the idea that the brain is the only part of us that can gather, process, and share information, more specifically emotional messages. Based on her findings that the peptides and other informational or chemical substances and their receptors are found in the body's nerves of all kinds, it would then follow that emotions could be stored and mediated by other parts of the body. Therefore, Pert hypothesizes that "we could no longer consider the emotional brain to be confined to the classical locations of the amygdala, hippocampus, and hypothalamus. ... These recent discoveries are important for appreciating how memories are stored not only in the brain, but in a *psychosomatic network* extending into the body ... all the way out along pathways to internal organs and the very surface of our skin. I'd say that the fact memory is encoded or stored at the receptor level means that memory processes are emotion-driven and unconscious (but, like other receptor-mediated processes, can sometimes be made conscious)" (pp. 141, 143). According to Pert,

> What this translates into in everyday experiences is that positive emotional experiences are much more likely to be recalled when we're in an upbeat mood, while negative emotional experiences are recalled more easily when we're already in a bad mood. Not only is memory affected by the mood we're in, but so is actual performance.... It doesn't take an expert in emotional theory to recognize that there is a very close intertwining of emotions and memory. For most of us, our earliest and oldest memory is an extremely emotion-laden one.

This recognition that emotion and memory are clearly linked, whether these functions are based primarily in the brain or throughout our bodies, could have enormous implications for how we understand learning in adulthood.

CONNECTIONS TO LEARNING

Connecting what we know about the brain and related systems to learning in adulthood is at best a set of working hypotheses. Although some educators have tried to make very direct correlations by devising what they term *brain-based learning programs* (for example, Caine and Caine, 1994), we still have a long way to go before we can make any really useful linkages that will affect large numbers of adults. This gap between the theoretical knowledge of how the brain and related systems work, and practical applications of that knowledge, has created questionable educational practices.

The major issue has been the simplistic applications some educators have made based on supposed factual knowledge about the brain. As Bruer (1997, p. 4) argues, "Currently we do not know enough about brain development and neural function to link that understanding directly, in any meaningful, defensible way to instruction and educational practice." He observes that even neuroscientists, "while interested in how their research might find application outside the laboratory and clinic, are more guarded in their claims, [and] often ... puzzled by the neuroscientific results educators choose to cite, by the interpretations educators give those results, and by the conclusions educators draw from them." For example, one of the major applications of brain research to learning has been related to brain hemisphere differences and specializations. The idea that our brains are divided into two hemispheres, or halves, has led some educators to design full programs for the left versus the right brain. By the end of these programs, sponsors claim that people have more fully developed their untapped right or left brain potential. Although there are indeed hemispheric specializations, a number of researchers have pointed out that both hemispheres are active and involved in most tasks and situations (Farley, 1988; Restak, 1995; Springer, 1987; Sylwester, 1995). "For example, the left hemisphere (in most people) processes the objective content of the language— *what* was said—while the right hemisphere processes the emotional content of facial expressions, gestures, and language intonation—*how* it was said. By processing related information from different perspectives, the hemispheres collaborate to produce something that becomes a unified mental experience" (Sylwester, 1995, p. 49).

MERGING RESEARCH FROM THE COGNITIVE AND NEUROBIOLOGICAL SCIENCES

Rather than relying on either neurobiology or cognitive sciences, the promise of connecting what we know about how the brain functions and learning comes primarily from the merger of the two sciences (Bruer, 1997; Crick and Koch, 1992; Kandel and Hawkins, 1992; Siegler, Poon, Madden, and Welsh, 1996; Smith, 1996). Bruer (1997) has used the metaphor of the bridge to illustrate this point. On the one hand we have a "well-established bridge" of knowledge about learning from the cognitive sciences. We have a newer bridge between "cognitive psychology and neuroscience. This newer bridge is allowing us to see how mental functions map onto brain structures. When neuroscience does begin to provide useful insights for educators about instruction and educational practice, those insights will be the result of extensive traffic over the second bridge. Cognitive psychology provides the only firm ground we have to anchor these bridges" (Bruer, 1997, p. 4). He goes on to observe that in the future "we should attempt to develop an interactive, recursive relationship among research programs in education, cognitive psychology and systems neuroscience.... In the meantime, we should remain skeptical about brain-based educational practice and policy" (p. 15).

Two areas that hold some promise for further investigation within this framework are the emotional and attentional mechanisms of the brain (Pert, 1997; Sylwester, 1995; Taylor, 1996). For example, Taylor (1996) describes "from a physiological perspective, the interdependent relationship that exists between emotion and reason based on a review of the contemporary research in neurobiology" (p. 301). He concludes from this review that "without emotions, rationality cannot work.... Without the emotional value that gives salience to positive and negative decisions, people are unable to reason" (p. 303). Pert (1997) goes even further and asserts that "emotions are constantly regulating what we experience as 'reality.' The decision about what sensory information travels to your brain and what gets filtered out depends on what signals the receptors [for emotion] are receiving" (p. 1997). She goes on to state that "fortunately, however, [these] receptors are not stagnant.... This means that even when we are 'stuck' emotionally, fixated on a version of reality that does not serve us well, there is always a biochemical potential for change and growth" (p. 146). Those writing about emotional intelligence (for example, Gardner, 1983; Goleman, 1995), also ground their assertions in this study of the emotional mechanisms and processes of the brain.

Emotion can be seen in addition as part of the attentional mechanism, in both our conscious and unconscious processes of learning. "Our emotions allow us to assemble life-saving information very quickly, and thus to bypass the extended conscious and rational deliberation of a potential threat.... Emotion also has an important positive side that can move life beyond mere survival into a much more pleasant sense of joie de vivre.... We may accept grief, but we tend to move toward those things that give us joy—music, games, jokes, dances, caresses, sunsets, celebrations, vacations" (Sylwester, 1995, pp. 73, 74). In addition to the emotional component of the attentional mechanism, it is important to investigate other neurobiological elements for such processes as getting and sustaining our attention on important situations and tasks, and knowing when and how to shift our attention quickly when new information arrives. By gaining clearer biological explanations of emotional, attentional, and other physiological mechanisms that facilitate memory and learning, we should gain a better understanding about how the mind works and adults learn.

SUMMARY

Understanding the internal workings of the learning process have fascinated scientists for decades. Researchers from the cognitive sciences have the longest history of research in this important arena, and more recently scholars from the neurobiological sciences are offering new hypotheses about how the brain and related systems are involved in learning. Perhaps the most exciting new arena of study, with the greatest potential for expanding our knowledge base of the internal processes of learning, are the combined efforts of cognitive scientists and neuroscientists working together to address how and where learning happens in the brain.

Cognitive scientists, primarily from the discipline of psychology, describe how people receive, store, retrieve, transform, and transmit information. Most of the work from this framework has focused on memory and aging, with the resulting conclusion that there are some apparent losses as we age in both working and long-term memory. How this loss affects the everyday learning activities of adults is still unanswered, except that we know that most older adults take a longer time to process complex information. Other important aspects of cognition reviewed in this section are the concepts of schemas, the effect of prior knowledge and experience on learning, and cognitive and learning-style theories. The concept of schemas has provided a useful framework for thinking about both the forms of knowledge (declarative and procedural) adults have accumulated over time and how that knowledge is transformed and used. In exploring the effects of prior knowledge and experience on learning, the concepts of novice and expert learners were stressed. The differences between cognitive and learning styles were discussed as well, with the resulting observation that learning styles seem to be a more useful concept. The learning-style inventories, although many have questionable reliability and validity from a research standpoint, appear to have proved effective in helping both learners and instructors gain some basic understanding of their strengths and weaknesses as learners and instructors.

Neurobiologists, from fields such as anatomy and physiology, have provided some fascinating descriptions of how the brain is organized and functions. Especially with the newer technologies, such as MRI and PET, we can catch glimpses of how our brain operates during differing types of learning episodes. Direct connections between what we see and have learned about the brain, and learning interventions are still yet to come. What we have now are tentative hypotheses about the neurobiology of learning.

With this caveat in mind, we first described the most current theories of how the brain is organized and how information is exchanged within the structures of the brain. We then commented on how educators have tried to apply this knowledge, with limited, if any, success because of this lack of definitive knowledge about the relationships between brain functioning and learning. We closed with a discussion of two areas, that of the emotional and attentional mechanisms of the brain, that hold the most promise for further collaborative work among cognitive and neuroscientists and could inform our practice as adult educators. It is hoped that we will be able to draw from this work helpful observations and techniques, and possibly even biological interventions, that could assist adults in the learning process.

ESTABLISHING INCLUSION AMONG ADULT LEARNERS

RAYMOND J. WLODKOWSKI

> *When a system of oppression has become institutionalized it is unnecessary for individuals to be oppressive.*
>
> *Florynce Kennedy*

When we are teaching, exclusion is usually an indirect act, an omission of opportunity or of someone's voice. We're usually not mean-spirited but, more likely, unaware that a perspective is missing, that a biased myth has been perpetuated, or that we aren't covering topics of concern to certain adults. In fact, most adult learners, usually those who have been socialized to accommodate our method of instruction, may like our course or training. Things seem pretty pleasant. Why go looking for trouble?

We need to be mindful about our instruction because, as Adrienne Rich (1984) has so eloquently said, "there is no way of measuring the damage to a society when a whole texture of humanity is kept from realizing its own power." When it comes to the perspective of this book, I believe that enabling people to realize their own power relates to our obligation to create an equitable opportunity to be motivated to learn as well as to have the right to an equitable education. The two are inseparable. To begin, I believe we have to be vigilant about the patterns we see in our courses and training. Are some people left out? Do particular income groups or ethnic groups do less well than others? Who are the people whose motivation to learn is not emerging or seems diminished among the adults we teach or train? How might we be responsible for or contribute to these trends?

My experience is that teaching or training begins with relationships, respectful relationships. For most adults, the first sense of the quality of the teacher-student relationship will be a feeling, sometimes quite vague, of inclusion or exclusion. Upon awareness of exclusion, adult learners will begin to lose their enthusiasm and motivation. If you'd like to appreciate this tendency by working directly with adults themselves, try the exercise called Marginality and Mattering (Frederick, 1997). Ask adults to remember a moment in the recent past (a week to a month) when they felt marginal, excluded, or discounted—"the only one like me in a group, not understood or, perhaps, unaccepted." Ask them to reflect on this and then to pair off and discuss the following questions: How did you know? How did you feel? How did you behave? Then ask them to remember a moment when they felt that they mattered, were included, or were regarded as important to a group. Ask the adults to reflect on this and then to pair off again to discuss the questions, How did you know? How did you feel? How did you behave? Ask the adults to reflect on both situations and to discuss the patterns of thinking, feeling, and behaving that emerged, the influence of those patterns on their motivation and enthusiasm, and how the changes in motivation and enthusiasm might relate to learning and teaching. As this exercise will demonstrate, our motivation is constantly influenced by our acute awareness of the degree of our inclusion in a learning environment.

Feelings of cultural isolation often cause adult motivation to learn to deteriorate. In a course or training seminar, a sense of community with which all learners can identify establishes the foundation for inclusion. Our challenge as instructors is to create a successful learning environment for all learners that (1) respects different cultures and (2) maintains a common culture that all learners can accept. We are fortunate, because adults are community-forming beings. Our capacity to create social coherence is always there (Gardner, 1990). We need community to find security, identity, shared values, and people who care about us and about whom we care. As more and more adults sandwich their education between work and family, adult education settings provide critical opportunities to experience community and a sense of belonging. But mere contact with those different from us does little to enhance intercultural appreciation. Mutual respect and appreciation evolve from the nature of our contact. The norms we set as instructors and the strategies we use to teach will largely determine the quality of social exchange among our learners. Those norms should be supportive of equity, collaboration, and the expression of each learner's perspective (Wlodkowski and Ginsberg, 1995). It simply makes sense to set a tone in which learners can come together in friendly, caring, and respectful ways.

The strategies that follow contribute to establishing a *climate of respect*. In this atmosphere, intrinsic motivation is more likely to emerge because learners can voice the things that matter to them. Their well-being is more assured. They can begin to develop trust. Relevant learning is possible. These strategies also enable learners to *feel connected* to one another. This feeling of connection draws forth learners' motivation because their social needs are met. Feeling included, people are more free to risk the mistakes true learning involves as well as to share their resources and strengths. Before we discuss these strategies, we need to look at the dimensions of cultural variation often critical to effective intercultural communication. Your understanding of these important dimensions should increase your capacity to sensitively apply the strategies to establish inclusion. To describe these dimensions, I have summarized an essay by Peter Andersen (1997, pp. 244–256).

UNDERSTANDING DIMENSIONS OF CULTURAL VARIATION

As we enter the third millennium, contact between people from various cultures is increasing. International migration is at an all-time high. International trade increased 400 percent between 1965 and 1995 (Brown, Kane, and Roodman, 1994). The amount of intercultural contact in today's world is unprecedented, making the study of intercultural communication more important than ever.

Two of the most fundamental nonverbal differences in intercultural communication involve space and time. Time frames of cultures may differ so dramatically that if only these differences existed, intercultural misunderstandings could still be considerable. In general, time tends to be viewed in the United States as a commodity that can be wasted, spent, saved, managed, and used wisely. Many cultures have no such concept of time. In many traditional cultures and in many cultures in developing countries, time moves to the rhythms of nature, the day, the seasons, the year. Human inventions like seconds, minutes, and hours may have no real meaning.

Research has documented that cultures differ substantially in their use of personal space, the distances they maintain, and their regard for territory (Burgoon, Buller, and Woodall, 1989). Considerable intercultural differences have been reported in people's *kinesic* behavior, including their facial expressions, body movements, gestures, and conversational regulators. Stories abound in the intercultural literature of gestures that signal endearment or warmth in one culture but are obscene or insulting in another. Differences in kinesic behavior come into play in a learning environment; they can determine how one gets the floor in conversation, shows deference or respect, indicates agreement or disagreement and approval or disapproval. For the teacher, these norms of participation may seem obvious and their derivation from European American norms of conduct unimportant, but to a learner from another culture, such expectations may be alienating or exhausting (because of the relentless anxiety of determining how to behave appropriately), especially if learners are directly called on to recite and are graded for oral participation in class.

Along with genetics, culture is the most enduring, powerful, and invisible shaper of our communication behavior. Initial research has shown that cultures can be located along dimensions that help explain intercultural differences in communication. Most of the adult learners we work with will probably not be international students; however, they will often have ethnic backgrounds and histories of immigration that make the dimensions discussed in the sections that follow quite informative about their differences in communication and nonverbal behavior.

Immediacy, Expressiveness, and Contact Cultures

Immediacy behaviors are actions that simultaneously communicate warmth, closeness, and availability for communication and approach rather than avoidance (Hecht, Andersen, and Ribeau, 1989). Examples of immediacy behaviors are smiling, touching, making eye contact, being at closer distances, and using more vocal animation. Some scholars have labeled these behaviors *expressive* (Patterson, 1983). Cultures that display considerable interpersonal closeness or immediacy have been labeled *contact cultures,* because people in these cultures stand closer and touch more (Hall, 1996). People in *low-contact cultures* tend to stand apart and touch less.

It is interesting that contact cultures are generally located in warmer countries, low-contact cultures in cooler climates. Considerable research has shown that high-contact (more expressive and immediate) cultures are found in most Arab countries, the Mediterranean region, the Middle East, Eastern Europe, Russia, and virtually all of Latin America (Jones, 1994). Low-contact (less expressive and immediate) cultures are found in most of Northern Europe and virtually every Asian country; white Anglo-Saxons (whose culture is the primary culture of the United States) and traditional American Indians also have low-contact cultures. These findings are painted with a fairly broad brush; they will become more detailed as we review the other dimensions of cultural variation.

Individualism and Collectivism

One of the most fundamental dimensions along which cultures differ is their degree of individualism as opposed to collectivism. The main cultures of Europe, Australia, and North America north of the Rio Grande tend to be individualistic. The main cultures of Latin America, Africa, Asia, and the Pacific Islands tend to be collectivist. Individualists are oriented toward achieving personal goals, by themselves, for purposes of pleasure, autonomy, and self-fulfillment (Triandis, 1995). Collectivists are oriented toward achieving group goals, by the group, for the purposes of group well-being, relationships, togetherness, and the common good.

The United States is considered the most individualistic country on earth (Hofstede, 1982). As Bellah and his associates (1985, p. 142) have written, "Anything that would violate our right to think for ourselves, judge for ourselves, make our own decisions, live our lives as we see fit, is not only morally wrong, it is sacrilegious." Many people in the United States find it difficult to relate to a culture in which interdependence may be the basis of a sense of self. Although individualism has been argued to be the backbone of democracy, it has also been considered to be largely responsible for problems of crime, alienation, loneliness, and narcissism in U.S. society.

Different ethnic groups in the United States vary along the dimensions of individualism and collectivism. For example, most African Americans tend to be individualistic, whereas most Mexican Americans place greater emphasis on group and relational solidarity (Hecht, Andersen, and Ribeau, 1989).

The degree to which a culture is individualistic or collectivistic affects adult communication and nonverbal behavior. People from individualistic cultures are more remote and distant proximally. People from collectivist cultures tend to work, play, live, and sleep in closer proximity to one another. Lustig and Koester (1993, p. 147) maintain that "people from individualistic cultures are more likely than those from collectivist cultures to use confrontational strategies when dealing with interpersonal problems; those with a collectivist orientation are likely to use avoidance, third party intermediaries, or other face saving techniques." People in collectivist cultures may suppress both positive and negative emotional displays that are contrary to the mood of the group, because maintaining the group is a primary value. Individualistic cultures encourage people to express emotions because individual freedom is a paramount value. In the United States, flirting, small talk, smiling, and initial acquaintance are more important than in collectivist countries, where the social network is more fixed and less reliant on individual initiative.

Gender

The gender orientation of a culture has a major impact on role and communication behavior, including the types of expressions permitted by each sex, occupational status, the ability to interact with strangers or acquaintances of the opposite sex, and all aspects of interpersonal relationship between men and women. *As conceptualized here, rigidity refers to the rigidity of gender rules.* In rigid cultures, masculine traits are typically such attributes as strength, assertiveness, competitiveness, and ambitiousness, whereas feminine traits are such attributes as affection, compassion, nurturance, and emotionality (Hofstede, 1982). In less rigid cultures, both men and women can express more diverse, less stereotyped sex-role behaviors.

Considerable research suggests that androgynous (both feminine and masculine) patterns of behavior result in more social competence, success, and intellectual development for both men and women (Andersen, 1988). Nonverbal styles through which both men and women are free to express both masculine traits (such as dominance and anger) and feminine traits (such as warmth and emotionality) are likely to be healthier and more effective for lowering stress (Buck, 1984).

Power Distance

The fourth fundamental dimension of intercultural communication is power distance. Power distance, the degree to which power, prestige, and wealth are unequally distributed in a culture, has been measured in a number of cultures using the Power Distance Index (PDI), developed by Hofstede (1982). In cultures with high PDI scores, power and influence are concentrated in the hands of a few rather than more equally distributed throughout the population. Most African, Asian, and Latin American countries have high PDI scores. The United States is slightly lower than the median in power distance. Cultures differ in terms of how status is acquired. In many countries, such as India, class or caste determines one's status. In the United States, power and status are typically determined by money and conspicuous material displays (Andersen and Bowman, 1990).

Cultures with high power distance will foster and encourage emotions that present status differences: for example, in high power distance cultures, people are usually expected to show only positive emotions to high-status others. The continuous smiles of many Asians are a culturally inculcated effort to appease superiors and to smooth social relations that are appropriate to a culture with a high PDI. As students, many Asians are expected to be modest and deferential in the presence of their instructors. Vocal cues are also affected. A loud voice in a high-PDI culture may be offensive to higher-status members.

Uncertainty

For the purposes of this discussion, uncertainty is a cultural predisposition to value risk and ambiguity (Hecht, Andersen, and Ribeau, 1989). People with intolerance of ambiguity or with high levels of uncertainty avoidance want clear, black-and-white answers. Disagreement and nonconformity are not appreciated. Emotional displays are usually tolerated less in countries with high levels of uncertainty avoidance. Cultures with tolerance of ambiguity and with low levels of uncertainty avoidance are more tolerant, accept ambiguous answers, and see many shades of gray. In general, the higher uncertainty avoidance is among people, the greater their fear of failure and the lower their risk taking in academic situations.

The majority culture of the United States is low in uncertainty avoidance. When people from the United States communicate with people from a country like Japan or France (both high in uncertainty avoidance), the people from the United States may seem excessively nonconforming and unconventional, whereas their Japanese and French counterparts may seem too controlled and rigid (Lustig and Koester, 1993).

High and Low Context

The last dimension of intercultural communication we will discuss is that of context. A high-context (HC) communication is a message in which most of the information is either in the physical context or internalized in the person. Very little is in the coded, explicit part of the message (Hall, 1976). Lifelong friends often use HC messages that are nearly impossible for an outsider to understand. A gesture, a smile, or a glance provides meaning that doesn't need to be articulated. Low-context (LC) messages are just the opposite. Most of the information is in explicit code and must be elaborated and highly specific, like a legal brief. Very little of the communication is taken for granted.

The lowest-context cultures are found in Switzerland, Germany, Canada, and the United States. Placing a high value on Aristotelian logic, these cultures are highly verbal and preoccupied with specifics and details. The highest-context cultures are found in Asia (notably China), Japan, and Korea (Hall, 1984). Strongly influenced by Zen Buddhism, these cultures place a high value on silence, on less emotional expression, and on unspoken, nonverbal parts of communication. American Indian cultures with migratory roots in East Asia are like these cultures in their use of HC communication.

Communication is quite different in HC and LC cultures, and frequently one culture will misattribute the causes for the behavior of the other group. People from LC cultures are often perceived as excessively talkative, belaboring the obvious, and redundant. People from HC cultures may be perceived as secretive, sneaky, and mysterious. The people from HC cultures are particularly affected by contextual cues. Facial expressions, tensions, movements, speed of interaction, location of interaction, and other "subtleties" are likely to be perceived and may have meaning for people from HC cultures that people from LC cultures may remain unaware of.

In addition to these dimensions of cultural variation is the issue of language and dialect. We frequently use our own language as a normative reference; that is, we may consider "standard English," for example, as *the* language rather than *a* language. Thus, as instructors, we may see adults who speak a different version of English as "language deficient." Instead of asking ourselves, How do we respectfully teach these students in the area of standard English where necessary? we may see the learners as impaired. This view can lower our expectations for these adults, leading to their lower motivation and learning, a well-documented self-fulfilling prophecy (Good and Brophy, 1994).

Perhaps, like me, you realize how daunting it is to understand someone from another culture. You may also be joyful about the number of possible ways there are to be human. I benefit (not without anxiety) from knowing that my teaching is shaded by a persona that is more rigidly masculine than I like, fairly expressive with a median PDI, tolerant of ambiguity, low context, and leaning leftward toward collectivism. This self-analysis makes me more mindful of the dimensions of cultural variance and gives me a better chance to provide instruction compatible with the norms and values of learners from other cultures. By being conscious of these tendencies, I believe I'm less likely to impose them on others as expected norms. Continuing to learn and understand these dimensions of cultural variation helps me select educational practices that accommodate the communication styles of those adults whose socialization has been different from my own. The following discussion of the motivational strategies will take into consideration these dimensions of cultural understanding.

ENGENDERING AN AWARENESS AND FEELING OF CONNECTION AMONG ADULTS

The core characteristics of empathy and cultural responsiveness will significantly influence the degree to which we engender a feeling of connection among adults. Raising an awareness of what we have in common and instilling a sense of mutual care are essential. A good place to begin preparing ourselves is to consider the learners we expect to be teaching and our own *positionality* in the group—that is, the cultural group identities we have that may influence our own outlook as well as how these learners will look upon us (Johnson-Bailey and Cervero, 1997). These identities are usually the more visible dimensions of race, gender, age, and physical ability or disability, but they also include ethnicity, class, and sexual orientation as well as some of the cultural variations discussed in the preceding sections.

For example, when I teach an extension course, I need to realize that being a male, middle-class, European American academic gives me a certain perspective that may be quite different from that of the African American, working-class women who are some of the students in my course. I probably have very different experiences regarding such issues as health, education, safety, and economic security. If I merely follow personal opinions and familiar routines, I may give an advantage to one group of students over another in the topics I choose, in the time or opportunity students have to speak, and in the feedback I give. Indeed, for certain groups of students, I may not have the "expertise" in matters of personal psychology and social relations I think I have. Yet if I think only of these sorts of things or that I must know every detail, I can feel overwhelmed and immobilized. I want also to hold in my mind the large strands of life that I and all my students hold in common: the mutual desire for good health, education, and security; the emotions of sorrow, joy, and love; the experiences of family, death, birth, and illness; and the reason we all came together—to learn. That desire, my awareness of difference and common ground, and the knowledge that I can flex and plan make me realistically enthusiastic. And I know where I can begin. I like to start with introductions. (Please note that I have numbered the strategies throughout this text for organizational purposes, not to indicate an order of preference or a particular sequence to follow. The selection of each strategy you use will depend on your philosophy, situation, and goals.)

STRATEGY 1: *Allow for introductions.*

Introduce yourself. This is definitely for the first meeting of the group and seems quite obvious, but it is amazing how many instructors fail to extend this common courtesy. Say a few things about who you are, where you're from, why you're conducting the course or training session, and by all means, welcome the group. This really shouldn't take more than a couple of minutes. It is also a good idea to give the learners a chance to introduce themselves as well. This emphasizes their importance and your interest in them as people. It also helps people start to learn each other's names (name tents are a valuable supplement to this strategy) and significantly reduces the tension so often present at the beginning of most courses and training sessions. Scores of articles (Johnson and Johnson, 1996) have been written describing different exercises for helping people get acquainted in new social situations. My particular favorite among such devices is multidimensional sharing, the next strategy I describe.

STRATEGY 2: *Provide an opportunity for multidimensional sharing.*

Opportunities for multidimensional sharing differ from many icebreakers. They tend to be less game-like and intrusive. For adults from backgrounds that value modesty, introductory activities that require self-disclosure or the sharing of deeper emotions may seem contrived and psychologically invasive. I remember being in a teaching workshop where a well-meaning trainer asked us as part of the introductory activity to "share about one person who loves us." Rather than encourage connection, this request tended to stall the development of mutual care among us.

Opportunities for multidimensional sharing are those occasions, from introductory exercises to personal anecdotes to classroom celebrations, when people have a better chance to see one another as complete, evolving human beings who have mutual needs, emotions, and experiences (Wlodkowski and Ginsberg, 1995). These opportunities give a human face to a course or training, break down biases and stereotypes, and provide experiences in which we see ourselves in another person's world.

There are many ways to provide opportunities for multidimensional sharing, depending on the history, makeup, and purpose of the group. Informal ways include potluck meals, recreational activities, drinks after class, and picnics. For introductory activities, anything that gets people to relax and to laugh together or helps them learn each other's names deserves our serious attention. Here are two introductory activities I have often used.

Learners usually need some time to think before they begin this activity, which can be a small- or large-group process. Each person introduces himself or herself and recommends (1) one thing he has read (such as an article, story, or book) *or* (2) one thing he has seen (such as a TV program, film, or real-life experience) *or* (3) one thing he has heard (such as a speech, musical recording, or song) that has had a strong and positive influence on him. Each person concludes by stating the reasons for recommending his choice.

The second activity, which I learned from Margery Ginsberg, is called Decades and Diversity. People in the group divide themselves into smaller groups according to the decade in which they would have or did graduate from high school (the fifties, sixties, seventies, and so on). Each smaller group brainstorms a list of items in three to five areas of experience at that time: popular music, clothing styles, major historical events, weekend social opportunities (What did you usually do on a Saturday night?), and standards (What was considered significant immoral behavior for you as an adolescent—a no-no in the eyes of your family?). Then each group reports on its list. The activity concludes with a discussion by the members of the entire group about their insights, the possible meanings of the lists, and the process they engaged in. The powerful influence of age and its accompanying time of socialization consistently emerges as part of the groups' perceptions.

These activities are most inclusive and motivating when they validate the experiences of the adults involved and establish a sense of affiliation with you and other learners. The more natural and appropriate such opportunities feel, the more likely a genuine sense of community can evolve.

STRATEGY 3: *Concretely indicate your cooperative intentions to help adults learn.*

Almost everyone who has something to learn from somebody is vulnerable to a nagging fear—what if I really try, and I can't learn it? Adults commonly experience this fear, because so much of what they must learn will directly influence their job performance or family relations. For instructors to let learners know at the outset that there is a concrete means of assistance available will help learners reduce their fear and save face. Be it announcing our availability during office hours or at breaks in a workshop, arranging tutorial assistance by appointment, or creating a device whereby learners who are having difficulty can use special materials or aids—essentially, our message is, "As instructor and learner, we are partners in solving your learning problems. I want to help you, and it's OK to seek help." We are telling the learners that their vulnerability will be safeguarded and that they will have a nonjudgmental and interested response to their requests for assistance (Johnson, 1980). With this strategy, we offer immediate evidence that we do care about the people who learn with us.

STRATEGY 4: *Share something of value with your adult learners.*

The next time you go to hear a professional speaker, whether it is at a banquet or a conference, check to see how much time elapses before that person tells a joke or a humorous anecdote. It will probably be less than three minutes, and it will happen about four out of every five times. Professional speakers know the value of *sharing humor.* It does far more than break the tension between speaker and audience. It says, if you can laugh with me, you can listen to me. You can identify with me. You can see I am a human being and that I have emotions too. All sharing has this potential—to break down images and to allow the learner to experience our common humanity without self-consciousness. Humor is a very efficient means to this end. It also tells the learner that there are at least times when we do not take ourselves too seriously, that we have some perspective on life, and that the way we teach will allow for the vitality of laughter in the learning process.

Another type of effective sharing is to relate a *credible intense experience.* This may be some trouble we have had on the job, a difficult learning experience, a crisis within our family, an unexpected surprise, an accident—something that tells the learners that we have mutual concerns and a shared reality. This form of sharing should relate to the topic at hand, or it will seem forced. I sometimes tell about problems I have had with apathetic learners. I know most of my audience has had similar problems, and this gives me a chance to share what I have learned from these dilemmas. This type of sharing has also taught me how much of this process is a two-way street. Seeing the concerned faces in the audience increases my identification with them as well.

Sharing *your involvement with the subject matter*—problems, discoveries, research, or new learning—is a way to show your enthusiasm as well as your humanity. Adults are interested in seeing how their investment in the subject matter will pay off for them. When we share our involvement with the topic at hand, we model this potential for them and reveal something about our real selves as well.

Another powerful, ongoing form of sharing is to give adult learners *our individual attention.* When we do, we are committing one of our most valuable assets as instructors to our learners—our time. Being available to learners before, during, and after class directly tells them we care about them. Also, one-to-one contact creates a more personal and spontaneous situation.

In general, sharing *something about our real selves,* when done tactfully and appropriately, gives adult learners a chance to see us beyond the image of an instructor. Most people are a bit surprised when they see their instructors in common settings like supermarkets, shopping centers, and theaters. Part of this surprise is due to novelty, but part is also due to how dramatically set apart most learning environments seem from the real world. By wisely self-disclosing our reactions to common experiences—television shows, sporting events, travel, maybe even a little trouble we've had with life along the way—we give adult learners a chance to identify positively with us and become more receptive to our instruction (Jourard, 1964).

STRATEGY 5: *Use collaborative and cooperative learning.*

Although there are a wide variety of *collaborative learning methods,* most emphasize the learners' exploration and interpretation of course material to an equal or greater extent than they do the instructor's explication of it. When everyone participates, working as partners or in small groups, questions and challenges to create something energize group activity. Instructors who use collaborative procedures tend to think of themselves less as singular transmitters of knowledge and more as colearners.

Among the many collaborative learning possibilities, *cooperative learning* represents the most carefully organized and researched approach. More than one-third of all studies comparing cooperative, competitive, and individualistic learning have been conducted with college and adult learners. David Johnson and Roger Johnson (1995) have found in an analysis of 120 of these investigations that cooperative learning significantly promotes greater individual achievement than do competitive or individualistic efforts. When adults learn cooperatively, they tend to develop supportive relationships across different ethnic, language, social class, and gender groups. Cooperative learning groups create a setting in which learners can

- Construct and extend understanding of what is being learned through explanation and discussion of multiple perspectives.
- Use the shared mental models learned in flexible ways to solve problems jointly.
- Receive interpersonal feedback as to how well they are performing procedures.
- Receive social support and encouragement to take risks in increasing their competencies.
- Be held accountable by peers to practice and learn procedures and skills.
- Acquire new attitudes.
- Establish a shared identity with other group members.
- Find effective peers to emulate.
- Discover a "voice" to validate their own learning (Rendon, 1994).

As its practitioners strenuously emphasize, cooperative learning is more than merely placing learners in groups and telling them to work together (Johnson, Johnson, and Smith, 1991). Positive interdependence and individual accountability are fundamental components of effective cooperative learning. Groups lacking either of these two features are properly identified as engaged in a form of collaborative learning, not cooperative learning. To organize lessons so learners do work cooperatively requires an understanding of five components—positive interdependence, individual accountability, promotive interaction, social skills, and group processing—and their rigorous implementation in the group and in the lesson. It is also of paramount importance that a significant amount of cooperative learning take place within the learning environment to permit monitoring by the instructor and to allow groups to initially establish themselves while they can receive needed support.

1. *Positive interdependence.* When learners perceive that they are linked with groupmates in such a way that they cannot succeed unless their groupmates do (and vice versa) and that they must coordinate their efforts with the efforts of their partners to complete a task (Johnson, Johnson, and Smith, 1991), they are positively interdependent. They sink or swim together. Each group member has a unique contribution to make to the group because of his resources, role, or responsibilities. For example, in the popular *jigsaw procedure,* a reading assignment is divided among the group, with each member responsible for comprehending a separate part and explaining or teaching that part to all other members of the group until the entire group has a coherent understanding of the total reading assignment. The following three approaches are additional ways to create positive interdependence in a cooperative learning group.

Positive goal interdependence: the group is united around a common goal, a concrete reason for being. It could be to create a single product, report, or answer, or it could be general improvement on a task so that all members do better this week than they did last week. Outcomes might include a skill demonstration, a media product, an evaluation summary, a problem solution, an action plan, or just about anything that leads to greater learning and that the group members can produce and hold each other responsible for.

Positive resource interdependence: each group member has only a portion of the resources, information, or materials necessary for the task to be accomplished, and the members have to combine resources in order for the group to achieve its goals. The metaphor for this approach is a puzzle, and each group member has a unique and necessary piece to contribute to the puzzle's solution. For example, for an upcoming exam, each member of a group might be responsible for a different study question; when the group convenes, members share their knowledge of the question and check to make sure all groupmates have satisfactorily comprehended this knowledge.

Positive role interdependence: each member of the group selects a particular role that is complementary, interconnected, and essential to the roles of the other group members. Suppose, for example, that the learning goal is the development of some form of skill, such as interviewing. One group member is the person practicing the skill (the interviewer), another person is the recipient of the skill (the interviewee), and a third person is the observer-evaluator. In this manner, each person has an essential contribution to make in terms of either skill practice or feedback. Roles can easily be rotated as well.

In all cooperative learning groups, it is extremely important that the learners are very clear about the assignment, goal, and role involved. Especially with diverse groups of learners, checking for this kind of understanding can make the difference between a satisfying or a confusing learning experience. Positive interdependence works best when all group members understand that each person has a part to do, that all members are counting on each other, and that all members want to help each other do better.

2. *Individual accountability.* This is present when the learning of each individual in the learning group is assessed, the results are shared with the learner, and the learner is responsible to groupmates for contributing a fair share to the group's success. One of the main purposes of cooperative learning is to support each member as a vital, competent individual in his or her own

right. Individual accountability is the key to ensuring that all group members are strengthened by learning cooperatively and that they have a good chance to effectively transfer what they have learned to situations in which they may be without a group support.

Some texts emphasize individual accountability as a means to prevent *hitchhiking,* the situation in which a learner contributes little of worth to the total success of a group's learning experience and overly benefits from the contributions of other group members. My experience is that this seldom occurs when cooperative norms are well in place and competitive assessment or grading procedures are eliminated. A powerful extrinsic reward denied to most members of a group will undermine cooperation and encourage individuals to seek the greatest amount of external gain for the least amount of effort. They do not count playing time in the championship game when they hand out those Super Bowl rings: every team member receives one.

Specific ways to enhance individual accountability include the following:

- Keep the size of the groups small. Keep the role of each learner distinct. Typical size is two to four members.
- Assess learners individually as well as collectively.
- Observe groups while they are working.
- Randomly request individuals to present what they are learning, either to you or another group.
- Request periodic self-assessments and outlines of responsibilities from individual group members.
- Randomly or systematically ask learners to teach someone else or you what they have learned.

A simple and positive way to support individual accountability and prevent related conflict among group members is to brainstorm answers to the question, How would we like to find out if someone in our cooperative learning group thought we were not doing enough to contribute to the benefit of the total group? What are some acceptable ways of letting us know? Then write the possible actions on the chalkboard and discuss them. Such a procedure can go a long way to avoid unnecessary suspicion or shame.

3. *Promotive interaction.* When members of cooperative groups encourage and assist each other with information and emotional support and also deliberate to reach relevant goals, they are engaged in promotive interaction. Mutual care should permeate this interaction: as it does, for example, when someone in a cooperative writing group hears a fellow member read her own words and offers sincere and helpful suggestions to improve the manuscript. This sort of interaction allows different perspectives and commitments to take hold.

4. *Social skills.* Cooperative work depends on communication that enables group members to reach goals, get to know and trust each other, communicate accurately, accept and support each other, and resolve conflicts constructively (Johnson, Johnson, and Smith, 1991). Even though adults want to cooperate, they may not be able to do so effectively if they lack conventional social skills.

My experience with diverse adults is that when the norms of collaboration and "no blame" are discussed and made explicit, they create (along with *ground rules,* discussed later in this section) a learning climate that significantly reduces aggressive conflict. There is then far less need for direct training in conventional interpersonal skills, such as *active listening,* which often feel contrived and alien to many people, especially those who do not identify with the dominant culture. It is appropriate for an instructor to intervene in a group, when necessary, to suggest more effective procedures for working together. Yet instructors should not intervene any more than is necessary. I often find that if everyone exercises a little patience, cooperative groups work their way through their own problems and construct not only timely solutions but also methods for solving similar problems in the future. Sometimes, simply asking group members to set aside their task, describe the problem as they see it, and come up with a few solutions and then a decision as to which one to try first is enough to get things moving along satisfactorily.

5. *Group processing.* Cooperative learning benefits from group processing—that is, members' reflecting on their group experience to describe actions that were helpful and unhelpful and to make decisions about what actions to continue or change. When groups with the same members continue over longer periods of time (more than a few hours) or are significantly diverse, discussing group functioning is essential (Adams and Marchesani, 1992). Adults need time to have a dialogue about the quality of their cooperation, to reflect on their interactions, and to learn from how they work together. This *processing time* gives learners a chance to receive feedback on their participation, understand how their actions can be more effective and cohesive, plan for more helpful and skillful interaction for the next group session, and celebrate mutual success. As instructors, we need to allow enough time in the learning environment for this activity to take place and to provide some basic structure for it—for example, by suggesting the group discuss a few things it is doing well and one thing it could improve.

In general, heterogeneous groups tend to work well. Unless projects or special reasons prevail, regularly remixing groups at the beginning of new activities often has a revitalizing affect and makes working with different people a course norm. However, practical reasons may sometimes override the benefits of heterogeneity. Students' interest in a specific topic, accessibility for meetings outside of class, very limited skills, or language acquisition issues might predicate more homogeneous groups. For projects or activities with significant assessment consequences (for example, if they represent a large proportion of a course grade), I usually accept individual completion as an option. I do this to respect the more individualistic or absolutist orientations among class members. In addition, for some activities, I find that letting students form their own groups (ranging from two to four members) allows smaller groups and a greater comfort level for those adults less at ease with cooperative learning.

Once cooperative learning groups start working, our role as the instructor is that of colearner, observer, adviser, and consultant. Without being obtrusive, we should watch cooperative groups, especially as they *begin* their tasks. Sometimes we can see that certain groups will need clarification or guidance. Otherwise we remain available, always keeping in mind that it is the learners themselves who are the major resources for support and assistance to one another.

Exhibit 4-1, an outline for planning cooperative learning activities, is an adaptation of the Cooperative Lesson Planning Guide from *Active Learning* (Johnson, Johnson, and Smith, 1991).

Exhibit 4-1. Cooperative Lesson Planning Guide.

Step 1: Select an activity and desired outcome(s).

Step 2: Make decisions.

    a. Group size:_____

    b. Assignment to groups: _____

    c. Room arrangement:_____

    d. Materials needed for each group: _____

    e. Roles: _____

Step 3: State the activity in language your students understand.

    a. Task: _____

    b. Positive interdependence: _____

    c. Individual accountability: _____

    d. Criteria for success: _____

    e. Specific behaviors to encourage:_____

(continued)

Exhibit 4-1. Cooperative Lesson Planning Guide. cont'd

Step 4:   Monitor.

   a. Evidence of cooperative and encouraged behaviors:_____

   b. Task assistance needed: _____

Step 5:   Evaluate outcomes.

   a. Task achievement:_____

   b. Group functioning:_____

   c. Notes on individuals: _____

   d. Feedback to give: _____

   e. Suggestions for next time: _____

   _____

   _____

Source: Adapted from Johnson, Johnson, and Smith, 1991, pp. 4:35–36.

Many different types of groups can be structured as cooperative learning groups. The following is a list of possibilities.

- *Special interest groups:* groups organized according to categories of participants' interests for the purposes of sharing information and experiences and of exploring common concerns.
- *Problem-solving groups:* groups organized to develop solutions to substantive problems of any nature.
- *Planning groups:* groups organized to develop plans for activities, such as field trips, guest speakers, resource use, and the like.
- *Instructional groups:* groups organized to receive specialized instruction in areas of knowledge or skill. The instructional task cannot be taught in a large-group setting, such as in a science laboratory, human relations seminar, or machine operation training course.
- *Investigation or inquiry groups:* groups organized to search out information and report their findings to the entire learning group.
- *Evaluation groups:* groups organized for the purpose of evaluating learning activities, learner behavior, or any issue that requires feedback or decision making on the part of the learning group or instructor.
- *Skill practice groups:* groups organized for the purpose of practicing any set of specified skills.
- *Tutoring or consultative groups:* groups organized for the purpose of tutoring, consulting, or giving assistance to members of other groups.
- *Operational groups:* groups organized for the purpose of taking responsibility for the operations of activities important to the learning group, such as room arrangements, refreshments, preparation of materials, operation of equipment, and the like.
- *Learning-instruction groups:* groups that take responsibility for learning all they can about a particular content unit and instructing themselves, the rest of the learning group, or both.
- *Simulation groups:* groups organized to conduct an intergroup exercise to increase knowledge or build skills, such as role playing, a game, or a case study review.
- *Learning achievement groups:* groups organized to produce a learning product that develops the members' knowledge, skills, or creativity.
- *Cooperative base groups:* cooperative learning groups that remain together for the duration of a course, have a stable membership, and foster individual accountability as they provide support, encouragement, and assistance in completing course responsibilities (Johnson, Johnson, and Smith, 1991).

- *Learning communities:* a form of block scheduling that enables college students to take more than one course together to give them an opportunity to work as a study team over a period of a semester or longer (Tinto, 1998).

Considering the length of this section on cooperative learning, you might infer that I think competitive and individualistic learning should be abandoned in adult education and training. On the contrary, I like competitive activities *when my peers and I can freely choose to participate or not to participate.* I fondly remember those movies of the fifties in which the Step Brothers or Fred Astaire and Gene Kelly would engage in a friendly rivalry of dancing, each person topping the other only to see the other person dance to an even more fantastic choreography. That's what good competition is about: choosing to elevate others and oneself to a higher plane of performance, whether it is in dancing, basketball, debate, or making wine—knowing you need each other because achieving your very best vitally depends on someone else accomplishing his or her very best.

Also, for less consequential learning, for drill practice, and for enjoyment, when the stakes are not very high (the most you can win is a round of applause), individual and intergroup competition can be quite effective. For any learning task where students' individual differences and abilities are significant, as in math or writing, an individualized approach may be more helpful to some learners. Also, there are occasions when cooperative learning can take too much time to structure and operate. What matters most is that cooperation is the norm for learning, that we are a community of learners who care about the learning of our peers as we do about our own learning. The more intellectually and socially connected we feel, the more we will persist to learn (Tinto, 1998).

Life's most important goals demand cooperation. The nurturing of our children, the quest for peace, the safeguarding of the environment, and the daily press for a stable economy all rely on mutual goodwill. Whether or not these aspirations are ever met relates profoundly to the way we learn.

STRATEGY 6: *Clearly identify the learning objectives and goals for instruction.*

As soon as adults know the objectives of an instructional unit, they begin to form a personal theory about the choices and competencies necessary for accomplishing those tasks. They ask themselves such questions as, Where do I begin? Am I able to do this? What do the other people in this course seem to know about these objectives? These reflections influence their attitude as well as their sense of inclusion. Academically, the objectives have a unifying force. These goals set the purpose for which the learners are there and show them, at the very least, what they presently hold in common, no matter their background. Objectives provide the mutual bond for learning and are why cooperation makes sense. Learners can more clearly understand and discuss their expectations. For nonnative speakers of English, clear objectives are even more critical.

Entire books have been written about how to construct learning objectives. I understand them to have at least three possible forms: clearly defined goals, problem-solving goals, and expressive outcomes.

1. *Clearly defined goals.* When specific objectives, skills, or competencies are appropriate and meaningful, especially in technical areas such as medicine and engineering, clearly defined goals can heighten learners' sense of control and capability. These goals let learners know what skills they need to acquire and inform them about what is necessary to achieve those skills. The three essential elements (Caffarella, 1994) for constructing a learning objective are *who* (the learners), *how* (the action verb), and *what* (the contents): for example, "As a result of this workshop, participants [the learners] will create [the action verb] a résumé containing their professional achievements [the contents]." Adults studying to be medical technicians are likely to appreciate

knowing that they (the learners) are going to take (the action verb) blood samples indicating blood type and Rh factor (the contents). Performance or product learning goals are often more clear when demonstrated with examples, models, or films: a dance routine, a graphic design, or an experimental procedure—whatever it takes so that confusion does not detract from learners' expectation to succeed.

Dick and Carey (1990) suggest two more elements of specific learning objectives: conditions under which the learning is to be demonstrated and the criteria for acceptable performance. Examples of given conditions are

With the following problem …

Using this software …

When a patient declines assistance …

Some examples of criteria for acceptable performance are

… with 80 percent correct

… with three or fewer errors

… with completion in thirty minutes

2. *Problem-solving goals.* Much of what we aspire to and cherish as human beings is not amenable to uniform and specific description. How could one convincingly define integrity or describe how water tastes? As Eisner (1985, p. 115) states, "To expect all of our educational aspirations to be either verbally describable or measurable is to expect too little."

The problem-solving goal differs in a significant way from the conventional instructional objective (Schön, 1987). In working on a problem-solving goal, the learners formulate or are given a problem to solve. *Although the goal is clear (solve the problem), the learning is not definite or known beforehand.* For example, in a social science course, learners might be asked how to reduce crime in a particular area, or in a design seminar, learners might be asked to create a paper structure that will hold two bricks sixteen inches above a table. In both situations, there is a range of possible solutions and learning. Problem-solving goals place a premium on intellectual exploration and the higher mental processes while supporting different cultural perspectives and values. Students' alternative solutions offer explicit evidence of the benefit of diverse talents and viewpoints. Relevant and genuine problems are most likely to elicit learner motivation.

3. *Expressive outcomes.* Another type of educational goal identified by Eisner (1985) focuses on expressive outcomes, learning objectives that emerge as the result of an intentionally planned activity. In these instances, learning goals do not precede an educational activity; they occur in the process of the activity itself. They are what we and the learners construct after some form of engagement. How many times have we read a book, seen a film, or had a conversation with learners the resonance of which affords so many questions and inspirations that to limit learners to our own educational intention is a confinement of imagination? Encouraging expressive outcomes allows us to share reciprocally with learners various media or experiences derived from our own lives, such as critical incidents (Brookfield, 1995). Afterwards, through dialogue, we can mutually decide what direction learning should take.

Problem-solving goals and expressive outcomes support the preeminence of adult self-determination and perspective in defining relevant learning goals. These forms of establishing a learning purpose are an excellent means to initiate transformative learning (Mezirow, 1997) and critical teaching (Freire, 1970). They more readily allow knowledge to be examined and constructed rather than prescribed. I once began a course in adolescent psychology by watching with the class a few excellent films in which adolescents were the main characters. After this viewing and through the compelling dialogue that evolved, we constructed the course topics, reading list, and projects to facilitate learning. The resulting course proved so powerfully informative that it was expanded the next semester to include two seniors from the local high school as coteachers.

STRATEGY 7: *Emphasize the human purpose of what is being learned and its relationship to the learners' personal lives and contemporary situations.*

Adults will feel a part of something that is relevant to them. They will want to belong to a group because it meets their personal needs. Finding a human purpose in what they are learning that is connected to their real world gives them something to care deeply about and to work in common to achieve. This purpose has the potential to be a shared vision, one that inspires cohesion, participation, and action.

This strategy is based on the assumption that *anything* that is taught somehow bears a relationship to a human need, feeling, or interest. Otherwise why else would we instruct or train for it? For us as instructors the question is, What are the human ramifications of what we are helping learners know or do? Once we have an answer to this question, the relevance of what we instruct will be clearer, and we can think of ideas to make this meaning part of the learning process. Whether we are teaching people how to wire a circuit, how to speak a foreign language, or how to write a complete sentence, there are human purposes that these skills and knowledge serve. If we can understand these qualities, especially as they may relate to the daily lives of our learners, we have some guidance in selecting those social aspects of the learning experience we may wish to emphasize.

Giving a human or social perspective to a learning experience infuses it with value beyond the technical requirements of the task and changes it from an expendable, isolated activity into a potentially valued source of personal satisfaction for the learner (Kitayama and Markus, 1994): for example, "We are not just studying how to use a new telecommunications system; we are learning a dynamically more effective and efficient way to communicate that benefits ourselves and our clients." If this viewpoint is sincerely portrayed by the instructor and embraced by the learner, the instructional activity has acquired a transcendent meaning. In plain words, this makes learning special. In fact, the structure of the previous quotation can be used to help glean the human ramifications for any specific learning objective: "We are not just studying [a specific topic or skill]; we are learning [human purpose]."

When human beings are in any way the topic of study, do their morals, values, decisions, problems, feelings, and behavior bear a relationship to similar qualities in our learners? If so, it may be worth the time to ask our learners to deal with these aspects of human existence through reflection, discussion, writing, or any other learning process. When our topics are in the realm of the physical and natural sciences, such as biology, chemistry, physics, and geology, showing how this knowledge relates to understanding challenges faced by humanity or how it can make life more sane and peaceful for everyone bonds learners in common cause. For skills from math to medicine, using human problems and concerns to illustrate and practice these useful tools can stimulate teamwork as well as emotional responsiveness in learners (Wilkerson and Gijselaers, 1996). In the technological fields, such as computer programming and database management, accentuating the contributions these processes make to human endeavors can diffuse their mechanistic isolation and humanize the learning process.

In the previous examples, we discussed emphasizing the human dimension of what is being learned so that learners can more easily identify with the topic at hand. Probably more emotionally relevant is any learning situation in which what is being learned has an immediate relationship to the *personal daily lives of adults* (Freire, 1970). If an instructor is conducting a seminar on alcoholism as a community problem, what are the implications of this information for the communities of those adults present and, more important, for their own families? In a similar vein, when an instructor is demonstrating a sales technique, why not demonstrate it with the type of client most often encountered by those sales personnel who are learning the technique? Consider a basic education instructor teaching the difference between a circle and a square. This may seem a highly abstract concept, but if, as a point of discussion, the instructor asks the learners to think of important circles and squares in their own lives, something abstract instantly becomes relevant. The closer we bring our topics and skills to the personal lives of our learners in the here and now, the more available their emotional involvement and sense of common purpose will be.

CREATING A CLIMATE OF RESPECT AMONG ADULTS

Across most cultures, to be respected in a group means, at the minimum, that you have the freedom to express your own integrity without fear of threat or blame and that you know your opinion matters. When mutual respect is present in a learning environment, adults normally feel safe, capable, accepted, and able to influence the situation when appropriate or necessary. Among people with good intentions, misunderstanding is probably the most common enemy of respect. The first recommended strategy helps all members of a learning group avoid misapprehending their situation at the most vulnerable time in their tenure, the beginning.

STRATEGY 8: *Assess learners' current expectations and needs and their previous experience as it relates to your course or training.*

Although we may already have conducted a needs assessment of the learners, they may still have perspectives they haven't voiced or important interim experiences of which we are not aware. I vividly remember conducting a workshop on motivation for a group of teachers a few years ago. I did not know they were going to strike that same afternoon. Needless to say, things weren't going very splendidly, and I hadn't a clue why. Until I asked the participants what was going on, my enthusiastic self-admonition, "Carpe diem!" made no difference.

We can confirm or alter our prior expectations or assessments with information gathered face-to-face during the opening segment of the learning experience. We can do this as part of the introductions; we can simply say, "When you are introducing yourself, please include your expectations for the course." Asking learners to fill out a short questionnaire or to answer a few questions placed on the overhead projector is also a possibility. Giving learners the chance to describe areas of worry or concern can often provide insight into the perspectives and issues they may hold regarding the course or training.

For learning experiences during which there is likely to be controversy, we may want to provide a private way for learners to convey their expectations and needs. Maurianne Adams (Adams, Bell, and Griffin, 1997, p. 317), who teaches courses in social justice, offers a good example of this approach:

At the end of the first class, I give students time to write to me, telling me whatever they want me to know about themselves, such as their background or preparation for the class, their goals for themselves in this class, any worries they may have about the class, or any physical or other disabilities they want me to know about so I can adjust assignments and activities. These are confidential. Then during the semester, I ask them to write again, telling me how they are doing, what they are struggling with, what questions or problems they have, what aspects of my teaching they find helpful, and what they wish I would change.

Adams's description emphasizes the importance of *checking in* with learners during a course or training. My experience has been that the more diverse the group, the more important it is to check in early and often to see how successfully the course and I are meeting expectations. For example, for a three-day workshop, I will check in every day no matter how well things seem to be going. When we are working with diverse learners, it is often easy to leave people out in terms of their goals and experiences without realizing it. Unless respectfully invited, people from cultures with high power distance usually are not forthcoming with this kind of information. Frequent checking in helps us adjust our instruction with minimum difficulty for learners and for us. My experience is that most adults see checking in as a caring and respectful thing to do.

STRATEGY 9: *Explicitly introduce important norms and participation guidelines.*

Every learning group is as unique as a fingerprint. It develops its own internal procedures, patterns of interaction, and limits. To some extent, it is as if imaginary lines guide and control the behavior of learners in a group. Norms are the group's common beliefs regarding appropriate behavior for its members (Johnson and Johnson, 1996). These *shared expectations* guide the perceptions, thinking, feeling, and behavior of group participants and help group interaction by specifying the kinds of responses that are expected and acceptable in particular situations. All learning groups have norms, set either formally or informally. For a group norm to influence members' behavior, members must recognize that it exists, be aware that other group members accept and follow the expectation, and feel some internal commitment to the norm.

Norms are the core constructs held in common that can ensure safety and build community among learners. Norms can create the kind of atmosphere that allows charged feelings and disagreements to be buffered as well as respectfully considered. The norms of collaboration, sharing the ownership of knowing, and a nonblameful view are critical to fostering inclusion among diverse adult learners (Wlodkowski and Ginsberg, 1995). However, a norm can be confusing to people whose culture has not socialized them for it. People who are more oriented toward individualism, high power distance, or uncertainty avoidance may feel perplexed as well as distressed by the norms just mentioned. That's why these and all important norms should be made explicit. Knowing the boundaries in a group helps members immensely in guiding their behavior.

There are several ways to implement norms (and participation guidelines) in a group. One common method is simply to state them as the rules that govern the behavior of the group. Certainly, we want to offer a rationale for them and an opportunity for discussion, remaining flexible where appropriate. We can support norms through modeling. Our formal and informal behavior toward learners has a powerful effect on the norms of the learning group. Another method is to incorporate the institutional norms of group members into the learning group. This is a common method in business settings. Learners often assume that the norms that govern their behavior in a particular institution will transfer to learning events sponsored by that institution.

Norms can also be established through consensus. Learners might suggest which norms are needed or which need editing or specific discussion. The instructor can then lead the group through a decision-making process to gain the group's consent for acceptable recommendations. Two group skills extremely important for appropriately handling this process are conflict negotiation and consensual decision making (Johnson and Johnson, 1996). Generally, adults will more actively accept norms they have helped establish. Ownership gives them a sense of personal choice, an understanding that the norms reflect their values, and a better awareness of the need for their support to maintain the norms. Finally, the more clearly they see how a norm aids in the accomplishment of a salient goal to which they are committed, the more readily adults will accept and internalize the norm.

When course or training content is challenging and the learning process is experiential and interactive, adults appreciate *participation guidelines.* By clearly identifying the kinds of interactions and discussion that will be encouraged and discouraged, the instructor and learners create a climate of safety, ensuring that everyone will be respected.

The first meeting is an appropriate time to establish these guidelines and to request cooperation in implementing them. The following rules usually prove to be acceptable as well as extremely beneficial to establishing inclusion (Wlodkowski and Ginsberg, 1995; Griffin, 1997b):

- Listen carefully, especially to different perspectives.
- Keep personal information shared in the group confidential.
- Speak from your own experience, saying, for example, "I think …," or, "In my experience I have found …," rather than generalizing your experience to others by saying, for example, "People say …," or, "We believe …"
- Do no blaming or scapegoating.

- Avoid generalizing about groups of people.
- Share airtime.
- Focus on your own learning.

I have found that instructors who use participation guidelines usually have a few that are nonnegotiable (Tatum, 1992). This makes sense because everyone is safer when we as instructors know what our professional limits are. Although the list is sometimes longer or shorter, most adults accept and generate these guidelines because these rules reduce feelings of fear, awkwardness, embarrassment, and shame. They also provide a safety net for critical discourse. Leaving participation guidelines open to further additions and referring to them when necessary keeps the boundaries of the learning environment clear and dynamic.

STRATEGY 10: *When issuing mandatory assignments or training requirements, give your rationale for these stipulations.*

Adults hate busywork. Many of them have had teachers who were simply authoritarian and handed out assignments without rhyme or reason. Because requirements demand time, energy, and responsibility, even the most motivated adult learner will feel cautious when the assignments are handed out. (Notice how quiet it gets!)

When we state the rationale for stipulations, learners will more likely know that we have carefully considered the matter; that we realize the obligations, benefits, and results of the requirements; and most important, that we respect learners and want to share this information. It is also no mean advantage to us that by revealing the rationale, we are more likely to ensure that learners won't misinterpret the motive or purpose of the assignment.

As in most matters of communication, difficult news is best received when it is delivered directly and concisely. Here are two examples. An instructor might say: "At the end of this unit, I will ask each of you to role-play a conflict management situation in a small-group setting. Each of you will be asked to resolve this problem by applying the suggestions for conflict management that are most relevant to a collectivist culture. This will give me the opportunity to give each of you guided practice and feedback so that you can refine your skills and have a chance to test this approach under simulated conditions." Or an instructor might say: "In addition to the readings in your textbook, I've assigned three outside articles and put them on reserve at the local library. I realize this may be somewhat of an inconvenience for you. However, each of these articles contains a case study that is far more realistic and comprehensive than any of those found in your text. These case studies will provide much better examples of the principles you are studying and give you a chance to explore the benefits of these theories in situations much closer to your own real-life experiences."

Even with the clearest rationale behind them, assignments are assignments, and usually no one applauds after they are given. This silence often simply reflects the realistic concern of adult learners who are accepting a new responsibility.

STRATEGY 11: *To the degree authentically possible, reflect the language, perspective, and attitudes of adult learners.*

Counselors call this practice *pacing and mirroring.* It is considered essential to establishing rapport with other people (Pedersen, 1994). In pacing and mirroring, the instructor matches the verbal and nonverbal behavior of adult learners—literally reflecting their speech, mannerisms, and perceptions. Specialists in intercultural communication refer to this process as *anticipatory communication* or *receiver centeredness:* the ability to capture and mirror the implicit meaning of other people, a sensitivity much valued by those from high-context cultures (Yum, 1997).

Friends mirror each other naturally. They "understand" each other, usually have something in common, and speak a similar language. Strangers striking up a relationship follow a similar pattern. They cast about for some common interest—the weather, sports, or current news. When they hit a common chord, they share perspectives that may lead to some shared viewpoint that further intensifies the relationship. Feeling connected with someone usually means finding mutual interests, values, and outlooks in that person. Friends who have not seen each other for a long time often talk about the "old days," using shared past experiences to renew their sense of rapport. People are sometimes accused of "talking shop" at parties, but this professional rapport is usually the true foundation for their relationship. It might be difficult for them to have a genuine conversation without referring to the workplace.

One of the easiest things we can do to gain the acceptance of adult learners is to fluently use their language and their perspective. People understand other people by their own definitions and their own attitudes. They not only have a difficult time understanding someone who speaks differently than they do but also have a more difficult time trusting that person. This is a universal, historical fact. Our assuming the language and perspective of our adult learners makes us more clearly understandable, more trustworthy, and more effective as models. This is why listening is so important. Until we really understand someone, it is difficult to accurately use his or her language. We are not talking down or up to anybody but being sensitively aware of the predicates, figures of speech, interests, and values that adult learners have in common with us. We use our awareness of these factors to construct a language and perspective that we use with integrity to communicate effectively. If a person uses the expression *bottom line* to mean "personal limit" and displays a very analytical approach to a political question, we are wise to use a similar expression and approach if we want to be well understood regarding the same political question. The goal is not to be a chameleon but to select wisely from among what we hold in common with learners and to be willing to learn new perspectives and expressions from them. This approach encourages the use of the voice of the learners and gives us access to the knowledge and realities both of their world and our own. When we approach communication this way, we create a language to transcend our own limits, moving us toward greater learning for all.

STRATEGY 12: *Introduce the concepts of comfort zones and learning edges to help learners accommodate more intense emotions during episodes of new learning.*

The concepts of comfort zones and learning edges can support adults as they struggle to understand and explore their reactions to challenging class activities and to other learners' perspectives (Griffin, 1997b). When we are dealing with topics or activities with which we are familiar, we usually feel comfortable and without serious tension or anxiety. This is learning *within our comfort zone.* When we are solidly in our comfort zone and not challenged, we are usually not learning anything very new. When we are dealing with unfamiliar topics and activities or seeing familiar topics in new ways, we are *outside our comfort zone* or on its edge. If we are too far outside our comfort zone, we usually try to withdraw or to strongly resist the new information or experiences; we keep ourselves safe.

When we are on the edge of our comfort zone, we are in a very good place to stretch our understanding, take in a different perspective, and expand our awareness. This is our *learning edge.* It is important to recognize our learning edge, because the time when we are on it is an optimum time for new learning but is often accompanied by feelings of annoyance, anxiety, surprise, confusion, defensiveness, and sometimes anger. These emotions frequently are signs that our way of seeing things is being challenged. As Griffin (1997b, p. 68) wisely cautions, "If we retreat to our comfort zone, by dismissing whatever we encounter that does not agree with our way of seeing the world, we lose an opportunity to expand our understanding. The challenge is to recognize when we are on a learning edge and then to stay there with the discomfort we are experiencing to see what we can learn."

Comfort zones and learning edges are important concepts for adults to acknowledge. We normally don't like to have our beliefs challenged, because they are the sources of stability in our lives. Some courses and training push the learning edge more than others. I have found that in those courses I teach that deal with diversity or social issues, offering learners a chance to become familiar with the concepts of comfort zones and learning edges gives them a language and a means of adjustment that offers real relief for some of their anxiety. Taking a couple of minutes to exchange stories with a partner about times he or she has been on a learning edge with new information or skills (especially those he or she is now glad of having) gives learners a chance to familiarize themselves with these concepts from their own experience. Usually the discussions are about things like sports, dancing, new relationships, social issues, and tough academic courses. It is also helpful to ask learners to identify the internal cues that alert them to their learning edge. Pounding hearts, dry mouths, and shaky stomachs are universal experiences accompanying the birth of important new learning.

STRATEGY 13: *Acknowledge different ways of knowing, different languages, and different levels of knowledge or skill to engender a safe learning environment.*

One of the myths perpetuated about adults is that if you're older you know more. This fiction doesn't account for all we have learned that was wrong, incorrect, unethical, or misleading. It also doesn't cover for what we have forgotten and confused, not to mention those vast stores of irrelevance attached to our dendrites. (Does anyone really care that I can name every movie Gilbert Roland played in?) We may certainly know more about some things, but we do have our limits. At best, aging and wisdom are dubious partners. Nonetheless, the myth is an intimidating one, and many adults feel uncomfortable when they realize they may know less than other participants in a course or training. Often it's more a case of knowing things differently or with a different language. In teaching about research, for example, with its buckets of jargon, I have found adults openly relieved to know *reliability* means something as straightforward as consistency.

To relax things a bit, we can acknowledge to learners that we would appreciate knowing when there's a different way they understand something or a different language they use. As an example, I often qualify research findings by noting they are a particular way of knowing something and, at best, they can only inform our experience. We can also ask how our experience can inform this research.

For many learning experiences, from child psychology classes to computer training, adults in attendance also may differ extensively from one another in their experience and knowledge, some people being novices and others having more experience than the instructor. After performing some form of assessment to understand these disparities and acknowledging that the disparities are OK, we need to find a way to move forward together. We may do this using special project work, grouping systems, cooperative learning, or panel discussions—whatever allows us to learn most effectively and remain a mutually respectful community.

As I close this section, it is probably a good time to say a few words about resistance in a learning group when it occurs in the beginning of a course or training. Resistance often comes up because the learning experience is required or because people believe they have been unfairly mandated to attend. The group feeling tends to be some version of "we don't need this" or "this is going to be a waste of time." In these circumstances, it is usually best to openly acknowledge the situation and the possible feelings that may be occurring in the group. If appropriate, we might pace and mirror the learners as we listen. Then we can plan or engage in learning that emphasizes immediate relevance and choice for them. These procedures have a good chance of moving the group forward.

The challenge of inclusion is to find ways to allow all adults to be respected as part of a learning community, without diminishing their spirit, their experience, their perspective, and their feeling. A mere strategy does not create such a milieu. Inclusion is the result of a determined living harmony, a constancy of practices blended with ideals from the beginning to the end of every lesson of every session of every course.

SECTION FIVE

HELPING ADULTS DEVELOP POSITIVE ATTITUDES TOWARD LEARNING

RAYMOND J. WLODKOWSKI

Exhortation is used more and accomplishes less than almost any behavior-changing tool known.

Robert F. Mager

We all spend a great deal of our time trying to influence other people's attitudes, especially the attitudes of those for whose work or effort we have some responsibility. We talk, show evidence, list logical reasons, and in some instances, actually give personal testimony to the positive results of this desired attitude. We are trying to be persuasive. Intuitively, we know it is best for people to like what they must do. Instructors want learners to feel positively toward learning and the effort it takes to accomplish it. However, exhorting, arguing, explaining, and cajoling are usually very inefficient means of helping someone develop a positive attitude toward learning. All these methods have a glaring weakness: they are simply words—"talk," if you will—that have nowhere near the impact of the consequences, conditions, and people involved in the learning task itself. When successful, the *process* and *outcomes* of learning are what tell the story for the learner. When unsuccessful, persuasion becomes a form of linguistic static, badgering, or nagging that undermines the development of a positive attitude in the adult learner.

In general, it is probably best not to try to talk adults into learning. There are far more powerful things we can do in the presentation of the subject matter as well as in our treatment of adults to help them build positive attitudes toward their learning and themselves as learners. This section will examine a number of strategies that encourage adults to look forward to learning and, perhaps most important, feel eager to learn more.

FOUR IMPORTANT ATTITUDINAL DIRECTIONS

Attitudes predispose adults to respond favorably or unfavorably toward particular people, groups, ideas, events, or objects. From a sociocultural view, relevance and choice are two of the qualities that most determine a positive attitude among adult learners. When relevance and choice are present, most adults initially perceive the learning as appealing, as an activity they would freely endorse as something they want to do. From a more analytic, individualistic view, we can say that adult attitudes usually move in one or more of four directions, which together determine how appealing learning is for adults: (1) toward the instructor, (2) toward the subject, (3) toward the adults themselves as learners, and (4) toward the adults' expectancy for success.

This more cognitive-behavioral understanding is limited in its sensitivity to culture (Okun, 1990) but offers a well-researched, useful interpretation of attitude as a combination of a perception with a judgment that often results in an emotion that influences behavior (Ellis, 1989). The examples in Table 5-1 illustrate the influence that attitudes can have on behavior and performance in learning tasks.

Whenever we instruct, we want to establish a learning environment in which these four important attitudinal directions are positive and unified for the learner. We want adults *to like and respect us and the subject matter and to feel confident as learners who realistically believe they can succeed in the learning task at hand.*

If any one of these four attitudinal directions becomes seriously negative for the adult, his or her motivation to learn can be impaired. A person could respect the instructor, feel confident as a learner, and objectively expect to do well but still intensely dislike the subject area. This sometimes happens with required courses or training; competent instructors find capable adults disinterested and apathetic. In a similar vein, an adult could like the instructor and the subject and be confident

Table 5-1.   Attitudinal Directions.

Perception	+	Judgment	→	Emotion	→	Behavior
I see my instructor.		He seems helpful.		I feel appreciative.		I will cooperate.
The instructor announces the beginning of a new unit on family relations. (subject matter)		Learning more about being an effective parent is helpful to me.		I feel interested.		I will pay close attention.
It is my turn to present my project to the seminar. (self as learner)		I am knowledgeable and well prepared for this.		I feel confident.		I will do a good job and give a smooth and articulate presentation.
The instructor is giving a surprise quiz. (expectancy for success)		I have not studied this material and will probably flunk this quiz.		I feel very anxious.		I can't think straight and won't be able to answer the questions.

as a learner but realize there is not enough time or proper materials to prepare and be successful in the learning task. It is quite likely that this person's overall motivation to learn will be significantly reduced, and his trying hard will probably lead only to frustration. This situation often arises when someone has to compete against someone else whose preparation and material advantages seem far superior to his own.

In most instances, adults experience their attitudes immediately, without premeditation or serious reflection. They hear or see something, and the attitude begins to run its course. The instructor introduces the topic, and the learner's attitude toward that topic emerges. The instructor assigns homework, and the learner quickly has an attitude toward the assignment. "Wait and see" makes a great deal of sense, but that is not how attitudes work. We use this self-administered advice in an appeal for caution because we understand how instantly attitudes (including erroneous ones) influence us. "Wait and maybe I can change this attitude" is probably a more accurate self-admonition. Once a person has had an experience, the attitude will occur, like it or not. It may be only a vague feeling, but it is still an influence on behavior. That is why we as instructors have to be aware of what can be done to influence learner attitudes positively at the beginning of any learning experience. The attitudes will be there from the very start. Having them *work for* learners and us gives the best chance for motivated learning to occur. Although most of the following strategies can be implemented throughout the learning experience, the discussion here will stress their use at the beginning of learning and training activities.

CREATING A POSITIVE ATTITUDE TOWARD THE INSTRUCTOR

Even in the case of distance education, learning is significantly associated with the instructor (Dillon and Smith, 1992). We want that association to be positive. It is more difficult for adults to accept what they are offered when the person who is giving it to them is someone they do not like or respect. A learner's negative attitude toward an instructor makes that instructor a barrier between the material to be learned and the learner. Instead of feeling consonant and at ease because a respected instructor is offering an attractive lesson, the learner may feel dissonant and psychologically tense because a disliked instructor is offering an attractive lesson. The same principle occurs in everyday behavior. We feel uneasy purchasing a car from a salesperson we don't like or accepting a gift from someone we disrespect. In most instances, it seems better for us not to buy the car or not to accept the gift, because then our actions are consistent with how we feel toward the person. In learning situations, adults will be more open, accepting, and responsive to materials and tasks they receive from an instructor they like and respect. They will be quite the opposite with an instructor they don't like or respect. Optimal motivation for learning will probably decrease.

The core characteristics of expertise, empathy, and cultural responsiveness will be major influences in establishing a positive attitude toward the instructor. Because the learners' relationship to the instructor bears so strongly on learners' sense of inclusion, the strategies directed toward creating a positive attitude toward the instructor appeared under the title Establishing Inclusion Among Adult Learners (Section four) (which discusses strategies that establish inclusion). They are summarized here:

- Allow for introductions. (Strategy 1)
- Concretely indicate your cooperative intentions to help adults learn. (Strategy 3)
- Share something of value with your adult learners. (Strategy 4)
- When issuing mandatory assignments or training requirements, give your rationale for these stipulations. (Strategy 10)
- To the degree authentically possible, reflect the language, perspective, and attitudes of adult learners. (Strategy 11)
- Acknowledge different ways of knowing, different languages, and different levels of knowledge or skill to engender a safe learning environment. (Strategy 13)

BUILDING A POSITIVE ATTITUDE TOWARD THE SUBJECT

Please read the following words out loud:

English	Grammar	History
Computers	Math	Reading
Biology	Music	Spelling
Writing	Algebra	Chemistry

Which word evoked the strongest emotional reaction in you? Was it a positive or a negative feeling? Most of the listed subject areas are common to the educational experience of adults. Adults have taken such courses, and they usually have distinct attitudes toward them. Any new learning that involves elements from these former subjects will cause immediate attitudinal reactions on the part of adults. That is why adults so often ask questions like these at the beginning of new courses and training sessions: How much reading will I have to do? What kind of math does this training require? What will I have to write? Adults have strong opinions about both their capabilities and their feelings toward such requirements. They carry attitudes toward them that often are decades old and very entrenched (Smith, 1982). New learning often causes mixed reactions in adults. They might want to learn about innovative uses of computers but honestly have real fears if any math is involved in the training.

To some extent, new learning goes against the grain of the personal autonomy and security of adults. Older adults have usually found a way to cope with life and have formulated a set of convictions (Schaie and Willis, 1996). New learning often asks them to become temporarily dependent, to open their minds to new ideas, to rethink certain beliefs, and to try different ways of doing things. This may be threatening to them, and their attitudes can easily lock in to support their resistance.

It has also been documented that adults may react with apprehension to specific areas of content, such as math and foreign languages (Smith, 1982). For some, speaking in front of the group is a real ordeal. Others find specific learning techniques, such as role playing and videotaping of themselves, to be quite anxiety producing.

Whatever we can do as instructors to minimize adults' negative attitudes and to foster the development of their positive attitudes toward the subject and the instructional process will improve their motivation for learning. Invigorated by our enthusiasm, the following strategies are a means to this end.

STRATEGY 14: *Eliminate or minimize any negative conditions that surround the subject.*

Mager (1968) once wrote that people learn to avoid the things they are hit with. It is a common fact of learning that when a person is presented with an item or subject and is at the same time in the presence of negative (unpleasant) conditions, that item or subject becomes a stimulus for avoidance behavior. Things or subjects that frighten adults are often associated with antagonists and situations that make them uncomfortable, tense, or scared. Therefore, it is best not to associate the subject with any of the following conditions. These tend to support negative learner attitudes and repel adult interest:

- *Pain:* acute physical and psychological discomfort, such as continuous failure (where learner effort makes no difference), poorly fitting equipment, or uncomfortable room temperature
- *Fear and anxiety:* distress and tension resulting from anticipation of the unpleasant or dangerous, such as threat of failure or punishment, public exposure of ignorance, or unpredictability of potential negative consequences
- *Frustration:* an emotional reaction to the blockage or defeat of purposeful behavior, such as occurs when information is presented too quickly or too slowly or when the learner receives unannounced tests or inadequate feedback on performance
- *Humiliation:* an emotional reaction to being shamed, disrespected, or degraded, such as occurs when a person receives sarcasm, insult, sexist comment, or public comparison of inadequate learning
- *Boredom:* a cognitive and emotional reaction to a situation in which stimuli impinging on a learner are weak, repetitive, or infrequent, as occurs when learning situations lack variety, cover material already known, or contain excessively predictable discussion respondents (the same people talking over and over again)

This list is quite dismal. However, just as a slate must be wiped clean before clear and lucid new writing can be set down, learning environments must have these negative conditions removed before positive conditions can effectively occur. Otherwise, the best efforts of motivating instructors can be contaminated and diffused by the mere presence of such oppressive elements.

STRATEGY 15: *Ensure successful learning with mastery learning conditions.*

It is difficult for anyone to dislike a subject in which they are successful. Conversely, it is rare to find anyone who really likes a subject in which they are unsuccessful. Competent learning in a subject is probably one of the surest ways to sustain a positive attitude toward that subject. According to Bloom (1981), most learners (perhaps more than 90 percent) can master what is generally taught. The important qualification is that some learners take a great deal more time to learn something than others do. In general, Bloom's studies indicated that slow learners may take six times longer to learn the same material as faster learners do. With effective instruction and efficient use of learner time, he estimated this ratio could be cut down to three to one.

Some adults may be discouraged when they realize how much extra time and effort they will need to expend to master what we are teaching. However, we can positively influence their attitudes as well as those of our faster learners when we guarantee the following three conditions: (1) quality instruction that will help them learn if they try to learn, (2) concrete evidence that their effort makes a difference, and (3) continual feedback regarding the progress of their learning.

In addition, it helps us as instructors to realize that few adults know for certain how much time and effort it will take to master a particular subject. When the three conditions just cited are present from the very beginning of a course, learners have a much better chance to experience success. Here are Bloom's *guidelines* (1981) for establishing these conditions:

- In addition to your main instructional techniques (laboratory and discussion, textbook, and so forth), have a number of alternative instructional processes available to meet the needs of individual learners. The following are some alternatives:

  Group study procedures might be available to learners as they need them. Small groups of learners (two or three) could meet regularly to go over points of difficulty in the learning process. If you use group study, avoid competitive forms of evaluation, so that everyone feels able to gain from cooperating with the others.

  Other suggested textbooks might offer a clearer or better-exemplified discussion of material the learner is having difficulty grasping in the adopted textbook.

  Workshops, programmed instruction units, and computer-assisted instruction might provide the drill and specific tasks that regular instruction cannot. Some learners need small steps and frequent reinforcement to overcome particular learning difficulties.

  Media, films, and the Internet might sometimes provide the illustrations and vivid explanations not found in regular learning procedures.

  Tutorial help is often a last resort but is certainly a legitimate and helpful one for many learners.

- Set clear (that is, understandable) standards of mastery and excellence. When adults know the criteria by which their learning will be evaluated, they know better what to do in order to do well in a particular subject.

- Avoid competition for scores and grades. When adults do not have to fear each other's progress to protect their self-esteem, an extra and valuable corps of instructional assistants becomes available in the learning environment.

- Break down courses or training into smaller units of learning. Such a learning unit may correspond to a chapter in a book, a well-defined content portion of a training seminar, or a particular time unit. Segmenting instruction into smaller increments allows the learner to perceive progress more easily, just as gauging a minute on a clock is easier to do than gauging an hour. Every time we can help our learners say that they have concretely learned something, we have helped them feel a sense of progress. This also helps them maintain their concentration.

- Frequently use *formative evaluation*. These are exams and tests, written, oral, or performance, that are used only to diagnose progress (meaning they are *not graded*). They are meant to assess learner progress and to indicate points of learner difficulty or instructional inadequacy; they are tailored to the particular unit of learning. For those learners who have mastered the unit, formative evaluation will give them positive feedback. They can honestly say, "With that instructor, I really know how well I'm doing." For those learners who lack mastery of a unit, formative evaluation will point out the particular ideas, skills, and processes they still need to work on and the instructional delivery the instructor may need to alter. Bloom found that learners respond best when the instructor refers them to particular instructional materials or processes intended to help them correct their difficulties. They can at least say, "I know where I am, and I know what I have to do to help myself."

Ensuring successful learning is a powerful strategy. Success breeds interest and motivation for further learning. Research indicates that using this approach can enhance learner attitudes and achievement, particularly for those who have difficulty in conventional college learning environments (Kulik, Kulik, and Bangert-Drowns, 1990).

STRATEGY 16: *Positively confront the erroneous beliefs, expectations, and assumptions that may underlie a negative learner attitude.*

Some learners have mistaken beliefs that support their negative attitudes. For example, learners may think, "If I have to do any math in this course, I won't do well in it," or, "Communications training has never helped anyone I know," or, "If I make a mistake, I'll really look bad." Assumptions of this sort can cause learners to fear and resist a subject (Ellis, 1989). People maintain their negative attitudes by repeating such beliefs to themselves. If you think an individual or a group is holding such beliefs, you can engage in an appropriate discussion along the following guidelines to help reduce the negative attitude:

1. Tactfully find out what the learner might be telling herself that leads to the negative attitude. ("You seem somewhat discouraged. Could you tell me what might be happening or what you might be thinking that's leading to such feelings?")
2. If the learner appears to have a self-defeating belief, point out how negative feelings would naturally follow from such a belief. ("If you believe making a mistake will really make you look foolish in front of your peers, you probably feel fearful and anxious about trying some of the group exercises.")
3. Suggest other assumptions that might be more helpful to the learner. ("You might tell yourself that this is guided practice, where everyone including your instructor expects some mistakes, and that the purpose of the exercises is to refine skills, not to demonstrate them at a level of perfection.")
4. Encourage the learner to develop beliefs, based on present reality, that promote well-being. ("When you start to feel discouraged or negative, check out what you are telling yourself and see if it really helps you. Consider whether there might be some other beliefs or expectancies that would do you more good. You might want to discuss this with me so that I can give you feedback and other possible ways of looking at the situation that might be more helpful.")

Sometimes it's useful to ask the learner "what might have to happen" for her to believe she could do well or to change her attitude in a positive direction. This question may help the learner describe relevant examples of evidence that will fit her perspective and produce a shift in attitude. At a workshop, I once asked this question of a group of reluctant college faculty. They anonymously wrote their answers on cards, which I read back to them. Midway through the deck I found myself reading one that stated, "A public hanging of the dean." Fortunately, she graciously laughed. Her sense of humor and compassion took us to another level of discourse, and the workshop progressed with much more effectiveness.

STRATEGY 17: *Use assisted learning to scaffold complex learning.*

Assisted learning is a pragmatic blend of individualistic and socioconstructivist thinking. Vygotsky (1978) realized there were certain problems and skills that a person could solve or master when given appropriate help and support. Such learning, often called assisted learning, provides *scaffolding*—giving clues, information, prompts, reminders, and encouragement at the appropriate time and in the appropriate amounts and then gradually allowing the learner to do more and more independently. Most of us naturally scaffold when we teach someone to drive a car or play a card game. The *zone of proximal development* is the phase in a learning task when a learner can benefit from assistance (Wertsch, 1991). The upper limit of the zone is the place at which the learner can perform the task independently; the lower limit is the place where the learner can perform the task but needs assistance. Most of us learned to drive a car with someone in the seat next to us who prompted and reminded us of what to do and when to do it as we navigated a road. In the beginning, this "coach" usually had to scaffold pretty intensely: "Check your speedometer"; "I think you're speeding"; "Watch out for that car"; "If you don't stop, we are going to have an accident." We were obviously in the lower limit of our zone of proximal development for driving. But eventually most of us required less coaching; we reached the upper limit and began to drive independently.

Myriad other learning tasks strongly benefit from scaffolding. Whether adults are learning to solve math problems, conduct experiments, or use a personal computer, our assessing their zone of proximal development and structuring the appropriate scaffold can lead to success. Adults deeply appreciate the support assisted learning offers because it tends to be concrete, immediate, and tailored to their obvious needs. The following are some of the methods specific to assisted learning that can be used to scaffold more complex learning (Association for Supervision and Curriculum Development, 1990). The description of each method includes an example in which I model assisting students to learn to write a research report.

- *Modeling:* the instructor carries out the skill while the learners observe, or the instructor offers actual examples of learning outcomes, such as finished papers or solved problems. (I ask the learners to read two previously completed reports. One is excellent, the other is satisfactory.)
- *Thinking out loud:* the instructor states actual thought processes in carrying out the learning task. (I talk about some of the goals and criteria I would consider before writing the report. I ask the learners why one report was considered excellent and the other only satisfactory. I supplement the learners' perceptions with my own.)
- *Anticipating difficulties:* as the learning proceeds, the instructor and learners discuss areas where support is needed and mistakes are more likely to occur. (Because the sections of the report that discuss findings and statistical analyses seem most challenging to learners, we discuss how these sections were done in the two reports and arrange for prompt feedback on the learners' initial drafts of these sections in their own reports.)
- *Providing prompts and cues:* the instructor highlights, emphasizes, or structures procedural steps and important responses to help learners clearly recognize their place and their importance to the learning task. (I provide an outline for writing a research report with exemplars from previous reports.)
- *Regulating the difficulty:* the instructor introduces a more complex task with simpler tasks and may offer some practice with these. (I give the learners a basic research scenario, a hypothesis, data, and an analysis scheme and ask them to write a brief research report with this information.)
- *Using reciprocal teaching:* the instructor and the learners rotate the role of instructor; in that role, each learner provides guidance and suggestions to others. (While I monitor, each learner presents his or her brief research report to a learning partner who acts as the instructor and gives supportive feedback. Then they reverse roles. The same process is carried out with the first draft of their actual research report.)
- *Providing a checklist:* learners use self-checking procedures to monitor the quality of their learning. (I give the learners a checklist of questions and quality criteria to consider as they write their reports.)

Consider the possible metaphors for the provider of assisted learning: sensitive tutor, seasoned coach, wise parent—all people who tell us just enough, what we need to know when we need to know it, trusting us to chart the rest of our journey to learning. Assisted learning conveys an underlying message: "You may stray, but you will not be lost. In this endeavor, you are not alone." The image is not one of the rugged individualist or the solitary explorer. Rather, assisted learning embraces a vision of remarkable possibility nurtured by a caring community.

DEVELOPING A POSITIVE SELF-CONCEPT FOR LEARNING

Goethe believed that the greatest evil that can befall a person is that he should come to think ill of himself. Some learners may not have a negative attitude toward their instructor or the subject, but they may have a negative attitude toward themselves. They may believe their capabilities to perform a task and succeed at it are inadequate. A person holding such negative beliefs is often said to have a "poor self-concept." His or her motivation to learn is often diminished.

Among adults, self-concept tends to be situation-specific (Pintrich and Schunk, 1996). A person might feel quite physically adept but very incompetent in academic situations. This kind of breakdown exists within the academic self-concept as well. A learner might feel quite superior in English and very inferior in math. Adults constantly modify their self-concepts in specific areas of learning, which means that during our instructional or training session we have a chance to positively affect a person's self-estimation.

There are some cautions. The adult has a firmer and more fully formed self-concept than does the child (Brundage and MacKeracher, 1980). It is not uncommon for adults to harbor doubts about their personal learning ability. They often underestimate and underuse their capacities (Knox, 1977). Their own family members may reinforce their self-doubts by questioning their abilities or need for certain learning. Later adulthood and old age are periods when many learners are more prone to this source of anxiety.

Regardless of the state of the adult's self-concept on entering our learning situation, we can provide the experiences from which each adult can derive self-confidence as a learner. Before we move to particular strategies, it is important to emphasize again the strategies of *ensuring successful learning* and *scaffolding* (Strategies 15 and 17, respectively). These strategies powerfully affect both the learner's attitude toward the subject and the learner's attitude toward the self as learner. In fact, we should consider them prerequisites for all the strategies that follow. The fundamental basis for acquiring a positive self-concept for learning in any area is realistically seeing oneself as a *successful* learner from one's own perspective.

STRATEGY 18: *Encourage the learner.*

We can use this strategy with a group or an individual. Encouragement is any behavior on our part by which we show the learner (1) that we respect the learner as a person, no matter what is learned, (2) that we trust and believe in the learner's effort to learn, and (3) that the learner *can* learn. An adult who perceives that the instructor's respect is contingent only on learning performance will feel dehumanized. Such a criterion for acceptance by the instructor denies the adult's other worthy qualities and makes the person into a "thing" that learns without feelings or dignity. The primary foundation for encouragement is our caring about and acceptance of the learner. This caring and acceptance creates the context in which we choose ways to show confidence and personal regard for the learner's effort and achievement. These ways include the following:

Giving recognition for effort.

Any time a person seriously attempts to learn something, that individual is taking a risk. Intentional learning is a courageous act. No one learns 100 percent of the time. Some risk is usually involved. We can help by acknowledging learners' effort and by respecting their perseverance. Any comment that says, "I like the way you try," can help learners understand that we value their effort. When insecure learners know that we honestly esteem their effort during the time preceding eventual achievement, it does a great deal to reduce their performance anxiety and its debilitating effects.

Minimizing mistakes while the learner is struggling.

Sometimes learning is like a battle. The critical edge between advancement and withdrawal or between hope and despair is fragile at best. Our emphasis on a learner's mistakes at such a critical moment will accentuate whatever pessimistic emotions the learner is already feeling and is a sure way to encourage self-defeat.

Emphasizing learning from mistakes.

Help adults see a mistake as a way to improve future learning. When we actually help them learn from a mistake, we directly show them how thinking and trying are in their best interest and that we have confidence they will learn.

For each learning task, demonstrating a confident and realistic expectancy that the learner will learn.

Essentially we are conveying the message, "You can do it," but without implying that the task is easy or simple. Whenever we tell a person that something is easy, we have placed that person in a lose-lose dilemma. If the person successfully does the task, she feels no pride, because the task was easy in the first place. If the person fails, she feels shame, because the task was implied to be simple.

Showing faith in the adult's capacity as a learner.

This faith translates into "sometimes it may be difficult, but I believe you can learn, and I will work with you toward that goal." Whenever we give up on a learner, we also give up on ourselves as instructors. Realistically, some of our learners actually may prefer that we give up. It makes it easier for them to stop trying. By showing consistent trust in the learner's capacity to achieve, we maintain our responsibility as instructors, and we emphasize the learner's responsibility for continued effort.

Working with the learner at the beginning of difficult tasks.

It's amazing what can be lifted and moved with just a little help. Sometimes a learner might be momentarily confused or not know what to do next. As a form of early scaffolding, our proximity and minimal assistance can be just enough for the learner to find the right direction, continue involvement, and gain the initial confidence to proceed with learning.

Affirming the process of learning.

This means acknowledging all parts of the learning endeavor—the information seeking, the studying, the practicing, the cooperating, and so forth. If we wait for the final product—the test results, project, or whatever the final goal is—we may be too late. Some learners may have given up by this time. Our delay also implies that the learner should wait until the end of learning to feel good about learning. Even waiting for some minimal progress can sometimes be a mistake. Learning does not follow a linear progression; there are often wide spaces, deep holes, dead ends, and regressions. Real encouragement says the task of learning is itself important and emphasizes the intrinsic value of the entire process of learning.

STRATEGY 19: *Promote the learner's personal control of the context of learning.*

It is very important for learners to be successful and to feel encouraged, but for people to build confidence as learners, they usually need to realize that their own behavior is most responsible for their learning. This is especially the case for those with individualistic values; they are more compelled to feel a sense of personal causation in the process of learning—that they mainly *control* how, what, and when they learn (Deci and Ryan, 1991). At first, this may seem obvious: if a person pays attention, studies, and practices, of course the person will feel responsible for any successful achievement. However, when we remember that instructors usually establish requirements, issue assignments, give tests, generally set the standards for achievement, often control the learning environment, and sometimes pressure learner involvement, it is not too difficult to understand how a learner could come to believe it is the instructor who is most responsible for achievement. Even when a person is successful, he or she may feel very dependent as a learner and consequently bound to the demands and directions of the instructor for future learning. In this way, a person can feel like a pawn while learning and not develop self-confidence as a learner.

Adults are inclined toward autonomy in many aspects of their daily lives; the following methods to increase their sense of personal causation while learning should effectively complement this tendency.

The learner plans and sets goals for learning.

Planning validates the individual as the originator and guide of the process.

To the extent appropriate, the learner makes choices about what, how, with whom, where, and when to learn something.

Choice is the essence of responsibility. It permits the learner to feel ownership of the learning experience. The learner can choose topics, assignments, with whom to learn, when to be evaluated, how to be evaluated, and so forth.

The learner uses self-assessment procedures.

When a learner can appraise mistakes and successes while learning, she experiences a concrete sense of participation in the learning act. Sometimes learners can get the feeling that mistakes are created by the instructor more than committed by the learner. Self-assessment procedures can prevent this misperception and give the learner a sense of control from the beginning to the end of the learning experience. When a person can determine for herself whether she is really learning something, she feels more responsible for that learning.

The instructor helps the learner identify personal strengths while learning.

For example, "You have a number of assignments to choose from, but it seems to me you have a real talent for explaining things well and could probably give a very interesting oral presentation. What do you think?" A learner who knows and takes advantage of personal assets while learning feels a real sense of power and confidence.

The learner logs personal progress while learning.

This allows the learner to feel personal growth and learning concretely, as they take place.

The learner participates in analyzing potential blocks to progress in learning.

For example, the instructor might ask, "What do you think the difficulty might be?" or, "In your estimation, where do you think the confusion begins?" By participating in solving the learning problem, the learner feels more commitment to its resolution and is more aware of her role in the learning process. An added plus for instructors—adult learners frequently know better than we do where problems in learning are occurring.

When advisable, the learner makes a commitment to the learning task.

This accentuates the learner's personal choice. It prevents denial or withdrawal of personal responsibility for learning. When we ask a learner, "Are you sure you're going to do it?" or, "Can I feel certain that you're going to try?" and we receive a sincere affirmative answer, we are helping to amplify the learner's sense of self-determination. However, use this technique sparingly and with careful forethought. If it lacks integrity, it becomes a mere manipulation and an insult to the learner.

The learner has access to prompt feedback.

Prompt feedback during learning leads to stronger feelings of personal control and responsibility. This is one of the main reasons computer-assisted instruction can be fantastic for increasing motivation. The computer has the mechanical ability to give immediate feedback. The learner has moment-to-moment awareness of progress in learning. This constant back-and-forth *dialogue* between computer and learner gives the learner a strong sense of control in the learning process. In so many ways, the computer tells the learner it will not respond until the learner responds first. The learner's personal control is undeniable.

In contrast, the longer it takes for a person to know if a response has had an effect, the more difficult it can become to know whether that response had any effect at all. Imagine having a conversation with someone who waited at least a minute or longer to answer any question you asked. It is likely that you would wonder if you were actually being heard. Anything an instructor can do to ensure the best possible pace of accurate feedback will concretely help emphasize learner responsibility. See "Engendering Competence Among Adult Learners" (Section Five) for a more comprehensive discussion of the appropriate use of feedback.

The purpose of these methods is to emphasize that the *majority* of responsibility for learning is under the control of the learner. For an adult to feel "I can do it" when it comes to future learning, he or she has to have felt "I did it" during previous experiences in learning.

STRATEGY 20: *Help learners accurately attribute their success to their capability, effort, and knowledge.*

Whereas the last strategy dealt with the *context* of learning, this strategy focuses on the *outcome* of learning. That outcome is *success,* and I use the term here in its broadest sense. Success can mean passing a test, receiving an excellent grade, completing a fine project, satisfactorily demonstrating a new skill, correctly answering a problem—any achievement that turns out well in the eyes of the learner.

Adults frequently think about the consequences of their behavior. *If they have a success, they will often reflect on a reason or a cause for that success.* Some cognitive psychologists call these inferred causes *attributions* and have created a theory and body of research to demonstrate their significant effects on human behavior (Weiner, 1992). For instructors, the important understanding is this: when people have had a learning success, it will probably best enhance their self-concept and their motivation to believe that the major causes for that success are their capability, effort, and knowledge. We might suppose that if learners had a good deal of personal control over the learning context and were successful, at least they would take credit for their effort. Certainly this is probable, but some learners find such attributions as luck, easiness, and fear just as plausible. There is no way to guarantee what a person will think. Because of this unpredictability, it is vital that we do whatever we can to directly help learners see their capability, effort, and knowledge as the causes of their learning success.

There are a number of reasons why the adult learner benefits from believing capability, effort, and knowledge are the causes of personal academic success. Belief in these causes is *realistic* self-understanding. It usually is some combination of capability, effort, and knowledge that makes learning success possible. Because the learner internally controls those causes, he or she can feel genuine pride. Capability also has a stable quality to it (it lasts), and the adult can feel more confident when similar learning tasks arise. Effort and knowledge are less stable (sometimes it's difficult to persevere or remember), but it is probably these aspects of behavior over which the learner feels the most control. Knowing that knowledge or skill can be gained through study and practice and that effort is often a matter of will reduces the learner's feelings of helplessness and increases persistence. Attributions to effort and knowledge provide realistic hope.

Here are some ways to help learners attribute their success to capability, effort, and knowledge.

- Provide learners with learning tasks suitable to their capabilities. "Just within reach" is a good rule of thumb. These kinds of tasks challenge learners' capabilities and require knowledge and moderate effort for success.

- Before initiating a learning task, stress the importance of learners' effort and knowledge for success. This should be a reminder and not a threat: for example, "Considering the challenge of this task, we'll have to practice and become proficient before we apply what we know." This alerts the learners to their responsibility and increases the likelihood that learners will attribute their success to effort and knowledge.
- Send verbal and written messages to accentuate learners' perceptions of capability, effort, and knowledge in relation to their success. Here are a few examples: "Great to see your hard work pay off." "Your skills made a real difference." "That's a talented performance." "Your knowledge is apparent in your writing." "I know a lot of perseverance went into this project." *Knowledge can also mean skill or strategy.* The great thing about such statements is that they can be distributed all the time.

Certain subjects, such as math, writing, and art, are conventionally understood to be *aptitude-driven* when in reality they greatly benefit from effort and strategy. For example, knowing there are five interesting ways to begin an essay (with a statistic, quotation, question, anecdote, or revelation) is a strategy that can make starting a new paper an enjoyable challenge rather than an oppressive frustration. When we attribute effective learning to an attainable skill or strategy, we can build learners' confidence as well as contribute relevant knowledge.

STRATEGY 21: *When learning tasks are suitable to learners' capability, help learners understand that effort and knowledge can overcome their failures.*

The term *failure* is used here in its broadest sense—mistakes, errors, lack of completion, poor test results, low grades, unskilled performance, or any lack of achievement that turns out poorly in the eyes of the learner. If a learner experiences an unsuccessful learning outcome, there is very little he can do to improve unless he believes further personal effort or knowledge can make a difference. To paraphrase Seligman (1975), intelligence, no matter how high, cannot manifest itself if the person believes that his own actions will have no effect. If a person believes failure is due to lack of aptitude, then more effort will seem to make little difference, because ability, in the eyes of most people, is very difficult to change. The result will be discouragement. Bad luck, too difficult a task, and poor materials are all attributions learners might make that indicate personal effort will only have a small impact on their future performance. Sometimes these attributions are correct, but sometimes they are rationalizations that ease learners' guilt and frustration.

If we have honest reasons to believe greater effort will improve performance, we need to let the learner know. Strategic knowledge can also be extremely encouraging. The idea of "working smarter" rather than just harder has its appeal. Whether they are following an outline or using the Internet, adults can see how these strategies make learning easier as well as more informative. Attributions of effort and knowledge evoke real hope for future performance. The ability to tactfully reveal them to the learner is an immeasurable asset: for example, "I realize you might be feeling quite bad about how this assignment turned out, but my honest estimation of your performance is that with continued effort you can definitely improve. Here are the units that seem to need further review...." So often what seems like defeat can actually lead to a higher level of creativity and learning.

ESTABLISHING EXPECTANCY FOR SUCCESS

It is possible that a learner could initially like a subject, feel positively toward the instructor, have a good academic self-concept, and still not expect to succeed. The person simply might decide there is not enough time to study for the training or course. For adults, time is a critical issue because of their many other roles and responsibilities. The decision to invest time in a learning activity may be as important as the decision to invest money or effort (Lowe, 1996). Sometimes learners do not understand what is necessary to do well in a course, and this confusion leads to discouragement. Sometimes the materials and training are so new and different to the learners that many of them actually have difficulty seeing themselves as potential performers in the necessary learning tasks.

There are many different reasons why adult learners might not expect to succeed. And when they don't have this expectation, they probably consider it in their best interest not to get enthusiastic. If they do, they will experience greater pain and disappointment if they fail. In fact, for people to try at something they do not believe they can do is usually not very intelligent behavior and is often a waste of time. When expectancy for success is low, learners tend to protect their well-being by remaining withdrawn or negative. Instructors often interpret this as apathy or resistance, but for the learners it is usually self-protection, more to do with realistic doubt than with being ornery. In such instances, our demonstrating clearly that the learning task is concretely possible to achieve is a significant positive influence on learners' attitudes.

STRATEGY 22: *Make the criteria of assessment as fair and clear as possible.*

Assessment is thoroughly discussed under the title "Engendering Competence Among Adult Learneers" later in this section. However, because learning goals and assessment procedures go hand in hand in the beginning of most adult education courses and training, we need to pay some attention to assessment as an attitudinal issue. In the view of most adults, how they are assessed will play a crucial role in determining their expectation for success. The outcomes of assessment in the form of grades and quantitative scores can powerfully influence their self-determination, sense of self-worth, and access to careers, further education, and financial aid (for example, scholarships and grants). Therefore, assessment criteria are extremely relevant to developing or inhibiting a positive attitude toward learning. Whenever we formulate learning goals, we should simultaneously address assessment procedures and criteria.

If learners understand the criteria and agree to them as fair, they know which elements of performance are essential. They can more easily self-assess and self-determine their learning as they proceed (Wiggins, 1993). This should enhance their motivation, because they can anticipate the results of their learning and regulate how they learn (for example, studying, writing, practicing, and so on) with more certainty.

In general, we ought to demonstrate how we or the learners can go about assessing the quality of their learning: what is being looked for in the assessment, how it is valued, and how this value will be indicated. This discussion of evaluation usually entails clarifying terms, standards, and calibration of measurement, so that all of us come to a common understanding and agreement about how these indicators of learning are applied, scored, and integrated.

The less mystery there is surrounding evaluation criteria, the more likely learners are to direct their own learning. We are wise to allow for questions and suggestions about assessment. It is very beneficial to make available some examples of concrete learning outcomes—past tests, papers, projects, and media—that you have already evaluated using the same criteria, thus giving learners realistic illustrations of how you have applied them. Exemplary models of other learners' accomplishments often hold the power to inspire adults. When I look back on my teaching, it is clear that demystifying the criteria of assessment and providing exemplars of past student learning have been among the most powerful strategies I have ever learned for enhancing adult motivation and performance.

STRATEGY 23: *Use relevant models to demonstrate expected learning.*

Because many adults often find learning new as well as abstract, they honestly wonder if they can do it. Any time we can provide examples of people who are similar to the learners enthusiastically and successfully performing the expected learning activity, we have taken a significant step toward enhancing learners' expectancy for success (Pintrich and Schunk, 1996).

This strategy is derived from the research of Bandura (1982, pp. 126–127): "Seeing similar others perform successfully can raise efficacy expectations in observers who then judge that they too possess the capabilities to master comparable activities.... Vicariously derived information alters perceived self-efficacy through ways other than social comparison.... Modeling displays convey information about the nature and predictability of environmental events. Competent models also teach observers effective strategies for dealing with challenging or threatening situations."

With film and video technology, we have wonderful ways to organize and demonstrate what we want our learners to achieve. Former students and trainees are another source for live modeling sessions. If something can be learned and demonstrated, be it a skill, technique, or discussion, today's technology enables us to bring it to our learners and to raise in a concrete way their expectations for success.

STRATEGY 24: *Announce the expected amount of time needed for study and practice for successful learning.*

As we have discussed, time is precious to adults. It is often very difficult for adult learners to estimate the amount of time a given course, assignment, or practice regimen might take. Some will overestimate. Some will underestimate. Others will procrastinate, as busy people often do. If a learning activity will require a significant amount of time, it is best for learners to know this so that they can plan more effectively, realize their responsibility, avoid procrastination, and attribute their success to effort.

STRATEGY 25: *Use goal-setting methods.*

This is a more individualized approach to increasing learners' expectancy for success and their self-efficacy. Bandura (1986, p. 391) defines *self-efficacy* as "people's judgements of their capabilities to organize and execute courses of action required to attain designated types of performances." Adults who perceive low self-efficacy for a task tend to avoid that task, whereas those who believe they are capable are likely to get involved. Efficacious learners persist longer, especially when they encounter difficulties.

The advantage of goal setting is that it brings the future into the present and allows the learner to become aware of what he needs to do to have a successful learning experience. Goal setting not only prevents the learner from making an unrealistic expectation but also gives him a chance to evaluate and plan specifically for those obstacles that prevent success. Using the goal-setting model, the learner feels more control and can calculate what to do to avoid wasting time or experiencing self-defeat. Thus, before even beginning the learning task, the learner knows that the effort he expends will be worthwhile and that there is a good probability for success. As postsecondary education evolves into a greater number of alternative forms and as learning more frequently involves projects and complex tasks, goal setting is a real asset to the instructor and the adult learner.

There are many different methods of goal setting (Locke and Latham, 1990). The one that follows is an eclectic adaptation of various models in the literature. If the learner is to have a good chance of reaching the learning goal (and therefore of initiating the learning experience), instructor and learner should consider the following criteria together. In order to take these criteria beyond abstract suggestions, I present an actual case from my experience to exemplify how the criteria can be applied.

Yolanda Scott-Machado, whose tribal affiliation is Makah, is an adult learner in a research course. To learn more about a variety of skills and concepts including research design, validity, reliability, sampling procedures, statistical analysis, and operationalization,

Yolanda wants to design, conduct, and report a research study in an area of personal interest. She has questions about the concept of learning styles, especially as it is applied to American Indians. She wants to carry out a study to determine if urban American Indian high school students, when compared to urban European American high school students, score significantly higher in the field-sensitive mode as measured by Witkin's Group Embedded Figures Test. This is an ambitious study for a beginning research student. We launch the goal-setting process by examining the criterion of achievability.

1. Discuss whether the goal is achievable.

Can the learner reach the learning goal with the skills and knowledge at hand? If not, is there any assistance available, and how dependable is that assistance?

Yolanda feels confident, and her competent completion of exercises in class substantiates that confidence. She is also a member of a class cooperative learning group and values her peers as knowledgeable resources. We work out a plan that includes a preliminary conference with peers to garner their support, and a follow-up call to me.

Is there enough time to reach the goal? If not, can more time be found, or should the goal be divided into smaller goals?

This question is a bit tricky. Yolanda will need at least fifty students in each of her comparison groups. At the minimum, she will need to involve two high schools. Can she get the necessary permission? Who will do the testing, and when? The bureaucratic maneuvering and testing could drag on and complicate the study.

2. Determine how progress will be measured.

In what specific ways will the learner be able to gauge progress toward the achievement of the goal? In many circumstances, this measure can be something as simple as problems completed, pages read, or exercises finished. To respect learners' different ideas of how to accomplish their long-range goals, you should schedule meetings to talk about their evolving experience.

We decide that the most important "next step" is for Yolanda to write a research proposal and bring it in for a meeting with me. Then we might work out a schedule for her completion of the study.

3. Determine how much the learner desires the goal.

Why is the goal important? Is the goal something the learner wants to do? The learner may have to do it or perhaps should do it, but is the goal wanted as well? If it isn't, then the learner's satisfaction level and sense of self-determination will be less. Goal setting can be used for "must" situations, but it is best handled if you are clear about it and admit to the learner the reality of the situation to avoid any sense of manipulation. When possible, aligning the goal with other, desired goals is helpful. This alignment can increase a learner's motivation, much as a railroad engine gains power by hooking up with another moving engine.

Yolanda wants to do this study. She believes that certain teaching practices derived from learning styles research may not apply to some Northwest American Indian tribes or urban American Indians. Because educators so often advocate these methods for teaching American Indians, Yolanda believes more caution about their use may be necessary. In addition, she is considering advanced graduate study in psychology and views research skills as an important addition to her résumé.

4. Create a consistent way to focus on the goal (optional).

Some learners feel the need for a daily plan that keeps the goal in their awareness; the plan helps them avoid forgetting or procrastinating. For others, such an idea may seem oppressive. Possible reminders are outlines, chalkboard messages, and daily logs.

Yolanda finds this option unnecessary.

5. Preplan to consider and remove potential obstacles.

The question for the learner is, "What do you think might interfere with reaching your goal?" Obstacles may include anything from other obligations to lack of a quiet place to study. Planning ahead to reduce these barriers should decrease their obstructive force and give the learner added leverage to contend with them.

When I ask Yolanda about potential obstacles, she remarks that her "plate is pretty full," and probably the biggest obstacle would be to take on something else while she is conducting the research project. We joke about practicing to say no and eventually decide to leave this possibility to her best judgment.

6. Identify resources and learning processes with the learner.

Engaging the learner in a dialogue about how she would like to reach the learning goal can be a very creative process. This is the time to consider the learner's various talents and preferred ways of knowing. Will accomplishing the learning goal involve media, art, writing, or some other possibility? What form should it take—a story, a research project, or a multimedia presentation? Identifying outside resources—such as library materials, local experts, exemplary models, or films—aids and sometimes inspires the entire learning process.

Yolanda decides to review the literature on learning styles, especially as it refers to American Indians and other native people. She also chooses to interview a professor at another university and an American Indian administrator at a local school district. She decides that her format for reporting her study will be the conventional research thesis outline.

7. The learner makes a commitment.

This is a formal or informal gesture that indicates the learner's acceptance of the learning goal. It can range from a shared copy of notes taken at the meeting to a contract. This affirms the learner's self-determination and acknowledges the mutual agreement between the learner and the teacher, building trust, motivation, and cooperation for further work together.

Yolanda composes a contract, which we agree on at our next meeting. (Her contract appears as an example in the discussion of Strategy 26.)

8. Arrange a goal review schedule.

To maintain progress and refine learning procedures, the learner and the instructor may need to stay in contact. Because of the way time varies in its meaning and feeling to different people, contact can occur at regular or irregular intervals. The main idea is that trust and support continue. If progress has deteriorated, reexamine the criteria. Asking, for example, "What did you do instead?" may help uncover hidden distractions or competing goals.

We have three meetings at irregular intervals prior to Yolanda's completion of an excellent study. To find a large enough sample for her research, she eventually involves five high schools. Her research indicates that urban American Indian high school students are more field-independent than European American high school students, suggesting the possibility that previous research conducted on Native American learning styles is far from conclusive across tribes and regions.

STRATEGY 26: *Use contracting methods.*

Learning contracts often complement goal setting. They are considered by practitioners in adult education to be a significant means for fostering self-direction and expectancy for success (Knowles, 1986). They are effective for assisting adults in understanding their learning interests, planning learning activities, identifying relevant resources, and becoming skilled at self-assessment (Brookfield, 1986). The ability to write contracts is a learned skill, and teachers may have to spend considerable time helping learners focus on realistic as well as manageable activities. My experience as a teacher supports Brookfield's observation (pp. 82–83): "Particularly in institutions where other departments and program areas conform to a more traditional mode, learners will often find it unsettling, inconvenient, and annoying to be asked to work as self-directed learning partners in some kind of negotiated learning project. Notwithstanding the fact that learners may ultimately express satisfaction with this experience, initially, at least, there may be substantial resistance. It is crucial, then, that learners be eased into this mode ... and faculty must make explicit from the outset the rationale behind the adoption of these techniques."

Learning contracts can individualize the learning process and provide maximum flexibility for content, pace, process, and outcome. They usually detail in writing what will be learned, how the learning will be accomplished, the period of time involved, and frequently the criteria to be used in assessing the learning. Learners can construct all, most, or part of the contract depending on the learner's and teacher's knowledge of the subject matter, the resources available, the restrictions of the program, and so on. For example, what is learned (the objective) may not be negotiable, but how it is learned may be wide open to individual discretion.

The contract document often follows the outline of categories shown here (O'Donnell and Caffarella, 1990):

1. Learning goal or objective. (What are you going to learn?)
2. Choice of resources, strategies, and activities for learning. (How are you going to learn it?)
3. Target date for completion.
4. Evidence of accomplishment. (How are you going to demonstrate that you have learned it?)
5. Assessment of the learning. (What are the criteria by which you will judge the learning, and who will be involved in the judging process?)

The following are two examples of learning contracts. The first covers a specific skill to be accomplished in a short period of time in an undergraduate communication skills course. The second is the contract submitted by Yolanda Scott-Machado.

Sample Contract: Paraphrasing Skills

Learning goal: To apply paraphrasing skills to actual communication situations.

Learning resources and activities: View videotapes of paraphrasing scenarios. One hour of role playing paraphrasing situations with peers.

Target date: End of one week (date specified).

Evidence of accomplishment: Participate in paraphrasing exercise under teacher's supervision.

Assessment of learning: Can contribute appropriate paraphrasing responses to 80 percent of the communicated messages, to be validated by teacher.

Sample Contract: Research Project of Yolanda Scott-Machado

Learning goal: To conduct a research study to determine if urban Native American high school students when compared to urban European American high school students have a significant perceptual difference as measured by Witkin's Group Embedded Figures Test.

Learning resources and activities: Conduct a review of the literature on learning styles, especially as this concept relates to Native Americans. Interview a professor at the University of Washington who specializes in the relation of learning styles to people of color. Also, interview a local Native American school administrator who has responsibility for a number of projects involving Native American students. Carry out the research, remaining in communication with my cooperative learning group and our teacher.

Target date: Two weeks before the end of the semester, to allow for revisions.

Evidence of accomplishment: Completed research study according to the design agreed on by me and my teacher.

Evaluation of learning: A self-evaluation indicating what I learned and why it was important to me. Validation by the teacher regarding the quality of my research design and analysis and the soundness of my discussion and conclusion as drawn from the research evidence.

O'Donnell and Caffarella (1990) have some helpful ideas about the use of learning contracts with learners who are inexperienced or unfamiliar with them.

- Enlist the aid of those learners more familiar with designing learning contracts to help those beginning this process.
- Give those with less experience more time to develop their plans.
- Allow the less experienced learners to develop a mini-learning plan first and then complete a more in-depth one.
- Give learners clear guidelines for developing contracts. Supply a number of diverse samples to encourage a variety of learning processes and outcomes.

In general, the use of learning contracts is, like good writing, often a process of revision and refinement. Using collaborative groups and remaining open to feedback from learners about contracts and their formats are ways to ensure their effective use.

CREATING RELEVANT LEARNING EXPERIENCES

The next section emphasizes relevance and choice. The strategies described here could have been placed along with those aligned with *attitude toward the subject* (Strategies 14 through 17). However, these strategies originate more from literature and research related to a sociocultural perspective. Each is an approach to creating learning activities that respect the learner's perspective and unique talents. Also embedded in these strategies is a concern for maintaining a connection between what is learned and the ongoing use of that learning by the learner in the real world (Wiske, 1998).

To be truly relevant, instruction has to go beyond adult interests; it must ensure that learning is accessible through the person's ways of knowing. It requires us to teach to a range of profiles of intelligences (see Gardner, 1993, chap. 1) and learning styles. The following strategy helps us be responsive to the learning preferences and differences we will encounter in a group of diverse adults.

STRATEGY 27: *Use the five entry points suggested by multiple intelligences research as ways of learning about a topic or concept.*

When we offer adults only a single way of knowing a concept or problem, they are forced to understand it in a most limited and rigid fashion. By encouraging learners to develop multiple representations and having them relate these representations to one another, we can move away from the tyranny of the "correct answer" so often dominant in education and arrive at a fuller understanding of our world. Most knowledgeable and innovative practitioners of any discipline are characterized precisely by their capacity to access critical concepts through a variety of routes and apply them to a diversity of situations. In addition, this overall approach makes us colearners with our students and more likely to take their views and ideas seriously; all of us can thus develop a more comprehensive understanding.

Gardner (1993) proposes that any concept worth teaching can be approached in at least five different ways that, roughly speaking, map onto the multiple intelligences and allow all learners relevant access. He advocates thinking of any topic as a room with at least five doors or entry points. Awareness of these entry points can help us introduce the topic with materials and formats that accommodate the wide range of cultural backgrounds and profiles of intelligences found among a group of diverse adults.

Let us look at these five entry points one by one, using an example from the natural sciences (photosynthesis) and one from the social sciences (democracy) to show how each entry point might be used in approaching topics or concepts.

Using the *narrational* entry point, we present a story or narrative account about the concept in question. In the case of photosynthesis, we might describe with appropriate vocabulary this process as it occurs in several plants or trees living in our environment, describing differences as they are noted. In the case of democracy, we could trace its beginnings in ancient history and make comparisons with the early development of constitutional government in a selected nation.

Using the *logical-quantitative* entry point, we approach the concept with numerical considerations or deductive and inductive reasoning processes. We could approach photosynthesis by creating a time line of the steps of photosynthesis and a chemical analysis of the process. In the case of democracy, we could create a time line of presidential mandates, congressional bills, constitutional amendments, and Supreme Court decisions that broadened democratic principles among people in the United States or analyze the arguments used for and against democracy by relevant political leaders throughout history.

The *foundational* entry point explores the philosophical and terminological facets of a concept. This approach is appropriate for people who like to pose fundamental questions, of the sort that we often associate with young children and with philosophers. A foundational corridor to photosynthesis might examine a transformative experience of our own or of a relevant individual, family, or institution and compare it with the process of photosynthesis, assigning parallel roles as they fit (for example, source of energy, catalyst, and so on). A foundational means of access to democracy could ponder the root meaning of the word, the relationship of democracy to other relevant forms of decision making and government, and the reasons one might prefer or not prefer a democratic rather than a social political philosophy.

Using the *esthetic* entry point, we emphasize sensory or surface features that will appeal to learners who favor an artistic stance toward the experience of living. In the case of photosynthesis we could look for visual, musical, or literary transformations that imitate or parallel photosynthesis, and represent them in artistic formats that might include painting, dance, mime, video, cartooning, or a dramatic sketch. With reference to democracy, we could experience and consider the variations of artistic performance that are characterized by group control as opposed to individual control: an orchestra as compared to a string quartet, ballet compared to experimental modern dance, a stage play compared to improvisational acting, and so on.

The last entry point is the *experiential* approach. Some people learn best with a hands-on approach, dealing directly with the materials that embody or convey the concept. In studying photosynthesis, such individuals might carry out a series of experiments involving photosynthesis. Those learners dealing with democracy might consider a relevant news issue and "enact" a democratic procedure, whether a legislative, judicial, or executive process. Then they could enact another approach to the same issue, replicating a less democratic system from another country, and compare their experience of the two diverse processes.

As instructors, we can open a number of doors on the same concept. Rather than presenting photosynthesis only by example, or only in terms of quantitative considerations, we can make available several entry points at the beginning or over time. In this way, we improve the chances that diverse learners with different ways of knowing and differing intelligence profiles can find relevant and engaging ways of learning. Learners may also suggest entry points of their own design. The use of technology, such as films, microcomputers, and interactive video, further enhances these efforts. Exhibit 5-1 presents a planning format and another example of a concept with five entry points.

Although Gardner's scheme of multiple intelligences is acknowledged in adult education, it has not been widely applied (Torff and Sternberg, 1998). However, this theory is very promising. Its integration of multiple intelligences and culture provides a substantive, unified, and generally applicable way to understand many of the findings of learning styles research regarding how people prefer to perceive, organize, and process information.

Exhibit 5-1.   Learning Activities Based on the Five Entry Points from Multiple Intelligences Theory.

Concept: All living things are systemically related.

Related principle: All human behaviors affect the earth's land, water, and air.

Entry Point	Example
Narrational	Report incidents that reflect one's understanding of the effects of human behavior on other countries and on distant places. Identify behaviors according to whether they harm or benefit the planet. Based on interests generated, select relevant reading materials.
Logical-quantitative	Choose a harmful but controversial human systemic influence, such as overpopulation. After finding data that quantify various (population) trends and the effects that result from this systemic influence, search for cultural, economic, and political factors (possibly from a country of interest) that inhibit or exacerbate this influence.
Foundational	Reflect on one's personal influence on the local environment. Consider those behaviors that improve the environment and those that pollute it. Examine the beliefs, assumptions, and values that appear critical to each set of behaviors. Create a personal environmental philosophy. Sharing it in small groups is optional.
Esthetic	Choose from the following options: create a sketch, a photo journal, a video, or poetry to depict relevant systemic relationships in one's own environment.
Experiential	Create mini-environments in local yards, in terrariums, or both. Experiment according to relevant influences (for example, temperature, water, pollutants, pets, traffic, and so forth). Observe and report effects on various life forms.

STRATEGY 28: *Make the learning activity an irresistible invitation to learn.*

The first time people experience anything that is new or that occurs in a different setting, they form an impression that will have a lasting impact (Scott, 1969). It is essential that we make the first learning experience for a new instructional unit or workshop an irresistible invitation to learn. We achieve such an effect when the learning activity meets the following five criteria.

1. *Safe:* there is little risk of the learners suffering any form of personal embarrassment from lack of knowledge, personal self-disclosure, or a hostile or arrogant social environment.

2. *Successful:* there is some form of acknowledgment, consequence, or product that shows that the learners are effective or, at the very least, that their effort is worthwhile.
3. *Interesting:* the learning activity has some parts that are novel, engaging, challenging, or stimulating.
4. *Self-determined:* learners are encouraged to make choices that significantly affect the learning experience (for example, what they share, how they learn, what they learn, when they learn, with whom they learn, where they learn, or how they are assessed), basing those choices on their values, needs, concerns, or feelings. At the very least, learners have an opportunity to voice their perspectives.
5. *Personally relevant:* the instructor uses learners' concerns, interests, or prior experiences to create elements of the learning activity or develops the activity in concert with the learners. At the very least, a resource-rich learning environment is available to encourage learners' selections based on personal interest (for example, the library, the Internet, or a community setting).

I vividly remember experiencing this strategy in a workshop on adapting to the culture of another country. The initial learning activity focused on learning important expressions in the language of that country. The instructor began by asking the participants which expressions they most wanted to learn and recorded them on a flip chart ("Hello," "Good-bye," "Where is the bathroom?" "How much does this cost?" and the like). The instructor thus met the criteria of *personally relevant* and *self-determined.* After she taught us the expressions, she asked us to pick a partner and practice until we felt proficient. We could then move on to another partner for further practice. The instructor maintained *safety* by keeping the groups small (dyads). *Success* was immediate, and it was *interesting* (and fun) to practice with two different people. From that moment forward, participants used these expressions during breaks and free time.

I have found this strategy so useful that I have made it a mainstay in all my motivational planning. Every learning activity I create has to meet these five criteria. When an activity does not go well, I use the criteria to critique, refine, and improve the experience. A prototypical example of this strategy is brainstorming a relevant topic, because such brainstorming is

Safe	All answers are initially acceptable.
Successful	A list is created and acknowledged.
Interesting	Creative answers usually occur.
Self-determined	Answers are voluntary and self-chosen.
Personally relevant	The topic was selected because it was relevant.

STRATEGY 29: *Use the K-W-L strategy to introduce new topics and concepts.*

Originated by Donna Ogle (1986), the K-W-L strategy is an elegant way to construct meaning for a new topic or concept based on the prior knowledge of the learners. Adults have a storehouse of experiences that can give extraordinary meaning to novel ideas. The K-W-L strategy offers a simple and direct way to creatively probe adults' vast reservoir of knowledge.

During the first phase of the strategy, the learners identify what they think they *K*now about the topic. Whether the topic is black holes, the gross domestic product, phobias, or acid rain, this is a nonthreatening way to list some of the unique and varied ways adults understand something. It allows for multiple perspectives and numerous historical contexts. Just think of what the possibilities might be for a diverse group of adults initiating a unit on immigration law. The discussion of what adults *K*now about a topic can involve drawing, storytelling, critical incidents, and predictions.

In the second phase, the learners suggest what they *W*ant to know about the topic. This information may be listed as questions or subtopics for exploration and research. For example, if the topic were immigration law, some questions might be as follows: Where do most immigrants come from today? Ten years ago? Fifty years ago? What was the last significant immigration law enacted by Congress? Is there evidence that immigrants deny work opportunities to established citizens of the United States? What are some noteworthy contributions of recent immigrants? These questions can serve as ideas for using the five entry points discussed under the multiple intelligences strategy (for example, a narrational entry point could be used to look at immigration history and an experiential and logical-quantitative entry point could be used to conduct research on recent immigration patterns). The K-W-L strategy also meets the five criteria for irresistible learning.

In the last phase, the learners identify what they have *L*earned, which may be the answers to their questions, important related information, and perhaps new information that counters some inaccuracies they may have held prior to this learning.

STRATEGY 30: *Use brainstorming webs to develop and link new information.*

A brainstorming web is a visual tool: symbols graphically linked by mental associations to create a pattern of information and a form of knowledge about an idea (Clarke, 1991). Brainstorming webs can be linear or nonlinear and individually or collaboratively constructed on paper, board, or a computer screen. (Figure 5-1 shows an example.) They allow adults, especially those more visually oriented, to construct mental models that reflect the unique set of relationships an idea can generate in their minds.

Brainstorming webs are the most idiosyncratic of visual tools, allowing adults the freedom to create the form of graphics and the associations themselves (Hyerle, 1996). There are a number of webbing techniques; I will emphasize the *mindmapping* techniques of Tony Buzan (1979). His approach (as shown in Figure 5-1) begins with a key word or image in the center of the page (in this case, *economics*), followed by extensions expanding outward.

Arrows and lines in other areas of the map connect secondary ideas to each other; the more important concepts are drawn nearer to the center. All words are printed in capitals, and single words are suggested for each line. Brainstorming webs can be made more holographic through the use of such highlights as arrows, asterisks, question marks, geometric shapes, three-dimensional drawings, and personal images. Multiple colors can enhance the web as a mnemonic tool. These techniques can make recall easier and information more accessible, encouraging learners to create relevant, comprehensive views of connected information. We therefore should not overly prescribe the techniques and uses of brainstorming webs. For additional information about other visual tools and their uses, see *Visual Tools for Constructing Knowledge* (Hyerle, 1996).

In this section, we have looked at numerous ways to build more positive attitudes toward learning. Which strategies you select will be based on your sensitive awareness of yourself, your adult learners, and the learning situation. When your material is relevant and all four of the important attitudinal directions are positive—toward you, the subject, the learner's self-concept, and the learner's expectancy for success—you have motivational force to support any instructional endeavor. Also, because attitudes seem most consequential at the beginning of any human contact, executing these strategies early in your instructional design creates an advantage for both the learner and you.

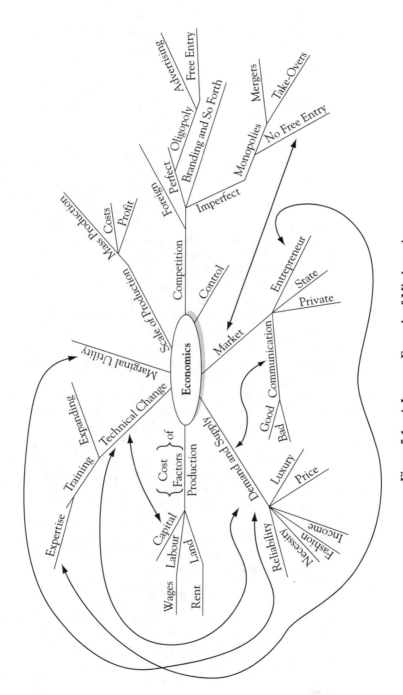

Figure 5-1. A Learner Example of Mindmapping.

Source: From USE BOTH SIDES OF YOUR BRAIN by Tony Buzan. Copyright © 1974, 1983 by Tony Buzan. Used by permission of Dutton, a division of Penguin Putnam Inc.

ENGENDERING COMPETENCE AMONG
ADULT LEARNERS

Raymond J. Wlodkowski

Only when we break the mirror and
climb into our vision,
only when we are the wind together
streaming and singing,
only in the dream we become with
our bones for spears,
we are real at last
and wake.

Marge Piercy

Being effective at what we value resonates with something beyond feeling competent. At some level, competence connects with our dreams, with that part of us that yearns for unity with something greater than ourselves. We want to matter. There are many ways to make this so: caring for someone we love, nurturing beauty, living with purpose, finding good in our work, and learning. Although we may do these things day in and day out, we need to believe we do them fairly well. If we do not, we must vaguely realize we are diminishing what makes life worth living and hope a constant in our midst. To be ineffective at what we value is a spiritual dilemma. By being competent we build the bridge that reconciles spiritual satisfaction, a moral life, and altruistic passion. The quest for competence starts with something as simple as a baby looking for a toy behind a pillow and ends in later life with what Erik Erikson called generativity, our desire to leave an enduring and beneficent legacy.

Competence is the most powerful of all the motivational conditions for adults. Competence is our reality check: it tells us what is possible by our own will. As adults we have a deep desire to be competent and often seek learning as a means to this end. *Across cultures, this human need for competence is not one to be acquired but one that already exists and can be strengthened or weakened through learning experiences.* Many people understand competence as individual proficiency, but others may conceive of it as a collective responsibility, carried out with regard for what is best for others—for future human and environmental well-being. Individual effectiveness is important, yet it is to be achieved with consideration of our interdependence with all things and our impact on the generations to come. This quest for a balanced sense of competence is found not only in many native cultures (Michelson, 1997) but also among many workers and employers who actively pursue social and environmental responsibility as an ethical commitment. The emphasis in this book is on finding ways to support adult competence while illuminating the socially redeemable aspects of the individual's increased effectiveness.

SUPPORTING SELF-DETERMINED COMPETENCE

Self-determination and building competence go hand in hand. The norm of individual freedom and responsibility is very strong in this society; therefore, when *most* adults see themselves as the locus of causality for their learning—as self-determined learners—they are much more likely to be intrinsically and positively motivated. Adults are experienced self-directed learners, especially when solving their own problems (Caffarella, 1993). Today's world of work increasingly requires people who can capably self-direct in their jobs.

However, sometimes instructors encounter adults who seem dependent, lacking in self-confidence, or reluctant to take responsibility for their learning. There are a number of possible reasons for this. Three of the most common are that (1) these adults have not been socialized to see themselves as in control of their own learning, (2) their experience in school or in the particular domain of learning has been generally negative or unsuccessful, and (3) they do not believe they have a free choice as to whether or not they engage in the learning or training experience. This last reason, very common among adults, is a *personal security* issue. In many instances, adult learners need courses and training not so much because they want them but because they need the jobs, the promotions, and the money for which these learning experiences are basic requirements. This is the reality for many adults, and it may be one about which they feel they have little choice. "Just tell me what to do," is their common refrain.

Strategies to support adults in taking ownership of their learning have been discussed earlier. Those strategies that relate to the motivational purposes of respect, self-concept, expectancy for success, and engagement and challenge are most effective in this regard. When combined with the following strategies to engender competence, they create a holistic system in which the competence and self-determination of adult learners mutually enhance each other. Proficiently applied, the strategies enable those adults who feel minimal control of their learning to grow in the realization that they do have a voice and can determine learning they value.

Permeating every competence strategy is the understanding that *informational* communication about a learner's effectiveness has the best chance to cultivate self-determination. According to the seminal work of Deci and Ryan (1991), when instructors tell adults about the quality of their work, these transactions can be either *informational* or *controlling*. Informational transactions tell learners something about their effectiveness and support their sense of self-determination for learning. Controlling transactions tend to undermine self-determination by making a learner's behavior appear to be dependent on implicit or explicit forces that demand, coerce, or seduce the learner's compliance. They encourage the learner to believe that the reason for learning is some condition outside the learner or the learning activity itself, such as a reward or pressure from the instructor. When verbally communicated, controlling transactions often contain imperative locutions such as *should* and *must*. For example, an instructor might say to an adult learner, "Your performance was excellent. As soon as you received concrete feedback, you were really able to apply your skill" (informational). Or the same instructor might say, "Your performance was excellent. As soon as I made the feedback concrete, you did exactly as you should do" (controlling). The difference between these two statements may seem subtle but is nonetheless very important. The former encourages self-determination, whereas the latter places much more of the emphasis on the instructor's control. The following competence strategies will always emphasize the informational approach, which not only nurtures self-determination but also promotes self-direction and is more likely to increase intrinsic motivation.

RELATING AUTHENTICITY AND EFFECTIVENESS TO ASSESSMENT

In training and more formal learning experiences, assessment exerts a powerful motivational influence on adults because it is the educational procedure to communicate about their competence in a socially sanctioned way. Historically, more than any other action, assessment by the instructor has validated learners' competence. Our comments, scores, grades, and reports affect learners in the present and the future. Assessment often leaves a legacy for adults, directly or indirectly, by having an impact on their careers, vocational opportunities, professional advancement, and acceptance into various schools and programs.

Adults tend to undergo more stress in testing situations than do youths (Smith, 1982). They often feel awkward and anxious taking exams. Test anxiety is a widespread problem among adults (Sarason, 1980). There are many reasons for this uneasiness. Among them are fears of revelation of ignorance, of negative comparison with peers, and of inability to meet personal standards and goals. (Robert Smith, 1982, has written some helpful suggestions for training adults to cope with exams.)

For assessment to be intrinsically motivating for adults it has to be *authentic*—connected to adults' life circumstances, frames of reference, and values. For example, if a case study were used as an authentic assessment, it would ask learners to respond to a situation that mirrors their work or community life with the resources and conditions normally there. A real-life context for demonstrating learning enhances its relevance for adults, appeals to their pragmatism, and affirms their rich background of experiences (Kasworm and Marienau, 1997). In contrast, one can easily see how an impersonal multiple-choice exam might seem tedious and irrelevant to most adults.

Effectiveness is the learners' awareness of their command or accomplishment of something they find to be important in the *process* of learning or as an *outcome* of learning. Therefore, both the processes and the results of learning are significant information for adults. How well am I doing? and How well did this turn out? are a critical duet for adult learning activities. In the example of the case study, to judge the quality of their thinking as they *process* the case, the adults would likely want feedback about how well their responses relate to the issues found in the case study. In addition, when they finally resolve the case, they would want to assess the quality of this *outcome* for its merits as well. Motivation is elicited when adults realize they have competently performed an activity that leads to a valued goal. Awareness of competence affirms the need of adults, across all cultures, to relate adequately to their environment in areas they value.

If we take an institutional perspective, the first aim of assessment is usually to audit adult learning. However, the first edition of this book and, more recently, other scholars (Wiggins, 1998) have asserted that assessment should primarily be used to enhance learning and motivation. With respect to this assertion, let's begin with feedback as a motivational strategy, because self-adjustment based on feedback is central to learning. Adults change or maintain *how* they learn and *how* they perform based on the feedback they receive. Through feedback they *become* more competent, as well as realize they *are* competent.

STRATEGY 48: *Provide effective feedback.*

Feedback is information that learners receive about the quality of their work. Knowledge about the learning process and its results, comments about emerging skills, notes on a written assignment, and graphic records are forms of feedback that instructors and learners use. Feedback appears to enhance the motivation of learners because learners are able to evaluate their progress, locate their performance within a framework of understanding, maintain their efforts toward realistic goals, self-assess, correct their errors efficiently, self-adjust, and receive encouragement from their instructors and other learners.

Some writers (Wiggins, 1998) distinguish feedback from the way the instructor might evaluate and guide the learners' performance. In their opinion, feedback is information about what exactly resulted from the learner's action. It reflects the learner's actual performance as opposed to the learner's ideal performance. Facts are fed back to the person about his or her performance without the addition of another adult's view of the value of the performance or of how to improve the situation (for example, "You've made thirteen of fifteen foul shots," or, "I wanted my entire audience in rapt attention while I spoke. The videotape shows at least 20 percent of them fidgeting and restless"). The advantage of this orientation to feedback is its emphasis on making feedback clear and self-evident in order to encourage learners' self-assessment and self-direction. For adults from more collectivist cultures and for those of us who desire the inclusion of other perspectives on our work, this orientation to feedback might seem too individualistic or minimalist.

Feedback is probably the most powerful process that teachers and other learners can regularly use to affect a learner's competence. In studies at Harvard, students and alumni overwhelmingly reported that the single most important ingredient for making a course effective is getting rapid instructor response on assignments and exams (Light, 1990). However, feedback is far more complex than a few words about a learner's progress during a learning project or at the end of an assessment. The following paragraphs describe the characteristics of effective feedback:

- Effective feedback is *informational rather than controlling.* As we have already discussed, our feedback should emphasize the learner's increasing effectiveness or creativity and self-determination. For example, we might say, "In your paper you've clearly identified three critical areas of concern; your writing is well organized and vivid; I appreciate how well you've supported your rationale with facts and anecdotes," rather than, "You're making progress and meeting the standards I've set for writing in this course."

- Effective feedback *provides evidence of the learner's effect relative to the learner's intent.* This most often is feedback that is based on *agreed-on* criteria, standards, and models. Learners can compare their work against a standard: a superbly written executive letter, a museum sculpture, a rubric for critical thinking, or a video of a political activist giving a rousing speech. Learners are then in a position to understand clearly what they have done and how it compares to their own goals. They can judge how well they have performed or produced in terms of a specific target. They are clear about the criteria against which their work is being evaluated and can explicitly indicate what needs to be done for further effective learning. Self-assessment leads to self-adjustment. Learners can thus use this information to guide their effort, practice, and performance more accurately. For example, in a welding course, each learner agrees to produce a ninety-degree corner weld to industry specifications. The standards are written out on paper and available. When the learner makes a weld that she judges to be up to this standard, she comes to a table to compare her weld to welds ranging from excellent to poor. Based on this comparison, the learner adjusts the necessary skills and improves the next weld or, if satisfied, moves on to a more advanced task. The instructor may give guidance if the learner requests it.

- Effective feedback is *specific and constructive.* It is difficult to improve performance when one has only a general sense of how well one has done. Most people prefer specific information and realistic suggestions for how to improve: for example, "I found your insights on government spending compelling. To emphasize your conclusion, you might consider restating your initial premise in your last paragraph." When you are giving guidance with feedback, it is important to keep in mind how much the learner *wants to* or *ought to* decide on a course of action relative to the feedback. In general, the more the learner can self-assess and self-adjust, the more self-determined the learner will be.

- Effective feedback can be *quantitative.* In such areas as athletics, quantitative feedback has definite advantages. It is precise and can provide evidence of small improvements. Small improvements can have long-range effects. One way to understand learning is by measuring *rate,* which indicates how often something occurs over a fixed time. For example, learners are told they completed thirty laps during a one-hour swimming practice. Another way is to decide what percentage of learning performance is correct or appropriate. Percentages are calculated by dividing the number of times the learning performance occurs correctly by the total number of times the performance opportunity occurs, as in batting averages and field goal percentages.

Another common form of quantitative feedback is *duration,* which is how long it takes a learning performance to be completed. For example, a lab technician might receive feedback on how long he takes to complete a particular chemical analysis. These are not the only forms of quantitative feedback that are possible, but they are a representative sample. Whenever progress on learning a skill appears to be slow or difficult to ascertain, quantitative feedback may be an effective means to enhance learner motivation.

- Effective feedback is *prompt.* Promptness characterizes feedback that is quickly given as the situation demands rather than immediately. Sometimes a moderate delay in feedback enhances learning because such a delay is simply culturally sensitive or polite. For example, some learners may experience discomfort with direct mention of specific performance judgments shortly after the occasion. Also, a short wait may allow learners to forget incorrect responses more easily or reduce their anxiety, as in the case of a public performance. In general, it is best to be quick with feedback but to pay careful attention to whether any delay might be beneficial.

- Effective feedback is usually *frequent.* Frequent feedback is probably most helpful when new learning is first being acquired. In general, you should give feedback when improvement is most possible. Once errors have accumulated, learners may see improvements as more difficult to accomplish. Also, once multiple errors become established, the new learning encouraged through feedback may seem overwhelming and confusing to learners, making further progress seem even more remote.

- Effective feedback is *positive.* Positive feedback places emphasis on improvements and progress rather than on deficiencies and mistakes. It is an excellent form of feedback because it increases learners' intrinsic motivation, feelings of well-being, and sense of competence and helps learners form a positive attitude toward the source of the information. Adults prefer positive feedback because when they are trying to improve, emphasis on errors and deficiencies (negative feedback) can be discouraging. Even when learners are prone to making mistakes, the instructor's pointing out a *decrease* in errors may be considered positive feedback. Also, positive feedback can be given with constructive feedback. For example, an instructor might say to a learner, "You've been able to solve most of this problem. Let's take a look at what's left and see if we can understand why you are getting stuck."

- Effective feedback is *related to impact criteria.* Impact criteria are the main reasons a person is learning something, the heart of the individual's learning goal (Wiggins, 1998). Often these are unique or strongly related to a cultural perspective. One person may produce a speech or a piece of writing to inspire, arouse, or provoke. Another may wish to create a design or a performance to be a gift for the family or friends. Assessment and feedback should support such goals and respectfully deal with what may be ineffable or accomplished only in a realm beyond mechanistic objectivity. We may need to give feedback that is more akin to dialogue or to what many artists do when they respond to how another's work affects them, rather than "evaluate" that work.

- Effective feedback is usually *personal and differential.* Differential feedback uses self-comparison and focuses on the increment of personal improvement that has occurred since the last time the learning activity was performed. In skill or procedural learning, such as writing, operating a machine, or learning a particular sport, emphasizing small steps of progress can be very encouraging to learner motivation. The amount of time that lapses before we give such differential feedback can be quite important. For example, learners are able to see larger gains and feel a greater sense of accomplishment when their improvement is reviewed on a daily or weekly schedule, rather than after each performance.

In addition to the specific characteristics of feedback just listed, some refinements in the composition and delivery of feedback may be helpful. For many skills, *graphing* or *charting* feedback can be encouraging to learner motivation because it makes progress more concrete and shows a record of increasing improvement.

We should always consider *asking learners what they would like feedback on,* especially when we are working with diverse populations. Their needs and concerns may be different from ours, and the knowledge gained from such discussion can make the feedback more relevant and motivating.

Learners' *readiness to receive feedback* is also important. If people are resistant to feedback, they are not likely to learn or self-adjust. For example, this may mean holding off on feedback until a personal conference can be arranged or until learners are more comfortable with the learning situation.

There are times when *checking to make sure our feedback was understood* can be important. This is certainly true for complex feedback or situations in which English is not the learner's first language.

Everything that has been said about feedback thus far could also apply to *group feedback.* Whether the group involved is a team, a collaborative group, or an entire class, feedback on total performance can influence each individual, and because group feedback consolidates members' mutual identification and sense of connection, it helps enhance group cohesiveness and morale.

As a final point, remember that sometimes the best form of feedback is simply to encourage learners to move forward to the next, more challenging learning opportunity. Too much comment by instructors tends to emphasize our power and can diminish our role as colearners.

STRATEGY 49: *Avoid cultural bias in assessment procedures.*

Probably nothing is more demoralizing to an adult than to realize she does not have a fair chance to demonstrate her knowledge or learning. The reality is that it is difficult to avoid bias in any test or assessment procedure that uses language, because the words and examples sway the learner toward a particular cultural perspective. This is especially true for paper-and-pencil tests. A common example of bias is content that favors one frame of reference over another (Ovando and Collier, 1997). These issues relate not only to ethnicity but also to age and gender. For example, items about baseball averages tend to give males an edge, whereas items of similar difficulty but focusing on child care may favor females (Pearlman, 1987). We need always to examine the assumptions embedded in the materials we create or select for assessment. We do not want to penalize anyone for not having been fully socialized in a particular culture. We know adult learning is derived from multiple sources and varied life experiences (Kasworm and Marienau, 1997). So when we are developing our assessment instruments, it is important to consider the following issues (as we should with all training and curricular materials):

- Invisibility
  Is there a significant omission of women and minority groups in assessment materials? (This implies that certain groups are of less value, importance, and significance in our society.)

- Stereotyping
  When groups or members of groups are mentioned, are they assigned traditional or rigid roles that deny diversity and complexity within different groups? (When stereotypes occur repeatedly in print and other media, learners' perceptions are gradually distorted, making stereotypes and myths seem more acceptable.)

- Selectivity
  Does offering or allowing for only one interpretation of an issue, situation, or group of people perpetuate bias? (We may fail to tap the varied perspectives and knowledge of learners.)

- Unreality
  Do assessment items lack a historical context that acknowledges—when relevant—prejudice and discrimination? (Glossing over painful or controversial issues obstructs authenticity and creates a sense of unreality.)

- Linguistic bias
  Do materials reflect bias in the English language? For example, are masculine examples, terms, and pronouns dominant? (The implication of invisibility is to devalue the importance and significance of women and minorities.)

Even directions for tests can constitute a form of bias. This is especially true for language-minority students. English-language learners of all ages can benefit from test instructions that are direct and simplified. Whenever possible, we want to avoid the passive voice and ambiguous comments. Test instructions should be in short sentences with clear and explicit ground rules. We also should allow adequate processing time for questions and directions to be understood.

STRATEGY 50: *Make assessment tasks and criteria known to learners.*

The time has come. No more secrets. If we genuinely want self-assessing, self-adjusting, and self-directed learners, we must make sure they comprehend the tasks and criteria by which they are assessed. Trainers in the business world do this frequently, and those of us in higher education must evolve in this direction as well. Adults greatly appreciate this approach because becoming competent is then no longer a guessing game, and they can more clearly assess and guide their own learning.

This strategy complements mastery learning, scaffolding, and contracting. Using it, we make criteria, examples, and models readily available to learners. Where scoring or grades are necessary, we ensure that all learners clearly understand the rationale for their assignment. In fact, one of the issues we need to consider when using this strategy is the degree to which learners participate in the creation and refinement of the assessment criteria. Certainly, we should discuss criteria and assessment procedures at the beginning of a course or training, remaining open to making changes to the process or criteria, based on the input from the learners. For example, discussion might reveal a lack of time, materials, or opportunities. These conditions may prohibit certain kinds of learning. Therefore, it's quite possible that we could not apply certain criteria fairly.

However, what about revision of criteria or assessment procedures because of differences in the learners' values or perspectives? I don't have an answer that I believe would fit most circumstances, but I do have a procedure that I often find helpful. I offer it not as a formula but as an example of how I have dealt with the complexity of asking adults to participate in shaping assessment criteria.

> In a research course, part of the assessment process is for students to critique a research article of their own choosing and also to create a research proposal in an area of interest. The major purpose of the course is for learners to develop an understanding of the primary assumptions, perspectives, and methods that guide research as it can be conducted in the social sciences.
>
> On the first day, I give the learners models of an excellent critique of a research article and an exemplary research proposal. After reading them, the class divides into small groups to discuss why these two examples might be considered commendable. They also reflect on other ways to critique an article or create a proposal that might vary from the examples I offered and still be laudable. During a whole-group discussion, we list both sets of these qualities. I then pass out the criteria I normally use, and we see which of their criteria match mine and which do not match. Then we talk further, and after this discussion, I make the agreed-on revisions to the criteria. Often the changes have to do with adding qualitative pieces, such as interviews and personal histories.

Transforming training and courses into educational settings where learners share responsibility and authority for their learning is an evolving process for learners as well as for instructors. It may often mean coming to the learning environment with a well-considered plan and set of assessment criteria but being willing to reinvent some of these elements according to the learners and situation we find there.

STRATEGY 51: *Use authentic performance tasks to enable adults to know that they can proficiently apply what they are learning to their real lives.*

Authentic performance tasks are one of the oldest forms of assessment and have been commonly used in training and adult education for many years (Knowles, 1980). Today we have a more sophisticated understanding of these procedures and their central idea: that assessment should resemble as closely as possible the ways adult learners will express in their real lives what they have learned. Thus, if a person is learning computer programming skills, we would assess his learning by asking him to program a personal computer in a relevant area.

The closer assessment procedures come to allowing learners to demonstrate what they have learned in the environment where they will eventually use that learning, the greater will be learners' motivation to do well and the more they can understand their competence and feel the self-confidence that emerges from effective performance. Providing the opportunity for learners to complete an authentic task is one of the best ways to conclude a learning activity because it promotes transfer of learning, enhances motivation for related work, and clarifies learner competence. An authentic task directly meets the adult need to use what has been learned for more effective daily living.

According to Wiggins (1998), an assessment task, problem, or project is authentic if it

Is realistic. The task replicates how people's knowledge and capacities are "tested" in their real world.

Requires judgment and innovation. People have to use knowledge wisely to solve unstructured problems, as a carpenter remodeling part of a house must do more than follow a routine procedure.

Asks the learners to "do" the subject. Rather than recite or demonstrate what they have been taught or what is already known, the learners have to explore and work within the discipline, as when they demonstrate their competence for a history course by writing history from the perspective of particular people in an actual historical situation.

Replicates or simulates the contexts that adults find in their workplace, community, or personal life. These contexts involve specific situations and their demands: for example, managers learning conflict resolution skills could apply them to their work situations, with consideration of the actual personalities and responsibilities involved.

Assesses the learners' ability to use an integration of knowledge and skill to negotiate a complex task effectively. Learners have to put their knowledge and skills together to meet real-life challenges. This is analogous to the difference between taking a few shots in a warm-up drill and actually taking shots in a real basketball game, or between writing a paper on a particular law and writing a real proposal to appropriate legislators to change the law.

Allows appropriate opportunities to rehearse, practice, consult resources, and get feedback on and refine performances and products. This is so important. Learning and, consequently, assessment are not one-shot enterprises! Almost all learning is formative, whether one is learning how to repair plumbing, write a publishable article, or bake a pie. We put out our first attempt and see how it looks, sounds, or tastes. We repeatedly move through a cycle of *perform, get feedback, revise, perform.* That's how most high-quality products and performances are attained—especially in real life. *We must use assessment procedures that contribute to the improvement of adult performance and learning over time.* Doing so means that much of the time assessment is separated from grading processes to assure learners that their mistakes are not counted against them but are a legitimate part of the learning process.

Exhibit 5-2 contains Wiggins's description of the differences between typical tests and authentic tasks.

STRATEGY 52: *Provide opportunities for adults to demonstrate their learning in ways that reflect their strengths and multiple sources of knowing.*

As adults, most of us are motivated to accomplish assessments in which we can use our strengths to demonstrate the depth and complexity of our learning. Such opportunities cannot use

Exhibit 5-2.   Key Differences Between Typical Tests and Authentic Tasks.

Typical Tests	Authentic Tasks	Indicators of Authenticity
Require correct responses only.	Require quality product or performance (or both) and justification.	We assess whether the learner can explain, apply, self-adjust, or justify answers, not just the correctness of answers using facts.
Must be unknown in advance to ensure validity.	Are known as much as possible in advance; involve excelling at predictable demanding and core tasks; are not "gotcha!" experiences.	The tasks, criteria, and standards by which work will be judged are predictable or known to the learner—as a recital piece, a play, an engine to be fixed, or a proposal to a client can be clearly understood and anticipated prior to assessment.
Are disconnected from a realistic context and realistic constraints.	Require real-world use of knowledge: the learner must "do" history, science, and so on in realistic simulations or actual use.	The task is a challenge with a related set of constraints that are authentic—likely to be encountered by the professional, citizen, or consumer. (Know-how, not plugging in, is required.)
Contain isolated items requiring use or recognition of known answers or skills.	Are integrated challenges in which knowledge and judgment must be innovatively used to fashion a quality product or performance.	The task is multifaceted and nonroutine, even if there is a "right" answer. It thus requires problem clarification, trial and error, adjustments, adapting to the case or facts at hand, and so on.
Are simplified so as to be easy to score reliably.	Involve complex and nonarbitrary tasks, criteria, and standards.	The task involves the important aspects of performance or the core challenges of the field of study (or both), not the easily scored; it does not sacrifice validity for reliability.
Are one-shot.	Are iterative: contain recurring essential tasks, genres, and standards.	The work is designed to reveal whether the learner has achieved real versus pseudo mastery and understanding versus mere familiarity over time.
Depend on highly technical correlations.	Provide direct evidence, involving tasks that have been validated against core adult roles and discipline-based challenges.	The task is valid and fair on its face. It thus evokes student interest and persistence and seems apt and challenging to learners and instructors.
Provide a score.	Provide usable (sometimes concurrent) feedback; the learner is able to confirm results and self-adjust as needed.	The assessment is designed not merely to audit performance but to improve future performance. The learner is seen as the primary beneficiary of information.

Source: Wiggins, 1998, p. 23.

one-dimensional, high-stakes paper-and-pencil testing formats because, by their very structure, tests of this sort reduce and constrict what we can show about what we know. We need either multiple forms of assessment (tests, products, portfolios, and journals) or multi-dimensional assessment (such as authentic performance tasks and projects) to adequately reveal the richness of the strengths and sources of our knowing.

    At times, the amount of professional time required to accomplish the assessments described here can seem overwhelming. Yet, if we make assessment a partner to exciting learning and continuing motivation for adults, rather than merely audits by which to assign grades or scores, assessments become important learning activities in and of themselves, worthy of everyone's time and effort. Nonetheless (I know you are thinking), time constraints will still be a challenge. With this problem in mind, here are some worthwhile activities and methods to support the use of authentic tasks or to be transformed into authentic tasks.

Assessment options based on Gardner's multiple intelligences. Adults have different profiles of intelligences. Their having the opportunity to select an assessment process that reflects their particular intellectual strengths should encourage their participation and enthusiasm for demonstrating their competence. The following menu of options, adapted from *Teaching and Learning Through Multiple Intelligences* (Campbell, Campbell, and Dickinson, 1992), is categorized by each intelligence.

Linguistic

Tell or write a short story to explain ...	Keep a journal to illustrate ...
Write a poem, myth, play, or editorial about ...	Create a debate to discuss ...
Create an advertising campaign to depict ...	Create a talk show about ...

Logical-Mathematical

Complete a cost-benefit analysis of ...	Write a computer program for ...
Design and conduct an experiment to ...	Create story problems for ...
Induce or deduce a set of principles on ...	Create a time line for ...

Musical

Create a song that explains or expresses ...	Revise lyrics of a song to ...
Collect and present music and songs to ...	Create a musical piece to ...
Create a music video to illustrate ...	Use music to ...

Spatial

Create a piece of art that demonstrates ...	Create a poster to ...
Create a videotape, collage, photo album of ...	Chart, map, or graph ...
Design a flag or logo to express ...	Create a scale model of ...

Bodily-Kinesthetic

Perform a play on ...	Build or construct a ...
Role-play or simulate ...	Use puppets to explore ...
Create a sequence of movements to explain ...	Create a scavenger hunt to ...

Interpersonal

Participate in a service project that will …	Offer multiple perspectives of …
Contribute to resolving a local problem by …	Teach a group to …
Use what you've learned to change or influence …	Conduct a discussion to …

Intrapersonal

Create a personal philosophy about …	Discern what is essential in …
Explain your intuitive hunches about …	Explain your emotions about …
Explain your assumptions in a critical incident …	Use a journal to …

Naturalist

Discover and describe the patterns in …	Create a typology for …
Relate and describe the interdependence of …	Create a flow chart for …
Use a field trip to analyze …	Observe and describe …

In addition to accommodating multiple intelligences, this assessment menu offers a range of performance actions that require higher-order thinking—*design, teach, discern, explain, analyze, write,* and the like. For example, a learner in a science course might *design* an experiment to analyze the chemicals in the local water supply and *write* an editorial based on the results for the local paper. These assessments provide opportunities for imaginative experiences that allow adults to use their unique preferences and strengths. Furthermore, with these assessments adults can develop deeper relationships between new learning and their cultural backgrounds and values.

Portfolios and process folios. Regardless of its purpose, a portfolio is a sample of a person's work or learning. It can provide more diverse evidence and an array of performance examples incorporating a longer time frame than a single test. Multiple indicators, such as tests, products, media, and self-assessments, can make up a portfolio and contribute to a deeper understanding of an adult's learning. Portfolios are an excellent means of assessing an adult's personal goals as they mesh with course goals in such programs of study as the arts and in vocational and graduate schools. The contents of a portfolio and the assessment criteria used to evaluate it will differ depending on the portfolio's purpose. The following is a list of some of the possible ways a portfolio can be used (Wiggins, 1998):

As a display of the learner's best work, as chosen by the learner, the instructor, or both

As a display of the learner's interests and goals

As a display of the learner's growth or progress

As documentation of self-assessment, self-adjustment, self-direction, and learning

As evidence for professional assessment of learner performance

A *process folio* (Gardner, 1993) goes beyond a traditional portfolio: it layers elements of the entire learning experience so that learners are able to document and reflect on challenges and understandings that emerge over time. The process folio documents three primary considerations: the content of learning (what is being learned), the context of learning (how what is being learned fits into a larger framework, possibly the learner's life and experiences), and perceptions of the process of learning (perceptions about various influences on the student's learning and ways in which learning was enhanced). This type of portfolio is a powerful tool for responding to the interests and concerns of diverse learners (Wlodkowski and Ginsberg, 1995).

The following are some guidelines to consider when working with portfolios:

1. Involve learners in the composition and selection of what makes up the portfolio.

    Learners may want to explore different aspects of a particular discipline. In a research course, for example, the learner might design an ethnographic study *and* an experimental study for her portfolio.

    Learners may choose among different categories, such as most difficult problem, best work, most valued work, most improved work, a soulful or spiritual experience, and so forth.

2. Include information in the portfolio that shows learner's self-reflection and self-assessment.

    A. Learners may include a rationale for their selections.
    B. Learners may create a guide for their portfolio offering interpretations, commentary, critique, and matters of contextual importance.
    C. Learners may include self- and peer assessments indicating strengths, areas for improvement, and relationships between earlier and later works.

3. Be clear about the purpose of the portfolio.

    A. Learners should be able to relate their goals for learning to the contents of the portfolios.
    B. Learners should be able to provide a fair representation of their work.
    C. Rubrics and their models for assessing portfolio contents should be clearly understood and available (see Strategy 53).

4. Exploit the portfolio as a process to show learner growth.

    A. Learners may submit the original, the improved, and the final copy or draft of their creation or performance.
    B. Using specific works, learners may make a history of their "movement" along certain dimensions in their growth.
    C. Learners may include feedback from outside experts or descriptions of outside activities that reflect the growth illustrated in the portfolio.

5. Teach learners how to create and use portfolios.

    A. Offer models of excellent portfolios for learners to examine but stress that each portfolio is an individual creation.
    B. Review portfolios regularly and give feedback to learners about them, especially early in the term or year when learners are initially constructing their portfolios.

Projects. We often use the term *project* to describe the major undertakings of businesses and institutions ("We're working on a new project," or, perhaps more critically, "This thing is turning into a project"). In education and training, it is magnitude and complexity that afford something the status of a project. From performing community service to making dramatic presentations, projects offer the multiple challenges, meanings, and creative resolutions that make learning motivating and capable of embracing cultural diversity. Because of their size and duration, projects provide the opportunity for active immersion across disciplines and the use of a wide range of profiles of intelligences. They easily can connect new concepts and skills with the real lives and goals of learners.

The investigation conducted by Daniel Solorzano (1989) and his students is a classic example of a collaborative project carried out with critical consciousness. In the late 1970s, Solorzano offered a sociology course at East Los Angeles College. Beginning with a discussion centering on the negative stereotypes of Chicanos in Hollywood gang movies, Solorzano and his students arrived at two questions: Why are Chicanos portrayed negatively in the mass media? and, Whose interests are served by these negative portrayals of Chicanos?

To conduct extensive research on these queries, the class divided itself into three research groups: (1) a library group to research contemporary and historical images of Chicanos in the media, (2) a group to research public information data on youth gangs in East Los Angeles, and (3) a group to research the film industry. After analyzing and discussing their research, the learners more clearly understood how film companies were exploiting Chicano stereotypes. Consequently, they organized a boycott against these films. Collaborating with outside organizations for assistance led to the founding of the ad hoc Gang Exploitation Committee. Solorzano reports that no new Chicano youth gang movies appeared in the decade after this class. Student learning was extensive, and the students succeeded in doing something they considered important and positive.

In the same vein, the investigation of learning styles designed and executed by Yolanda Scott-Machado is a fine representation of an individual project. Some guidelines to keep in mind for creating and carrying out projects are as follows:

- Whether the project is individual or collaborative, learners should be involved in its conception and planning.
- Consider goal setting or some of its elements as a means to explore and plan the project.
- Request an outline of the project that includes some schedule of agreed-on documentation and a completion date.
- Arrange for the presentation of the project to a relevant audience who can offer authentic acknowledgment and feedback.
- Assess the project from numerous perspectives, including a learner's self-assessment. Overall, assessment may involve the quality of project planning, execution, and presentation; the challenge level; creativity and originality; the employment of resources; what was learned. It may also incorporate the evaluation of other learners and knowledgeable people outside the course or training.

STRATEGY 53: *When using rubrics, make sure they assess the essential features of performance and are fair, valid, and sufficiently clear so that learners can accurately self-assess.*

When it comes to assessment, rubrics are "where the rubber meets the road." That is because rubrics often mean more than assessment; they mean evaluation. Assessment describes or compares, but evaluation makes a value judgment. In evaluation, we fix passing scores or criteria that determine how acceptable or unacceptable a given performance is. Grades or scores may be assigned and recorded according to the rubric. Evaluations often significantly affect an adult's promotion to or qualification for particular programs or positions.

A rubric is a set of scoring guidelines for evaluating a learner's work. It strongly *controls* learning because, as Wiggins (1998, p. 154) points out, many instructors use rubrics to answer the following questions:

By what criteria should performance be judged?

What should we look for to judge performance success?

What does the range in quality of performance look like?

How do we determine validly, reliably, and fairly what score should be given and what that score should mean?

How should the different levels of quality be described and distinguished from one another?

I've been carefully and cautiously using rubrics for about three years, and they can be deceptive even though they do not appear that way at first glance. They remind me of a large wall from a distance. You can't see the cracks until you get closer. Baseball averages afford a good example of the complexity and elusiveness of rubrics. A rubric comprises a scale of possible points along a continuum of quality. Batting average is a rubric in the sense that we evaluate how good batters are by their percentage of hits for times at bat. The higher the average, the better the player. But is a .300 hitter a good hitter? Well, that depends: How many times has the player been to bat? Does she get extra base hits? How does she hit when players are on base? At night? With two strikes? When the team is behind? Against left-handed pitching? As many managers know, you don't use batting average alone to evaluate a player—not even to judge only hitting. And that's how it is with rubrics: they may seem concrete, specific, and telling, but life's contexts and complexity can make the simplest performance a puzzle.

Yet rubrics answer a question that counts for many adults: What are you going to use to judge me? If rubrics are fair, clear, reliable, and valid and get at the essentials of performance, and learners can self-assess with them to improve before performance is evaluated, they enhance motivation because they significantly increase the probability of learners' achieving competence. However, rubrics need models and indicators to make each level of quality concretely understandable. And they need to be created or revised with input from learners if they are to be culturally sensitive. For example, if we use *smiles frequently* as one indicator for *very good* presentation style, we penalize someone who tends to be droll or someone from a culture where smiling frequently is more an indication of anxiety than of ease. Excellent rubrics are valuable but flawed assistants in making judgments about learning—flawed because language at best renders, but never duplicates, experience.

Let's look at one straightforward rubric for judging the clear expression of a main idea in an essay (Exhibit 5-3). (Other rubrics would be necessary for evaluating other dimensions of performance in the essay, such as critical thinking or writing skills.) This rubric will help us better understand some of Wiggins's guidelines (1998) for creating effective rubrics. These guidelines follow Exhibit 5-3.

If I were using this rubric (and had a model for the descriptor of each level of performance) to evaluate twenty essays *only for the main idea,* I should be able to

Use this rubric to discriminate accurately among the essays by assessing the essential features of performance. This makes the rubric valid.

Rely on the rubric's descriptive language (what the quality or its absence looks like), as opposed to relying on merely evaluative language, such as "excellent product," to make the discrimination.

Exhibit 5-3. A Rubric for Expressing an Idea Clearly.

Rating	Descriptor with Indicators
Exemplary = 4	Clearly communicates the main idea or theme and provides support that contains rich, vivid, and powerful detail.
Competent = 3	Clearly communicates the main idea or theme and provides suitable support and detail.
Acceptable with flaws = 2	Clearly communicates the main idea or theme, but support is sketchy or vague.
Needs revision = 1	The main idea or theme is not discernible.

Use this rubric to consistently make fine discriminations across four levels of performance. When a rubric can be repeatedly used to make the same discriminations with the same sample of performances, it is reliable. To maintain reliability, rubrics seldom have more than six levels of performance.

Make sure learners can use this same rubric and its descriptors (and models) of each level of performance to accurately self-assess and self-correct their work.

See that this rubric is parallel. Each descriptor generally matches the others in terms of criteria language used.

See that this rubric is coherent. The rubric focuses on the same criteria throughout.

See that this rubric is continuous. The degree of difference between each descriptor (level of performance) tends to be equal.

There is a cottage industry in books about how to write rubrics. At this time, I find most of these books overly linear and not culturally sensitive. However, I do find reading them helpful for understanding the creative variety of rubrics that are possible and for deepening my critical awareness about the uses, value, and possible harm of rubrics. Right now, the discipline of assessment and evaluation reminds me of the computer industry: there are vast changes and better models ahead.

STRATEGY 54: *Use self-assessment methods to improve learning and to provide learners with the opportunity to construct relevant insights and connections.*

In addition to the type of self-assessment in which learners compare their work against rubrics and make self-adjustments, there are reflective assessment methods that enable adults to understand themselves more comprehensively as learners, knowers, and participants in a complex world. These methods help learners weave relationships and meanings between academic and technical information and their personal histories and experiences. These forms of self-assessment allow adults to explore their surprises, puzzlement, and hunches, to explore the tension they feel when they experience something that does not fit with what they already know. Because integration of learning with identity and values is essential to adult motivation, this kind of self-assessment is a key process for deepening adult learners' feelings of competence: it can create the bridge that unites formal learning with learners' subjective world.

In general, learners appreciate clearly knowing what to focus on (and what might possibly be learned) in the process of self-assessment. It's a good idea to explain how we as instructors will evaluate or respond to self-assessments. Our interest and timely feedback encourage learners. Not everything needs to be read or commented on, but learners are more likely to strengthen their reflective skills if they receive expected, supportive, and specific feedback from us (or other learners). This is especially so in the beginning phases of any self-assessment process.

Self-assessment can be superficial when it is appended to a training or class as a single episode at the end of a long term. MacGregor (1994) advises instructors to build self-assessment into longer learning situations as an ongoing activity. There are several approaches we can use throughout a learning experience and then summarize from a longer perspective. Among them, I have found journals, post-writes, closure techniques, and the Critical Incident Questionnaire to be very beneficial.

Journals. Journals can take a number of forms. Consider, for example, a journal that is used in a science course to synthesize lab notes, address the quality of the work, examine the process(es) on which work is based, and address emerging interests and concerns. Journals document risk, experimentation with ideas, and self-expression. They are an informative complement to more conventional forms of assessment.

With respect to sensitivity to cultural differences and encouraging critical awareness of the origins and meanings of subject-specific knowledge, learners can use journals to address the following questions: From whose viewpoint am I seeing or reading or hearing? From what angle or perspective? How do I know what I know? What is the evidence, and how reliable is it? Whose purposes are served by this information?

Journals can address interests, ideas, and issues related to course material and processes, recurring problems, responses to questions from the instructor, responses to questions generated by the learner, and important connections that the learner is making. These important connections may be the learner's observations in the classroom, but optimally, connections are meanings that emerge as the learner applies course work to past, present, and future life experiences. If we wish to promote this level of reflection, then we must make the classroom a place where this can happen. Providing time in class for learners to respond in their journals to readings, discussions, and significant questions builds community around the journal process and sends yet another message that the classroom is a place in which the skills of insight and personal meaning are valued.

Journals require time and effort. Initially, it may be best for learners to pay less attention to the mechanics and organization and to whether or not their writing makes sense; they should simply try to get their thoughts and feelings down on paper where they can learn from them. Having sufficiently incubated, this material can be reorganized and summarized later.

Post-writes. Post-writes are reflections that encourage learners to analyze a particular piece of work, how they created it, and what it may mean to them (Allen and Roswell, 1989). For example, you might say, "Now that you have finished your essay, please answer the following questions. There are no right or wrong answers. We are interested in your analysis of your experience writing this essay."

What problems did you face in the writing of this essay?

What solutions did you find for these problems?

Imagine you had more time to write this essay. What would you do if you were to continue working on it?

Has your thinking changed in any way as a result of writing this essay? If so, briefly describe.

It is easy to imagine ways in which this technique could be applied across disciplines. Consider, for example, slightly redesigning the previous questions to allow learners in math or science to identify and reflect on a problem that posed a particular challenge.

Closure techniques. Closure activities are opportunities for learners to synthesize—to examine general or specific aspects of what they have learned, to identify emerging thoughts or feelings, to discern themes, to construct meaning, to relate learning to real-life experiences, and so forth. Essentially, learners articulate their subjective relationship with the course or training material. For example, at the end of a workshop, we might ask participants to formulate an action plan to apply what they have learned. Closure, then, becomes a way of building coherence between what people have learned in the workshop and their personal experience beyond the workshop. Another example of this might be to ask participants to identify one particular obstacle they must still overcome to be more proficient with what they have learned. Additional suggestions for positive and constructive closure follow.

- *Head, heart, hand* is a closure activity that allows learners to integrate different dimensions of a learning experience. After learners have had a short time for reflection, the activity may be conducted as a small- or large-group experience in which all learners have a chance to hear each other's voices. Learners may report out one or more of the following possibilities. For *head,* learners identify something they will continue to think about as a consequence of the learning experience. For *heart,* learners identify a feeling that has emerged as a result of the learning experience. For *hand,* learners identify a desired action they will take that has been stimulated by the learning experience.

- *Note-taking pairs* is a technique that can be used intermittently during a lecture or as a culminating activity (Johnson, Johnson, and Smith, 1991). Either way, two learners work together to review, add to, or modify their notes. This is an opportunity to cooperatively reflect on a lesson, review major concepts and pertinent information, and illuminate unresolved issues or concerns. It is especially beneficial after a lecture. Many learners, including but certainly not limited to students who speak English as a second language, benefit by summarizing their lecture notes to another person or vice versa. Students may ask each other such questions as, What have you got in your notes about this particular item? What are three key points made by the instructor? What is the most surprising thing the instructor said today? What is something that you are feeling uncertain about? and the like.

- *Summarizing questions* are informative questions for reflecting on an entire course or training program. The following are some examples (Elbow, 1986):

    What have you accomplished that you are proud of?

    Compare your accomplishments with what you had hoped for and expected at the start.

    Which kinds of things were difficult or frustrating? Which were easy?

    What is the most important thing you did during this program?

    Think of some important moments from this learning period: your best moments, typical moments, crises, or turning points. Tell about five or six of these, using a sentence or two for each.

    Who is the person you studied whom you cared the most about? *Be* that person and write that person's letter to you, telling you whatever it is they have to tell you.

    What did you learn throughout? Skills and ideas? What was the most important thing? What idea or skill was hardest to really "get"? What crucial idea or skill came naturally?

    Describe this period of time as a journey: Where did the journey take you? What was the terrain like? Was it a complete trip or part of a longer one?

    You learned something crucial that you won't discover for a while. Guess it now.

    Tell a few ways you could have done a better job.

    What advice would some friends in the course give you if they spoke with 100 percent honesty and caring? What advice do you have for yourself?

Critical Incident Questionnaire. I have adapted this self-assessment approach from the work of Brookfield (1995, p. 115). In training and teaching, it allows me to be more responsive as an instructor and helps learners be more reflective about their significant experiences.

The Critical Incident Questionnaire is made up of five questions, each of which asks learners to write details about important events that took place while they were learning. For college courses, Brookfield uses it at the end of each week. For intensive workshops and seminars, I have found value in using it at the end of each session (four hours or longer). The questions are printed on a form; there is space below each question for the learner's responses. Learners complete the questions anonymously and retain a photocopy or carbon copy of their answers for their own benefit.

The Critical Incident Questionnaire

1. At what moment in this workshop did you feel most engaged with what was happening?
2. At what moment in this workshop did you feel most distanced from what was happening?

3. What action that anyone (instructor or learner) took in the workshop did you find most affirming and helpful?

4. What action that anyone (instructor or learner) took in the workshop did you find most puzzling or confusing?

5. What about the workshop surprised you the most? (This could be something about your own reactions to what went on, or something that someone did, or anything else that occurs to you.)

I explore the papers looking for themes, patterns, and, in general, learners' concerns or confusions that need adjustments and responses on my part. I also look for the part of our learning and instruction that has been affirmed. I find hints and suggestions for areas to probe or deepen. Most important, my experience has been that this questionnaire gives me a more sensitive reading of the emotional reactions of learners and of those areas that may create controversy or conflict. However, I do realize that for some students, writing may inhibit their responses, and I publicly acknowledge this shortcoming of the process.

For the beginning of the session immediately following the distribution of the questionnaire, I outline the results in short phrases on an overhead projection and have a dialogue with the learners about these responses. This tends to build trust, further communication, and deepen learning. What I like most is that this form of self-assessment can be so fluidly used to build community. Brookfield (1997) has also developed the Critical Practice Audit, which uses a critical analysis approach to self-assessment for such practitioners as instructors and nurses.

A FEW WORDS ABOUT GRADES, ASSESSMENT, AND MOTIVATION

Although they serve no legitimate teaching purpose and do not accurately predict educational or occupational achievement, grades receive very high status in U.S. society (Wlodkowski and Ginsberg, 1995). For most adults, low grades, because they are threatening and stigmatizing, do more to decrease motivation to learn than they do to enhance it. For poor and working-class people, grades as an indication of intellectual merit reduce accessibility to higher education (American Association of University Women Educational Foundation, 1992). Topping off a thirty-year trend, grade inflation is growing at a rapid rate (Astin, 1998) and further eroding the worth of grades.

Yet, until we reform the grading system, many of us will have to give grades. Because contracts have a structure that allows for mutual understanding and agreement and a dialogue about the content, process, criteria, and outcomes of learning, I recommend using them to arrive at grades. If you are not able to use contracts but can use the assessment strategies described in this section to assign grades that stand for something fair, clear, stable, and valid, then the more pernicious motivational consequences of grading should be minimal.

In fact, as a set of interdependent practices, Strategies 48 through 54 align extremely well with the guiding principles for assessment of adult learning offered by Kasworm and Marienau (1997). In general, adults become more competent, feel more confident, and look forward to assessment when assessment procedures are

Related to goals they understand, find relevant, and want to accomplish

Reflective of growth in learning

Indicative of clear ways to improve learning without penalty

Expected

Returned promptly

Permeated with instructor and peer comments that are informative and supportive

Used to encourage new challenges in learning

COMMUNICATING TO ENGENDER COMPETENCE

The rest of the motivational strategies found in this section also enhance competence but are frequently used apart from assessment. Often they are straightforward communications given as the situation demands.

STRATEGY 55: *When necessary, use constructive criticism.*

Constructive criticism is similar to feedback but has a few more qualifications. It does emphasize errors and deficiencies in learning, but unlike basic criticism, it does not connote expressions of disapproval, disgust, or rejection. In general, criticism does not have to be used as often as we may think. Instructors may tend to overuse criticism when they do not know how to use feedback properly or have to work with learners who do not have proper entry-level skills for the learning task they are *required* to perform. The latter condition is best alleviated through more appropriate selection and guidance procedures, such as pretesting and interviews. However, there are still circumstances in which giving constructive criticism may be a necessary strategy for engendering competence:

When the learning process is extremely costly or involves a threat to human safety, mistakes cannot be afforded. Training with a particular machine, weapon, chemical, or medical procedure are examples of this type of situation.

When the learning performance is so poor that to emphasize success or improvement would be ridiculous or patronizing.

When the learning performance has significant errors and there are only a few remaining chances for improvement in the training or course.

When a learner directly requests criticism.

Constructive criticism may be a helpful and motivating way to deal with these situations. Like feedback, constructive criticism has the following qualities: it is informational, based on performance criteria, behavior specific, corrective, and prompt, and when possible, it provides efficient opportunities for improvement. Unless a state of emergency exists, it is given privately. In addition, where appropriate, constructive criticism has the following characteristics:

- It helps the learner see performance in the context of overall progress and not as an isolated failure: for example, "Your science exam indicates that 70 percent of the concepts are still unclear to you. I hope you keep in mind that you've already progressed through four units, and although this one may seem difficult, that's a pretty good indication you can more fully understand these ideas. Let's go over the material."
- It respectfully informs the learner of the conditions that lead to the emphasis on mistakes or deficiencies: for example, "This machine can be quite dangerous. For your own safety, before you get another chance to operate it, I think we'd better take a look at any mistakes you might have made," or, "You've got only one more chance to practice before you meet with the review committee. I think the best use of our time would be to check your performance on the last case study and to concentrate on any parts that may need improvement."
- It acknowledges the learner's effort: for example, "There's no doubt you've put a great deal of work into this report. Just the number of references you cite testifies to the effort and comprehensive research that went into this project. Yet it seems to need more organization. There's no unifying theme that ties all this evidence together. What generalization could you think of that might serve this purpose?"

- It provides emotional support: for example, "At the end of your last session, your client stated he felt frustrated as he left. Do you think you may have been trying too hard? You sounded a bit strident and didn't respond to the client's stated needs. We can analyze the videotape to see just where this happened. However, you did very well with the other two clients you worked with. Since you have only one more chance to practice in this seminar, let's be as careful as possible to understand what might not have worked so well. It's obvious you want to do your best, and I feel confident you'll learn from this situation."

When you are giving feedback and constructive criticism, adults benefit from knowing when more effort on their part or another learning strategy could significantly contribute to their learning. Strategy 20 explains why and how to make these attributions.

STRATEGY 56: *Effectively praise and reward learning.*

In this book, the term *praise* has the same meaning it usually has in everyday language: to commend the worth of or to express approval or admiration (Brophy, 1981). It is an intense response on the part of an instructor, one that goes beyond positive feedback to include such emotions as surprise, delight, or excitement as well as sincere appreciation for the learner's accomplishment. ("That's a remarkable answer. It's comprehensive, insightful, and extremely precise.")

As a strategy, the use of praise has had a controversial history. Some scholars have opposed praise and rewards on principle, viewing them as bribes for doing something that is often in the learners' best interest or in the best interest of society (Kohn, 1993). Others are critical of praise because it may contribute to a hierarchical relationship between learners and instructors. Instructors distribute praise because they are the judges and experts who deem learners as praiseworthy. This kind of social exchange may diminish the chances for colearning and for a more egalitarian relationship.

Although praise can enhance learners' motivation, there is considerable research to show it often does not serve this purpose (Kohn, 1993). Praise is frequently ineffective because it is not related to exemplary achievement, it lacks specificity (the learner does not know exactly why it was given), and it is not credible. For example, sometimes we may give it because learners seem happy and enthusiastic about their work and show it to us, and we do not know what else to say *(awkward-moment praise)*. Other times we may give it because we feel sorry for learners who are having difficulty and use it to boost their morale *(mercy praise)*.

Many competent adults do not want or expect praise. They want clear, positive feedback about their progress and may experience praise as annoying or patronizing *(snob praise)*. Furthermore, praise given too frequently and indiscriminately may begin to seem perfunctory and predictable to learners, encouraging them to interpret it as a form of instructor small talk or flattery *(jabber praise)*. The focus of praise on form rather than substance can cause a problem as well. Praise for turning in an assignment or for learning responses that agree with instructor values may seem controlling and manipulative *(puppet praise)*. In some instances, instructors have even used praise to *end* learner behavior: perhaps a discussion initiated by a learner has, in our opinion, gone on a bit too long; we toss out a compliment about what has been said to provide pleasant closure, and move on to something else *(terminator praise)*.

In general, to praise effectively we need to praise *well,* rather than necessarily *often.* The same could be said about rewarding effectively. In fact, praise is often considered to be a verbal reward (Pittman, Boggiano, and Ruble, 1983). Whether the reward is verbal (praise) or tangible (money, promotions, privileges) or symbolic (grades, trophies, awards), there are guidelines that can ensure the positive effects of these rewards on learner motivation. The six suggestions that follow are based on a continuing analysis by Brophy (1998), which has largely used studies done with children and adolescents. However, this material is supported by research with young adults (Morgan, 1984) and adults learning in the workplace (Keller, 1992).

Effective praise and rewards are

1. *Given with sincerity, spontaneity, variety, and other signs of credibility.* These characteristics may be more pertinent for praise than for other rewards. Rewards are often known ahead of time and given with more uniformity of procedure. However, the affect with which a reward is given is critical to its impact on the learner. An insincerely given reward or form of praise is really an insult to an adult. (A personal note: I have conducted hundreds of workshops in which I have asked instructors to volunteer the guidelines for effective praise. Without exception, sincerity has been listed as the number one guideline.)

2. *Based on the attainment of specific performance criteria.* This means that the learner has achieved a standard and can clearly understand what particular personal behaviors are being acknowledged. This approach not only makes the reward or praise informational but also significantly increases the person's chances of learning exactly which behaviors are important. For example, "Nice job" written on a paper is not as helpful as, "This paper has not a single spelling or grammatical error in it. I appreciate the meticulous editing this so obviously reflects."

3. *Adapted in sufficiency, quantity, and intensity to the accomplishments achieved.* Rewards that are less than what is merited can be insulting and demeaning. Rewards that are too much for what has been accomplished are excessive and disturbing. There are common expressions in everyday language to reflect adult embarrassment in response to inadequate or undeserved praise: "Damning with faint praise" (too little praise) and "Gushing over trivia" (too much praise).

4. *Given to attribute success to the apparent combination of the personal effort, knowledge, and capabilities of the learner.* Emphasizing these attributes increases the learner's sense of internal causality and implies the learner can continue such accomplishments in the future: for example, "Your design of this model is exceptional. It meets all the criteria for strength, durability, and esthetics. Would you mind sharing how you created it with the rest of the team? I think we could all learn from your approach."

5. *Given contingent on success at a challenging task.* This makes the learner's task *praiseworthy* and testifies to the competence of the learner. The praise implies that the learner overcame a real difficulty and deserves the recognition. If the task were not challenging, then the praise would be indiscriminate, and a reward, if given, would tend to be seen as likewise.

6. *Adapted to the preference of the individual.* Again, this characteristic may be more applicable to praise than to other rewards. Rewards are often given in a ritualistic manner, as in award ceremonies. However, one would certainly want rewards to be attractive and valued in relation to the learner's cultural preferences. For example, more collectivist cultures may prefer to receive praise indirectly rather than directly. In one study, Jones, Rozelle, and Chang (1990) found that Chinese adults did not want to be used as "good examples for others," whereas the group from the United States found that to be quite acceptable. When in doubt, it is probably best to give praise and other rewards privately.

There is a mnemonic device for remembering these six guidelines: 3S-3P, which stands for Sincere, Specific, Sufficient, Properly attributed, Praiseworthy, and Preferred. In sentence form, the mnemonic can be stated this way: praise (or other rewards) should be Sincere, Specific, Sufficient, and Properly attributed for genuinely Praiseworthy behavior, in a manner Preferred by the learner. In general, it is important to remember that the subjective viewpoint of the learner and the context in which praise and other rewards are given will immensely influence their effect (Morgan, 1984). As of now, there are no ways to accurately prescribe these conditions, except to encourage instructors to remain continually sensitive to their impact.

FURTHER MEANS OF AFFIRMING LEARNER COMPETENCE

There are important strategies to enhance aspects of adult competence that may not easily be measured by performance criteria but that are critical nonetheless, such as creativity or cooperation. In some instances, these aspects of competence emerge out of the human experience learners and instructors share from having worked and accomplished something together. The following strategies accommodate these less easily categorized outcomes of learning.

STRATEGY 57: *Acknowledge and affirm the learners' responsibility and any significant actions or characteristics that contributed to individual or group learning.*

The idea behind this strategy is as follows: if there is anything significant the learner has done or exemplified that has contributed to the individual's or group's learning, we want to reflect this back to the learner. The implication of this strategy is that standard means of providing feedback, assessment, praise, or other rewards were not sufficient to adequately reveal the learner's assets. Some specific ways to carry out this strategy are as follows:

- Interview learners for their opinions as to what the critical processes were that helped them to learn successfully. This method is especially useful with self-directed individual and small-group learning projects. It offers an excellent opportunity to include self-assessment materials, such as post-writes, journals, and closure techniques (see Strategy 54). A more formative approach to competence in ongoing self-directed learning activities is this set of four questions asked at an appropriate interval: What is your evaluation of what you have done so far? How can you still improve? How can you help yourself? How can I help you?
- Acknowledge the risk taking and challenge involved in the learning accomplishment. When adults deliberately choose a challenging learning goal, the process of learning becomes even more special because they have knowingly placed themselves at risk. This condition intensifies what they can learn about themselves. With further reflection, learners can build their self-confidence and experience the merit of their talents, strategies, and effort. If they do not accomplish the learning goal, the process can be a lesson in reality testing and self-appraisal. Learners can explore related issues through questions like these: What has been learned from attempting to accomplish the goal? Does the goal remain worthwhile? Is it reasonable to continue to strive for the goal? If not, what is a desirable next step? And so forth.

Taking on learning challenges that are reasonable and personally valued is a form of courage—the courage to persevere in the midst of ambiguity, the courage to extend personal boundaries, the courage to embrace learning for its own sake. These are not spontaneous human qualities. They are cultivated, and they evolve. As instructors, we can provide opportunities for adults to reflect on where these aspects of their learning occur and what their value may be.

- Affirm the strengths and assets of the learner that contribute to the learner's own achievements or to the accomplishments of others. When instructors and learners work together for a period of time, they begin to recognize in each other various qualities that are beneficial not only to learning but also to people's well-being. Many of these characteristics may not be easily classified under the performance criteria being applied. Also, they may not be praiseworthy by definition. However, they are significant enough to be recognized and influential enough to be appreciated. Helping learners see that they possess these assets can raise their self-awareness and make these strengths more available to them in future learning and work situations. Stating such an appreciation can be quite simple. For example, "I just wanted you to know I really enjoyed your sense of humor in this course" could suffice. We can make this kind of statement informally, one-on-one with the learner, or as part of a concluding group exercise in which each member of the learning group is allowed two statements of appreciation to anyone about anything that has occurred during the course or training.

The following are some strengths and assets learners often possess, and it may benefit learners to know they possess them:

Writing skills	Thinking skills
Physical skills	Integrity
Multiple intelligences	Cooperativeness
Personal traits	Creativity
Verbal skills	Math skills
Knowledge base	Sense of humor
Organizational skills	Kindness
Significant actions	Leadership skills

This list is more suggestive than exhaustive. The main point is not to miss the opportunity to give learners important information derived from the human interaction in a learning experience. Also, this approach encourages learner-to-learner feedback, which might have more impact on a person than anything an instructor could communicate.

STRATEGY 58: *Use incentives to develop and maintain adult motivation in learning activities that are initially unappealing but personally valued.*

One of the insights Peters and Waterman (1982) made about the use of positive rewards is that rewards are an excellent means to help people move in directions they are already headed. Positive reinforcement can be a gentle and precise way to develop and maintain adult motivation for learning that is personally valued but not initially appealing.

An *incentive* may be defined as an anticipated reward. It serves as a goal we expect to achieve as a result of some specific behavior. Incentives take many forms, such as recognition, money, relationships, and privileges. Incentives are frequently used in the workplace (Kemmerer and Thiagarajan, 1992). However, I use this concept only as it can be understood to support intrinsic motivation while learning—as a means to assist adults in becoming more effective at what they personally value. Incentive systems in the workplace are not necessarily created or implemented with this orientation as an essential element.

Adults' lives are filled with incentives. We frequently use rewards for performing activities we value but find tedious, difficult, or perhaps even painful—exercising easily comes to mind, but there's also dieting, studying, budgeting, and cleaning. We reward ourselves at certain points for performing these activities. The reward may be a piece of chocolate, a massage, a movie, a long distance call, or a walk outside. Knowing these kinds of incentives are coming at the end of our task makes the tedium or effort a little more bearable. Regardless of how many times I tell myself it's great to get my heart rate up and sweat like a steam whistle, seeing my favorite cold drink at the end of the workout is a far more fetching notion to keep me working out. But please keep in mind that I chose the activity, I value the activity, and I want to be competent at it. I'm using a reward to help me sustain an activity I'm intrinsically motivated to perform. And make no mistake about it: in my mind, the reward makes the whole experience better.

There are at least two situations in which incentives may be an effective and inviting means to encourage adult participation in a valued learning activity:

1. *The adult has had little or no experience with the learning activity.* Maybe the training or instructional program is very new or unique. Lack of experience can prevent the learner from enjoying or valuing what he is learning or cause him to feel cautious and apprehensive. Or perhaps the person is learning how to use a new machine or how to apply a different auditing process or how to work with recently invented technology. In this case, the learner anticipates the value of the activity but has not yet realized that value. Under such circumstances, incentives could actually contribute to the awakening of intrinsic motivation in the learner because there is no prior negative experience to lead the learner to believe that the incentive is being used as compensation for participation in an unpleasant learning task (Lepper and Greene, 1978). The learner is more likely to see the incentive as a reward for "trying out" or becoming competent in a new learning opportunity.

2. *The adult has to develop a level of competence before the learning activity can become enjoyable or interesting.* Some sports, such as tennis and swimming, are good examples of this situation, but the same could be said for learning to speak a foreign language or use a personal computer or play the trumpet. There are so many things that are valuable to learn but just not that appealing to do until the learner has achieved a level of competence. In such situations, incentives may be the only positive means available to sustain effort until the necessary level of proficiency provides its own pleasure and satisfaction. That is why parents applaud vigorously and unashamedly for their children at those, to say the least, imperfect music recitals and why an instructor might have to give extra attention and recognition to a struggling student in an adult basic education course.

One of the things we're learning from studies of the situated nature of learning (Greeno, Collins, and Resnick, 1996) and the sociocultural perspective is that we can't separate learning from its context, certainly not in the mind of the learner. So when rewards are external to the activity but enable adults to become competent in learning they value, they may see those rewards as necessary and functionally a very real part of the learning process. For example, I love basketball and want to improve my free-throw shooting average, and I have a coach who will take me out to lunch if I practice five hundred extra free throws. To some people, lunch and free throws seem unrelated, but to me they are part of the same idea: getting better at basketball while having a fun way to make the grueling monotony of practicing free throws more immediately worth it. When it comes to intrinsic motivation and incentives, the paramount issues to consider are the learners' value for the activity or for what the activity leads to, the probability of increasing competence through the activity, and the learners' view of the overall process.

PROMOTING NATURAL CONSEQUENCES AND POSITIVE ENDINGS

The concept of natural consequences comes out of reinforcement theory (Vargas, 1977). Natural consequences are changes in a person resulting from learning. Reading a book may have the natural consequence of producing new insights and expanded awareness in an adult. When working with natural consequences, we emphasize the result of learning (insights) more than the process of learning (reading). Sociocultural theory takes the perspective that both of these elements are intimately related and cannot be arbitrarily divided. For example, a person is motivated to solve a problem by both the pleasure of analyzing it and the satisfaction of arriving at a solution. In other words, it's both the trip and the destination that are motivating. Yet emphasizing natural consequences is an effective motivational strategy, because like a good tour guide, it helps adults more vividly understand the importance of their destination.

STRATEGY 59: *When learning has natural consequences, help learners to be aware of them and of their impact.*

One can see that natural consequences and feedback go hand in hand. However, because using natural consequences as a strategy includes *every* consequence that an adult can perceive as a result of learning, it encourages instructors to *make learning active as soon as possible* so that adults can quickly have natural consequences to increase and maintain their motivation. The remarkably successful Suzuki violin method does this for children, but so might any instructor of adults teaching any skill, ranging from sailing to surfing the Internet.

Many learning activities have natural consequences for adults that are not included in the performance criteria. To miss these would be a shame. It would be like serving a cake without the frosting. People often do not realize some of the consequences of their learning. In these situations, instructors can act as mirrors or magnifying glasses to reveal relevant consequences not readily apparent. The guiding question is, As a result of this learning activity, what else does the learner know or what else can the learner do that is important and worth pursuing? Suppose, for example, that an adult takes a course in technical report writing. The standard of performance is based on a readability index that is precise and provides excellent informational feedback. The adult achieves the standard of performance and successfully completes the course. It is also possible that because of the learning in this course, the adult is more confident as a writer, enjoys writing in general more than ever before, can more clearly communicate verbally, sees improvement in personal letter writing, and will now pursue a career in which writing is a requisite skill. When the instructor takes some time at the end of this course to discuss with the learners what other outcomes may have been achieved by them, they are likely to deepen their motivation and broaden their transfer of learning.

Discussion is not the only means of making natural consequences more conspicuous. Authentic performance tasks and simulations often reveal more than the specific expected learning. Using self-assessment strategies as well as videotapes and audiotapes to record progress and demonstrate before and after effects, we can highlight a variety of natural consequences. There is also the possibility of using examples in which a given skill or concept is applied outside the expected context, such as asking how a communication skill might be used with a learner's family as well as on the job.

STRATEGY 60: *Provide positive closure at the end of significant units of learning.*

A significant unit of learning can be determined by length or importance. In terms of length, when any entire course, seminar, or training program is terminating, a significant unit of learning has occurred. In longer courses there may be segments based on content or skill that each have a clearly delineated beginning and ending. For example, a course in marketing might be divided into units on promotion, sales, and contracts.

In terms of importance, a significant unit of learning is any segment of learning that has some characteristic that makes it special: the level of difficulty, cohesiveness, or creativity; the type of learning situation, structure, or process (special equipment, materials, location, grouping, or task); or the presence of such prominent individuals as an esteemed audience, lecturer, or evaluator.

In all these cases, something notable is coming to an end. Positive closure enhances learners' motivation because it affirms the entire process, verifies the value of the experience, directly or indirectly acknowledges competence, increases cohesiveness within the group, and encourages the surfacing of inspiration and other beneficial emotions in the learners themselves. Positive closure can be a small gesture, such as thanking learners for their cooperation, or something much more extravagant, such as an awards ceremony. Some ways to achieve positive closure are as follows:

- Celebrations. For people all over the world, festivals and holidays have been a joyous means of acknowledging the ending of seasons, religious periods, and harvests. There is no valid reason to avoid this in learning. Savor with learners their moment of triumph and accomplishment. This can be a pleasurable discussion, a party, a round of applause, sitting back and reliving the experience through "remember when" statements, or mild congratulations. But let the moment linger and enjoy it together. It is a happy occasion, not to be taken for granted. Celebrations are a wonderfully inclusive metaphor. They allow people to feel pleasure for whatever they personally accomplished or valued during the entire learning experience.

- Acknowledgments. These can be simple statements of gratitude and appreciation or more formal and ritualized awards. The goal is to recognize any learner contributions or achievements that were noteworthy during the span of the learning event (see Strategy 57). Depending on the situation, acknowledgments can be given by the instructor, the learners, or both.
- Sharing. Sharing is anything the instructor and learners might do to show their caring and sensitivity to the special quality of the learning experience and those involved in it. Some have cooked dinner for their learning group. Others have brought in personal collections or demonstrated their musical or artistic abilities. More frequently, this type of sharing takes the form of a poignant final statement that may include an eloquent poem or an inspirational quotation. When something has gone well, it deserves a fitting form of closure.

TRADITIONAL DEVELOPMENTAL STRATEGIES

P. CRANTON

Traditionally, developmental strategies for educators focused on the improvement of skills and the acquisition of new knowledge and techniques. Although these activities are an essential part of professional development, the recent emphasis in the adult education literature on critical reflection and transformative learning gives us new insights into how educators learn. If adults learn by transforming their perspectives (Mezirow, 1991) or by reconstructing their experiences (Tennant and Pogson, 1995), then we should be able to apply our understanding of these processes to learning about educational practice. We can integrate our learning into our practice—learn about teaching while we are teaching—and reconstruct what we know in addition to acquiring new knowledge.

At the end of a day of organizing and leading training seminars, the trainer goes to an adult education course at the local university and discusses in small groups the meaning of self-directed learning. After a busy spring spent running the performance appraisal system in the department, the human resource developer goes to a conference retreat to learn about innovative techniques in the field. When the semester is over and the final grades submitted, the college instructor is invited to a series of professional development workshops on planning courses and constructing tests.

Thus although a lot of our learning takes place apart from doing, we know that "learning by doing," or learning from experience, is critical. What we tend to do is incorporate learning-by-doing activities into learning experiences that are actually isolated from the workplace or the rest of the life of the learner and hope that they can be transferred back to practice. This does happen, of course, but many factors can interfere, including the culture of the educator's organization.

Professional preparation schools are grounded in a model of education that separates learning from doing, and this way of thinking has been carried into professional development experiences as well. In our childhood education, we perceived schools as the place of learning; we went to school in a separate building at predetermined times of the day and year. When school was over, learning was finished. Professional education (for teachers, nurses, social workers, and the like) is largely conducted by colleges and universities outside of the schools, hospitals, and social service agencies, even though practice teaching, clinical experiences, and fieldwork are inserted into the programs. Trades training comes closer to incorporating on-the-job experiences directly into the program, but the isolated school component remains the determining factor in learners' success at the trade; it is here that the evaluation takes place. The German apprenticeship model (Wilson, 1992) is well known for its learning-on-the-job philosophy, but still, "[t]he dual system is a combination of practical and theoretical vocational training at two places of learning with different legal and structural characteristics: in-plant and in-school training" (p. 33). It is not my intent here to argue that our preparatory systems are wrong, but rather to demonstrate that our thinking about educator development naturally follows from our experiences of preparatory education, in which learning was mostly isolated from practice.

In describing learning about work, Jarvis (1992b) reminds us that there are two forms of experience: primary and secondary. "The latter involves experiences in which interaction or teaching occurs over and above the primary experience. Hence, in the workplace there can be two simultaneous experiences: that which the workers are experiencing and that skill that they are being taught in a human resource development or continuing professional education program" (Jarvis, 1992b, pp. 180–181). Marsick and Watkins (1990) describe the learning that takes place from primary experience in the workplace as incidental or unintended. In Schön's (1983) work, professionals are described as learning during their practice (through reflection-in-action), but it is acknowledged that this process may not be viewed as learning by the professionals themselves.

With this background in mind, I review traditional developmental strategies. I examine each strategy in terms of the likelihood of its leading to the types of knowledge and I analyze each in relation to its congruence with practice. I argue that frequently our developmental strategies emphasize instrumental knowledge and take place separately from actual practice. If we can also critically examine our practice in its own context, we can further enhance development.

I have selected for discussion some of the most commonly used developmental strategies: manuals, guides, newsletters, and how-to books; workshops; retreats; training programs; and evaluations and performance appraisals. I have deliberately excluded individual consultation between developer and educator, as its nature is unique to the people involved and it is difficult to make generalizable comments.

MANUALS, GUIDES, NEWSLETTERS, AND HOW-TO BOOKS

What does a professional do when in doubt? Search for an answer or a suggestion in print. Human resource developers, instructional developers, training consultants, and nursing educators often turn to printed materials for the answers to educational problems. Consequently, we have seen a proliferation of how-to materials for educators over the last three or four decades. Imel (1991, p. 15) is prompted to write: "The task of keeping up with the professional literature in adult education may create information anxiety. Rapid expansion of the field's literature base makes it difficult to keep abreast of the latest publications as well as to evaluate their relevance to any ongoing work."

The expectation that we can turn to a manual to find a solution to an educational problem, in much the same way that we turn to a computer manual to find out why the machine does not behave as we want, may be rooted in our perception of what a profession is. For the last three hundred years, Western thought has been shaped by the rise of science and technology. It has been our belief that through technical rationality, we could cure the ills of the world. Traditionally, professions have been defined in terms of the extent to which they utilize technical rationality, or instrumental knowledge. In an important book on the professions, Moore (1970, p. 56) wrote that a profession "involves the application of general principles to specific problems, and it is a feature of modern sciences that such general principles are abundant and growing." Glazer (1974) distinguished between major or "near-major" professions—such as medicine, law, business, and engineering—and minor professions—such as social work, education, and town planning—on the basis of technical rationality. The minor professions are described as being unable to develop a base of scientific knowledge. The knowledge base of a real profession is seen to be specialized, firmly bounded, scientific, and standardized.

The conceptualization of professional knowledge as being best learned through reflection on practice (as described by Cervero, 1989; Harris, 1993) has not been at the core of definitions of a profession.

Education wants to be a major profession, or at least a near-major profession. What better way than to strive for general principles that can be applied to specific problems? Thus, we have what Stubblefield (1991) describes as the procedural literature in adult education. He writes: "Adult education as a procedural discipline provides guidelines for practice, and its literature is prescriptive" (p. 28), and "Beyond prescriptions for effective practice lies a more generic question about the nature of professional practice itself" (p. 29). It seems that we hope to define ourselves as professionals by being able to provide clear-cut answers to educational problems.

Type of Knowledge

An examination of manuals, guides, newsletters, and how-to books supports the notion that we hope to have an instrumental knowledge base in adult education. Indeed, there may well be aspects of our practice that can be described in terms of cause and effect. As an example, we may accept that continuous and ongoing feedback is conducive to learning and that perhaps this is a generic principle of effective education. However, even this principle can be questioned. Do all learners benefit from continuous feedback? What kind of feedback? Are there times when feedback is inappropriate?

As one illustration, in the procedural literature we find Piskurich (1993, pp. 64–65) writing, "I'm not going to go too deeply here into the *correct* way to write objectives. There are plenty of books on the subject, and in all honesty, I don't think there is one correct way…. However, there are three rules for the writing of objectives for self-directed learning materials that I think are inviolable." He then identifies the three rules: write objectives for the trainees, use performance-based verbs (a list of appropriate verbs is provided), and use a valid job analysis.

There are dozens of examples of books, manuals, and guides on how to be a better educator. Many, of which Piskurich's book is one example, demonstrate our desire to know how to do things right. We do need to have our own rules and procedures, and beginning educators acquire this knowledge from books as well as the other developmental strategies. However, as we continue to grow and develop as educators we often begin to question those rules, to reconstruct our experience, and to reconsider our assumptions. The "how-to" manuals no longer meet our changing learning needs.

Congruence with Practice

Educators rarely think of or describe their practice as being predictable, regulated, or explained by rules and principles. Every professional developer knows the common reaction to a suggested technique: "Oh, that won't work with my group," followed by a description of the content, the learners, or the organization. Every educator sees her or his teaching context as unique, and indeed it is.

Brookfield (1990a, p. 1) describes teaching as a complex and passionate experience: "Passion, hope, doubt, fear, exhilaration, weariness, colleagueship, loneliness, glorious defeats, hollow victories, and above all, the certainties of surprise and ambiguity—how can one begin to capture the reality of teaching in a single word or phrase." He goes on to say, "The idiosyncratic messiness of classroom reality is … far removed from the orderly textbook version (in which teachers carefully apply systematic methods in the pursuit of unequivocal objectives)." Some days a strategy will work, the classroom will be 'alive with conversation, activity, and interested learners; the next day or the next week the same strategy can yield blank stares or the glazed-over eyes indicating boredom. In the same group, one individual can love a visualization technique, another feels that it is a personal intrusion, and several others feel silly but try anyway. I consider myself to be a good educator generally, but some days I simply have no idea what went wrong. When I ask the group, they may say, "It has nothing to do with you; we're upset about what happened to Shirley yesterday," or perhaps, "We're just tired of group work tonight." The how-to book cannot include these irregularities.

Schön (1983, 1987) approaches this issue from a slightly different angle. He argues that we intuitively make decisions about our practice while we are practicing. He describes teaching as an art, not a set of skills or techniques. In fact, he argues that viewing teaching, or other professional practice, as technical expertise limits our potential for reflection: "Many practitioners, locked into a view of themselves as technical experts, find nothing in the world of practice to occasion reflection. They have become too skillful at techniques of selective inattention, junk categories, and situational control, techniques which they use to preserve the constancy of their knowledge-in-practice. For them, uncertainty is a threat; its admission is a sign of weakness" (Schön, 1983, p. 69).

Recent research into teachers' thinking and knowledge about teaching in the public school setting supports the notion that educators recognize the complexity of their practice (Hargreaves and Fullan, 1992; Russell and Munby, 1992), or, as Brookfield calls it, "the chaos" (1990a, p. 1). New educators also describe their practice as ambiguous and unpredictable (for example, see Eble, 1988). In the face of the complex nature of our practice, it is natural to seek guidelines and principles to restore order. Teaching tips and guidelines perform this function well and are especially useful for new educators as a starting point. But they cannot be congruent with practice because they cannot take into account the almost infinite variations in what we do. Sometimes, a belief in the expert's advice may even lead us to a sense of insecurity, as we try to implement the expert's sure-fire formula and see that it does not turn out.

Many educators who call or drop into the office of a human resource developer or faculty developer want a quick answer. They may ask for a handout on how to increase learner participation or how to hold more effective staff meetings. Understandably, people expect a professional developer to have answers. If not, can he or she be considered an expert or a professional? The developer, of course, accepts the client's request and often works from there to encourage reflection. Perhaps what we also need to do is change the focus in our materials. Manuals, guides, newsletters, and books can emphasize critical questioning, reflection, and the "chaos" of educator practice, as does, for example, Brookfield's (1990a) *The Skillful Teacher.*

Workshops

Workshops may well be the most common professional development activity. In an early literature review on the improvement of teaching in higher education, Levinson-Rose and Menges (1981) noted that workshops were the most common faculty development format and, further, that the only evaluation of their effectiveness was participant satisfaction ratings. Workshops tend to be one-half or one-day sessions, though they may be as short as one hour or as long as several days. Generally, they focus on techniques or strategies, such as how to adopt an appropriate leadership style, write objectives, assess performance, ask questions, or improve relations with staff.

As the label *workshop* implies, these sessions are meant to include experiential or hands-on learning. The original meaning of the term was a room or building in which work, especially mechanical work, was carried on. We now tend to use the term to describe a session that emphasizes the exchange of ideas and the demonstration and application of techniques and skills. Some workshops lean toward lectures or presentations, with a token group activity thrown in to justify the title.

The literature on workshops is mostly from the 1970s (for example, see Davis, 1974) and addresses the practicalities of conducting good sessions. Zuber-Skerritt (1992, p. 178) describes workshops as "ideal for discussion in small, leaderless groups." She discusses the advantages of one-time workshops in which staff can be introduced to a topic or problem which they are specifically interested in, but she points out that an integrated series of workshops allows for more in-depth and individualized discussion. Zuber-Skerritt also emphasizes that the skill of the workshop leader is critical to the success of the session, a point that can hardly be argued. It is interesting that she refers to what could be a description of transformative learning: "The process of 'unfreezing' old behaviour, trying out alternative behaviours and arriving at new, improved, deliberate and controlled action must be at the core of all PD [professional development] workshops if they are to effect real change" (p. 180).

Type of Knowledge

By definition, the workshop format is intended for the attainment and practice of techniques and skills. The format is derived from the carpenter's or the auto mechanic's workshop where tradespeople learn how to use their tools and equipment. When it follows this tradition, the workshop emphasizes instrumental knowledge.

A typical workshop might include the following agenda items: introductions and an ice-breaker in which participants get to know each other and state their expectations of the session; a short presentation by the workshop leader on the topic; a group activity in which participants apply the concepts to their practice; a reporting back by the small groups and a general discussion of their work; and a summary and integration by the workshop leader. Sometimes, longer sessions repeat this cycle as often as the time allows. This format follows the original notion of "workshop" in which learners might be introduced to a new piece of equipment, have a chance to try it out, and report back to the instructor on their experiences.

Workshops in the social sciences have evolved and are considered useful by both educators and developers. Dirkx, Lavin, Spurgin, and Holder (1993), for example, report on educators' perceptions of continuing education workshops and conclude that the participants' expectations of helpful activities were consistent with the practical perspective of continuing education. Of course, there is a tremendous diversity of workshop formats and styles, and generalizations do not hold true for every workshop. Often in education, practical or communicative knowledge is emphasized. The use of group work and discussion fosters communication among individuals and a sharing of their experiences. Such activities can stimulate emancipatory or transformative learning, especially when the workshop is held over time in an integrated-series format.

Congruence with Practice

In a discussion of traditional instructional development activities in higher education, Amundsen, Gryspeerdt, and Moxness (1993, p. 329) comment that "techniques were taught and evaluated in isolation without any attempt to fit them into the wider context of the teaching-learning process or within the professor's existing knowledge of instruction." Similarly, in a discussion of the preparation of professionals, where workshops are often used, Cavanaugh (1993) describes the discontinuity of education and practice. Although professional development workshops vary greatly across contexts, they have some common characteristics that could be related to their becoming isolated from practice. The workshop is often planned in advance of the leader's meeting the participants. It may be advertised or promoted throughout an organization or professional association. People then choose to attend based on the description of the workshop, a description that is designed to attract participants. Even though every good workshop leader asks participants what their expectations are at the beginning of a session, it is difficult to change an agenda if people's needs are very different from what has been planned. In this case, congruence with practice depends on the accuracy of the advertising and the reasons people had for deciding to attend.

When the group is more homogeneous, such as in a workshop for one department of an organization or for, say, literacy volunteers, it is more likely that the content will be congruent with the participants' practice. This depends in part on the degree to which the workshop leader is familiar with the educators' context and expectations, and in part on the kind of preplanning that is done. For example, if participants are involved in the planning, and if the agenda remains open to change as the workshop progresses, congruence can increase.

Retreats

Retreats are sessions held away from the educators' normal workplace. They tend to be of a longer duration than workshops, and they often include some social activities in addition to the discussions, presentations, and group work. Retreats may be organized by one organization or institution for their educators or trainers; they may be organized by professional associations or more informal groups and thus be available to participants from different organizations. Some retreats precede or follow professional conferences.

The formats that retreats can take vary widely. They may have a specific topic or theme; they may be brainstorming, needs-assessment, or problem-solving sessions; they may be wide-open discussion groups; or they can involve practical, experiential learning of a new method or medium, such as a computer technology. One advantage that retreats have over workshops is their longer duration, and hence their potential to foster critical reflection. A second advantage is that participants are away from the routines and distractions of their usual practice. A retreat will stand out as a special event, and the learning may, by association, also stand out in participants' subsequent reflection on their practice. There is no guarantee, of course, of particular kinds of learning occurring at a retreat; as with any session this depends on the purpose, the participants, the facilitators or leaders, and the nature of follow-up events.

Although retreats are a common professional development approach, there is little literature on their content, style, or effectiveness. Selman and Dampier (1991, p. 137) discuss the general advantages of residential centers for learning, commenting that "there are numerous such centres across Canada, and all exhibit the same support for learning." The authors do not provide further details. One example that I am familiar with is the Niagara Institute, a nonprofit organization that offers three-day retreats for managers from business, industry, and government. The retreat is described as a "proven program to develop the attitudes, techniques and strategies required to be the new kind of leader" (Niagara Institute, 1994, p. 1). It is promoted as "interweaving theory, practical information, discussion, personal reflection and action planning to create a life-changing experience" (p. 1).

For university educators, an example of the use of retreats can be found in the Lilly Teaching Fellows Program, which includes, among other components, spring weekend conferences held at different sites throughout the eastern United States. Austin (1992) conducted a survey of participants in this program, interviewed selected faculty, and made site visits to assess the effectiveness of the program. Austin found that participants' "personal teaching philosophies expanded as they read the research literature related to teaching" (p. 95) and included quotations from faculty about "philosophical shifts." Participants also mentioned learning about instructional methods and design, confidence building, and increased commitment to teaching as among the benefits of the program.

Type of Knowledge

Retreats have the potential to foster critical reflection if the activities, discussions, or group work are designed with that goal in mind. However, if a retreat is a one- or two-day event, with no follow-up activities, the likelihood of its leading to sustained critical reflection may decrease. Mezirow describes what a program designed to foster communicative learning would help learners do:

Decontextualize

Become aware of the history, contexts, and consequences of their beliefs

Become more reflective and critical

"Bracket" preconceived ideas

Make better inferences, more appropriate generalizations, and more logically coherent arguments

Be more open to the perspectives of others

Rely less on psychological defense mechanisms (Mezirow, 1991, p. 215)

In addition, transformative learning includes a critique of the premises that need reassessment and a revision of distorted assumptions or values. This is a difficult bill to fill in a one-time session, even if it is of several days' duration.

I argue, nevertheless, that a retreat format for development work could be a good starting point for emancipatory learning. Decontextualization, self-awareness, bracketing of ideas, and critical questioning would be enhanced by being away from the workplace. In the process of working toward transformative learning, the individual needs to step outside of himself or herself—examine long-held beliefs through different eyes or from a fresh perspective. A change in environment and an intensive focus on one's practice could enhance such an effort. In the three-day retreat offered by the Niagara Institute mentioned earlier, the managers are staying and working in an attractive rural setting usually quite distant from their workplace. They engage in an assessment of their leadership style, psychological type, communication skills, and career goals as a part of the retreat. The combination of self-assessment and distance from work has the potential to stimulate critical self-reflection and transformation. If the process is continued rather than treated as an isolated event, emancipatory development could occur.

Congruence with Practice

The degree to which the retreat format for developmental work is congruent with educators' practice depends on the design and the activities included. By its very nature, the retreat is isolated from practice in the way that a workshop is, or perhaps even more so. On the other hand, the longer time available allows the use of strategies such as simulations, critical incidents, role play, and case studies, all of which can be designed to bring in problems, experiences, and issues from participants' practice. Mezirow (1991, p. 214) warns us, though, that simply bringing in role plays does not necessarily foster communicative learning about one's practice: "The assumption seems to be that these things are learned in much the same way as any other behavioral skill except that practice occasionally requires the use of hypothetical reality contexts such as role playing, which are unnecessary in learning to operate a lathe or perform other manual tasks."

In my experience, retreats generate considerable enthusiasm about making changes to practice—often committees and task forces are set up at the end of a retreat to implement new ideas. However, participants may then return to the workplace, comment for a few days or even weeks about what a good retreat they had, and gradually lose sight of the insights and plans they had made. The retreat can be a stimulating experience, but the nature of the work and the culture of the organization to which the educators return can separate the learning from practice. If the developmental activities are a part of actual practice, this separation cannot occur as easily.

Training Programs

Training programs for educators are found primarily in business and industry and are often referred to as "train-the-trainer" programs. Sometimes government departments and health professionals also use this approach to educator development. Programs for training the trainer vary significantly in their approach, content, and duration, as do workshops and retreats. They have, though, some underlying assumptions in common which warrant special treatment here.

In writing about the "art of managing," Schön (1983) makes comments that are equally relevant to trainers in organizations: "The field of management has long been marked by a conflict between two competing views of professional knowledge. On the first view, the manager is a technician whose practice consists in applying to the everyday problems of his organization the principles and methods derived from management science. On the second, the manager is a craftsman, a practitioner of an art of managing that cannot be reduced to explicit rules and theories" (pp. 236–237). He notes that the "first view has gained steadily in power" (p. 237).

Traditional train-the-trainer programs tend to view the trainer as a technician. Mager (1962) is the father of this perspective; it is one that has generated an enormous literature on systematic, objectives-based approaches to training. Training itself is generally based on the underlying assumption that problems in an organization are caused by knowledge or skill deficits that can be remedied through instrumental learning. As can be expected, this model is also applied to learning about training. One example is Bard, Bell, Stephen, and Webster's *The Trainer's Professional Development Handbook* (1987). This book contains a directory of learning aids and materials as well as specific guidelines on how to develop learning plans to increase professional competence.

Wilson (1992) provides some examples of train-the-trainer programs. They range in nature from twelve- to fifteen-week courses to one-day sessions. Examples of the topics are the concepts, principles, and techniques of assessing training and development needs; design and delivery of effective training programs; the role and scope of government-funded training programs; and effective training strategies for coping with technological change. Programs are offered by in-house trainers, training managers, private practitioners, or professional associations. Wilson (1992, p. 55) describes the offerings as "outcome-oriented, pragmatic and issue-specific, rather than general in nature."

Type of Knowledge

Technical interests are expressed through the medium of work. Carr and Kemmis (1986) describe instrumental knowledge as necessary for modern industry and production processes, and as "scientific explanation" (p. 134). It is not surprising therefore that many training programs for educators in business, industry, hospitals, and government agencies focus on instrumental knowledge. The systems within which trainers work have technical interests. The goal of the organization is to maintain the most efficient and effective outcomes. Trainers are often individuals who have worked in other aspects of the organization before taking on a trainer's role; they bring the goals and values of the organization's culture with them.

On the other hand, many programs that retain the label "train the trainer" have moved away from the technical approach. With the increased emphasis on teamwork, empowerment, and participative decision making (see Watkins and Marsick, 1993, for example), a strictly technical approach is no longer seen as valid. At times, though, concepts such as the-worker-as-decision-maker are used as rhetoric aimed at increasing labor productivity rather than at meaningful change in training (Wells, 1987).

The design of training programs may be driven by the notion that in a given situation there is an appropriate technique to be applied that will lead to people obtaining pre-determined knowledge or skills. Ewert (1991, p. 350) writes: "With student achievement as the objective, the instrumental approach focuses on tools, resources, environments, techniques, teachers, and students as the means to that given end. Education systems are viewed as an input-output system, where resources and raw materials enter at one end and the finished product, an achieving 'educated' student, issues from the other. Within this delivery system, educational problems are viewed as blockages, caused by inappropriate teacher behaviors, student inadequacies, or inefficient resource uses." As Watkins and Marsick (1993) advocate, training can be redesigned to encourage continuous learning based on a partnership among executives, human resource developers, and managers.

Congruence with Practice

It may be the emphasis on instrumental knowledge in some organizations that maintains the congruence between trainers' development and their view of their practice. If "human performance technology" (Butler Research Associates, 1989) is the new and emerging focus for trainers, it is also likely that they view the development of their own practice in the same way. "The new human performance technology assumes that the purpose of training is to improve job performance and, more importantly, to impact on the organization's bottom line (be it dollars, service, or reputation). Performance technology's aim, then, is not to provide training nor merely to improve performance, it is to make a positive contribution to the outcome of the organization" (Geis, 1991, p. 16). With this as the purpose of training, the goal of training the trainer will be to increase that person's performance in getting others to have an impact on the organization's bottom line. This leads to congruence between development and practice for the trainer, as long as the underlying approach of instrumental learning is not questioned.

Many programs for trainers are designed to keep the content and activities congruent with trainers' practice. Some graduate-level programs even have a curriculum that reflects the instrumental approach. To give one example, the core courses of Concordia University's Ph.D. program in Educational Technology are Instructional Design, Human Resources Development, Research Methods and Practices, Educational Cybernetics, Systems Analysis and Design, Theory, Development and Research in Educational Media, Distance Education, and Thesis Research. Other programs, of course, take a more developmental and nonlinear approach (as examples, the University of Texas at Austin and the University of Calgary's continuing education master's degree).

As I discussed earlier, workshops and retreats can be isolated from educators' practice by virtue of their being held at the end of the day or away from the workplace. This is also true of many train-the-trainer programs, especially those where the trainers go to a university, college, or professional association center. It could be that the specific information and activities are not directly related to individuals' practice even though the underlying philosophy may be in tune with the trainers' approach. In-house training programs are less likely to create this schism between content and practice.

When trainers encounter programs based on a different perspective, they can experience a dramatic conflict between their practice and the program. To illustrate this, I describe Bob, who enrolled in a seminar in adult education last year.

Bob is a trainer in a government department. In the group of twenty-five, there were three other self-described trainers, one from the health professions, one from private industry, and one from an entrepreneurship center at a college. It was Bob who most strongly felt the discrepancy between his practice and the content of the seminar. He initially stated his goal for the seminar as being "to obtain better facilitation skills." As we read, discussed, and worked with the concepts of self-directed learning, personal autonomy, critical reflection, and transformative learning, Bob devoted his energies to drawing specific skills and techniques out of the content and the process. He would often ask others in the group what technique they would use in a situation. He was interested in why the facilitator was doing what she was doing, and he observed her closely. This served Bob well for the first semester. He simply extracted what he could, while considering the theoretical discussions not relevant to his work.

We did not expect Bob back for the second semester, but he arrived. This time it was not as easy for him. As the group discussed and planned the topics they wanted to work with during the seminar, it was clear that Bob's voice was almost unheard. Over the semester, he gradually withdrew, attending more and more infrequently, choosing to find things to read on his own that better suited his goals. Some weeks later, Bob told me that he had had difficulty trying to reconcile the discrepancy between his perspective of training and others' perspectives of education.

EVALUATIONS AND PERFORMANCE APPRAISALS

There can be no question that evaluation of educators' performance has been the most common entry into developmental activities over the past three decades. In a recent edited volume, Banta and Associates (1993) provide a comprehensive overview of the impact that evaluation has had on teaching in higher education. Theall and Franklin (1991) dedicate one-third of their *Effective Practices for Improving Teaching* to evaluation. Centra (1993, p. 19) argues that "[e]valuation can play an important role in developing teaching effectiveness" and presents a model for enhancing teaching through formative evaluation.

In higher education, students' ratings of teaching are the most common form of evaluation. An extensive literature addresses the reliability and validity of student ratings; many scholars dedicate their careers to the study of this form of evaluation; Centra (1993) provides a good recent summary of this research. Other formats for the evaluation of educators' practice are encouraged in most institutions but used much less frequently. For example, faculty sometimes use peer review of their course materials, others' (peers, instructional developers, or administrators) observations of their teaching, videotape analyses, interviews or discussions with students, input from professional organizations, or follow-up studies of how alumni perceived their courses.

In business, industry, government, and health-professional organizations, *performance appraisal* is the term most often used for evaluation of individuals' practice (Robbins and Stuart-Kotze, 1994). Rating scales are also commonly used, but not to the extent that they are used in higher education. Ratings are given by staff, peers, or supervisors. Other methods include written essays or reports; critical incidents, which focus on critical behaviors that separate effective from ineffective performance; and multiperson comparisons, in which individuals are ranked or ordered in comparison to others' performance (Robbins and Stuart-Kotze, 1994).

The emphasis on rating scales for evaluation comes from the belief that quantitative data are more objective and more precise. It is based on the assumption that educators' practice can be measured empirically. I witnessed an extreme example of this approach in an organization in which ratings were averaged across items, giving each educator one number to describe their effectiveness. People would receive an overall average rating of 2.82 or 3.24. Part-time people, hired on contract for specific programs or sessions, were then rank-ordered according to this number, and those on the bottom were not rehired regardless of the absolute value of the number or the size of the difference between their number and another person's number.

In all settings, evaluations are conducted both to provide feedback to the individual (formative evaluation) and to make administrative decisions (summative evaluation), although I have argued elsewhere (Cranton, 1993) that this distinction is not a useful one for educators to make. It is possible to view all evaluation of educator practice as developmental, except in cases where evaluation procedures are abused, as in the example given in the preceding paragraph. It is rare that real administrative decisions are made based on evaluation results: even the promotion and tenure process in higher education can be viewed as developmental. Nevertheless, when the formative-summative distinction is made, it is formative evaluation that is linked to educator development, as one would expect. This link is so strong that some human resource developers have performance appraisal as their major responsibility, and some instructional development centers in higher education dedicate the majority of their time to conducting evaluations. The expectation is that when people receive feedback on their practice, they will be moved to make changes in areas where the feedback is negative. Early behavioral approaches to teacher education (for example, Gage, 1977) followed this model. Microteaching, a technique in which teacher trainees are videotaped conducting short instructional segments, remains a popular strategy. Yet there is resistance to this kind of developmental work. This is perhaps because, as Centra (1993, p. 11) states, "Most information, whether from students or from colleagues, is long on judgment and short on helpful advice." It is also because educators receiving feedback about their practice do not necessarily know how to change. If learners tell me that the organization of my courses is poor, how do I know what to do to change that? It is easier to blame the learners for not having the intelligence to see what organization I used, or blame the institution for requiring that I cover too much material in one course. Despite the good intentions, many results from evaluations or performance appraisals are filed and forgotten.

Type of Knowledge

Evaluation has the potential to lead to communicative or emancipatory learning about educator practice. Communicative learning could be fostered through the collection of qualitative information about practice, that is, through critical incidents, open-ended written or verbal comments from learners or peers, or reflective self-evaluation in a journal or log. Emancipatory or transformative learning could be stimulated through ongoing discussions with learners about the teaching and learning experience, or through extended discussions with a professional developer.

The most common format for evaluation of educator practice is the rating scale. Most rating scales focus on specific behaviors and skills. All rating scales, by definition, quantify people's perceptions of practice. Centra (1993, p. 176) writes: "For some psychometricians, it seems that an object or an effect does not exist unless it can be measured. Yet an old adage seems more applicable to many of life's phenomena: Not everything that counts can be counted and not everything that can be counted counts." Mezirow (1991) argues that if our goal "is to foster transformative learning, dogmatic insistence that learning outcomes be specified in advance of the educational experience in terms of observable changes in behavior or 'competencies' that are used as benchmarks against which to measure learning gains will result in a reductive distortion and serve merely as a device of indoctrination" (pp. 219–220). In other words, quantitative behavioral measures, such as rating scales, cannot be used to assess transformations in a person's perspective on practice. They are a means of determining learners' perceptions of the educator's observable behaviors.

Congruence with Practice

Last semester, I had two very different instructional development clients. By coincidence, I would frequently meet with them on the same day, heightening the contrast between them in my mind. One client consistently presented me with student evaluations that were decidedly poor. On a 5-point scale, average ratings tended to be around 2. Open-ended comments were as devastating as "This is the worst teacher I've ever had" and "I don't know why this person is allowed to teach." The second client, on the same scale, received average ratings of over 4 on all items and had mostly rave reviews in the comments section of the form. The first client dismissed her results, claiming to be a good teacher and blaming the nature of her discipline for the learners' responses. The second client also dismissed his results, claiming that the learners were just being "nice." Perhaps the extent to which evaluations are congruent with practice is dependent both on the nature of the evaluation and the individual's perspective on his or her practice.

Evaluations that involve observation and discussion of teaching or analyses of videotapes of teaching are more likely to be or become congruent with educators' perspectives of their practice than are the results of rating scales. This is the rationale behind the use of microteaching, for example (Gage, 1977). It is harder to dismiss a videotape of yourself being domineering and aggressive than it is to dismiss a person's low rating of your interpersonal skills.

When evaluation is an interactive process with learners, the use of evaluation as a developmental strategy can become fully integrated with practice. An educator can collect open-ended comments from learners midway through a course or program, summarize these comments, make his or her comments in writing, and hold a discussion with the group about the meaning of the results, discrepancies between the learners' and the educator's views, and what kinds of changes could be made in the sessions. The same interactive process can be used in a performance appraisal process. In one such project (Cranton and Knoop, 1993), staff and managers are presented with information about evaluation in preparatory sessions. The sessions are interactive and provide the opportunity for people to discuss fears, anxieties, or other concerns about evaluation. Staff and sometimes peers provide ratings as well as open-ended comments; managers complete a self-evaluation. Each individual receives a report on the results, including numerical, narrative, and interpretive components. With the report, he or she receives guidelines such as how to hold a discussion with staff about the report and how to develop an action plan for change through interactions with staff. Managers then meet individually or in small groups with a consultant to discuss their results, how their own discussions with staff are proceeding, and their action plans. At this time they are also provided with printed materials on how to make changes in a variety of aspects of their practice. Human resource personnel, who previously saw evaluation as a "necessary evil" in their lives, began to see the process as being a part of their practice.

The connection between evaluations and other resources for development is another critical factor in determining how likely it is that evaluations will lead to change. As I mentioned earlier, it is one thing to be told by your learners that you are not well-organized. It is quite another to know what to do about it. If evaluation processes are linked with support systems, discussion groups, printed resources, or peer consultation programs, there is a higher likelihood that this strategy will be seen as congruent with educator practice.

When evaluations and performance appraisals are isolated from practice, they can fail to relate to our communicative and emancipatory interests. They become a routine requirement of an institution or organization, with little attention being paid to their results. When they are integrated into practice through discussions with learners and when they are linked to other resources for development, they can be a meaningful strategy.

BUILDING ON TRADITIONAL DEVELOPMENTAL STRATEGIES

I have been critical of traditional developmental strategies to the extent that they are focused solely on the acquisition of skills rather than encouraging critical reflection on practice and to the extent that they are separated from practice. Even new educators, who may benefit most from skills acquisition, also have many years of experience in educational systems (including being a learner) and learn through questioning their experiences. Nevertheless, it would be unfair to leave this section without drawing together and summarizing the characteristics of traditional strategies that provide meaningful experiences for educators. Regardless of whether we call something a workshop, a training session, or a retreat, the process can have potential for critical reflection. What are some characteristics that are needed for a professional development experience to be transformative?

- The inclusion of a variety of perspectives. Written materials can include alternative points of view; opposing theoretical positions can be presented and discussed in a retreat or workshop.
- The articulation of assumptions. The author of developmental materials and the training leader can make their own assumptions open as well as encourage participating educators to do the same.
- Discussion. Educators who talk to other educators and to their learners about their practice can clarify their own perspectives, receive support from others, and gain awareness of other points of view. Discussing the results of a performance appraisal with one's staff is one example; small-group interaction in a workshop is another.
- A critical attitude. We sometimes shun being critical, not wanting to be negative. But if critical questioning of what anyone says, including ourselves and including the experts, becomes a part of our developmental work, we can move away from our technical interests.
- Activities based on practice. When educators' own practice and experience is used in workshops, retreats, and training programs, there is a greater possibility of people using their learning to change their practice.

SUMMARY

Commonly used development strategies for educators have been how-to materials, workshops, retreats, training programs, and evaluations and performance appraisals. Over the decades, there has been very little clear evidence that these strategies have a meaningful impact on practice. Possible reasons have been discussed in this section.

How-to books tend to be an expression of our hope that there is an instrumental-knowledge base in education. If only we can find the right technique and use it at the right time, we will become better educators. However, educators do not tend to see their actual practice as ordered and regulated by rules; the information in the how-to books may not be congruent with their perspective on practice unless it addresses the complexity of teaching. There is a societal value that objective and scientific knowledge is of more worth than dynamic, changing, or chaotic knowledge; this leads us to look for "truths" that may not exist.

Thousands of workshops are given somewhere every day, and there are good guidelines for designing workshops (Sork, 1984). Although they do not need to do so, often workshops tend to focus on the technical aspects of teaching. They can be isolated from practice, in part because of the type of knowledge conveyed and in part because they are usually held outside of working hours and the workplace.

Retreats have more potential than workshops to foster communicative or emancipatory learning, primarily because they are longer in duration and are usually conducted in an atmosphere conducive to reflection. Yet if there is little or no follow-up from a retreat, they can be regarded as an isolated event, apart from practice.

Train-the-trainer programs tend to be modeled on general training programs. Because they are connected with the world of business and industry, the "world of work," they traditionally represent people's technical interests: how can we increase the productivity of this organization? There are recent trends away from this perspective. The type of knowledge sought in train-the-trainer programs leads to congruence with trainers' perceptions of their practice. On the other hand, this perspective may not be the most appropriate for their own practice.

Evaluations and performance appraisals are commonly used as a starting point for educator development. Especially in higher education, considerable research has been done to address the usefulness and validity of student ratings of teaching. When evaluations are only quantitative in nature, they tend to emphasize educators' observable teaching behavior. However, evaluations and performance appraisals can take on many different formats, and when the educator is truly involved in understanding his or her practice through getting feedback from others and discussing that feedback with them, the process can be quite congruent with practice and can lead to communicative and emancipatory learning.

I have intended to argue in this section that we can enhance our developmental strategies by considering educators' communicative and emancipatory interests. In What Motivates Adults to Learn (Section Six), Establishing Inclusion Among Adult Learners (Section Four) and Helping Adults Develop Position Attitudes Toward Learning (Section Five), I view educator development from the perspective of adult learning: as an adult learner, the educator can draw from the theoretical work on self-directed learning, critical reflection, and transformative learning.

SECTION SIX

LEARNING OPPORTUNITIES IN ADULTHOOD

Whenever we ask adults about their learning, they most often mention education and training programs sponsored by the workplace, colleges and universities, public schools, and other formal organizations. They first picture classrooms with "students" learning and "teachers" teaching in a highly structured format. Yet when we ask these same adults about what they have learned informally over the last year, they typically respond with descriptions of learning activities outside these formal settings. They discuss, for example, remodeling a house, which has involved everything from reading and talking with friends to conversations with carpenters, plumbers, and electricians. Or they may focus on a major change in their life, such as an illness, parenthood, or divorce, which has precipitated numerous learning events, sometimes over an extended period of time. In considering the spectrum of learning opportunities available to adults, it is important to acknowledge all of these arenas of learning, from the highly structured to the more informal ways adults go about learning.

Why is it important that educators of adults recognize that learning happens in so many and varied places in the lives of adults? First, appreciating and taking into consideration the prior knowledge and experience of learners has become a basic assumption of our practice as educators of adults, wherever this knowledge was learned (Knowles, 1980). In working with welfare recipients, for example, instructors might recognize that parents on welfare have had to learn how to take care of their children on constrained budgets, keep their families safe and healthy under difficult living conditions, and in general make do with very little. Rather than asking questions about how they have learned to do this successfully, what is focused on most often is their lack of formal education and skills training. Formal schooling and skills training are important, but so are the ways they have informally learned about life skills that have kept them fed and clothed. Likewise, workshop leaders putting on staff development programs in schools might learn as much as possible about the background and experience of the teachers in that school and what their knowledge base is with respect to the content of the workshop. There is nothing that turns off teachers more in these programs than being treated as if they know very little about the subject matter, especially if they have been dealing with it on a daily basis.

Second, if educators assisted learners in recognizing the many places and ways they have gone about learning in adulthood, more adults might see themselves as active learners. As a result, they may be less cautious about learning new things and even be more willing to enter formal programs of learning. One of our favorite stories is about a duck carver who was interviewed as part of a study on self-directed learning (Berger, 1990). This man, who considered himself both a nonreader and "definitely not a very good student," taught himself how to carve ducks. He started this process by carving some ducks by himself and then taking them to duck carving shows, where he could talk with other artists about his initial attempts. In addition, he read every book he could get his hands on related to duck carving (and remember that he thinks of himself as a nonreader). He now raises ducks so he can have live models, in itself another learning project. As a result of the interview process, this man saw himself as much more of a learner than he had before. Our hope is that as more individuals view themselves as active and competent learners, at least in some areas, they might be better able to address the many life challenges that come in adulthood, through both formal and informal learning modes.

In exploring the spectrum of learning opportunities in adulthood, we first discuss each of the major arenas in which adult learning occurs: learning opportunities sponsored by formal institutions, nonformal community-based learning activities, and learning that is more informal or self-directed in nature. This is followed by a description of how these learning opportunities are designed for adults. The section closes with an exploration of a new site for learning: the learning organization.

WHERE LEARNING OCCURS

In this section we present a framework for three types of opportunities within which learning occurs for adults: formal institutional settings, nonformal settings, and informal or self-directed contexts. This framework is an adaptation of one proposed by Coombs, Prosser, and Ahmed (1973), in which they classified lifelong learning according to three broad categories. The major difference between their conceptualization and our framework is that we have added the concepts of self-directed learning (which is synonymous with their definition of informal learning) and indigenous forms of learning. Although we are aware of the problems of trying to divide the landscape of learning opportunities into three separate categories, we are assuming that all three categories are of equal importance in the adult learning enterprise. There will always be overlaps among the three major categories of the framework, something educators of adults can capitalize on when designing educational activities.

Formal Institutional Settings

For most people, learning in adulthood brings to mind classroom settings. We envision adults encased in four walls of various shapes and sizes, learning in a variety of ways, from formal lectures to small-group interactions. When we ask participants what they remember as positive about learning in formal settings, they often cite well-organized, knowledgeable, and caring instructors; participatory instructional methods and well-crafted lectures; relevant and useful materials; and respect for them as adults and learners. And, conversely, when we ask participants to recall some of their worst experiences, they talk about arrogant instructors who have no sense of them as people or learners, poorly delivered content whatever the method used, and poorly organized and irrelevant materials.

In more recent years, as the use of technology has increased in the delivery of learning programs, our picture of learning in formal settings has expanded dramatically. We now see learners doing individualized or group learning in computer labs, participating in interactive teleconferences, and interacting from their homes with fellow participants and instructors via the Internet. So, too, have our participants' reactions to learning in formal settings changed. They now add to the traditional comments from the positive side hardware and software that is user friendly and works, and on a more negative note, the continuing crashing of systems or unintelligible software programs. The stand-alone and interconnected systems of formal settings for adult learning have indeed become very differentiated and complex.

Numerous writers have described systems for classifying the vast array of formal settings that provide learning opportunities for adults (Merriam and Brockett, 1997). One of the most useful categorizations of formal institutional settings has been given by Darkenwald and Merriam (1982). Building on the work of Knowles (1964), they describe a four-part typology:

1. *Independent adult education organizations.* These organizations exist for the primary purpose of providing learning opportunities specifically for adults. They can be community based—for example, learning exchanges and grassroots organizations—or they can be private, such as literacy groups (Literacy Volunteers of America, Laubach Literacy International, and the like) and proprietary schools or residential centers such as the Highlander Center for Research and Education, which fosters social change and encourages thoughtful community citizenship.

2. *Educational institutions.* This category includes educational institutions, including public schools and postsecondary institutions of all sorts, that have had as their primary mission serving youth. In more recent years, the populations of some of these institutions have changed so dramatically that they are now reaching more adult learners than the traditional-age students, such as many community colleges and selected postsecondary institutions. In addition, some educational institutions have been established for the primary purpose of serving adults (for example, Empire State College in New York). The Cooperative Extension Service, whose primary mission is "to disseminate and encourage the application of research generated knowledge and leadership techniques to individuals, families, and communities" (Forest, 1989, p. 336), is also included in this category.

3. *Quasi-educational organizations.* Whether public or private, these organizations consider the education of the public to be an integral part of their mission, and they view education as an

allied or corollary function of their primary mission. This category includes cultural organizations (libraries, museums, and the mass media) and community organizations such as service clubs and religious and civic organizations.

4. *Noneducational organizations.* These are similar to quasi-educational organizations in that their primary mission is not educational; the difference is that rather than viewing education clearly as an allied function, noneducational organizations consider it a means to some other end. Furthermore, educational opportunities are mostly geared to the organization's employees instead of to the public, although they may sponsor some educational activities for the general public. For example, business and industry exist to make a profit. To the extent that education (more often called "training" or "performance improvement programs" in this setting) can increase profits, these institutions support it. Government agencies at the local, state, and federal levels are also engaged in extensive training and education, as are the armed forces, unions, and correctional institutions (Merriam and Brockett, 1997, pp. 106–107).

Although these settings are considered to be of a formal nature, some could also be more appropriately categorized as nonformal learning opportunities for adults, even those that are labeled independent adult education organizations. For example, some programs for adults offered by the Young Women's Christian Association (YWCA) or many community-based social action adult education programs could be categorized as nonformal learning settings. We go back to one of our assumptions about the framework we have chosen to use: there will always be overlaps among the three major categories of the framework.

Nonformal Settings

The term *nonformal education* has been used most often to describe learning opportunities outside formal educational settings that complement or supplement the needs of underserved adults or learners in developing nations (Bock and Bock, 1989; Brennan, 1997; Kidd, 1982; Merriam and Brockett, 1997). Typically, according to Merriam and Brockett (1997, pp. 169–170), the nonformal adult learning opportunity is "less structured, more flexible, and more responsive to localized needs. It also is expressly concerned with social inequities and often seeks to raise the consciousness of participants towards social action." Early programs of nonformal education were often associated with literacy initiatives and other community development programs in Third World countries.

Although this description of nonformal education is accurate for nonformal learning opportunities in most developing nations and for some programs in the more developed countries, in these latter countries many of the adult learning opportunities that could be placed in this nonformal category often more closely resemble programs in formal educational institutions. So does using this term *nonformal learning opportunities* have utility today? We believe that it does, both in terms of recognizing the many educational programs in developing nations as well as focusing on the community-based programs of adult learning in all environments that fit the parameters of less structure, more flexibility, and concern with social inequalities. In addition, another type of learning usually associated with nonformal education, that of indigenous learning, is again being recognized as an important form of learning (Brennan, 1997). Therefore, in describing nonformal educational learning opportunities, we focus principally on two types of these opportunities: community-based adult learning programs and indigenous learning.

Community-Based Learning Opportunities.

Varied pictures come to mind when we talk about community-based learning opportunities (*Adult Learning,* 1996; Beder, 1996; Cunningham and Curry, 1997; Galbraith, 1990; Hamilton and Cunningham, 1989; Harris, 1997; Hill, 1998; Peterson, 1996). We see people gathered in churches, the local community center, or the town square organizing to overcome a specific problem or issue they believe to be important in improving life in their community. These problems have ranged from addressing racial hatred and inequality to ensuring adequate housing and sanitary living conditions. Other images of community-based learning programs include men and women learning to read and write while at the same time gaining marketable job skills; farmers being introduced to new methods and crops as a way to build economic control over their lives; and spouses who batter being taught nonviolent ways of handling their anger and frustration. In addition, some traditional organizations, such as the Red Cross and the YMCA, also offer nonformal educational programs.

A common thread to all of these programs is their focus on social action and change for the betterment of some part of the community. Educators who work in these programs believe that education and training can be a powerful tool in assisting learners to take control over their own lives. Sometimes these programs are not welcomed by the mainstream community, especially if one of their major purposes is to challenge the existing way of life, including the current social and economic structures of that community. Vivid examples include the worldwide human rights movement, the continuing struggle to eliminate poverty and hunger, and the end to discriminatory practices based on race, class, and gender.

Working with adults in community-based learning settings has both its blessings and its curses. Being able to exercise flexibility in administration and programming is often recognized as its major benefit. Because these types of organizations "start small and are typically organized as free-standing organizations with fairly simple structures …, they can often move relatively quickly to identify problems and develop programmatic solutions" (Hemphill, 1996, p. 21). This can translate into quicker response times, in terms of both developing funding proposals and getting resources to where they are needed. "New people can be brought in (or unfortunately let go more quickly) as needed. Curricula can be rapidly developed or revised. Teaching assignments can be quickly modified" (Hemphill, 1996, p. 22). Being able to move more quickly does mean that checks and balances must be in place to ensure both a focused program direction based on community needs and quality learning opportunities that are useful. In addition, people attracted to work in community-based adult learning programs, whether paid or volunteer staff, often come with a passion for a cause that gives them the drive to stay with this work, even under the most trying conditions. On the downside, the very nature of many community-based organizations often puts them on the path of the unending search for resources. This continuing search for and worry about resources, in combination with long and often difficult working conditions, can lead to staff burnout very quickly, even for the most committed of individuals.

Indigenous Learning.

Indigenous learning is learning linked with a culture. It refers to processes and structures people within particular societies have used to learn about their culture throughout their history (Brennan, 1997). Often steeped in oral traditions and art forms, conscious use of indigenous forms of learning can enhance nonformal and perhaps even formal educational programs. Storytelling, for example, is often used by African American women to teach about the joys and sorrows of life. When teaching these women, instructors could incorporate storytelling as a major method of learning about the topic at hand, from surviving in modern-day organizations to basic literacy skills.

Descriptions of indigenous forms of learning can be found in both scholarly and more popular literature (Brennan, 1990; Cajete, 1994; Kidd and Coletta, 1980; Morgan, 1994; Ocitti, 1990). Cajete (1994) eloquently describes the tribal foundations of American Indian education, which he sees as "shared by Indigenous cultures of the world" (p. 33). In tracing these foundations, Cajete observes:

> We are tracking the earliest sources of human teaching and learning. These foundations teach us that learning is a subjective experience tied to a place environmentally, socially, and spiritually. Tribal teaching and learning were intertwined with the daily lives of both teacher and learner. Tribal education was a natural outcome of living in close

communion with each other and the natural environment. The living place, the learner's extended family, the clan and tribe provided the context and source for teaching.... Informality characterized the greater part of American Indian teaching and learning.... However, formal learning was usually required in the transfer of scared knowledge.

Hahoh is a Tewa word sometimes used to connote the process of learning. Its closest English translation is to "breath in." *Hahoh* is a sacred metaphor describing the perception of traditional Tribal teaching—a process of breathing in—that was creatively and ingeniously applied by all tribes.... Through these methods [such as storytelling, dreaming, tutoring, and artistic creation], the integration of inner and outer realities of learners and teachers were fully honored, and the complementary educational processes of both realities were fully engaged. [pp. 33–34]

Cajete beautifully expresses what teaching and learning mean to him: "A parable that often flashes through my memory during times of quiet, deep relaxation, or just before I fall asleep: 'It is an essential, life-sharing act of each generation of a People to nurture that which has given them Life and to preserve for future generations the guiding stories of their collective journey to find life'" (p. 187).

Brennan (1997, p. 191) has observed "that the lack of attention to the indigenous learning structure may have been initially the work of missionaries who viewed indigenous culture as inferior and non-Christian and therefore to be ignored or if necessary repressed." He goes on to suggest a four-stage process for recognizing indigenous learning as an essential part of the nonformal system of learning for adults. In Stage One, approaches or techniques that may be relevant to educational or developmental activities are identified—for example, the role of traditional dance and music and the use of legends, myths, tales, and proverbs (Adams, 1987, as cited by Brennan, 1997; Kidd, 1982; Kidd and Coletta, 1980). Stage Two involves classifying these approaches and techniques into a system that educators in more formal settings can understand and integrate into their own ways of thinking. "The third stage," he writes, "is associated with advocacy for the exploration of a broader indigenous learning 'system' [and] the fourth stage is represented by the development of more detailed and comprehensive learning 'systems' for a particular cultural group (Brennan, 1997, pp. 192–193). Indigenous forms of learning could also be seen as informal or self-directed learning as was described by Cajete and is examined in the following material.

Informal or Self-Directed Contexts

Informal learning or self-directed contexts are the last form of learning opportunities we discuss. Although these two terms have not often been used interchangeably, both describe similar phenomena. What characterizes both informal and self-directed learning from learning in formal and nonformal settings is that this form of learning occurs most often in learners' natural settings and is initiated and carried through primarily by the learners themselves (Candy, 1991; Coombs, 1985; Merriam and Brockett, 1997; Watkins and Marsick, 1993). Although well accepted today as the way most adult learning happens, many times adults do not even recognize they are learning even when they are actively engaged in informal or self-directed learning activities at work or at home. What also confounds understanding this form of learning is that incorporating methods of self-directed learning into formal and nonformal settings has become a major focus of practice for some adult educators. We describe first informal or self-directed learning carried forth primarily through learner initiatives and actions, then present an overview of how instructors in formal settings have organized their instructional processes around tenets of self-directedness.

Independent Pursuit Of Learning.

Charlie has a passion for model railroading. He spends hours in his basement planning his layout, tinkering with his equipment, and laying track. He subscribes to every railroad magazine published and talks shop with acquaintances who also have model trains. Every once in a while, he attends a model railroad show, but for the most part, this is a hobby he enjoys pursuing on his own. Over the years he has learned a great deal about model railroading and is proud of his layout, though as he says, "I'll never be totally satisfied. There are always new things coming out which I like to fiddle with."

Trudy has just learned that she has breast cancer. Once over the initial shock, she decides to take an active role in planning her treatment. So that she can speak intelligently with the myriad of medical personnel she knows she must face, she gathers as much information as she can about the disease from a number of sources, including the American Cancer Society, her local Reach for Recovery Program, the Internet, and an oncology nurse who is a friend of a friend. Moreover, she learns of a local support group for cancer patients and decides to join for both information and emotional solace, thereby choosing a nonformal learning opportunity as part of her own self-directed efforts. Her husband and best friend have joined her in her fight, and both are reaching out to a number of different sources for advice and counsel.

These scenarios, representing the independent pursuit of learning in natural settings, with or without the support of institutional resources, are very common in adult life (Candy, 1991; Percy, Burton, and Withnall, 1994). Yet even with the many verification studies that have been completed (Brockett and Hiemstra, 1991; Caffarella and O'Donnell, 1987), self-directed learning in this form is not recognized by many adults, or even some educators of adults, as "real learning." There are a lot of Charlies out there, learning all kinds of things on their own, from model railroading to making quilts and crafting clay pots. Some find friends or independent mentors to assist them in their learning, and some deliberately choose institutional resources that might be helpful to them as part of their self-directed activities. There are also numerous Trudys whose self-directed learning activities "arise from and seek to resolve a problem or situation" (Candy, 1991, p. 199). These learners often combine resources in their natural environments with those supplied by institutions, from educational materials to people who can assist them with their learning. What becomes evident is that this independent pursuit of learning does not necessarily mean learning alone, a major myth about this form of learning (Brockett, 1994). Rather, adults often use other people and even groups, whether they are institutionally based or not, in their self-directed learning pursuits.

A Way Of Organizing Instruction.

The majority of descriptions of how instructors of adults have capitalized on adults' independent pursuit of learning, to capture and maximize in their classes and activities what adults already do in informal or self-directed contexts, are of programs in formal settings (Brockett and Hiemstra, 1991; Candy, 1991; Straka, 1997). Only a few authors have addressed implementing informal or self-directed learning approaches in nonformal settings (for example, Rowland and Volet, 1996). The following scenarios represent two different ways that instruction has been organized in formal settings to use what we know about how adults typically go about learning in their natural settings.

Carolyn has asked her students in a graduate class in adult education to work with her in designing the class. As part of this process, she has requested that students choose from learning objectives that she has developed for the class and/or develop their own. In addition, she has challenged them to think about how they would like to learn the material and be evaluated on their learning. Carolyn has provided them with written resources to help guide them through this process, and she has suggested that some students may want to design their own program of study, while others may feel comfortable using the more structured course syllabus materials she has provided. However students choose to put together the class for themselves, she has asked that a formal learning contract be developed by either individuals or teams of students. In addition, Carolyn has agreed to facilitate the class according to what needs are expressed by the students, as well as to present some basic concepts and ideas that she believes are appropriate for all students to understand about the subject they are studying.

Barbara, director of training for a large health care organization, has been asked to develop self-directed learning options for staff as part of the company training program. One of the guidelines for this program is that the training must relate directly to the organization's mission and product orientation; otherwise she has been given free rein to complete this task. She and her team of people from throughout the organization have identified several options that allow staff to work individually or in small work teams. Among these options are individual professional development plans, self-directed work project teams, computer-assisted packages, and collaborative action research projects.

What is common in both of these scenarios is that the instructor and program manager are working to give more control to learners about what and how they learn, and on what criteria and who should evaluate that learning. In addition, these educators are trying to foster within their learners a more independent way of going about the learning process, whether these learners choose to learn on their own or within self-selected dyads or groups. In fact, many types of organizations, from colleges and universities to business and industry, use informal or self-directed ways of learning, in many forms, as a way to organize instruction (Caffarella and Caffarella, 1986; Cranton, 1994a; Piskurich, 1993; Wilcox, 1996).

In summary, we have presented a framework that encompasses three types of settings or contexts within which learning in adulthood occurs. The first two settings, formal and nonformal, involve some form of organizational or community sponsorship. The third opportunity, informal or self-directed learning, is more of a hybrid. Although the majority of learning opportunities within this last category are planned and initiated primarily by learners in natural settings (such as the home, on the job, or through recreational pursuits), the learning processes and methods used in self-directed and informal learning have been incorporated by some formal and nonformal settings into the way they carry through their instructional programs.

THE DESIGN OF LEARNING OPPORTUNITIES

Understanding how learning is designed in formal, nonformal, and informal or self-directed ways is a good way to gain a clear picture of the range of learning sites and opportunities that are available to adults and the overlapping nature of our categories. To that end, we describe how learning opportunities are designed for adults. Houle (1996) has provided the most comprehensive categorization of educational design situations, ranging from a focus on the individual to mass audiences. Note, from Table 6-1, which outlines Houle's eleven major categories of design situations, the emphasis on both self- and other-designed situations, including the formation of new

---

Table 6-1.   Major Categories of Educational Design Situations.

Individual

  1. An individual designs an activity for herself
  2. An individual or a group designs an activity for another individual

Group

  3. A group (with or without a continuing leader) designs an activity for itself
  4. A teacher or group of teachers designs an activity for, and often with, a group of students
  5. A committee designs an activity for a larger group
  6. Two or more groups design an activity that enhances their combined programs of service

Institution

  7. A new institution is designed
  8. An institution designs an activity in a new format
  9. An institution designs a new activity in an established format
 10. Two or more institutions design an activity that enhances their combined programs or service

Mass

 11. An individual, group, or institution designs an activity for a mass audience

---

Source: Adapted from Houle, 1996, p. 57.

institutions to address the learning needs of adults. These design categories can be used to think through the most effective way to design educational programs for adults, whether they are housed within formal and nonformal settings or are more informal or self-directed in nature.

Within Houle's categories for educational design situations is a recognition of self- and other-designed learning opportunities. In terms of thinking through this central theme of other- versus self-designed learning opportunities, Knowles (1980, 1987), Pratt (1988), Hiemstra and Sisco (1990), and Hiemstra (1994) have provided clear guidelines. In instructor-designed learning activities, the teacher or facilitator of the learning activity is primarily responsible for planning, implementing, and evaluating the learning experience. Instructor-designed activities may be done by individual instructors or by a team of instructors. This instructor-designed learning is what adults have come to expect in formal settings.

When more self-directed methods are introduced, some learners at first shy away from being involved. Some even feel cheated and angry; they think that they are being asked to do what they consider to be the "teacher's job." Other adults in formal settings readily embrace the more learner-centered form of planning learning activities, and like the opportunity to have a greater voice in what and how they will learn. This greater control by individual learners can be seen in such practices as self-directed work teams, individually designed professional growth plans, and classes where instructors and participants mutually plan their learning activities (Caffarella, 1993a; Maher, 1994; Piskurich, 1993).

The andragogical model of instruction, described by Knowles (1975, 1980, 1987), is the best-known learner-centered or learner-directed model of instruction. In addition, this model has been applied to more informal and self-directed learning arenas (for example, Caffarella, 1993b; Rowland and Volet, 1996). Although on the surface this model is similar to other instructional models (diagnosing learning needs, formulating objectives, designing a pattern of learning experiences, evaluating results), there is one key difference: the learner is viewed as a mutual partner or, when learning in natural settings, as the primary designer of the learning activities. Although Knowles himself (1984, 1987; Knowles and Associates, 1984), as well as others (Brookfield, 1986; Hiemstra and Brockett, 1994; Hiemstra and Sisco, 1990), have provided rich descriptions of how his model and its variations have been used in formal settings, we believe that the andragogical model of instruction has not been used a great deal in actual practice, except in nonformal or self-directed situations. Adult learning in formal settings, whether that learning is face to face or through the use of various instructional technologies, remains primarily instructor designed and directed.

There has been a call for the merging of these two extremes of instructor-directed and learner-directed designs to account for the learners' characteristics and skills and the content being taught (Candy, 1987, 1991; Grow, 1991; Pratt, 1988). Pratt (1988) has provided the most comprehensive framework for combining these two ways of designing learning activities. As illustrated in Figure 6-1, he proposes four ways of looking at learning situations based on the direction and support needed by the learner: (1) learners need both direction and support, (2) learners need direction, (3) learners need support but are reasonably self-directed, and (4) learners are at least moderately capable of providing their own direction and support. The key variable that separates each quadrant is the learner's competence in deciding what to learn and how to carry out the learning process and his or her commitment and confidence to do so.

Pratt's framework can be helpful for both instructors and planners in formal and nonformal settings and for individuals and groups of learners who want to plan their own learning activities. In choosing whether to use more instructor-directed or learner-directed instruction in formal settings, educators and trainers must assess learners' abilities and commitment to planning and carrying out specific learning activities. In designing a class on woodworking, for example, an instructor may give free run of the shop to expert hobbyists who have told her they want to become more creative in their work. In contrast, she may require those who have never done woodworking before to follow her specified regimen for learning the basic skills. Instructors who are willing to use a combination of instructor-directed and learner-directed approaches must be capable of

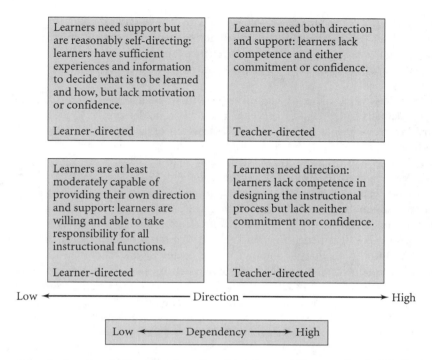

Figure 6-1. **Instructional Situations Based on Direction and Support Needed by Learners.**
Source: Pratt, 1988, p. 167. Adapted with permission.

assuming a variety of instructional roles and using a range of formats and techniques. And learners in more nonformal programs or those learning on their own could see where they fit in Pratt's framework in terms of the amount and types of assistance they may need for their learning projects. The following questions would be helpful for them to think about:

- How much do they know about the content or skill to be learned?
- Do they really want to learn this?
- Are they confident they can learn the material or skill on their own? If not, what kind of assistance might be useful?
- Do they have a sense of how to go about learning what it is they want to know or do?

In responding to these questions, learners can determine if they really can go about learning this material on their own, or if they might better combine some formal educational program with their own learning strategies.

Although the major focus of designing learning activities has been for individual learners or groups of learners, a recent trend has been to look at the organizational unit itself as a learning entity. This has led authors to speculate on what these learning organizations are all about and what educators of adults can do to foster learning organizations.

NEW FRONTIERS IN LEARNING OPPORTUNITIES: THE LEARNING ORGANIZATION

Attention in the literature and in practice to the concept of the learning organization has grown over the past decade. Watkins and Marsick (1993, p. 8) define the learning organization as "one that learns continuously and transforms itself. Learning takes place in individuals, teams, the organization, and even in the communities with which the organizations interact. Learning is a continuous, strategically used process—integrated with, and running parallel to [the] work [of the organization]." This learning capability improves an organization's capacity to respond quickly and in novel ways, thus increasing its ability to foster innovation and change. Organizations with this ability to make rapid changes may have a competitive advantage in the marketplace (Moingeon and Edmondson, 1996).

There is skepticism and even controversy as to whether organizations can really learn or whether "it is actually individuals in organizations that do the learning" (Rowden, 1996a, p. 107). Yet evidence is growing that understanding the learning organization is critical to fostering the growth and development of organizations and people who are associated with these organizations (Di Bella and Nevis, 1998; Leithwood, Leonard, and Sharratt, 1998; Senge, 1990; Watkins, 1996).

Grounded in the early work of Argyris and Schön (1974, 1978), among others, numerous writers have described what is needed to create a learning organization (Di Bella and Nevis, 1998; Moingeon and Edmondson, 1996; Pedler, Burgoyne, and Boydell, 1991; Senge, 1990; Starkey, 1996; Watkins and Marsick, 1993). One of the most often quoted sources is Senge's book, *The Fifth Discipline* (1990). It is Senge's contention that "organizations learn only through individuals who learn" (p. 140). With that assumption at the center of his theory, he describes five core disciplines, or "component technologies," that individuals must adopt for the learning organization to become a reality. Senge views systems thinking as the cornerstone of the learning organization. He believes that it is critical for people to shift their thinking from "seeing parts to seeing wholes, from seeing people as helpless reactors to seeing them as active participants in their reality, from reacting to the present to creating the future" (p. 69). Without this shift in thinking, he views the other four disciplines (developing personal mastery, changing mental models, building shared vision, and participating in team learning) as useless.

In a similar vein, Watkins and Marsick (1993) have outlined six "action imperatives" needed to create and sustain learning organizations. The first imperative is to create continuous learning opportunities at all levels of the organization. These opportunities range from on-the-job learning experiences to hosting global dialogue teams, with the goal that learning becomes an integral part of the everyday work life. To promote this continuous learning, two other action imperatives are brought into play: inquiry and dialogue, and collaboration and team learning. These learning strategies seem to form the heart of most organizational learning efforts, with the emphasis on the collective and interdependent nature of these processes. The fourth imperative, establishing systems to capture and share learning, involves "building organizational capacity for new thinking that is then embedded and shared with others" (Watkins and Marsick, 1993, p. 15). This fourth imperative, along with the fifth, of empowering people toward a collective vision, mirrors Senge's disciplines of changing one's mental models and building shared vision. The final imperative, connecting the organization to its environment, acknowledges the connections between the organization and its external constituents, including its customers and the various local, national, and international communities that affect the work of the organization. These connections are symbiotic; not only do the external constituents affect the organization, but the organization also affects these external groups.

In emphasizing the collective nature of organizational learning, Dixon (1997) has offered the metaphor of the hallway as a useful analogy for thinking about the process of building and sustaining learning organizations. She defines hallways as "places where collective meaning is made—in other words, meaning is not just exchanged, it is constructed in the dialogue between organizational members" (p. 25). Although the dissemination of complete and accurate information is needed to enable this process to work, it is not sufficient to promote shared meanings among people. Dixon contrasts this accessible meaning of the hallways to that of private meaning, which is knowledge known only to individuals and not accessible to others. Collective meanings of organizational members are held in what she terms the organization's storeroom. This collective meaning, which includes norms, strategies, and assumptions about how the organization functions, is the glue that holds the organization together. She acknowledges that this collective meaning, if not allowed to be questioned, can have a negative impact on organizations' being able to learn and change. Dixon goes on to assert that "hallways are the only spaces in which it is possible for an organization to learn" (p. 27) and outlines various examples of hallway learning, from "whole systems in the room" to the use of action learning, learning maps, and the appreciative inquiry approach. Finally, Dixon outlines seven critical elements that characterize hallway learning: (1) reliance on discussion, not speeches; (2) egalitarian participation; (3) encouragement of multiple perspectives; (4) nonexpert-based dialogue; (5) use of a participant-generated database; (6) the creating of shared experiences; and (7) the creation of unpredictable outcomes. We find the last element especially intriguing; it asks those of us who choose to create learning organizations to move away from the predictable aspects of learning and into the realm of reframing problems in unexpected ways and finding possibilities never thought of before.

In addition to providing opportunities for hallways of learning in organizations, authors have cited other factors that facilitate the creation of learning organizations. Di Bella, Nevis, and Gould (1996) have provided the most comprehensive list of these facilitating factors. Their first three items are similar to those indicated by Senge (1990) and Watkins and Marsick (1993): scanning imperative (of external happenings in one's environment), continuous learning, and a systems perspective. They also include seven other factors (Di Bella, Nevis, and Gould, 1996, p. 43):

1. *Performance gap.* Shared perceptions of a gap between actual and desired performances are viewed as opportunities for learning.
2. *Concern for measurement.* Discourse over defining specific, quantifiable measures when venturing into new areas is seen as a learning activity.
3. *Experimental mind-set.* Changes in work processes, policies, and structures are viewed as a continuous series of tryouts, and small failures are encouraged.
4. *Climate of openness.* Information is accessible, problems and errors are shared and not hidden, and conflict is acceptable.
5. *Operational variety.* Pluralistic, rather than monolithic, definition of valued internal capabilities (for example, response modes, procedures) is fostered.
6. *Multiple advocates.* Top-down and bottom-up initiatives are possible.
7. *Involved leadership.* Leaders at significant levels articulate vision and are actively engaged in implementing that vision.

In contrast, there are a number of barriers or inhibitors to creating learning organizations (Marsick and Neaman, 1996; Marsick and Watkins, 1994; Watkins and Marsick, 1993). Among the most critical are the inability of organizational members to recognize and change their existing mental models, the lingering power of individualism in organizations versus the spirit of collaboration and team learning, the lack of skills and developmental readiness by people to undertake "system-wide learning," and "truncated learning or the ghosts of learning efforts that took root because they were interrupted or only partially implemented" (Watkins and Marsick, 1993, p. 240).

We believe that the concept of the learning organization offers a whole new way of working and thinking for educators in both formal and nonformal settings. It allows us to move beyond planning just for individuals and groups of learners in terms of affecting both learning processes and outcomes. Creating learning organizations, whether we are associated with educational, quasi-educational, or noneducational institutions, provides a way to foster learning communities that are open to change and innovative practices.

SUMMARY

Learning opportunities for adults are found in a variety of settings, from formal institutions to one's home or place of employment. The importance of understanding this vast array of learning opportunities for adults is twofold: acknowledging prior knowledge and experiences of learners wherever gained is important to the practice of adult educators, and individual learners, even those without formal schooling, may be better able to recognize their abilities and skills as lifelong learners.

There are three major types of opportunities in which learning occurs for adults: formal settings, nonformal settings, and informal or self-directed contexts. Although the categorization of these learning opportunities and the language used within these categories helps us to think about learning, what is more crucial is the recognition that learning opportunities come in many sizes, shapes, and forms. The most critical actions that educators of adults can take is to recognize the equal importance of the various types of adult learning and advocate that people use them in whatever situation or setting they find themselves.

Designing and facilitating educational activities, no matter what the setting or context, can be done in a number of ways, whether the primary planners are individuals, informal groups, or people in institutional settings. Instructor-designed learning, where the teacher or program planner is primarily responsible for planning, implementing, and evaluating the learning, is predominant in formal settings. In contrast, learner-centered design crosses all three arenas of learning, although it is primarily used in the informal or self-directed context. More recently there has been a call for the merging of these two design frameworks, with both educators and learners making informed choices about what planning process to use depending on the specific situation and the learner's prior knowledge, abilities, and motivation.

The section concluded with an exploration of the learning organization as the newest frontier in educational opportunities for adults. In learning organizations, learning—whether done by individuals, groups, or the organization as a whole—is a central, valued, and integral part of organizational life. The heart of the learning organization is the willingness of organizations to allow their employees and other stakeholders related to the organization to suspend and question the assumptions within which they operate, then create and examine new ways of solving organizational problems and means of operating. This process requires that people at all levels of the organization be willing to think within a systems framework, with the emphasis on collective inquiry, dialogue, and action. Creating learning organizations could allow educators of adults, whether they are associated with formal or nonformal settings, to develop learning communities in which change is accepted as the norm and innovative practices are embraced.

WHAT MOTIVATES ADULTS TO LEARN

RAYMOND J. WLODKOWSKI

> *The map of the self is different in each culture, and each culture could be said to require its own separate psychological science.*
>
> ## Andrew Lock

As a discipline, motivation is a teeming ocean. A powerfully influential and wide-ranging area of study in psychology, motivation at its core deals with *why people behave as they do*. But in terms of scholarly agreement and tightly controlled boundaries of application, motivation swarms the field of psychology with abundant and rich and often dissimilar ideas. Theoretical assumptions relying on a view of human beings as rational, materialistic, pragmatic, self-oriented, and self-directed coexist with views of human beings as irrational, spiritual, altruistic, community-oriented, and other-directed (Gergen, Gulerce, Lock, and Misra, 1996).

This state of affairs has been brought about by the complexity of human behavior, the influence of socialization processes on any human endeavor, and a growing realization that claims for knowledge in the human domain are relative to the culture in which they are spawned. Currently, *socioconstructivism* is a growing theoretical force in understanding ways to improve learning in formal settings such as schools and professional seminars (Hickey, 1997). Incorporating views from sociology and anthropology, this perspective acknowledges the impact of collaboration, social context, and negotiation on learning. Critical to this view is the understanding that people learn through their interaction with and support from other people and objects in the world. As psychologists, we are aware that to better understand learning may require us to perceive a person's thinking and emotions as inseparable from each other and from the social context in which the activity takes place. For example, would I have these thoughts (writing clearly about adult motivation) and feelings (mild anxiety—maybe I won't) if I were not in front of a word processor surrounded by research journals and texts and aware of my history as a teacher of adults? It seems unlikely that I would. However, I am still an individual with my own thoughts, guided by personal interests and goals. I live as a socially constructed being with an individual identity. Both ways of being human exist at the same time.

From Piaget to Vygotsky, from Aristotle to Foucault, there are myriad theories to support each of these two major perspectives: a more mechanistic, individualist framework or a more contextual, socially constructed framework. Rather than choosing one to displace the other, I believe that *both* an individualistic worldview and a socioconstructivist worldview can inform educational practice, much as both Eastern and Western views of health inform medical practice. As time passes, these views are likely to become more closely integrated. Already in many instances, originally individualistic ideas, such as personal relevance, fit snugly into a socioconstructivist perspective. What a person finds relevant is often directly related to individual values, which are social constructions.

In general, both of these views can embrace intrinsic motivation and the tenets that human beings are curious and active, make meaning from experience, and desire to be effective at what they value (McCombs and Whisler, 1997). Because promoting learning among all adults is most possible through culturally responsive teaching based on intrinsic motivation, the motivational strategies documented from either of these perspectives are considerable assets to instructors of adults. Motivational strategies are deliberate instructor actions that enhance a person's motivation to learn. *The strategy contributes to stimulating or creating a motivational condition: a mental/ emotional state of being* in which the learner is desirous of information, knowledge, insight, and skill. For example, an intriguing question (strategy) might provoke curiosity (motivational condition); or a relevant example (strategy) might elicit interest (motivational condition) in a person. It is the interest and curiosity—the motivational conditions—that energize the individual's learning and foster engagement in such learning processes as reflection and dialogue.

What is most important to create, then, is a framework that combines essential motivational conditions in a way that is intrinsically motivating for diverse adults in formal learning situations. The strategies from an individualistic or socioconstructivist perspective can then be assigned and understood according to the condition to which they most obviously contribute. Let's begin by discussing the essential conditions; we will then describe the framework and conclude by applying that framework to an actual instructional situation. The descriptions of the specific strategies that contribute to creating each of the essential motivational conditions will follow in the material ahead.

Numerous social science theories and their related research have shown at least four motivational conditions to be substantially enhancing of adult motivation to learn—inclusion, attitude, meaning, and competence.

HOW INCLUSION FOSTERS INVOLVEMENT

Inclusion is the awareness of learners that they are part of an environment in which they and their instructor are *respected by and connected to one another.* Social climate creates a sense of inclusion. Ideally, learners realize that they can consider different, possibly opposing, perspectives as part of their learning experience. At the same time, there is a mutually accepted, common culture within the learning group and some degree of harmony or community. The atmosphere encourages learners to feel safe, capable, and accepted.

Respect is not a well-developed concept in psychology. Mentioned but seldom defined, *respect* rarely appears in the indexes of most psychology textbooks. Nonetheless, its importance to human beings is irrefutable. To be free of undue threat and to have our perspective matter in issues of social exchange are critical to our well-being and learning. Unless learners know that they can express their true selves without fear of threat or humiliation, they will not be forthcoming with their perceptions of their own reality. In such circumstances, an instructor does not find out learners' understanding of the world or their true ideas. If there is no meaningful dialogue and if no relevant action is possible, learners become less motivated, as well they should.

Connectedness in a learning group is perceived as a sense of belonging for each individual and an awareness that each one cares for others and is cared for. There is a shared understanding among group members that they will support each other's well-being. In such an environment, people feel trust and an emotional bond with at least a few others; because of this, there exists a spirit of tolerance and loyalty that allows for a measure of uncertainty and dissent. When the attribute of connectedness is joined with respect, it creates a climate in a learning group that invites adults to access their experience, to reflect, to engage in dialogue, and to allow their histories to give meaning to particular academic or professional knowledge—all of which enhance motivation to learn.

Telling and hearing our stories is essential to human nature. It is the way we make sense of things. It is compelling. With a sense of inclusion, most adults can publicly bring their narratives to their learning experiences. They can personalize knowledge—use their own language, metaphors, experiences, or history to make sense of what they are learning (Belenky, Clinchy, Goldberger, and Tarule, 1986). They can be involved knowledge builders rather than alienated knowledge resisters. When learners are encouraged by the learning atmosphere to use their own social and cultural consciousness, they can construct the cognitive connections that make knowledge relevant and under their personal control (Vygotsky, 1978).

Aside from research (Poplin and Weeres, 1992) and our common sense, which tell us that learners who feel alienated achieve less than those who do not, consider your own experience of being a minority. On those rare occasions when I have been, even when it's not a matter of ethnicity but when I simply have a different point of view, I remember my own struggle to make myself heard and understood as I wanted to be understood. My anxiety was usually palpable. I also remember those occasions when the instructor created an atmosphere that allowed my differences to be respectfully heard. I spoke more easily, learned more, and was certainly more open to learning more. Unless we are the ones discounted, we are often unaware of how motivationally debilitating feeling excluded can be to adults. Ask any group of adults about their motivation in a course where they felt excluded. The answers are searing.

The foundation of any learning experience resides in the nature of the teacher and student relationships. On a moment-to-moment basis, probably nothing is quite as powerful. We are social beings, and our feelings of inclusion or exclusion are enduring and irrepressible.

HOW ATTITUDES INFLUENCE BEHAVIOR

In general, an *attitude* is a combination of concepts, information, and emotions that results in a predisposition to respond favorably or unfavorably toward particular people, groups, ideas, events, or objects (Johnson, 1980). For example, an accountant is required by her company to take an in-service training course. A colleague who has already taken the training tells her that the instructor is authoritarian and arrogant. The accountant finds herself a little anxious as she anticipates the new training. At her first training session, the instructor matter-of-factly discusses the course and its requirements. The accountant judges the instructor's neutral style to be cold and hostile. She now fears the instructor and resents the mandatory training. This accountant has combined information and emotions into a predisposition to respond unfavorably to a person and an event. If the accountant's colleague had told her the instructor was helpful and caring, it is less likely that the same outcome would have occurred.

Attitudes powerfully affect human behavior and learning because they help people make sense of their world and give cues as to what behavior will be most helpful in dealing with that world. If someone is going to be hostile toward us, it is in our best interest to be careful of that person. Attitudes help us feel safe around things that are initially unknown to us. Attitudes also help us anticipate and cope with recurrent events. They give us guidelines and allow us to make our actions more automatic, making life simpler and freeing us to cope with the more unique and stressful elements of daily living. In psychology, this is called the *least effort principle:* whenever possible, apply past solutions to present problems or, whenever possible, apply past reactions to present experiences. This kind of reacting not only helps us cope but also to be consistent in our behavior, which is a vital need for human beings.

Needs influence attitudes because they make certain goals more or less desirable. For example, if managers are taking a training seminar because they feel a need to improve relations with workers, they will more likely have a positive attitude toward the learning experience than those who believe their relations with employees are completely satisfactory. Also, whenever physical or safety needs are under threat, as in the case of hungry or exhausted students or workers facing an imminent layoff, adults are not usually in the mood for learning unless it will concretely and immediately resolve these concerns.

Although attitudes can be influenced by such situational factors as strong needs, drugs, or illness, they are, for the most part, learned. They are acquired through such processes as experience, direct instruction, identification, and role behavior (teacher-student, parent-child, employer-employee, and so forth). Because attitudes are learned, they can also be modified and changed. New experiences constantly affect our attitudes, making them shift, intensify, weaken, or reverse. They are part of a dynamic process in which people, the media, and life in general constantly impinge on them. Attitudes can be personally helpful, as in the case of a positive expectancy for success, or they can be personally harmful, as in the case of an intense fear of failure. Attitudes are with us all the time, and they constantly influence our behavior and learning.

Attitudes are of great importance in understanding adult development because they predispose one's choices of activities, companions, and environments across the life span. Strongly related to adult attitudes and adaptation are *change events,* events in people's lives that affect their cognitive representations of themselves and others (Costa and McCrae, 1989). These change events alter previous goals, attitudes, and behaviors, transforming the quality of adult life. Education introduces many change events as people adjust to new ideas, challenging courses, and the consequences of acquired degrees and related career shifts.

New learning is usually risky business; the outcome is seldom a certainty. For adults, this risk may be even higher because the new learning is required for a job, a promotion, or some important personal goal. In unpredictable situations, people's attitudes are very active, because they help people feel more secure. As an instructor of adults, you can be quite assured that students' attitudes will be an active influence on their motivation to learn from the moment instruction begins. Adult learners will immediately make judgments about you, the particular subject, the learning situation, and their personal expectancy for success. However, beyond knowing that their attitudes are a constant influence on learners' motivation and learning, it is difficult to make broad generalizations about the attitudes of adults with respect to learning in general.

Hayes and Darkenwald (1990) found that women and people with a higher level of initial education show a more positive attitude toward adult education than do men and the less formally educated. However, we need to keep in mind that many less traditionally educated adults are marginalized learners for reasons of race, ethnicity, or class. They may distrust "education" because of having encountered difficulties in their earlier education, brought about in part by being denied their own interests, history, and ways of knowing. Because so many adults have had previous negative experiences with formal education, two of the most important criteria for developing a positive attitude among *all* learners are *relevance* and *choice*. Irrelevant learning can startle, annoy, or frighten us. We not only find such learning unimportant or strange but also implicitly know we are doing it because of someone else's domination or control. This knowledge triggers or develops a negative attitude. If we had some degree of choice in the learning situation, we might alter its irrelevant aspects to better accommodate our perspectives and values.

Personal relevance is not simply familiarity with learning based on the learners' prior experience. Because of media saturation, people could be familiar with a particular television program or magazine yet find it totally irrelevant. People perceive personal relevance when their learning is contextualized in their personal and cultural meanings, allows their voice to remain intact, and reflects their construction of reality. In other words, the learning is connected to who they are, what they care about, and how they perceive and know. In this process, the instructor and learners figuratively become coauthors, taking neither their own view nor the view of the other to be specially privileged but entering into a genuine dialogue, with each standpoint having its own integrity (Clifford, 1986).

When learners can act from their most vital selves, their curiosity emerges. They want to make sense of things and seek out challenges that are in their range of capacities and values. This leads to what human beings experience as interest, the emotional nutrient for a continuing positive attitude toward learning. When we feel interested, we have to make choices about what to do to follow that interest. Such choosing or self-determination involves a sense of feeling free in doing what one has chosen to do (Deci and Ryan, 1991). For the process of learning—thinking, practicing, reading, revising, studying, and other similar activities—to be desirable and genuinely enjoyable, adults must see themselves as personally endorsing their own learning. Global history and social science merge to support this observation: people consistently struggle against oppressive control and strive to determine their own lives as an expression of their deepest beliefs and values. Learning is no exception.

HOW MEANING SUSTAINS INVOLVEMENT

According to Mezirow (1997, p. 5), "a defining condition of being human is that we have to understand the meaning of our experience." Making, understanding, and changing meaning are fundamental aspects of adult development that continuously take place in a sociocultural context (Gilligan, 1982; Tennant and Pogson, 1995). But what is meaning from a motivational perspective? In relationship to learning, what is the meaning of meaning itself?

There are a number of ways to unravel this concept. One way to understand meaning is to see it as an increase in the complexity of an experience or idea that relates to people's values or purposes. This meaning may be beyond articulation, as in the realm of the creative or spiritual.

Emotion, art, and spirituality are essential to human experience and have incontestable meaning that is often inaccessible in words. For example, as I grow older, the meaning of friendship increases in conceptual complexity (different types of friendship) as well as in emotional and spiritual impressions I cannot easily describe in words.

Deep meaning implies that the experience or idea increasing in complexity is connected to an important goal or ultimate purpose, such as family survival or the meaning of life. As the philosopher Susanne Langer (1942) has posited, there is a human need to find significance. Across many cultures, achieving purpose appears fundamental to a satisfying life (Csikszentmihalyi and Csikszentmihalyi, 1988). When we assist learners in the realization of what is truly important in their world, they access more passionate feelings and can be absorbed in learning. Emotions both give meaning and influence behavior. If, for example, learners become troubled as they discover that certain tax laws create economic inequities, the complexity of their understanding has increased, and they may now find their agitation propelling them toward further reading about tax legislation. In general, however, because many adults prefer to avoid distress, more positive emotions, such as wonder and joy, are often more likely to deepen interest and nurture involvement.

Another way to understand meaning is to conceive of it as the ordering of information that gives identity and clarity, as when we say that the word *castle* means a large fortified residence or when we recognize our telephone number in a listing. This kind of meaning embraces facts, procedures, and behaviors that contribute to our awareness of how things relate or operate or are defined but do so in a way that doesn't deeply touch our psyche. In the words of Whitehead (1979), this is "inert knowledge." A good deal of foundational and professional knowledge is inert knowledge. It easily becomes boring. By recasting this knowledge in a context of goals, concerns, and problems relevant to adults, we can infuse it with deeper meaning. There are also motivational strategies that enhance the meaning of initially irrelevant information by stimulating learners' curiosity and insight.

Adults can feel included and have a positive attitude toward learning, but their involvement will diminish if they do not find learning meaningful. By making their goals, interests, and perspectives the context of learning, we create a system that evokes meaning and involvement in learning. A challenging learning experience in an engaging format about a relevant topic is intrinsically motivating because it increases the range of conscious connections to those interests, applications, and purposes that are important to learners. The enhancement of meaning is at the core of learning and motivation because human beings by their very nature need to maintain an ordered state of consciousness (Csikszentmihalyi, 1997), a harmony within themselves and with others.

HOW COMPETENCE BUILDS CONFIDENCE

Competence theory (White, 1959) assumes people naturally strive for effective interactions with their world. We are genetically programmed to explore, perceive, think about, manipulate, and change our surroundings to promote an effective interaction with our environment. Practicing newly developing skills and mastering challenging tasks engender positive emotions, *feelings of efficacy* that are evident even in early infancy. Researchers have demonstrated that babies as young as eight weeks old can learn particular responses to manipulate their environment. In one such study (Watson and Ramey, 1972), infants were placed in cribs with a mobile above their heads. By turning their heads to the right, they activated an electrical apparatus in their pillows, causing the mobile to move. These children not only learned to "move" the mobile but also displayed more positive emotions (smiling, cooing) than did the infants for whom the mobile's movement was controlled by the experimenter.

This innate disposition to be competent is so strong that we will risk danger and pain to accomplish a more able relationship with our environment. Consider the one-year-old who continually falls attempting to walk and, while still crying from a recent tumble, strives to get up and go at it again. Or the adult who, on gaining proficiency at one level of skiing, swimming, climbing, or running, "naturally" moves on to the next level, often putting body or being in jeopardy.

The history of the human race is a continuous, colorful catalogue of bold scientists and adventurers who have relentlessly reached out to explore their world. We humans are active creatures who want to have a part in shaping the course of our lives.

As adults, we most frequently view competence as the desire to be *effective at what we value*. Our socialization and culture largely determine what we think is worth accomplishing (Deci and Ryan, 1991). As we move from childhood to adulthood, our feeling competent more and more involves social input. Parents and teachers and schools and jobs, the unavoidable stuff of growing up, increasingly replace independent play and toys.

Because awareness of competence is such a powerful influence on human behavior, adults who are learning and can feel an actual sense of progress are usually well motivated to continue their efforts in a similar direction. Because adults enter educational programs with a strong need to apply what they have learned to the real world, they are continually attentive to how effectively they are learning. They know their families, jobs, and communities will be the arenas in which they test this new learning. Therefore, they are more motivated when the circumstances under which they assess their competence are *authentic* to their actual lives.

In formal learning situations, adults feel competent when they know they have attained a specified degree of knowledge or a level of performance that is acceptable by personal standards, social standards, or both. This sense of competence usually comes when adults have had a chance to apply or practice what they are learning. When they have evidence (through feedback) of how well they are learning and can make internal statements, such as "I really understand this" or "I am doing this proficiently," adults experience feelings of efficacy and intrinsic motivation because they are competently performing an activity that leads to a valued goal. This experience of effectiveness affirms their innate need to relate adequately to their environment.

The process and the goal are reciprocal—one gives meaning to the other. If someone wants to learn how to use a computer because it is a valued skill, that awareness of how valuable computer skills are will evoke his motivation as he makes progress in learning computer skills. However, the gained competence, the progress itself, will increase the value of the goal, making computer skills more valuable; the person could eventually enter a career that was before unimaginable (perhaps prompting that common existential question, How did I get here?).

When people know with some degree of certainty that they are adept at what they are learning, they feel confident. This confidence comes from knowing that they have *intentionally* become proficient. Their self-confidence emanates from such internal statements as, "I know this well," or, "I will be able to do this again."

The relationship between competence and self-confidence is mutually enhancing. Competence allows a person to become more confident, which provides emotional support for an effort to learn new skills and knowledge. Competent achievement of this new learning further buttresses confidence, which again supports and motivates more extensive learning. This can result in a spiraling dynamic of competence and confidence growing in continued support of each other. To feel assured that one's talents and effort can lead to new learning and achievement is a powerful and lasting motivational resource. It is also the mark of a true expert or champion in any field. Instructors can help adults learn to be confident by establishing conditions that engender competence. It is a wonderful gift.

ORGANIZING THE ESSENTIAL MOTIVATIONAL CONDITIONS: THE MOTIVATIONAL FRAMEWORK FOR CULTURALLY RESPONSIVE TEACHING

We have seen how important and complex the relationship of motivation and culture is to adult learning. Instructors need a model of teaching and learning that respects the inseparability of motivation and culture. The Motivational Framework for Culturally Responsive Teaching provides this understanding (Wlodkowski and Ginsberg, 1995). It dynamically combines the essential motivational conditions that are intrinsically motivating for diverse adults (see Figure 6-2). It provides

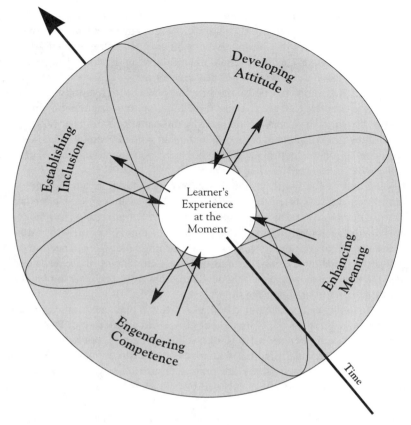

Figure 6-2. The Motivational Framework for Culturally Responsive Teaching.
Source: Wlodkowski and Ginsberg, 1995, p. 29.

a structure for planning and applying a rich array of motivational strategies. Each of its major conditions is supported by numerous theories and by related research that documents that condition's powerful influence on learner motivation.

The Motivational Framework for Culturally Responsive Teaching is respectful of different cultures and capable of creating a common culture that all learners in the learning situation can accept. It is a holistic and systemic representation of four intersecting motivational conditions that teachers and learners can create or enhance. The essential conditions are as follows:

1. *Establishing inclusion:* creating a learning atmosphere in which learners and teachers feel respected and connected to one another
2. *Developing attitude:* creating a favorable disposition toward the learning experience through personal relevance and choice
3. *Enhancing meaning:* creating challenging, thoughtful learning experiences that include learners' perspectives and values
4. *Engendering competence:* creating an understanding that learners are effective in learning something they value

People experience motivational influences polyrhythmically—that is, as a simultaneous integration of intersecting realities on both conscious and subconscious levels. You meet a friend you have not seen for many years. As you embrace your friend, many emotions rush through you—

joy, sorrow, love, perhaps regret. In that moment, your perceptions of your friend intersect with a history of past events recalled in your mind. A number of feelings arise from this dynamic network. How many of them affect you at this or any given moment? No one really knows.

From Buddha to Bateson, scholars and thinkers have understood life and learning to be *multidetermined.* As we have discussed earlier, researchers increasingly view cognition as a social activity that integrates the mind, the body, the process of the activity, and the ingredients of the setting in a complex interactive manner (Lave, 1988). Meeting your friend alone in an airport might be a very different emotional experience from meeting this same person in her home with her family present. Scholars in the field of situated cognition understand human beings to frequently act without deliberation; our perception and action arise together, each coconstructing the other (Bredo, 1994). *Much of the time we compose our lives in the moment.*

The conventional psychological model—perceiving, thinking, acting—describes a linear process that may occur far less often than earlier theorists have imagined. Understanding how the social and historical can be so vital to a person's thinking and learning helps us realize why dialogue and reflection may not be enough to change adult attitudes and behavior, why we need to remain humble as we attempt to unravel the mystery of adult learning, and why we need to do motivational planning. Because the four motivational conditions work in concert and exert their influence on adult learning in the moment as well as over time, instructors would be wise to plan how to establish and coordinate these conditions when possible.

Motivational planning can be integrated with instructional planning, or it can be used in addition to instructional planning. Motivational planning helps us avoid a serious pitfall common to teaching: blaming the learners for being unresponsive to instruction. With no motivational plan to analyze for possible solutions to motivational difficulties that arise during instruction, especially with adults who are culturally different from ourselves, we are more likely to place responsibility for this state of affairs on them. It is difficult for us to be openly self-critical. Defense mechanisms like rationalization and projection act to protect our egos. Motivational planning helps us keep our attention on the learning climate and on how we instruct and what we can do about that instruction when it is not as vital as we would like it to be. This focus diminishes our tendency to blame, which is a common reaction to problems that seem unsolvable.

APPLYING THE MOTIVATIONAL FRAMEWORK FOR CULTURALLY RESPONSIVE TEACHING

Let us take a look at the Motivational Framework for Culturally Responsive Teaching in terms of the teaching-learning process. Because most instructional plans have specific learning objectives, they tend to be linear and prescriptive: instructors sequence learning events over time and predetermine the order in which concepts and skills are taught and when they are practiced and applied. Although human motivation does not always follow an orderly path, we can plan ways to evoke it throughout a learning sequence. In fact, because of motivation's emotional base and natural instability, we need to painstakingly plan the milieu and learning activities to enhance adult motivation, especially when we face a time-limited learning period. For projects, self-directed learning, and situational learning (as in the case of problem posing), we may not be so bound to a formal plan.

The most basic way to begin is to transform the four motivational conditions from the framework into questions to use as guidelines for selecting motivational strategies and related learning activities to include in the design of your instructional plan:

1. *Establishing inclusion:* How do we create or affirm a learning atmosphere in which we feel respected by and connected to one another? (Best to plan for the *beginning* of the lesson.)
2. *Developing attitude:* How do we create or affirm a favorable disposition toward learning through personal relevance and choice? (Best to plan for the *beginning* of the lesson.)

3. *Enhancing meaning:* How do we create engaging and challenging learning experiences that include learners' perspectives and values? (Best to plan *throughout* the lesson.)
4. *Engendering competence:* How do we create or affirm an understanding that learners have effectively learned something they value and perceive as authentic to their real world? (Best to plan for the *ending* of the lesson.)

Let us look at an actual episode of teaching in which the instructor uses the motivational framework and these questions to compose an instructional plan. In this example, the teacher is conducting the first two-hour session of an introductory course in research. The class takes place on Saturday morning. There are twenty adult learners ranging in age from twenty-five to fifty-five. Most hold full-time jobs. Most are women. Most are first-generation college students. A few are students of color. The instructor knows from previous experience that many of these students view research as abstract, irrelevant, and oppressive learning. Her instructional objective is as follows: *students will devise an in-class investigation and develop their own positive perspectives toward active research.* Using the four motivational conditions and their related questions, the instructor creates the sequence of learning activities found in Exhibit 6-1.

Exhibit 6-1. An Instructional Plan Based on the Four Questions from the Motivational Framework for Culturally Responsive Teaching.

Motivational Condition and Question	Motivational Strategy	Learning Activity
Establishing inclusion: How do we create or affirm a learning atmosphere in which we feel respected by and connected to one another? (Beginning)	Collaborative learning	Randomly form small groups in which learners exchange concerns, experiences, and expectations they have about research. List them.
Developing attitude: How do we create or affirm a favorable disposition toward learning through personal relevance and choice? (Beginning)	Relevant learning goals	Ask learners to choose something they want to research among themselves.
Enhancing meaning: How do we create engaging and challenging learning experiences that include learner perspectives and values? (Throughout)	Critical questioning and predicting	Form research teams to devise a set of questions to ask in order to make predictions. Record questions and predictions.
Engendering competence: How do we create or affirm an understanding that learners have effectively learned something they value and perceive as authentic to their real world? (Ending)	Self-assessment	After the predictions have been verified, ask learners to create their own statements about what they learned about research from this process.

Let's look at the narrative for this teaching episode. The teacher explains that much research is conducted collaboratively. The course will model this approach as well. For a beginning activity, she randomly assigns learners to small groups and encourages them to discuss any previous experiences they may have had doing research and their expectations and concerns for the course *(strategy: collaborative learning)*. Each group then shares its experiences, expectations, and concerns as the teacher records them on the overhead. In this manner, she is able to understand her students' perspectives and to increase their connection to one another and herself *(motivational condition: establishing inclusion)*.

The teacher explains that most people are researchers much of the time. She asks the students what they would like to research among themselves *(strategy: relevant learning goal)*. After a lively discussion, the class decides to investigate and predict the amount of sleep some members of the class had the previous night. This strategy engages adult choice, increases the relevance of the activity, and contributes to the emergence of a favorable disposition toward the course *(motivational condition: developing attitude)*. The students are learning in a way that includes their experiences and perspectives.

Five students volunteer to serve as subjects, and the other students form research teams. Each team develops a set of observations and a set of questions to ask the volunteers, but no one may ask them how many hours of sleep they had the night before. After they ask their questions, the teams rank the five volunteers in order of the amount of sleep each had, from the most to the least *(strategy: critical questioning and predicting)*. When the volunteers reveal the amount of time they slept, the students discover that no research team was correct in ranking more than three volunteers. The students discuss why this outcome may have occurred and consider questions that might have increased their accuracy, such as, "How much coffee did you drink before you came to class?" The questioning, testing of ideas, and predicting heighten the engagement, challenge, and complexity of this learning for the students *(motivational condition: enhancing meaning)*.

After the discussion, the teacher asks the students to write a series of statements about what this activity has taught them about research *(strategy: self-assessment)*. Students then break into small groups to exchange their insights. Their comments include such statements as, "Research is more a method than an answer," and, "Thus far, I enjoy research more than I thought I would." Self-assessment helps the students extract from this experience a new understanding they value *(motivational condition: engendering competence)*.

This snapshot of teaching illustrates how the four motivational conditions constantly influence and interact with one another. Without establishing inclusion (small groups to discuss concerns and experiences) and developing attitude (students choosing a relevant research goal), the enhancement of meaning (research teams devising questions and predictions) might not occur with equal ease and energy, and the self-assessment to engender competence (what students learned from their perspective) might have a dismal outcome. Overall, the total learning experience encourages equitable participation, provides the beginning of an inclusive history for the students, and enhances their learning about research.

In this class session, the strategies and their related activities work together holistically as well as systemically. Removing any one of the four strategies and the motivational condition it evokes would likely affect the entire experience. For example, would the students' attitude be as positive if the teacher arbitrarily gave them the task of researching sleep among themselves? Probably not, and this mistake would likely decrease the research teams' efforts to devise questions.

One of the values of the Motivational Framework for Culturally Responsive Teaching is that it is not only a model of motivation in action but also an organizational aid for designing instruction. By continually attending to the four motivational conditions and their related questions, the instructor can select motivational strategies from a wide array of theories and literature to apply throughout a learning unit. The teacher translates these strategies into a set of sequenced learning activities that continuously evoke adult motivation (as well as teach).

Exhibit 6-1 is an example of a fully planned class session in which the learning activities are derived from and aligned with motivational strategies. To use this framework, *pedagogical alignment*—the coordination of approaches to teaching that ensures maximum consistent effect—is critical. The more harmonious the elements of the instructional design, the more likely they are to sustain intrinsic motivation. That's why one strategy—cooperative learning or self-assessment, for example—is alone unlikely to evoke intrinsic motivation. It is the mutual influence of a combination of strategies based on the motivational conditions that elicits intrinsic motivation.

As Exhibit 6-1 shows, there are four sequenced motivational strategies, each based on one of the four motivational conditions. Each strategy has been translated into a learning activity. The Motivational Framework for Culturally Responsive Teaching allows for as many strategies as the instructor believes are needed to complete an instructional plan. The instructor's knowledge of the learners' motivation and culture, the subject matter, the setting, the technology available, and the time constraints will determine the nature of and quantity of the motivational strategies. This framework provides a holistic design that includes a time orientation, a cultural perspective, and a logical method of fostering intrinsic motivation from the beginning to the end of an instructional unit.

For projects and extended learning sessions, such as problem solving or self-directed learning, the sequence of strategies may not include all four motivational conditions. For example, inclusion and attitude often have been established earlier through previous work, advising, or prerequisite classes. These conditions may need less cultivation, and the conditions of meaning and competence may be most important to foster.

The Motivational Framework for Culturally Responsive Teaching is the foundation for a pedagogy that crosses disciplines and cultures to respectfully engage *all* learners. It reflects the value of human motivation and the principle that motivation is inseparable from culture. The framework is a means to create compelling learning experiences in which adults can maintain their integrity as they attain relevant educational success.

STRATEGIES FOR SELF-DIRECTED DEVELOPMENT

P. CRANTON

Susan is a human resource developer in a large government department. She has learned about her practice primarily by working with a more experienced colleague, a woman she describes as her mentor. As time goes on, Susan begins to question some of the practices she and her colleague use. She thinks about trying different things. But Susan feels awkward bringing these ideas up with her colleague—she has always respected and followed in the footsteps of her mentor and worries that criticism would lead to resentment. When her colleague takes a maternity leave, Susan is both frightened and excited. Will she be able to carry out the work by herself? Can she use this time to experiment with alternative ideas? What if she fails?

Sometimes a person needs to be self-directed in order to reflect critically on practice. Sometimes becoming self-directed in one's practice is a transformation. Sometimes transformation is stimulated through the direction of another person but is in the end a self-directed process. Each of these alternatives could be the case for Susan.

I discuss self-directed learning before critical reflection and transformative learning not because there is a linear sequence to the process in learning—the concepts are interrelated in many ways—but rather because theoretically each concept builds on the previous one.

Independence, freedom, autonomy, empowerment, self-direction: in one form or another these have always been seen as the goals of human development and thus of education. Just as existentialist philosophers have struggled to define freedom (Macquarrie, 1973), so have adult educators struggled to define self-direction (Candy, 1991). The concept of self-direction has remained evasive. There is no common understanding among adult educators or scholars in adult education as to what they mean by self-direction. Yet this does not diminish its importance or the extent to which it has become a part of educators' espoused theories of practice. It would be rare to find an educator in Western culture who would not agree that he or she wanted learners to be more self-directed, more independent, or freer. These notions are an integral part of our social norms. Candy (1991, pp. 46–47) writes that self-direction "in the broadest sense seems to have captured the spirit of the times—that is, to embody a number of contemporary issues that have flowed together. These include the democratic ideal, the ideology of individualism, the concept of egalitarianism, the subjective or relativistic epistemology, the principles of humanistic education, and the construct of adulthood."

Educators are expected to be independent, self-directed professionals. We expect them to maintain an up-to-date expertise in their discipline, to initiate and implement innovations in their institution or organization, to contribute to their profession and their community, and to be responsible for their own professional development. However, traditional development strategies do not tend to encourage or even allow educators to have control over their own development. They may have a choice of which workshop to attend or which book to read, but it is often assumed that others know best what they need to learn.

If educator development is to be emancipatory or transformative, it is important that educators have control over their learning and access to the resources they need for learning. In Susan's case, she felt unable to transform her practice without having control, but she also would not have been able to do so without the experience she had gained with her mentor. These two criteria are used by Brookfield (1993) to define self-directed learning as a political concept. Simultaneously, the process of becoming a self-directed learner of one's practice may be transformative learning for educators. Susan's anxiety about being on her own could be the beginning of that process for her. If we are used to being told what we should do in order to work more effectively with our learners, and if we believe that our expertise lies in our subject area rather than in education, to change that perspective is transformative learning.

If educators see self-directed learning as a goal of their work with learners and do not see themselves as self-directed learners of educational practice, there is a discrepancy in their perspective. Mezirow (1991) describes perspective transformation as development. He writes, "transformation can lead developmentally toward a more inclusive, differentiated, permeable, and integrated perspective and that, insofar as it is possible, we all naturally move toward such an orientation. *This is what development means in adulthood* (emphasis in the original). It should be clear that a strong case can be made for calling perspective transformation the central process of adult development" (Mezirow, 1991, p. 155). Educators' professional development, when it moves beyond the acquisition of new techniques, is transformative learning. In order for this development to take place, educators need to develop as self-directed learners; this development, too, is transformative learning.

In this section, I first briefly review the variety of perspectives on self-directed learning, although it is not my intent to provide a full literature review. Candy (1991) and others do this well. I then use Candy's four dimensions of self-directed learning (1991) as a framework to discuss strategies for educators' development. He refers to "four distinct (but related) phenomena: 'self-direction' as a personal attribute (personal autonomy); 'self-direction' as the willingness and capacity to conduct one's own education (self-management); 'self-direction' as a mode of organizing instruction in formal settings (learner-control); and 'self-direction' as the individual noninstitutional pursuit of learning opportunities in the 'natural society setting' (autodidaxy)" (Candy, 1991, p. 23). Each of these phenomena is related to educator development as transformative learning.

DEFINING SELF-DIRECTED LEARNING

Jarvis (1992b, p. 130) notes that self-directed learning "is one of those amorphous terms that occurs in adult education literature but that lacks precise definition." Knowles (1975, 1980) introduced the term to practitioners, and his definition was pervasive in the literature until the late 1980s. His conceptualization follows an instructional design model, with the learners participating in or making the decisions. He saw self-directed learning as being a process in which learners "take the initiative, with or without the help of others" (1975, p. 18) in diagnosing their needs, setting objectives, selecting resources, choosing learning strategies, and evaluating their progress. Unfortunately, Knowles's work was misconstrued by researchers and practitioners alike. It was interpreted at times as independent learning, equivalent to modularized instruction or computer-managed instruction. Knowles actually emphasized people working together. Others assumed that adults were automatically self-directed, but Knowles had described their need or desire to take responsibility for their learning while acknowledging that people may not have the skills or the confidence to do so. What Knowles intended was similar to saying that people want to be free from constraints and oppression, but perhaps they are not or cannot be for various reasons.

During the 1980s, the concept of self-directed learning split into two related but conceptually different notions. It was seen as a characteristic of people, as in "She is a self-directed learner," and a method of learning, as in "He is using a self-directed approach in his course." The first concept, that of self-direction as a personal characteristic, led to researchers' attempts at quantification. Guglielmino's Self-Directed Learning Readiness Scale, or SDLRS (1977), and Oddi's Continuing Learning Inventory, or OCLI (1984), are two well-known examples of instruments designed to measure self-directedness. The SDLRS, in particular, has been used extensively in a variety of research studies (two of many examples are Long, 1987; and West and Bentley, 1989) and has provoked criticism and debate (Field, 1989). Three questions need to be considered regarding this line of inquiry:

1. What do such instruments measure?
2. Can self-directedness be quantified (which implies that it is instrumental knowledge)?
3. Can self-directedness be considered as a characteristic that is free of the learning and social context?

The second concept, that of self-directed learning as a method, led to the phenomenon of researchers conducting methods-comparison studies (for example, Rosenblum and Darkenwald, 1983). The learning and degree of satisfaction of participants who were and were not involved in the planning of learning were compared. This line of research resembled the 1960s experiments on the effectiveness of learner control (see Campbell, 1964). The early investigations of learner control generally revealed no measurable differences in learning as a result of method (Dubin and Taveggia, 1968). It is not surprising that comparing the self-directed learning "method" with other methods of instruction yields no meaningful results. Why would we expect groups of individuals, each with their distinct learner characteristics, experiences, and knowledge of and attitude toward the subject area, to respond predictably and consistently to being given responsibility for their own learning? As Candy (1991, p. 437) notes, "That such preoccupations are manifest in the literature on self-direction seems particularly ironic, in view of the nature of the phenomenon being studied."

Brookfield (1986) initiated the change in thinking about self-directed learning. He attempted to untangle the concepts of self-directedness as a measurable and assumed characteristic of adults, self-directed learning as a method, and self-directedness as an aim of education. He also questioned each of these assumptions. Candy (1991) then provided a thorough analysis of the various threads and dimensions of self-directed learning, drawing the factions together again into a four-faceted model. He argued against the positivistic approach to the study of self-directed learning, and consequently against attempts to measure self-directedness. In 1993, Brookfield clearly reconnected self-directed learning to the critical practice of adult education, or, in other words, emancipatory learning. He wrote, "The case for self-direction as an inherently political concept rests on two assumptions. First, that at the intellectual heart of self-direction is the issue of control, particularly control over what are conceived as acceptable and appropriate learning activities and processes. Second, that exercising self-direction requires that certain conditions be in place regarding access to resources, conditions that are essentially political in nature" (Brookfield, 1993, pp. 232–233).

At about the same time, Jarvis (1992b) attempted to "refine the notion of self-directed learning" by examining it through his analysis of "free will and freedom to act" (p. 131). He developed a model of self-directed learning in which he isolated nine major elements, seen as forming a variety of sequences of events shaping the learner's tendency to be self-directed or other-directed. The elements include

- Disjuncture, or discrepancy between past and present experience
- Decision to learn
- Type of participation, through an educational institution or independently
- Aims and objectives, whether they be determined by learners, others, or through negotiation
- Content, again whether it is determined by learners, others, or through negotiation
- Method
- Thought/language, a broad category including communicative interaction
- Assessment
- Action/outcome

Jarvis sees learners as being able to take various paths through each of these elements, being either self-directed or other-directed in each element.

Early in his writing, Mezirow (1985) described a self-directed learner as developing a more authentic meaning perspective, or in other words, engaging in critical self-questioning of underlying assumptions. He also related self-direction to the communicative aspect of transformative learning: "There is probably no such thing as a self-directed learner, except in the sense that there is a learner who can participate fully and freely in the dialogue through which we test our interests and perspectives against those of others and accordingly modify them and our learning goals" (Mezirow, 1985, p. 27).

Generally, self-directed learning has now been reintegrated with communicative learning and again seen to be a process concomitant with transformative learning. However, the branch of thinking in which self-direction is a quantifiable characteristic and a precise method remains in place. Long and his associates (1994) describe Brookfield's writing as the interjection of a "myth" into the literature. Long (1994, pp. 2) writes, "Unfortunately, the critical mythology continues to persist with little critical analysis" and "It is even more critical, however, when these myths are accepted to such a degree that they interfere with the development of research and practice. The myth gradually must be replaced with corrective information" (pp. 2–3). Piskurich's recent guide (1993) to the design and implementation of self-directed learning provides another example of this approach.

In an earlier book, I described self-directed learning as occurring when the learner

- Chooses to learn
- Consciously changes behavior, values, or knowledge
- Makes choices as to how to apply, what to read, what to do
- Is conscious of change and growth and can describe them
- Is free to speak, listen, interact, and consult
- Is free to challenge or question (Cranton, 1992, p. 55)

Self-directed learning is a goal, a process, and a learner characteristic that changes with the nature of the learning. Candy's framework of four distinct but interrelated phenomena (1991) may best capture and clarify the complexity of self-directed learning; I use this framework to discuss strategies for educator development.

PERSONAL AUTONOMY

Drawing on the writing of several philosophers, Candy (1991, pp. 108–109) comes to the conclusion that an individual is seen to have personal autonomy to the extent that he or she

- Conceives of goals and plans independently of pressure from others
- Exercises freedom of choice in thought or action
- Uses the capacity for rational reflection to make judgments on the basis of morally defensible beliefs, as objectively as possible, and using relevant evidence
- Has the will and capacity to carry through plans of action arrived at through the process described above
- Exercises self-mastery in the face of reversals, challenges, and setbacks
- Has a concept of himself or herself as autonomous

Candy views this definition as an ideal, one which is not likely to be attained by the majority of individuals; not only are there many external threats to personal autonomy, but it is impossible to escape socializing influences on attitudes, values, and beliefs. Autonomy is also situation-specific, as are the other components of self-directed learning. A person can be more autonomous in career than in marriage, or more autonomous in learning about work-related topics than in learning new or abstract knowledge.

Educator Development and Personal Autonomy

As personal autonomy is viewed as both a goal and a process, I will maintain these two themes here. That is, one goal of development is to increase personal autonomy; a person works toward independence and freedom from constraints. Also, the process of development itself involves autonomous learning; a person grows and learns, in part, on his or her own. It is also important to note, however, that "autonomy should not be endorsed or promoted as a goal to the detriment of social interdependence" (Candy, 1991, p. 109).

Autonomy as a Goal

If educator development is to lead to autonomy, what might this mean for developmental strategies? In order to be autonomous, educators would need to

- Have the knowledge and skills to develop their own goals for professional development independently of any pressure
- Be free from inward or outward constraints or restrictions
- Be able to choose objectively from among alternatives based on their own beliefs and experiences
- Be able to develop a plan of action for development
- Be able to face reversals and challenges
- See themselves as autonomous

Clearly this is an ideal, for what educator would describe himself or herself as completely free from constraints, or being independent of any pressure from others? Most educators who work within institutions or organizations would not be able to achieve these goals. Perhaps this is why Mezirow (1985) writes, "There is probably no such thing as a self-directed learner" (p. 27). Yet, as goals, these aspects of personal autonomy are completely congruent with Mezirow's notion of transformative learning: "transformation can lead developmentally toward a more inclusive, differentiated, permeable, and integrated perspective" (1991, p. 155).

What can educators do to work toward personal and professional autonomy? Some aspects of developing autonomy can be individual projects, but others are enhanced by working with others. Candy (1991, p. 119) suggests that still other aspects of autonomy, such as "emotional autonomy or perseverance, are partly innate or, in any case, are rooted deeply in people's very earliest experiences at home and school." It is also clear that engagement in autonomous activities does not necessarily lead to personal or professional autonomy for all individuals. Similarly, no person can "make" another person autonomous; it is an individual goal.

Some strategies that have the potential to lead educators to the goals of personal autonomy are

- Developing the knowledge and skills for goal setting by reading thought-provoking books and articles
- Talking to experts, attending conferences, or otherwise gaining knowledge about educational practice through discussions with others
- Considering all the things that are seen to be outward constraints or restrictions (such as organizational policies, lack of resources, or shortages of money), and questioning the extent to which they are actually constraining practice
- Working with a trusted friend or colleague to discuss and question perceived inward constraints and restrictions—for example, insecurities, anxieties, fear of failure
- Listing all possible alternative approaches to practice (for example, different ways to structure a group, resources from the media, a change in physical location) based on one's own knowledge, beliefs, and experiences
- Choosing, from the listed alternatives, some approaches to try in practice and discussing the outcomes with a friend or colleague
- Developing a personal professional development plan based on the strategies already listed
- Preparing for reversals and challenges through self-reflection (perhaps keeping a journal) or through the development of a support network of colleagues
- Thinking of oneself as autonomous in practice while remembering that this does not imply solitude or indifference to the opinions of others

Autonomy as a Process

Educator development, when it leads to transformative or emancipatory learning, is an autonomous learning process. In other words, no other person can "teach" someone self-awareness, although another person can challenge, question, support, and otherwise foster the process. But because transformative learning involves changing underlying assumptions, beliefs, and values, it must essentially be directed by the self. It is a developmental process.

Drawing on the work of Piaget and others, Candy (1991, p. 118) summarizes the characteristics of heteronomy and autonomy. The features of heteronomy include egocentrism, unilateral respect, conformity, rigidity, blind faith in authority, other- directedness, and dependence. The characteristics of autonomy, on the other hand, include:

- Cooperation
- Mutual respect
- Individual creativity
- Flexibility
- Rational criticism
- Inner-directedness
- Independence

We can take this list and use it to describe educator development as an autonomous process. In such a developmental process, educators would

- Work cooperatively and collaboratively to learn more about their practice
- Respect the expertise of their colleagues and others working in educational development
- Be respected by their colleagues and others
- Be creative in their approach to their practice
- Be flexible and open to change in their practice
- Critically question their own practice and the practice of others
- Be open to critical questioning of their practice by others
- Possess an inner drive to develop their practice
- Work independently, without pressure from others, on the development of their practice

We would all probably like to see ourselves learning in this way, but it is one thing to list these ideals and quite another to engage in a learning process that has such characteristics. Some strategies that might foster this process are

- Organizing a professional discussion group in which ideas about practice are exchanged
- Setting up a list of peers and others who have particular expertise in one or more aspects of practice, and consulting those individuals as needed
- Sharing one's own knowledge, skills, and beliefs about practice
- Trying new strategies in one's practice, and being open about this with learners
- Changing and experimenting with one's practice based on discussions with learners and peers
- Questioning and reflecting on one's practice after each session, perhaps with the help of a journal or log
- Requesting comments from others, learners and peers, on one's practice
- Developing a personal vision of what practice would be like in an ideal state (without constraints) and deliberately working toward that vision
- Setting up a development plan independently of any other person's request or expectation

Educator Development and Personal Autonomy: An Illustration

Jo Anne is a trainer for a medium-sized industrial company. Her main responsibility is disseminating information about safety, new government regulations, and technological upgrading. Jo Anne has always been very interested in improving her practice and has been frustrated by the seeming lack of understanding demonstrated by the workers who are her learners. She sees herself as responsible when someone reports a violation of the safety procedures. Jo Anne has always attended any workshop or conference for which she could get funding from her company. She subscribes to *Training and Development* from her personal funds.

Although Jo Anne felt that she learned something from each workshop she attended and from some of the journal articles, it never seemed quite the same in her workplace. Worse, she did not have anyone else with whom she could discuss these concerns. Her supervisor consistently told her she was doing "a great job" and not to worry so much.

Jo Anne finally took a big step. She called a nearby university and asked if there was anyone there who specialized in training. She was given a name, and made an appointment to speak with him. The meeting began with Jo Anne saying, "I wondered if you could help me to get my learners to learn more." After some discussion of her practice and considerable questioning about the problem, Jo Anne was given some references and the names of two other trainers in the area with whom she could discuss her practice. Jo Anne was somewhat disappointed; she had hoped that the expert would be able to give her some simple things to try.

When I last spoke with Jo Anne, she had become extremely enthusiastic about Stephen Brookfield's *The Skillful Teacher,* and she was meeting "once in a while" with a colleague from another company. The most striking thing about that conversation with Jo Anne was that she said, "I realize I have to do it on my own—I always thought someone else should be able to show me. This just feels better, even though I really don't know any more than I did, and that's still frustrating."

SELF-MANAGEMENT

Self-management is defined as the willingness and capacity to conduct one's own education (Candy, 1991). As a goal, this means development of the competence to direct one's learning, whether it be inside or outside formal educational settings. As a process, self-management involves making one's own decisions about learning. The relationship between personal autonomy and self-management is clear: the autonomous learner would engage in self-management. But what are the competencies that give a person the capacity to make learning decisions?

A considerable amount of research has been conducted in an attempt to describe the characteristics of individuals who direct their own learning. This was a primary focus of adult education research throughout the late 1960s and the 1970s. For example, in 1967, Miller linked Maslow's hierarchy of needs (1954) with Lewin's force-field theory (1947), creating a model to predict the extent to which learners would choose to participate in educational activities. The model includes a combination of personal factors and social forces, as does an early model developed by Boshier (1973). Cross (1992) incorporated life events and transitions as well as environmental factors into her chain-of-response (COR) model. Researchers continue to struggle with this issue. Henry and Basile's results (1994) emphasize the importance of social and institutional factors, rather than personal characteristics. Stalker (1993) presents data to indicate that more adult learning is other-directed than we believe. She concludes that researchers should consider the "concept of voluntary participation in terms of its complex and multi-dimensional elements" (p. 74).

Educator Development and Self-Management

When educator development is self-managed, individuals have the goal of developing the competence to direct their own development, and they make their own decisions about the nature of the learning.

Self-Management as a Goal

Based on a survey of twenty authors' research, Candy (1991, p. 130) summarized the competencies that people would ideally have in order to manage their learning. They would

- Be methodical and disciplined
- Be logical and analytical
- Be reflective and self-aware
- Demonstrate curiosity, openness, and motivation
- Be flexible
- Be interdependent and interpersonally competent
- Be persistent and responsible
- Be venturesome and creative
- Show confidence and have a positive self-concept
- Be independent and self-sufficient
- Have developed information-seeking and retrieval skills
- Have knowledge about, and skill at, learning generally
- Develop and use defensible criteria for evaluating learning

Candy (1991) discusses the criticisms of the research on which this list is based, including, as examples, class and gender bias and a neglect of situational characteristics. However, if we consider the list as presenting possible self-management goals, rather than as profiling a self-directed learner, individual educators can reject those items that are irrelevant or inappropriate for themselves personally, for their contexts, or in specific situations.

How can we become "methodical and disciplined"? Some strategies that educators could try in order to move toward the goal of self-management include

- Developing a time management system which gives priority to the professional development activities of interest—for example, time for reading, one evening a week for a course, time for reflection after each session
- Setting specific professional development goals and developing a plan to work toward them
- Using a logical problem-solving model to determine what professional development activities would be most meaningful in a given context
- Engaging in activities that promote reflection and awareness, such as keeping a journal, videotaping and reviewing sessions, or writing educator autobiographies
- Being curious about educational practice: questioning others, soliciting alternative viewpoints, or watching others teach
- Being willing to change strategies when one strategy does not appear to be leading to further development
- Trying new things and taking risks, especially risking the possibility of appearing foolish or being wrong
- Turning to others for their expertise and ideas, whether it be a long-term mentor relationship, a group of colleagues, or a one-time consultation with an individual
- Not giving up just because a strategy does not produce immediate results; becoming more self-directed can involve difficult changes
- Describing one's developmental goals and activities positively to others
- Seeing and describing oneself as a person interested in developing practice
- Developing independence and self-sufficiency by engaging in some professional activities on one's own
- Learning how to access the literature and other resources through journals, libraries, and computer networks
- Developing a comfortable system for assessing learning, whether it be through feedback from others or self-analysis of journals, videotapes, and teaching materials based on defensible criteria

Self-Management as a Process

When educator development is a self-managed process, individuals make their own decisions about what they need to learn, how they will learn it, and if and when learning is taking place. This process is based on Knowles's original conceptualization of self-directed learning (1975). As with the other facets of self-directed learning, self-management is simultaneously a process and a goal.

The educator who is engaging in self-managed professional development could be

- Diagnosing development needs, with or without the assistance of others
- Setting development goals independently of pressure from others, but perhaps with the help of others
- Selecting sources of help for learning: materials, individuals, consultants, courses, or programs
- Determining what is personally meaningful, apart from the reward systems of the institution or organization
- Choosing to give up independent learning temporarily in order to gain basic knowledge and skills in a more formal setting
- Continuously reviewing the progress made in the chosen professional development activities
- Honestly acknowledging weaknesses and shortcomings
- Changing tactics when the current strategy is not meeting needs
- Evaluating professional development progress based on personal criteria

Educator Development and Self-Management: An Illustration

Michael is a counselor who has a private practice. One part of his practice involves leading what he calls "educational groups" in which he introduces participants to the various aspects of dysfunctional family dynamics. Over ten sessions, he leads people through a variety of role plays, simulations, and small-group activities to help them question their perceptions of their past and present roles in the family context. Some participants have been involved in individual counseling; others go on to individual counseling after the educational group has finished. Michael has formal training as a counselor but has been concerned for some time that he does not know enough about being an educator.

A friend suggested that Michael take an M.Ed. degree, but Michael did not want to give up that much of his time. Stimulated by this discussion, he decided to carefully analyze what he actually wanted to learn and then determine the best way of gaining that knowledge. He used a series of questions that he had prepared to help his clients untangle personal problems and applied those questions to his perceived practice problem. He discussed the results of this exercise with a friend, asking the friend to question him critically on each learning need that he expressed.

Michael came to the conclusion that he had, at least initially, two goals: he wanted to learn how people learn, and especially how individuals differed in the way they learned; and he wanted to know how to teach or present cognitive information. He felt that once he got started, he might refine these goals or add others.

In order to work toward the first goal, Michael decided to take an educational psychology course entitled "The Psychology of Human Learning." He applied for special-student status, since he was not interested in course credit. When considering the second goal, Michael felt that the context in which his group worked was so specific that a course or workshop on presentation skills might not be relevant. He arranged, instead, for the professional development consultant from the local college to come and watch his work with his group and discuss it with him after each session. In exchange, he offered to put on a workshop series on counseling skills for the faculty at the consultant's college.

Now midway through both of these activities, Michael reports that he is "learning a lot," but he sees his initial goals as too "naïve." He has been reading about learning styles and has noticed that learning styles seem to be related to psychological type, a construct that he uses in his counseling practice. He plans to expand his reading and has already selected his next course.

Michael's circular way of approaching self-management may be fairly typical (for example, see Baskett, 1991). The development of practice, too, cannot be viewed as a linear sequence of learning experiences.

LEARNER CONTROL

Learner control can be described as a "mode of organizing instruction in formal settings" (Candy, 1991, p. 23). This dimension of self-directed learning is usually thought of as a continuum (Millar, Morphet, and Saddington, 1986; Renner, 1983) ranging from almost total teacher control to almost total learner control. On one end of the continuum, when the educator is in control, he or she plays an expert role and uses methods such as lectures and demonstrations; on the other end, when the learner is in control, the educator may become a resource person or facilitator (Cranton, 1992). This concept of a continuum of learner control was popular in the 1960s, primarily in association with work on programmed and individualized instruction. As programmed instruction was based on the theoretical foundation of behaviorism, the concept of learner control was discarded along with behaviorism by the end of the 1970s. As I explored in my doctoral dissertation two decades ago (Cranton, 1976), the term was also used in relation to computer-assisted instruction; it still continues to be associated with computer-based education (see Gay, 1986). Candy (1991, p. 10) is careful to note that he does not intend to use this "specialized meaning," but in fact the concept is quite similar to his learner-control dimension. Within an organized setting, the degree of learner control is defined by the degree to which participants make decisions about the learning process.

Brookfield (1993, p. 233) sees learner control as a political issue: "Who controls the decisions concerning the ways and directions in which adults learn is a political issue highlighting the distribution of educational and political power. Who has the final say in framing the range and type of decisions that are to be taken, and in establishing the pace and mechanisms for decision making, indicates where control really resides." It is through this perspective that learner control moves beyond a mechanistic decision-making process and into an emancipatory learning process.

Educator Development and Learner Control

When educators are involved in formal development activities such as workshops, courses, and retreats, to what extent are they in control of the decision making about the content, structure, and methods of learning? As was discussed earlier, traditional development strategies tend to pay lip service at best to self-directed learning. We have all witnessed, too many times, the workshop leader who asks at the outset of the session for participants' expectations or objectives, writes them on chart paper, goes on to her or his own agenda, and perhaps or perhaps not refers to the list again at the end of the session.

As with the other dimensions of self-directed learning, learner control can be viewed as both a goal and a process. The goal is for educators to be able to make decisions about their professional development within institutions and organizations; the process is that of participating in that decision making.

Learner Control as a Goal

There are two aspects to learner control as a goal: one is that educators gain control over their professional development in organizations that may not encourage this; the other is that educators gain the knowledge and skills for decision making. The latter competencies are similar to those required for personal autonomy and self-management.

When control over developmental activities is a goal, educators can consider the following strategies:

* Working toward personal autonomy and self-management, using some of the suggestions presented earlier

- Inquiring in advance of registering in a workshop, course, or program as to the extent to which participants will have control over their own learning and selecting only those in which control is promised
- Making suggestions to the professional development person or office as to the kinds of activities that would be of interest
- Volunteering to assist with professional development planning
- Asking workshop and course leaders to "permit" participant decision making
- Conducting sessions for colleagues in which participants have control over decisions, so as to act as a model

Learner Control as a Process

In order for the educator to engage in learner-controlled development in a formal setting, that setting must obviously provide the opportunity for it to occur. Most workshops, courses, or programs for educator development are somewhere on the continuum between total learner control and total control by others. The extent to which the following characteristics are present in development sessions indicates the degree to which they are a learner-controlled process:

- Educators' learning interests and needs are explored in advance of planning, ideally through discussion or observation of practice rather than the traditional needs assessment survey.
- Participants in the session are responsible for setting goals or objectives based on individual and group learning interests.
- Goals or objectives are periodically reviewed by the participants and modified as appropriate.
- The sequence and pace of the activities are determined by the participants through ongoing dialogue and review.
- The learning strategies are selected by the group and include variation so as to conform to individuals' preferences.
- All individuals (including the leader or facilitator) have access to learning resources and materials.
- Participants reflect on, discuss, and evaluate their own learning and development.
- Participants reflect on, discuss, and evaluate the quality of the sessions.

Educator Development and Learner Control: An Illustration

Vimla is a doctoral student specializing in medical education. She grew up in India and completed her undergraduate degree there. She describes that program as completely teacher-directed. During studies toward her master's degree, Vimla was careful to choose courses that were known for their rigor, heavy workload, and structure. She saw herself as a high-achieving student with high standards.

In the doctoral program, things became somewhat confusing for Vimla. There was one formal ongoing course, simply called the "Ph.D. seminar," in which students chose the topics to be investigated and led sessions. Some faculty usually attended, but there was no one teacher. Doctoral students could take any other courses they chose, but none were required. It was expected that students would read widely, complete comprehensive examinations, choose their research topic, and then register for the thesis. With the exception of some university requirements, the program was learner-controlled.

Vimla felt frustrated, helpless, and inadequate. Her usual reward system for learning was gone. She did not know how to make decisions about her own learning; she had never done so. Vimla's faculty adviser suggested that she treat the whole thing as an assignment with the objective of learning how to control learning. It is not an easy path for Vimla. She feels that much of her development is "superficial," and she continually seeks others' approval of her decisions. However, Vimla sees the importance of being able to control her own learning, especially in terms of her career development.

AUTODIDAXY

If I decide to learn about organic gardening because the Tennessee grub worm continues to mow down my tomato plants, I might buy books or go to the library, consult with my neighbors, experiment with various organic remedies, take notes on their effect, buy more tomato plants, and try again. This would be an example of autodidactic learning. Candy (1991) defines autodidaxy as intentional self-education. He writes: "It appears that adults learn how to build, how to buy, and how to borrow; they learn about languages and lampshades; about cooking and camping; about making wine; about music, art, literature, history, science, and psychology. In short, no domain of human existence or inquiry is exempt from the self-educational efforts of these avid amateurs, whose serious self-set study often eclipses both the breadth and intensity of even the best-informed practitioners and scholars" (Candy, 1991, p. 159).

It was in Tough's (1979) well-known study on individual learning projects that autodidaxy was first operationalized and investigated. Despite the criticisms leveled against Tough's work, he did establish that a large proportion of adults engage in sustained and independent learning pursuits. He also sparked considerable interest in the research community; numerous studies were conducted in a variety of settings and with different subgroups of the population to replicate and refine Tough's investigation. Candy (1991, p. 159) concludes that "80 to 100 percent of the adult population" may engage in autodidactic learning, and that it "is not confined to any particular social, educational, occupational, or ethnic categories, but is widespread—almost universal—among adults."

Educator Development and Autodidaxy

Autodidaxy may be an ideal form of learning. One can see that if all constraints are removed and individuals have control, free will, and access to resources, autodidactic learning will be the natural ideal. Jarvis (1992b, p. 133) comments that in autodidactic learning, individuals "are responsible to themselves alone." Professional educators are individuals who would seem to be more likely to engage in autodidaxy than other subgroups (for example, see Addleton, 1984).

The goal-versus-process distinction may not be as clear in this facet of self-directed learning as it is in the other three facets. Working toward autodidactic learning as a goal means that the individual will also be engaged in independent learning. When autodidaxy is a goal of educators' development, they will strive to become independent of formal or organized developmental activities. As a process, autodidactic learning involves educators' initiating and carrying out their own development projects.

Autodidaxy as a Goal

What should the educator who wants to pursue independent learning projects do? Tough (1979) treated this question as an organizational one: selecting a space and time for learning, obtaining resources, and setting deadlines. However, if a person has always relied on formal settings to provide opportunities for learning, these preparatory steps may not address the issue. Individual educators will have different preferences as to how to work toward autodidactic learning as a goal. Some of the following strategies may be helpful:

- Keeping a notebook of ideas of possible learning projects
- Collecting resources of any kind that are relevant to areas of interest, including making notes of people who have expertise in appropriate areas
- Conducting a self-analysis of one's practice: deciding what areas are of interest for further learning and what areas are already strengths
- Obtaining any prerequisite knowledge through taking instruction in a formal setting
- Experimenting with small learning projects, perhaps projects unrelated to professional practice
- Writing a description of what are usually the obstacles or blocks to independent learning, and reflecting on the validity of this description

- Asking colleagues and friends about their independent learning projects and how they conducted them
- Writing about or describing oneself verbally as a learner, and having a colleague or friend ask critical questions
- Listing and experimenting with ways to conduct a learning project differently from how one usually learns

Autodidaxy as a Process

Researchers who have attempted to describe the process of autodidactic learning have looked for organized patterns of steps that people go through. Candy (1991) is critical of this approach, pointing out that respondents try to please the researcher in their answers, that they may report socially acceptable learning methods rather than those they use, and that they may not be conscious of how they engage in learning projects. Individual differences among educators as learners are probably greater than the regularities. For some, learning projects may resemble problem-solving processes; for others, their intuition might lead the way. Some educators will look for collaborative projects; others will prefer to work alone. I have argued elsewhere (Cranton, 1994a) that psychological type preference (Jung, [1921] 1971) may provide an explanation for the different processes individuals go through in their learning. In addition, the content and context of the learning will influence the process (see Danis and Tremblay, 1987).

Some strategies that educators can consider using in an autodidactic learning process are

- Developing a systematic action plan that includes objectives, resources, and methods of learning
- Finding a learning partner, a mentor, or a group of colleagues who are interested in the same topic
- Designing a practical experience or set of experiences from which to learn (for example, volunteering to work on a curriculum committee in order to learn about curriculum development)
- Exploring all possible learning strategies and letting intuition guide one through
- Setting aside a quiet time alone for reading, reflecting, and writing
- Asking for ongoing feedback from others (students, colleagues, a professional developer) to guide the process

Educator Development and Autodidaxy: An Illustration

Edgar describes himself as an environmentalist, an activist, and an enthusiastic member of the green movement—"No capitals," he usually adds, to separate himself from the Green Party. It is unclear to Edgar's acquaintances what he actually does, for he always seems to be running from one meeting or conference to another, rather than "working." Edgar involves himself in working with community groups, organizing campaigns against projects that he sees as detrimental to the environment, publishing a newsletter, and writing on a wide variety of issues of interest to him.

Edgar has a background in education. He once was an elementary school teacher but resigned when he found the system oppressive. He decided that his experience in working with children was not adequate to help him best work with his community groups. Edgar's view of formal educational institutions was not conducive to leading him to register in a course on adult education, so he decided to begin an exploratory independent learning project.

In his intuitive way, Edgar ferreted out all discussion groups in the region that bore any resemblance to adult education; he collected numerous books, articles, and reports on education and the philosophy of education; and he began simultaneously to meet adult educators, talk about adult education, and read the literature. He had no systematic plan and could not articulate goals aside from the general one of learning about adult education. Edgar never missed a discussion group. He enjoyed describing his work with community groups and asking others for comments on his practice. He circulated drafts of articles for feedback. In no way observable to another person,

Edgar must have decided that he had reached his goal; the last time I saw him, he was involved in another set of discussion groups on a different topic.

SUMMARY

In order for educators to engage in transformative developmental activities, self-directed learning needs to be a component of the process. Explicating one's assumptions about practice, questioning those assumptions, and possibly revising them can only be conducted by the educator himself or herself. This is not to say, of course, that professional development is a solitary activity or is not stimulated by direction from others, but rather that the process is finally directed and controlled by the individual.

After a brief look at the history of self-directed learning, I have adopted Candy's framework of four distinct but interrelated phenomena (1991) in order to discuss educator development. Self-direction is seen to have the dimensions of personal autonomy, self-management, learner control, and autodidaxy. Each dimension is both a goal and a process.

In order to foster personal autonomy in their development, educators work toward freeing themselves from constraints, both personal and institutional, but they work cooperatively and collaboratively with others. Self-management involves the development of competence to make one's own decisions about learning. When working in formal settings, educators may have some degree of control over the decisions made; learner control is another dimension of self-directedness that can be developed. Finally, educators pursue independent learning projects related to their practice and thus engage in autodidactic learning. For each of these dimensions, an illustrative case study has been presented.